AN INTRODUCTION TO ADA
Second (Revised) Edition

ELLIS HORWOOD SERIES IN COMPUTERS AND THEIR APPLICATIONS

Series Editor: Brian Meek, Director of the Computer Unit, Queen Elizabeth College, University of London

ELLIS HORWOOD BOOKS IN COMPUTING

Series Editor: A. J. Jones, Brunel University

AN INTRODUCTION TO ADA*

Second (Revised) Edition

STEPHEN J. YOUNG, M.A., Ph.D., M.B.C.S., C.Eng., M.I.E.E.

Department of Computation
University of Manchester Institute of Science and Technology

ELLIS HORWOOD LIMITED
Publishers · Chichester

Halsted Press: a division of
JOHN WILEY & SONS
New York · Brisbane · Chichester · Toronto

* Ada is a registered trademark of the US Government (Ada Joint Program Office)

Second Revised Edition first published in 1984.

Reprinted in 1985 by

ELLIS HORWOOD LIMITED
Market Cross House, Cooper Street, Chichester, West Sussex, PO19 1EB, England

The publisher's colophon is reproduced from James Gillison's drawing of the ancient Market Cross, Chichester.

Distributors:

Australia, New Zealand, South-east Asia:
Jacaranda-Wiley Ltd., Jacaranda Press,
JOHN WILEY & SONS INC.,
G.P.O. Box 859, Brisbane, Queensland 40001, Australia

Canada:
JOHN WILEY & SONS CANADA LIMITED
22 Worcester Road, Rexdale, Ontario, Canada.

Europe, Africa:
JOHN WILEY & SONS LIMITED
Baffins Lane, Chichester, West Sussex, England.

North and South America and the rest of the world:
Halsted Press: a division of
JOHN WILEY & SONS
605 Third Avenue, New York, N.Y. 10016, U.S.A.

© 1984 S. J. Young/Ellis Horwood Limited

British Library Cataloguing in Publication Data
Young, Stephen J.
An introduction to ADA. — 2nd (rev.) ed.—
(Ellis Horwood series in computers and their applications)
1. ADA (Computer program language)
I. Title
001.64'24   QA76.73.A15

Library of Congress Card No. 84-19147

ISBN 0-85312-804-9 (Ellis Horwood Limited)
ISBN 0-470-20112-6 (Halsted Press)

Typeset by Ellis Horwood Limited.
Printed in Great Britain by R. J. Acford, Chichester.

Table of Contents

Chapter 5 DECLARATIONS AND BLOCKS

Chapter 6 SUBPROGRAMS

Chapter 7 PACKAGES

Chapter 8 STRUCTURED DATA TYPES

Author's Preface

Ada is a new language designed primarily for programming embedded computer systems, that is, those systems in which the computer is an integral component performing on-line monitoring and/or control. It is a real time language so that as well as containing a complete set of general purpose language features it also provides facilities for multi-tasking, synchronising with real time and programming low level device hardware directly. Ada is not, however, restricted to the real time applications area. Indeed, its 'non-real' time facilities far exceed those offered by most existing languages in common use. It is likely, therefore, that Ada will find a wide variety of applications in such diverse areas as systems programming, commercial software, numerical analysis, teleprocessing, etc., as well as in the conventional real time areas of industrial control, communications and military systems.

Ada is based on Pascal. This does not mean that Pascal is a subset of Ada, in fact, hardly anything from Pascal has found its way unaltered into Ada. The principal inheritance from Pascal is its philosophy — that both algorithms and data structures should be specifiable precisely and clearly and that the logical consistency of a program should be ensured by the compiler wherever possible. Thus, Ada is concerned with readability, maintainability and above all, security.

Ada is a modern language designed to meet the needs of software engineers for many years to come. Virtually all existing languages in common use were designed a long time ago. Even Pascal is now ten years old. When these languages were designed, computer systems required software of relatively modest proportions. Computing hardware offered only restricted memory space and multiprocessor configurations were rare. Today, however, VLSI technology offers potentially unlimited processing power and memory capacity, with the result that more and more complex applications are being undertaken. There is now, therefore, a growing need for software tools which support the construction of very large programs. Ada meets this need by providing extensive facilities for program modularisation.

An Ada program is specified as a set of *packages*. Each package is an encapsulation of a collection of data objects and their related operations. Packages may, therefore, be used to implement the various resources needed by a program in its execution. Here the term *resource* is used in a very general sense. It includes such things as input-output operations, buffers, stacks, common data pools and also user-defined data types, particularly abstract data types. Every package has two parts: an *interface specification* and a *body*. The interface specification names those entities within the package which are accessible to the rest of the program. The body contains the full definitions of these entities and any further ones needed to implement the package. The package thus allows controlled access to a set of logically related entities and is therefore a powerful tool for program modularisation. The interface specification aids documentation and allows the compiler to check that all uses of a package are legal. Furthermore, Ada allows package specifications and package bodies to be separately compiled, thereby directly supporting top-down design methodologies, incremental system construction and programming by teams as well as by individuals.

Thus, the package is the central concept in Ada and the real key to its power. Packages dominate the way an Ada program is designed, the way it looks on paper and the way it is constructed, tested and subsequently maintained.

This book is aimed at students and experienced programmers alike. It provides a complete introduction to programming in Ada. All Ada language features are carefully explained and wherever possible illustrated by examples. A key feature of the book is the inclusion of an extended example at the end of each chapter. These are intended to give further clarification of the points covered in that chapter but more importantly they are used to illustrate how programs should be designed in Ada. In particular, strong emphasis is placed on the use of the package in supporting data abstraction. Finally, exercises are provided with each chapter, and solutions to a selection of these are given at the end of the book.

Ada is a large and complex language and the difficulties involved in learning how to use it effectively should not be underestimated. Nevertheless, the benefits to be gained are potentially enormous. The reader may be assured from the outset that the effort involved will be well worth while — not only will he have learnt Ada, but he will also have learnt a new and powerful program design methodology.

Finally, I would like to express my gratitude to Brian Meek for his helpful comments during the preparation of the manuscript of this book and to my wife for her unceasing encouragement and support.

S. J. Y., February 1982

Preface to Second Edition

In February 1983, a new definition of Ada was published. The purpose of the new definition was primarily to clarify a number of ambiguities and obscurities in the earlier 1980 definition to make it acceptable for standardisation by the American National Standards Institute (ANSI). At the same time, a number of changes were made to the language, particularly in the area of input/output. This new edition of *An Introduction to Ada* has been completely updated to take these changes into account.

S. J. Y., May 1984

To my Parents

1

The structure of an Ada program

1.1 INTRODUCTION

This chapter is intended primarily to introduce the basic ideas of program construction in Ada. This will be done principally via two examples of very simple but nevertheless complete Ada programs. The intention is to try to convey an overall picture before presenting the details of the language. Of course, many of the points illustrated will not be properly understood until they have been covered in depth later. Despite this, it is hoped that this overview will help the reader see how the various language constructs and examples given in the subsequent chapters fit into the overall framework.

Before doing this, however, it will be necessary to briefly discuss what software development involves and introduce some of the basic terminology. A computer program is essentially a set of instructions which describe the functions which the computer is to perform. These instructions are stored in the computer's memory as a sequence of binary codes. For a program of any size, the generation of these codes directly by the programmer is a largely impossible task. Hence, high level programming languages are used to express the required functions in a notation which is oriented towards the problem that is to be solved rather than towards the machine which is to be used.

The translation of a high level language into the corresponding machine code is performed automatically by a program called a compiler. Once this translation is complete, the final program can then be executed. There are thus two major phases in a program's development and these are usually called *compilation* and *execution*. Events which happen during compilation are said to have occurred at *compile-time* and events which happen during execution are said to have occurred at *execution-time* or more commonly, at *run-time*. The distinction between compile-time and run-time is particularly important with regard to errors. There are many kinds of errors which can occur in a program, spelling mistakes, grammatical errors, logical inconsistencies and so on. Ada is designed to enable as many of these to be detected at compile-time as possible. This is highly desirable because errors detected by the compiler are easy to locate and correct whereas run-time errors can be very difficult and time-consuming to trace. Furthermore, the detection of errors at run-time involves the computer in performing extra work. Ada's ability to detect many errors at compile-time therefore gives higher programmer productivity, higher reliability and greater efficiency.

Turning now to the construction of an actual Ada program, the solution to any computing problem requires two distinct pieces of information to be given. Firstly, the data which is to be processed must be precisely defined and secondly, the operations which are to be performed on that data must be specified. In Ada, therefore, a simple program consists of two parts as shown by the following outline:

```
procedure NAME is
       - - specification of the data to
       - - be used by the program
begin
       - - sequence of statements defining
       - - the actions to be performed
end NAME;
```

The first line of this program starts with the keyword **procedure** followed by the name of the program which is chosen by the programmer. Keywords are part of the Ada language and denote particular kinds of construct. In this case, the keyword **procedure** denotes the start of a piece of program which is to be executed. Notice that keywords are written in lower-case and programmer-defined words are written in upper-case. Following the procedure name is the keyword **is**, and then comes the specification of the data to be used by the program. The actions to be performed by the program on this data are then written as a sequence of statements between the keywords **begin** and **end**. Finally, for increased readability, the name of the program is given again at the end.

There are many different kinds of statement in Ada but a very common one is the assignment statement. This is used to assign a value denoted by an expression to a variable denoted by a name. For example, the statement

$$X := (Y + 1) * 2;$$

computes the value of the variable Y added to 1 and multiplied by 2 and then assigns the result to X. The actual assignment is denoted by the *becomes equal* symbol ($:=$). The symbols to the right of the $:=$ symbol constitute an expression, that is, a formula for computing a value. Of course, if this statement appeared in the above program outline then the variables X and Y would have to have been defined in the data specification part.

The execution of a program takes place in two stages. Firstly, all the declarations in the data specification part are *elaborated*. This is the process by which each individual declaration achieves its effect. In simple cases, this may simply involve associating a name with some data object and possibly giving it an initial value. Secondly, the statements are *executed*. During either of these phases, it may be necessary to *evaluate* expressions. For example, the initial value of a data object may be defined by an expression or, as shown above, the value to be assigned in an assignment statement is denoted by an expression.

Thus, there are three terms which must be remembered: *elaboration, execution* and *evaluation*. The key point, however, is that in order to execute the statements of any of the different kinds of program unit in Ada, the data declarations must first be elaborated and this may require a variety of sub-computations to be performed. Elaboration is not a passive activity but requires the computer to perform certain actions just as it does when executing the statement part.

Having established some of the basic terminology, an actual Ada program can now be presented.

1.2 A SIMPLE ADA PROGRAM

As a very simple example, the program shown below called PRINT_BRACKETS will read characters from the standard input device attached to the computer and print out any left or right brackets [that is, '(' and ')'] detected in the input stream. The end of the input is assumed to be marked by a full stop.

```
with TEXT_IO;
procedure PRINT_BRACKETS is
    CH: CHARACTER;
begin
    TEXT_IO.GET(CH);
    while CH /= '.' loop
        if CH = '(' or CH = ')' then
            TEXT_IO.PUT(CH);
        end if;
        TEXT_IO.GET(CH);
    end loop;
end PRINT_BRACKETS;
```

The basic structure of this program follows the outline given above. The data specification part consists of a single declaration "CH:CHARACTER;". This notation means that the program operates on a variable whose name is CH and whose type is CHARACTER. The type of a data object defines what sort of values the object can have and what sort of operations can be applied to it. In this case, the variable CH can only hold values which are characters. Between the **begin** and **end** are the actual statements defining the actions to be performed by the program. Thus, when this program is started, the declaration of CH is first elaborated and then the statements are executed. In this case, the elaboration phase simply involves associating the name CH with a location in memory which will be used to store its current value. The execution phase involves repeatedly reading a character from the input device and if the character is a bracket printing it. This continues until a full stop is read. The actual acts of reading and printing are performed by *procedure call statements*. For example, each character is read by the statement TEXT_IO.GET(CH). Here the name GET denotes another subprogram just like PRINT_BRACKETS. The only difference between the two is that PRINT_BRACKETS is executed automatically when the program is started whereas GET is executed only when required to do so by a procedure call statement. The effect of GET is to read the next character from the input and assign its value to the variable CH. The actual code which defines GET is located in a package called TEXT_IO. Because GET is defined in a package, in order to refer to it, the package name must be given as a prefix to the sub-program name, that is, TEXT_IO.GET. This package defines a whole range of facilities for input/output and is described in detail in Chapter 15. The point to emphasise here, however, is that TEXT_IO is just one of many packages which can be used to build an Ada program. Some of these packages will be pre-defined, as is TEXT_IO; others will be defined by the programmer to serve his own particular needs.

In fact, the overall structure of the PRINT_BRACKETS program is shown in Fig. 1.1. As can be seen, it consists of two packages in addition to the procedure PRINT_BRACKETS. The package STANDARD represents the pre-defined Ada environment. It contains definitions for all Ada pre-defined types and operations and is always implicitly available. For example, the type CHARACTER is defined in this package. The package TEXT_IO is a pre-defined library unit containing a set of operations for text input and output. The package STANDARD is unique in that the entities within it are always automatically accessible. All other packages required by a program must be listed in a so-called **with**-clause to make them available. Hence, the procedure PRINT_BRACKETS must be prefixed by the clause

    with TEXT_IO;

in order to access the text i/o package.

In general, an Ada program will utilise three classes of package: the predefined package STANDARD, predefined library packages such as TEXT_IO, and user-defined packages. The next section illustrates briefly how a user-defined package is written.

1.3 PACKAGES

As an example of the way that a package is written and used, suppose that the PRINT_BRACKETS example was to be modified so that instead of printing out

package STANDARD is

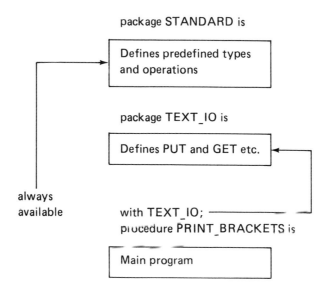

Fig. 1.1 – Structure of PRINT_BRACKETS

the lcft and right brackets in the input stream, it calculated the difference between the number of left and right brackets to check that they balance.

In order to do this, some form of counter will be needed. Of course, a simple integer variable could be used directly for this purpose, but here a solution using the methodology of "design by data abstraction" will be developed. This methodology is of vital importance in designing large well-structured programs, and many features of the Ada language have been introduced specifically to support it. In essence, it means that a program is designed top-down in a series of levels. At the top level, the program is specified in terms of one or more abstract data types and a set of appropriate operations for manipulating them.

By *abstract* type, what is meant is that thc actual internal structure of any variable declared of the type is not known, nor is it relevant at that stage of the design. All that is really being done is to introduce new data types which have just the properties that are needed to solve the current problem. Thus, in PRINT_ BRACKETS all that was needed was the ability to store character values. The pre-defined type CHARACTER was already available for storing character values and so there was no problem. If, however, the type CHARACTER had not been already available, then it could still have been used in exactly the same way, except that it would then be an abstract type. The design of PRINT_BRACKETS would not alter, but the programmer would ultimately have more work to do because, after designing PRINT_BRACKETS, he would then have to go on to design an implementation for the type CHARACTER.

By using abstract data types, irrelevant matters of detail are excluded from the top level design. At the first level of refinement, the internal structure and related operations of all abstract types used at the top level are defined. Where these types are quite complex, their definitions may need to be in terms of further (slightly less) abstract types. Hence, the process may be repeated, with each successive level being refined in a similar way, until all types are defined in terms of the built-in types provided by the language.

Returning now to the example, an abstract data type may be defined in Ada using a package. A package consists of two separate parts. Firstly, the package specification defines all the facilities provided within the package which are available to users of the package. Secondly, the package body defines how these facilities are actually implemented. The following package specification defines an abstract type called TOTAL, with the operations INIT, INCREMENT and DECREMENT defined for it. These operations are invoked by procedure call statements in just the same way that GET was used in the previous example. In addition, a function IS_ZERO is supplied to check the state of the counter.

```
package COUNTER is
    type TOTAL is private;
    procedure INIT(X: in out TOTAL);
    procedure INCREMENT (X: in out TOTAL);
    procedure DECREMENT (X: in out TOTAL);
    function IS_ZERO(X: TOTAL) return BOOLEAN;
end COUNTER;
```

The symbol **private** means that the internal structure of the type TOTAL is private to the package (that is, it is unknown to users of the package). Each of the operations INIT, INCREMENT, etc., has a single parameter defined for it, of type TOTAL. This allows the user of the package to specify which particular data variable of type TOTAL that he wishes to operate on. For example, the call COUNTER.INIT(X) will initialise the variable X.

Given this package specification, a program can now be designed in terms of the abstract type TOTAL, as follows:

```
with TEXT_IO,COUNTER;
procedure COUNT_BRACKETS is
    use TEXT_IO;          - - makes PUT and GET directly inaccessible
    use COUNTER;          - - makes TOTAL, INIT, etc. accessible
    CH:CHARACTER;
    NBRACKETS: TOTAL;     - - an object of the abstract type TOTAL
```

```
begin
    INIT(NBRACKETS); GET(CH);
    while CH /= '.' loop
        case CH is
            when '(' => INCREMENT(NBRACKETS);
            when ')' => DECREMENT(NBRACKETS);
            when others => null;
        end case;
        GET(CH);
    end loop;
    if IS_ZERO(NBRACKETS) then
        PUT("BRACKETS MATCH");
    else
        PUT("ERROR: BRACKETS DO NOT MATCH");
    end if;
end COUNT_BRACKETS;
```

The operation of this program may be explained in the following way. The variable NBRACKETS of abstract type TOTAL is used to count the difference between the left and right brackets encountered in the input stream. After initialising NBRACKETS and the current character CH, a loop is repeated until CH contains a dot. Within the loop a **case** statement allows the operations INCREMENT, DECREMENT or **null** to be selected, depending on the value of CH. The statement **null** indicates that no action is to be taken.

Notice that the **with**-clause prefixing COUNT_BRACKETS has now been extended to include the package COUNTER as well as TEXT_IO. Also, **use**-clauses have been added to the declarative part. These simply allow package entities such as PUT and GET to be referenced directly without having to give the package name as a prefix, for example, PUT rather than TEXT_IO.PUT.

Having established the top level design in terms of the abstract type TOTAL, the next level of refinement consists of defining TOTAL itself. This involves specifying both the type of TOTAL and the implementation of its operations. A suitable representation for TOTAL is an integer type which may be specified in Ada by

```
type TOTAL is new INTEGER;
```

This type declaration means that TOTAL has all the properties of the pre-defined type INTEGER, but is nevertheless a distinct type. Logically, this type declaration should go within the body of the COUNTER package since it contains information which should be hidden from users of the package. However, Ada requires that it be placed (for implementation reasons) in the package specification.[†] Hence, the specification of COUNTER given above is, in fact, incomplete. The full version is

```
package COUNTER is
     type TOTAL is private;
     procedure INIT(X: in out TOTAL);
     procedure INCREMENT(X: in out TOTAL);
     procedure DECREMENT(X: in out TOTAL);
     function IS_ZERO(X: TOTAL) return BOOLEAN;
private
     type TOTAL is new INTEGER;
end COUNTER;
```

where the declaration between the symbol **private** and the **end** is private to the package. Programs which use the package COUNTER have no access to the information given in the private part.

The implementation of the package COUNTER now consists of defining the supplied operations for the type TOTAL. Each operation has the same form as the main program itself except that, as it happens, none have any declarations in their data specification parts

```
package body COUNTER is
     procedure INIT(X: in out TOTAL) is
     begin
          X:= 0;
     end INIT;

     procedure INCREMENT(X: in out TOTAL) is
     begin
          X:=X+1;
     end INCREMENT;

     procedure DECREMENT(X: in out TOTAL) is
     begin
          X:=X−1;
     end DECREMENT;

     function IS_ZERO(X: TOTAL) return BOOLEAN is
     begin
          return X=0;
     end IS_ZERO;
end COUNTER;
```

[†]See, for example, *Real Time Languages*, S. J. Young, Ellis Horwood, 1982, Chapter 9, for an explanation of this problem.

The procedure COUNT_BRACKETS and the package COUNTER constitute a complete Ada program whose overall structure is illustrated in Fig. 1.2.

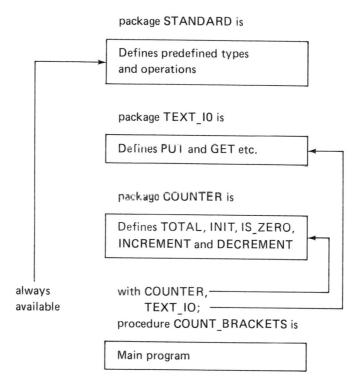

Fig. 1.2 – Structure of COUNT_BRACKETS

At this point the reader may be wondering why it is necessary to write 28 lines of code in order to implement a trivial operation like counting. The above example is very simple and, of course, the COUNTER package could easily be dispensed with. NBRACKETS could be declared as an INTEGER immediately and incremented and decremented directly within the COUNT_BRACKETS procedure. However, the point of this example is to illustrate how large programs may be built. Few abstract types are as simple as TOTAL and the separation of the implementation of such types from their use offers very real advantages. First and foremost, it offers a powerful strategy for designing programs by successive refinement. Secondly, the package allows the use of an abstract type to be protected. This allows the operation of a package to be verified in isolation from its working environment. Thirdly, the implementation part of a package can be changed without affecting the program that uses it thus simplifying program maintenance. For example, a check could be added to the COUNTER package to ensure that the count never goes negative without any modification to the procedure COUNT_BRACKETS. Finally, the division of a program into separate packages makes it very easy to apportion tasks to a team of programmers. The reader is, therefore, asked to use his imagination and to picture the above example not as a simple 40-line program, but as a cameo of the structure of a 40,000-line program!

This, then, is the basis of Ada programming. The overall design is defined in terms of a collection of functionally distinct modules. Each module is represented by a package, and its interface to the rest of the system is defined by the package specification. This interface defines the abstract properties of the module, that is, it identifies those entities which characterise the external behaviour of the module. Irrelevant implementation details are hidden inside the private part of the package specification and the package body. Actual Ada programs may exhibit rather more complex structures than that illustrated by Fig. 1.2. For example, packages will depend on other units besides the main program. Also, Ada allows parallel tasks to be initiated, and this considerably complicates the overall structure. Nevertheless, the basic principles involved in the use of packages remain unchanged.

The following chapters of this book describe the various features of the Ada language in detail. Most chapters conclude with one or more examples; however, very few of these represent complete Ada programs. Rather, they represent modules or subcomponents of modules. It is hoped that this introductory chapter has given the reader a clear enough picture of the overall construction of an Ada program to enable him to place these examples in a suitable context.

2

Notation

An Ada program consists of a sequence of basic lexical units or symbols. Each symbol is made up of one or more characters just like words in ordinary English. In this chapter, the rules for writing these symbols and their meaning will be described.

The symbols fall into six classes: identifiers, delimiters, numeric literals, character literals, strings and comments. Numeric literals and identifiers must be separated from other numeric literals and identifiers by a space or a newline; in all other cases layout characters are ignored. In general, the layout of a program should be carefully chosen to accentuate its structure — the examples given in this book may serve as a guide.

2.1 IDENTIFIERS

Most entities in an Ada program have a name which allows them to be referred to. A name is written as a sequence of letters, digits and underscore characters, starting with a letter and ending with a letter or digit. Names are one of the uses of identifiers: the other use is in denoting the keywords of the language. Identifiers denoting keywords are *reserved*, that is, they cannot be used as names. If upper and lower case are available, then by convention keywords are written in lower case and other names in upper case. For example in

procedure ID_EXAMPLE **is**

the identifiers **procedure** and **is** are keywords and ID_EXAMPLE is a programmer defined name. Note that the underscore character is significant: IDEXAMPLE would be treated as a different name. Upper and lower case are not, however, distinguished so that

        PROCEDURE   Procedure   procedure

all denote the same keyword.

The syntax of identifiers is given by the following diagrams

S1 ident

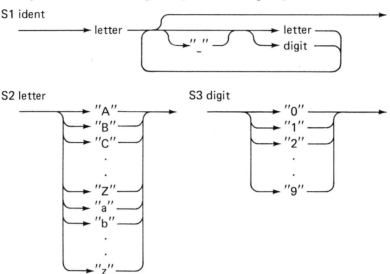

An aside for those unfamiliar with syntax diagrams:

Syntax diagrams such as those shown above are used throughout this book to describe the grammatical structure of the various Ada constructs. Each syntax diagram defines in graphical form the sequences of symbols which are legal for that syntactic unit. Starting from the entry point at the left side of the diagram, the arrows must be followed until the exit is reached on the right side. Each node in the diagram is labelled with either the name of some other syntactic unit or a terminal symbol, the latter being distinguished by the double primes. When the name of a syntactic unit is encountered in a diagram then it means that the diagram for that unit must be followed through at that point. When a terminal symbol is encountered then that symbol must be the current symbol on the input stream.

The act of determining whether a given input sequence is legal according to the syntax diagrams is called *parsing*. Suppose that it is required to determine whether or not AB_1 is a legal identifier. To find out, a path must be found through syntax diagram S1 which corresponds to the sequence of characters A, B, underscore, 1. If such a path can be found then the sequence does represent a legal identifier. The first node encountered in S1 is 'letter'. This is the name of another syntactic unit so the diagram for that unit must be followed through. Looking at S2, it can be seen that A is a legal letter, so the first character of the input sequence has been parsed. Now returning to S1, the path branches. One branch leads to the exit and the other leads into a loop. Since the input has not yet been fully parsed, the loop must be entered. Each time around the loop, either a letter or a digit must be parsed, optionally preceded by an underscore character. Thus, the first time around the loop B can be parsed and the second time _1 can be parsed. The input sequence will then be exhausted so the exit branch can be chosen to leave the syntax diagram. The sequence AB_1 has then been successfully parsed using S1, and hence it is a legal identifier.

In fact, from the programmer's point of view, such a detailed analysis is rarely necessary. He normally uses syntax diagrams as *recipes* for constructing grammatically correct Ada programs. For example, S1 shows that an identifier starts with a letter and is followed by any number of letters or digits optionally preceded by an underscore. Thus, following this recipe, AB_1 is clearly an identifier but 1_AB, _AB1, etc. are not.

Finally, note that the syntax diagrams in this chapter describe the basic lexical units of Ada, and therefore, their terminal symbols are characters. All the syntax diagrams in the rest of the book have these lexical units as their terminal symbols and describe how to put them into the proper sequences required to build the various Ada language constructs.

Examples

(a) programmer defined names

    MAX_SIZE   VEC0   PREVIOUS_VALVE_STATUS
    ITEM1_ENTRY46   I   ABC

(b) Reserved words — the following is a complete list of the 63 keywords used in Ada:

abort	else	mod	renames
abs	elsif		return
accept	end	new	reverse
access	entry	not	
all	exception	null	select
and	exit		separate
array		of	subtype
at	for	or	
	function	others	task
begin		out	terminate
body	generic		then
	goto	package	type
case		pragma	
constant	if	private	use
	in	procedure	
declare	is		when
delay		raise	while
delta	limited	range	with
digits	loop	record	
do		rem	xor

Finally, as noted in Chapter 1, Ada is designed to allow the production of highly readable and maintainable programs at the expense of some extra effort in writing. Thus, few abbreviations are used in Ada, for example, **constant** not **const** , **procedure** not **proc** , etc. Similarly, names should be carefully chosen to clearly indicate the nature and the purpose of the entity that they denote. Ada is intended for writing software with a potentially long life cycle. Some extra effort in the choice of names and avoiding the temptation to use obscure abbreviations can be a vital factor in the production of maintainable software. After all, a program is only written once, but it may be read many times.

2.2 DELIMITERS

Delimiters are used to denote syntactic symbols and operators. They are functionally similar to keywords except that they are represented by one or two special characters rather than by identifiers. The full set of delimiters used in Ada is as follows:

$$\& \quad ' \quad (\quad) \quad + \quad - \quad * \quad / \quad . \quad , \quad : \quad ; \quad < \quad = \quad > \quad |$$
$$\Rightarrow \quad .. \quad ** \quad := \quad /= \quad >= \quad <= \quad << \quad >> \quad <>$$

2.3 NUMERIC LITERALS

Numeric literals are used to denote integer and real values. They can be expressed either in a conventional decimal form or in a based form. All numeric literals containing a decimal point denote real values, all others denote integer values. Both integer and real literals may include an exponent but in the case of integers the exponent must be positive. Digit values for bases higher than ten are denoted by letters, that is, A=10, B=11, C=12, etc.

The syntax of numeric literals is given by the following diagrams

S4   numeric_literal

S5   decimal_number

S6   based_number

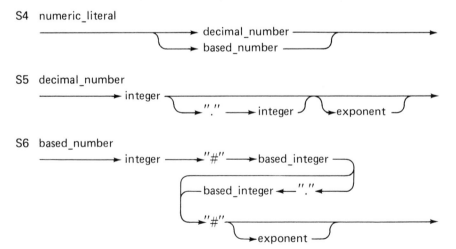

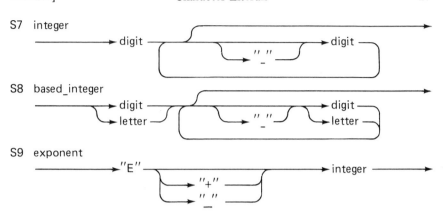

S7 integer

S8 based_integer

S9 exponent

Examples:

(a) Integer values

0	123	596	
10000	10_000	1E4	- - all the same value
8#77#			- - 63 in base 8
16#FE#			- - 254 in base 16

(b) Real values

3.0	123.0	3.14159	
10000.0	1.0E4	10_000.0	- - all the same value
16#F.FF#E+2			- - 4095.0 in base 16

Note that, unlike the case for identifiers, the underscore character is completely ignored in numeric literals. In based numbers, the actual base and exponent are always expressed in decimal. The exponent in a based number indicates the power of the base by which the preceding number must be multiplied to obtain the value of the literal. Hence, for example, 2#1#E1 means $1*2^1$ and not $1*10^1$ and is, therefore, equal to 2 and not 10.

2.4 CHARACTER LITERALS

A character literal denotes a character value. It is written as a single character enclosed by single quotes. The syntax diagram is as follows

S10 character_literal

$$\longrightarrow \text{"'"} \longrightarrow \text{ASCII GRAPHIC CHARACTER} \longrightarrow \text{"'"} \longrightarrow$$

Examples:

'A'	'a'	- - upper and lower case A
''''		- - the single quote character
' '		- - the space character

2.5 CHARACTER STRINGS

Character strings denote sequences of zero or more characters. They are written enclosed in double quotes. When the double quote itself must be included in a string it is written twice. A character string must not extend beyond one line; however, the catenation operator & may be used to catenate strings on adjacent lines. The syntax of a character string is as follows:

S11 character_string

Examples:

    "TEXT STRING"   -- a string of 11 characters
    "say " "Hello" " "   -- the string 'say "Hello" '
    " "   -- a null string
    "A"   -- not the same as 'A'
    "A very long string extending over" &
    "two lines"

Note also that the & operator can be used to catenate a string and a character, for example,

    "ABCD" & 'E'   -- same as "ABCDE"

An important use of this facility is that it allows control characters to be embedded within a string. For example, the carriage return and line feed characters are defined in a package called ASCII within STANDARD and are called ASCII.CR and ASCII.LF, respectively (see section 3.3). Hence, a new line could be inserted into a string by

    "1st line of string" & ASCII.CR & ASCII.LF & "2nd line of string"

2.6 COMMENTS

A comment starts with a double hyphen (minus sign) and is terminated by the end of the line.

Examples:

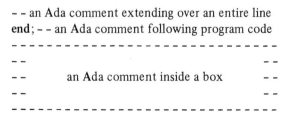

Note that it is not possible to interpose a comment between two symbols or before the first symbol on a line.

2.7 PRAGMAS

A pragma is used to issue a directive to the Ada compiler. A certain number of pragmas are defined as part of the formal Ada language. Any implementation of Ada, however, may introduce additional pragmas. The syntax of a pragma is

S12 pragma

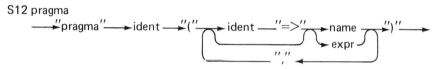

Examples:

      pragma LIST(OFF)   – – suppress list output
      pragma PACK(VECTOR)   – – minimise storage for VECTOR

A full list of the pre-defined Ada pragmas is given in Appendix B.

2.8 EXERCISES

(2.1) Which of the following are illegal symbols?

      (a) A_1000_000   (f) ' " '
      (b) UPPER_LIMIT   (g) " " "
      (c) 1000_E2   (h) 8#197#
      (d) 1.0E-2   (i) 23.E6
      (e) 1E-2

In each case state why the symbol is illegal and re-write it correctly.

(2.2) Express the binary pattern

      1011 0011 0000 1101

as a based integer number

      (a) in base 2
      (b) in base 8
      (c) in base 16

3

Discrete data types

Discrete data types are used to represent simple discrete scalar values. A scalar value is any value which has no internal structure. For example, the distance along the x-axis of a graph is a scalar quantity, whereas a position in the x-y plane is not since it requires two values to represent it. Discrete scalar values are those for which, over a given range, each value in the range can be enumerated. For example, integer numbers are discrete, whereas real numbers are not discrete. Over a fixed range, say 0 to 5, the integer values can be enumerated as 0, 1, 2, 3, 4 and 5 but there are an infinite number of real values in the same range.

Ada provides three pre-defined discrete types: integers, characters and Booleans plus an extensive set of facilities for allowing the user to define his own types appropriate to the problem at hand. Although the pre-defined types and the various mechanisms for building user-defined types each have their own special characteristics, there are a few basic principles on which the whole Ada typing system operates. The first section of this chapter explains these principles using the discrete types as examples. However, the reader should note that the principles are universal and apply to all Ada types. Subsequent sections then cover the details of defining and using discrete data types.

3.1 BASIC PRINCIPLES OF THE ADA TYPING SYSTEM

All computer programs are concerned primarily with the manipulation of data values and these data values may be of many different kinds. For example, one data object may take values which are integer numbers whereas another may hold character values. The set of values which may be assigned to a given object is denoted by its type. In Ada, the concept of type is exploited extensively in order to maximise security and reliability.

Ada is a strongly typed language. This means that
  (i) Every data object has a unique type;
  (ii) Each type defines a set of values and the set of operations which may be applied to these values;

(iii) In every assignment of a value to an object, the type of the value and the type of the object must be the same;

(iv) Every operator applied to a data object must belong to the set of operators defined by the object's type.

The effect of these rules is best illustrated by an example. Suppose that the following two objects are declared:

```
MYCHAR:CHARACTER;
IVAL:INTEGER;
```

where the notation means that MYCHAR is the name of a variable of type CHARACTER and IVAL is the name of a variable of type INTEGER. These two types are pre-defined Ada types denoting the values of the ASCII character set and whole numbers, respectively.

Typical assignments to these variables might be

```
MYCHAR := 'A';
IVAL :=0;
```

In both cases, the value on the RHS of the assignment belongs to the same type as the variable named on the LHS. Hence, they are both legal. Consider now, however, the following statements

```
MYCHAR :=0;                -- types do not match
IVAL := MYCHAR;            -- types to not match
MYCHAR := MYCHAR + '0';    -- illegal operator
```

Each of the above statements is illegal according to the strong typing rules and would be reported as an error by the Ada compiler. Thus, inadvertent errors such as mis-typing 0 instead of '0' are detected during compilation and many 'tricky' programming practices are quite rightly prohibited.

In any program of reasonable size, there will be a variety of different values being stored and manipulated. As a typical example consider a program which reads in a sequence of persons' names and their ages from some input device and stores these in a table. This program will have to manipulate the character values in each person's name and the integer values of each person's age. The strong typing rules given above ensure that there can be no possibility of mixing-up names and ages. However, the ages will not be the only integer values in the program. Each entry in the table will have a position number which will also be an integer value. If both ages and position numbers are represented by the type INTEGER then strong typing will not help detect inadvertent errors such as the assignment of a position number to an age.

This problem is overcome in Ada by allowing the user to define his own types. A simple way of doing this is by deriving the new type from an existing type. For example, the type declaration

type AGE_IN_YEARS **is new** INTEGER;

introduces a new type called AGE_IN_YEARS. This type has all the properties of the INTEGER type (that is, the same literal values and operations), but is nevertheless a distinct type. Hence, given

    AGE: AGE_IN_YEARS;
    TABLE_POSITION: INTEGER;

then,

    AGE := 0;

is legal but

    AGE := TABLE_POSITION;

is not legal because the types are different.

This kind of facility can be extremely useful in many programming situations. Essentially it allows a set of data objects to be grouped into a logically distinct class regardless of their underlying representation. Thus, although both AGE and TABLE_POSITION are represented as integer numbers, at the level of the program they are treated as logically distinct quantities.

As another example, suppose that a program needs to manipulate data representing the physical quantities of distance and velocity. In most languages other than Ada, both of these quantities would be denoted by the same real type, for example

    D1,D2:REAL;   - - distances
    V1,V2:REAL;   - - velocities

hence, there would be no way of detecting inconsistencies such as

    D1 := V1;

In Ada, however, distinct types can be introduced

    type DISTANCE **is new** REAL;
    type VELOCITY **is new** REAL;

Now the variables of distance and velocity can be declared with distinct types, namely

    D1,D2:DISTANCE;
    V1,V2:VELOCITY;

and the inconsistent assignment

    D1 := V1;

would now be detected by the compiler. Notice also that the declaration of explicit type names for distance and velocity aids readability to the extent that the supporting comments are no longer needed.

(At this point the reader may be wondering how calculations such as

time := distance * velocity

are computed since normally the operator * would require that both operands be of the same type and the result type would also be of this type. The answer to this is that Ada allows operators to be extended to cover the various combinations of operand and result types needed (see section 6.7).)

The second feature provided by Ada in its typing mechanism is the ability to selectively constrain the set of values which may be assumed by an object. Once again, this facility improves security and gives the reader of the program valuable additional information on the way that a variable is used. The actual kinds of constraint allowed depend on the class of type involved. In the case of discrete types, a constraint may be used to explicitly define the range of values that an object of that type may take. For example, if the variable TABLE_POSITION is known to take values only between 1 and 100 then it can be declared thus

TABLE_POSITION:INTEGER **range** 1. .100;

Subsequent to this declaration all values assigned to TABLE_POSITION are checked to be within the stated range. Thus,

TABLE_POSITION := 0;

would generate a compiler error message. However, range constraint errors cannot always be detected by the compiler. In an assignment such as

TABLE_POSITION:= IVAL;

the range check would normally have to be performed at run-time.

The use of range constraints in the declaration of variables is strongly recommended. In essence, the whole philosophy of Ada's typing system is based on the principle that any data object should be allowed to take just those values which are actually needed and no more. This principle gives improved program reliability and readability. In the case of TABLE_POSITION above, the declaration states that it is an INTEGER type restricted to the range of values 1 to 100. If a value outside this range is ever assigned to it, then an error will be raised. Presumably such an occurrence would be the result of a programming error. If the range constraint was omitted, this error could well have gone unnoticed for a long time. Hence, range constraints improve reliability. Readability is also improved because the stated range is valuable information for the reader when trying to understand what each variable is used for.

Where a group of objects require the same constraint then a sub-type can be introduced. For example,

subtype SMALL_INT **is** INTEGER **range** -128 .. 127;

introduces a sub-type called SMALL_INT. A variable declared of type SMALL_
INT then has an implicit range constraint applied to it, for example,

> I1:SMALL_INT;

is equivalent to writing

> I1:INTEGER **range** –128 .. 127;

It should be stressed that a sub-type does not introduce a new type. Hence,

> I1 := IVAL;

is a legal assignment. However, a distinct type can be introduced along with a
range constraint, by a derived type declaration, for example,

> **type** MY_INT **is new** INTEGER **range** –128 .. 127;

In this case, a variable of type MY_INT would be distinct from a variable of type
INTEGER or sub-type SMALL_INT. In fact, the above declaration is exactly
equivalent to writing

> **type** *** **is new** INTEGER;
> **subtype** MY_INT **is** *** **range** –128 .. 127;

where *** represents an anonymous identifier. Using this facility for associating
a range constraint directly with a derived type declaration, the type AGE_IN_
YEARS given earlier would be more precisely declared as

> **type** AGE_IN_YEARS **is new** INTEGER **range** 0. .150;

(assuming that 150 is a reasonable upper bound on a person's age!).

Finally, Ada provides an extensive set of attribute enquiries for determining
certain characteristics of types and sub-types. These are written in the form

S13 attribute

For example,

> INTEGER'FIRST

gives the first (that is, most negative) integer value supported by the implementation for the type INTEGER. Similarly,

> INTEGER'LAST

gives the last value. As an example of the use of such enquiries, Ada provides a
pre-defined sub-type called NATURAL defined as

> **subtype** NATURAL **is** INTEGER **range** 0 .. INTEGER'LAST;

Thus, the sub-type NATURAL includes all the positive integer values supported
by the implementation including zero.

In summary, Ada is a strongly typed language. A value can only be assigned to an object if their types are the same. Two types are the same if and only if they have the same name. New types can be introduced in terms of existing types by a derived type declaration. The set of values of a given type can be constrained by applying a range constraint to an object when it is declared or by introducing an explicit sub-type.

Formally, the syntax of type and sub-type declarations is given by the following diagrams

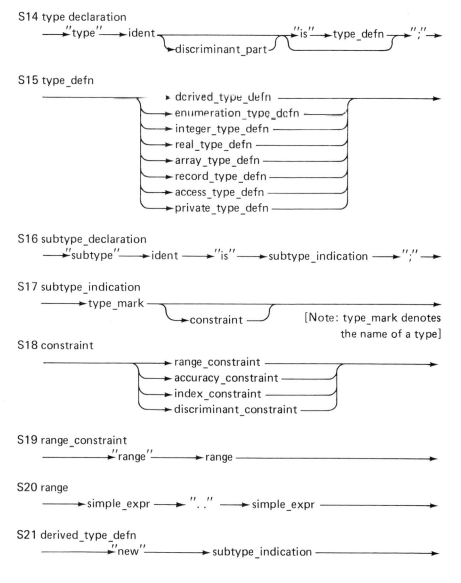

S14 type declaration

S15 type_defn

S16 subtype_declaration

S17 subtype_indication

    [Note: type_mark denotes the name of a type]

S18 constraint

S19 range_constraint

S20 range

S21 derived_type_defn

The various undefined type definitions and constraints will be described in subsequent chapters. Notice that a sub-type declaration need not include a constraint. In this case, the new sub-type name is just a synonym for the existing type name.

3.2 ENUMERATION TYPES

The most basic way of introducing a new type is to explicitly enumerate the set of values which it denotes. In Ada this is done by means of an enumerated type declaration, with the syntax shown by the following diagram

S22 enumeration_type_defn

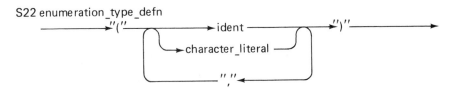

Ignoring for the moment the use of character literals, examples of enumerated type definitions are

> **type** DAY **is** (MON,TUE,WED,THU,FRI,SAT,SUN);
> **type** COLOUR **is** (WHITE,RED,YELLOW,GREEN,BLUE,BROWN,
>   BLACK);
> **type** ALARM_STATE **is** (GREEN,YELLOW,RED);

DAY is the name of a type with just seven values MON, TUE, WED, . . . SUN. Any object declared of type DAY must have one of these values and no other. For example, it is not possible to assign the value WHITE or the number 1 or the character 'A' to an object of type DAY. Similarly, COLOUR is the name of a type with values whose literals are the names of colours. ALARM_STATE is also a type with values that are colours but this is quite distinct from the type COLOUR. The same identifier can be used to name a value in more than one enumeration type. Such identifiers are said to be *overloaded*, the compiler determines which identifier is meant in a given situation from the context. For example, given

> ALARM:ALARM_STATUS;

then in

> ALARM := GREEN;

the type of the value GREEN is assumed to be the same as that of ALARM. However, there are occasions where the type of an overloaded identifier is ambiguous. In these circumstances, the compiler will report an error and a qualified expression must then be used as described in section 6.6.

If required, sub-types of enumeration types can be declared in the usual way, for example

subtype WORK_DAY **is** DAY **range** MON . . FRI;

and, of course, constraints can be applied directly in an object declaration, for example

ALERT_STATUS:ALARM_STATE **range** YELLOW . . RED;

The set of values denoted by an enumeration type is ordered. The first value in the set is given by the attribute FIRST and the last value by the attribute LAST. For example,

DAY'FIRST = MON
DAY'LAST = SUN

The preceding and succeeding values of an enumeration value are given by the attributes PRED and SUCC. For example,

DAY'PRED(WED) = TUE
DAY'SUCC(WED) = THU

Associated with each enumeration value is a number denoting its position in the ordered sequence of values. This position is given by the attribute POS. Thus,

DAY'POS(MON) = 0   - - the 1st position number is always 0
DAY'POS(TUE) = 1
DAY'POS(WED) = 2   etc.

The inverse function to POS is given by the VAL attribute, for example,

DAY'VAL(0) =   MON
DAY'VAL(1) =   TUE
DAY'VAL(2) =   WED etc.

All of the above 6 attributes can be applied to any discrete type but in practice they are mainly used with enumeration types.

Enumeration types are useful for describing non-numerical data such as that illustrated by the examples above. Of course, the days of the week could be represented by integer numbers rather than enumeration literals but this would lead to obscurity in the program design, would be rather less secure and more prone to error. The intention in Ada is always to allow the programmer to describe his data in as natural a way as possible.

3.3 CHARACTER TYPES

Ada provides a pre-defined type called CHARACTER which denotes the values of the ASCII character set. It may be noted that the syntax diagram for an enumeration type declaration given in the previous section allows a character literal to be used to denote an enumeration value. This allows the type CHAR-ACTER to be defined by enumeration. All printing characters in the ASCII set are denoted by character literals 'A', 'B', 'C', etc. All non-printing characters are denoted by mnemonic identifiers defined in a package called ASCII which, like the CHARACTER type, is given in the package STANDARD. The most commonly used non-printing characters are

```
LF              - - line feed
CR              - - carriage return
FF              - - form feed
```

In addition, the package ASCII provides names for some of the more unusual ASCII characters so that they can be introduced into a program using terminals which only provide a limited character set. For example,

```
LC_A            - - same as lower case 'a'
LC_B            - - same as lower case 'b'
    . .
    . . etc.

AT_SIGN         - - same as '@'
SHARP           - - same as '#'
QUERY           - - same as '?'
    . .
    . . etc.
```

Remember, however, that to use any of the character values defined in ASCII, the character name must be preceded by the package name (or a 'use ASCII' clause can be used − see 7.3). The complete contents of the ASCII package can be inspected in the listing of the package STANDARD given in Appendix C.

The attributes POS and VAL are particularly useful for converting between characters and their position values. For example, suppose that the character variable CH declared by

    CH:CHARACTER;

holds one of the characters '0' to '9'. Then the actual integer value represented by CH is given by

    CHARACTER'POS(CH) - CHARACTER'POS('0')

This type of conversion is often required in input-output routines.

Because Ada allows enumeration literals to be overloaded, the user can introduce his own character sets. For example,

    type HEX_DIGIT **is** ('0','1','2','3','4','5','6','7',
                '8','9','A','B','C','D','E','F');

defines a character type suitable for encoding numbers in hexadecimal format. Of course, the type CHARACTER could be used for this purpose but the introduction of a dedicated character set has several advantages. Firstly, the conversions between numbers and hex digits are trivial

> HEX_DIGIT'POS('0') = 0
> HEX_DIGIT'VAL(0) = '0'
> HEX_DIGIT'POS('F') = 15 etc.

Secondly, the type HEX_DIGIT offers greater security. If HEX_CH was a variable of type CHARACTER then an error such as

> HEX_CH := '@';

would pass undetected whereas if HEX_CH was of type HEX_DIGIT then the error would be detected by the compiler. Note that a sub-type of CHARACTER cannot help here because the digits and letters are not contiguous values. Finally, the use of an explicit problem-oriented character set improves program readability.

3.4 THE BOOLEAN TYPE

The logical values *true* and *false* are denoted by the pre-defined type BOOLEAN. Again, the definition of the type is by means of an enumeration type declaration, namely:

> **type** BOOLEAN **is** (FALSE,TRUE);

Notice that FALSE is ordered less than TRUE. The BOOLEAN type is used extensively for denoting the values of conditions in a variety of control structures (see Chapter 4).

3.5 INTEGER TYPES

As noted previously, Ada provides a pre-defined type called INTEGER representing integer values over an implementation dependent range. An Ada implementation must provide this type but it may also provide additional types such as SHORT_INTEGER and LONG_INTEGER with correspondingly smaller and greater ranges.

A classic problem with integer types is that because their ranges are implementation dependent, they are a potential source of non-portability. The ability to define one's own integer types in Ada allows this problem to be effectively solved. For example, suppose that a program requires that all integers cover at most the range -32768 to +32767 then a suitable integer type can be declared as follows

> **type** MYINT **is new** INTEGER **range** -32768 .. 32767;

Provided that the pre-defined type INTEGER in all implementations for which the program is to be used can accommodate this range then the program will work correctly without modification. However, if this is not the case, say for example, that a particular implementation only supports the range –4096 to +4095 then the type declaration for **MYINT** would have to be modified to, say,

type MYINT **is new** LONG_INTEGER **range** –32768 .. 32767;

To avoid having to redefine *portable* integer types in this way to suit the implementation, Ada allows a suitable parent type to be selected automatically by the compiler. To do this, a special syntax is provided for integer type declarations,

S23 integer_type_defn

————————————————▶ range_constraint ——————————————————▶

that is, for integer types, only the required range need be specified. Using this facility, the type **MYINT** would be declared as

type MYINT **is range** –32768 .. 32767;

The effect of this declaration is equivalent to writing

type MYINT **is new** "INTEGER_TYPE" **range** –32768 .. 32767;

where the compiler chooses a suitable pre-defined type for "INTEGER_TYPE" which is just big enough to support the requested range, that is, INTEGER, LONG_INTEGER, etc. as appropriate. In this way, truly portable programs can be written.

3.6 EXPRESSIONS

As with most programming languages, Ada allows values to be computed by applying various combinations of operators to other values in the form of expressions. In this section, the general rules concerning expressions will be given and the operators for discrete data types described. The syntax diagrams relating to expressions will be given in full here although some of the productions refer to other kinds of data types. These will be described in later chapters.

The syntax of Ada expressions is given by the following rules

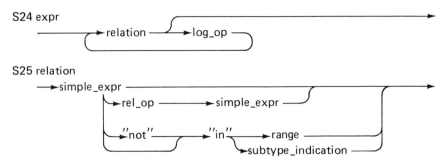

S24 expr

S25 relation

S26 simple_expr

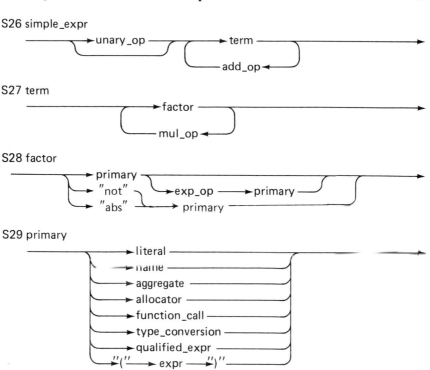

S27 term

S28 factor

S29 primary

As can be seen from examining these diagrams, the basic units of expressions are primaries. Each primary has a value and a type. Since only discrete types are of interest at the moment, the only two primaries which need to be considered here are literals and names. Literals denote fixed numeric, enumeration or character values

S30 literal

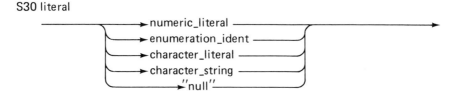

Character strings were described in Chapter 2; they will be discussed further when arrays are introduced in Chapter 8. The symbol **null** is used with access types as described in Chapter 11. Examples of literals of discrete types are

27	– – an integer literal
'A'	– – a character literal
GREEN	– – an enumeration literal
8#777#	– – an integer literal in based form

Names are used to denote objects. The simplest form of a name is just an identifier. The other forms will be dealt with later.

S31 name

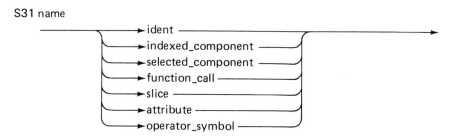

All Ada operators are divided into 6 classes, each class having a distinct precedence level

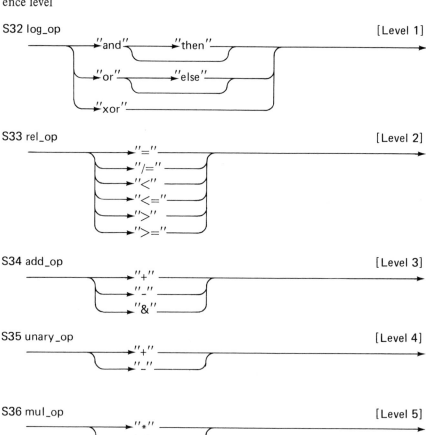

S37 exp_op   [Level 6]
————————————————→ ''**'' ——————————————————————————————→

where the precedence levels are shown in square brackets (1 is lowest). Note that
the **in** and **not in** operators given in diagram S25 have the same precedence as the
rel_op operators, and **not** and **abs** have the same precedence as the exp_op
operator.

As an example of an expression, consider the following

A + B**2 = C * D **or** E

The names A, B, C, D, E and the literal number 2 are primaries. S28 shows that
A, B**2, C, D and E are factors. S27 shows that factors can be combined with
multiplying operators to give terms. Hence, A, B**2, C*D and E are terms. S26
shows that terms can be combined with adding operators to give simple expressions. Thus, A + B**2, C*D and E are simple expressions. S25 shows that a
relation consists of either a single simple expression or two simple expressions
joined by a relation operator. Hence, A + B**2 = C * D and E are relations.
Finally, S24 shows that an expression is one or more relations joined by logical
operators. Hence, the original sequence of symbols is indeed an expression.

The above groupings of factors, terms, simple expressions and relations can
be shown more clearly by bracketing the expression as follows

((A + (B**2)) = (C * D)) **or** E

This equivalent form of the expression clearly shows the precedence levels
which are, in fact, implicit in the way that the syntax of expressions has been
defined. For example, the exponentiating operator ** must be applied first
(precedence 6), then the multiplying operator * must be applied (precedence 5)
and so on down to the logical operator **or** which must be applied last (precedence 1).

The way that expressions are constructed having been explained, the various
classes of operators will now be described.

Logical operators
These operators can be applied to operands of type BOOLEAN and give a
BOOLEAN result.

and	– – denotes logical conjunction
or	– – denotes logical inclusive disjunction
xor	– – denotes logical exclusive disjunction

Hence, given A and B of type BOOLEAN, the following table gives the result of
applying each of these operators to all possible values of A and B.

A	A	A and B	A or B	A xor B
T	T	T	T	F
T	F	F	T	T
F	T	F	T	T
F	F	F	F	F

where T=TRUE and F=FALSE. For example, if WAITING and FREE are of type BOOLEAN then the expression

(WAITING **and** FREE) **or** X=0

will be true if either both WAITING and FREE are true or the value of X is equal to zero. Notice here that the brackets must not be omitted. The form of logical expression denoted by

A **lop** B **lop** C **lop** D ...

is only allowed if the logical operator (denoted by **lop**) is the same in each case.

In addition to **and** and **or** the *short-circuit* forms **and then** and **or else** are provided. These short circuit forms have the same meaning as the corresponding normal forms but are evaluated differently. Consider the expression

E1 **or** E2

where E1 and E2 denote expressions. The language specification does not preclude the possibility that E2 will be evaluated even if E1 is already known to be true. In some circumstances, this may be embarrassing. For example, in the expression

$Y = 0$ **or** $X/Y > 1$

if $Y = 0$ and the compiler evaluates $X/Y > 1$ then an error will occur as a result of the attempt to divide by zero. The short-circuit forms allow this possibility to be excluded by writing

E1 **or else** E2

In this case, E1 is always evaluated first, E2 then only being evaluated if E1 is false; otherwise the expression is true. Hence expressions such as

$Y = 0$ **or else** $X/Y > 1$

are evaluated safely. The **and then** operator has a similar effect. In

E1 **and then** E2

E1 is evaluated first and E2 is only evaluated if E1 is true; otherwise the expression is false.

Relational operators

The relational operators used for comparing values are

=	- - equal
/=	- - not equal
>	- - greater than
>=	- - greater than or equal
<	- - less than
<=	- - less than or equal

The result of any comparison is always of type BOOLEAN. The operands may be of any discrete type, but both operands must be of the same discrete type. Examples are

26 > 3	- - false
TRUE > FALSE	- - true
'A' < 'n'	- - true
MON /= DAY'FIRST	- - false

In addition to these 6 relational operators, Ada provides two membership operations **in** and **not in**. These may be used to test whether or not a given value lies within a specified range or whether or not it satisfies a given subtype constraint. Examples are

N **not in** 0 .. 10	- - true if N<0 or N>10
WED **in** WORKDAY	- - true
WED **in** DAY **range** MON .. FRI	- - same test
CH **in** '0' .. '9'	- - true if CH is a digit

Adding operators

The adding operators + and - may be used to add and subtract operands of the same integer type (the & operator is used with arrays and is described later in section 8.3). Examples are

26 + 9 - 4	- - 31
DAY'POS(WED) - DAY'POS(MON)	- - 2

but note that the following is not allowed

WED - MON	- - illegal operand types

The type of the result of an integer addition or subtraction will be the same as the types of the operands. Different integer types may not be mixed in the same expression.

Unary operators

The unary operators + and - may be used to indicate the identity and negation of any integer type.

Multiplying operators

The operators * and / may be applied to integer operands to denote integer multiplication and division respectively. In the case of division, the result is truncated towards zero. Hence,

$$11/5 = 2 \qquad \text{and} \qquad -11/5 = -2$$

The operator **rem** gives the remainder after integer division. Formally it obeys the equality

$$A = (A/B)*B + (A \text{ rem } B)$$

where (A **rem** B) has the sign of A. The operator **mod** gives the mathematical modulus operation such that

$$A = B*N + (A \text{ mod } B)$$

for some integer value of N where (A **mod** B) has the sign of B. Note that if A and B have the same sign then both operators have the same effect. Some examples are

13 **rem** 5 = 3	13 **mod** 5 = 3
-13 **rem** 5 = -3	-13 **mod** 5 = 2
13 **rem** -5 = 3	13 **mod** -5 = -2
-13 **rem** -5 = -3	-13 **mod** -5 = -3

Exponentiating operator

The operator ** can be used to indicate the repeated multiplication of an integer type. The type of the result is the same as the left-hand operand. The right hand operand must be non-negative. Examples are

I ** 2	- - same as I*I
I ** 0	- - equals 1 always

The not and abs operators

In addition to the above, an **abs** operator is provided. It may be applied to any numeric type and yields the absolute value of its operand. Examples are

abs I	- - if I >=0 then I else -I
abs (-26)	- - 26

The operator **not** may be applied to a BOOLEAN operand to give the logical complement. For example,

not (I>0)	- - true if I <= 0

Note that **not** has a higher precedence than the relational operators: therefore the parentheses are essential.

3.7 TYPE CONVERSIONS

As indicated at the beginning of this chapter, Ada encourages the programmer to introduce many different types into his program to improve both security and clarity. Occasionally this can cause difficulties when a value needs to be copied from one related but distinct type to another. Type conversions allow such operations to be performed. They take the form of a function call with the type name as function name, that is,

S38 type_conversion
$$\longrightarrow \text{type\_mark} \longrightarrow {''}({''} \longrightarrow \text{expr} \longrightarrow {''}){''} \longrightarrow$$

To illustrate the rules applying to type conversion, consider the following type and variable declarations

```
type STATUS is (OFF,ON);
type SWITCH is (OFF,ON);
type BIT is new SWITCH;

type INT1 is range 0 . . 100;
type INT2 is range 0 . . 50;
subtype TINY_INT2 is INT2 range 0 . . 10;

ST:STATUS;   - - declare some objects of the above types
SW:SWITCH;
B:BIT;
I1:INT1;
I2:INT2;
T2:TINY_INT2;
```

Consider first the enumerated types STATUS, SWITCH and BIT. The types STATUS and SWITCH are completely unrelated — the fact that the names chosen for their enumeration literals are the same is merely coincidental. Hence, the value of ST cannot be assigned to SW (or vice versa), that is,

```
ST := STATUS(SW);        - - illegal type conversion
```

is not allowed. The types SWITCH and BIT, however, are closely related since one is directly derived from the other. In this case, type conversions are allowed, for example,

```
SW := SWITCH(B);
B   := BIT(SW);
```

are both legal.

In general, a type conversion may only be applied between two types if one is derived from the other. There are two exceptions to this rule. One concerns arrays and is dealt with later in section 8.6. The other concerns numeric types. All numeric types are considered to be closely related. Therefore,

    I1 := INT1(I2);   - - no range check needed

and

    I2 := INT2(I1);   - - range check needed

are allowed. Notice that a type conversion may require a range constraint check to be performed. In fact, the two types involved in a type conversion can be any numeric type, that is, an integer or a real type (reals are described in Chapter 16). When an integer type is converted to a real type (and vice versa), a change in representation as well as a range check is applied.

Finally, note that the type_mark specified in the conversion may be a sub-type name rather than a type name. For example, I1 could be assigned to T2 by

    T2 := TINY_INT2(I1);

3.8 EXERCISES

(3.1) In an operating system, all input/output operations include a code which denotes the type of input/output device involved. If the following devices are available, write a suitable type definition for representing device codes

| printer | terminal | disc |
| magnetic tape | card reader | card punch |

If ordinary users of the system are restricted to using only the printer, terminal and disc, then write a sub-type definition for representing user device codes.

(3.2) A program is required to measure the weights of certain objects in units of one gram where the maximum weight of an object is 10 000 grams. Define a suitable type for representing grams. Define a distinct type for representing weights in units of one kilogram. If the weight of an object in grams is given by W, write an expression denoting the weight to the nearest kilogram.

(3.3) Define a character type suitable for representing Roman numerals, for example, I, V, X, etc.

(3.4) Write expressions to compute the following

(a) The character digit corresponding to the integer value denoted by I where $0 <= I <= 9$.
(b) The test "I is odd and J is even" where I and J are of type INTEGER.
(c) The test "CH is a letter" where CH is of type CHARACTER.
(d) The value of INTEGER'LAST assuming that the type INTEGER is represented as an N bit 2's complement number.

(3.5) Evaluate the following expressions and state the type of the result assuming that

> **type** MY_INT **is range** -1000 .. 1000;
> **subtype** MY_POS **is** MY_INT **range** 0 .. MY_INT'LAST;
> **type** SIZE **is new** MY_INT;

and the following variables have the values and types given

I = 100,	type INTEGER
MI = -17,	type MY_INT
MP = 25,	subtype MY_POS
S = 6,	type SIZE

(A) I **mod** 6 ∗∗ 2
(B) (MI **in** MY_POS)=FALSE
(C) S + 1 <= 1
(D) MI **rem** MY_INT(S)
(E) MI **mod** MY_INT(S)

(F) MP > MI **and** S **not in** 0 .. 10
(G) 100 - SIZE(I)/S
(H) MY_POS(I) + MI
(I) I>0 **or not** S=6

If an expression is illegal, state why.

4

Statements

4.1 STATEMENT SEQUENCES

The actions to be performed by each of the various kinds of program unit (for example, task, etc.) in Ada are denoted by statement sequences. In the absence of any explicit transfer of control statement (described later), each statement in the sequence is executed in the order given. The syntax of a statement sequence is

S39 sequence_of_statements

The various kinds of statement are grouped into two classes: *simple* and *compound*. Simple statements specify a single discrete action, whereas compound statements may have further statement sequences nested within them. The syntax of a statement is given by the following diagram

S40 statement

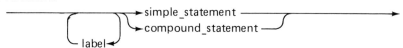

Any statement may be prefixed by a label. This facility is provided to allow a statement to be referenced by a **goto** statement (see section 4.4). Labels and **goto** statements should not be used in normal programming. They are included in Ada to allow programs to be written which automatically translate other programming languages into Ada. Labels are written in the form

S41 label

$$ \rightarrow ''<<'' \rightarrow ident \rightarrow ''>>'' \rightarrow $$

For example,

        `<<INC_X>>  X := X+1;`

is a statement with the label INC_X. All label names within a given scope must be distinct (see Chapter 9 for a discussion of the Ada scope rules). Note that no explicit declaration of a label name is required: the use of a label declares the name implicitly.

There are 11 kinds of simple statement and 6 kinds of compound statement, as shown by the following syntax diagrams

S42 simple_statement

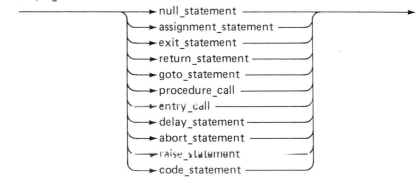

S43 compound_statement

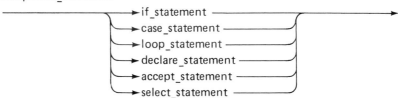

Of these only the **null**, assignment, **exit, goto, if, case** and **loop** statements are dealt with here. Declare statements are described in Chapter 5, procedure calls in Chapter 6, entry calls, **delay, abort, accept** and **select** statements in Chapter 12 and **raise** statements in Chapter 13. Code statements are implementation specific and are used to introduce machine code instructions into an Ada program. They are not covered in this book.

4.2 NULL STATEMENTS

The execution of a **null** statement has no effect. It is included to allow the programmer to indicate explicitly that no action is to be taken in the current context. Ada does not provide a dummy statement; that is, a statement sequence must include at least one statement. Hence, the **null** statement is essential in certain circumstances. Some examples of the use of **null** statements appear in later sections. The syntax of the **null** statement is just

S44 null_statement

Note that the **null** statement, like all Ada statements, must be terminated by a semicolon. In Ada, the semicolon acts as a statement terminator not a statement separator as in many other languages (for example, Pascal).

4.3 ASSIGNMENT STATEMENTS

An assignment statement enables the value computed by an expression to be assigned to a variable. The syntax is

S45 assignment_statement

$$\longrightarrow \text{name} \longrightarrow \text{":="} \longrightarrow \text{expr} \longrightarrow \text{";"} \longrightarrow$$

In all cases, the type of the expression must be the same as the type of the named variable. Hence, for example, the assignment statement

$$Z := X**2 + Y**2;$$

causes the values of X squared and Y squared to be added together and assigned to Z. X, Y and Z must all be of the same type.

4.4 GOTO STATEMENTS

As mentioned in section 4.1, **goto** statements are not used in normal programming. They are included here only for completeness: no examples of their use will be found in this book. The syntax diagram for a **goto** statement is

S46 goto_statement

$$\longrightarrow \text{"goto"} \longrightarrow \text{name} \longrightarrow \text{";"} \longrightarrow$$

The name must be that of a label. Execution of a **goto** statement causes control to be transferred to the statement prefixed by the specified label. This statement must be within the same program unit body as the **goto** statement. A **goto** statement cannot be used to transfer control into the sequence of statements within a compound statement.

4.5 IF STATEMENTS

The **if** statement is used to specify the execution of alternative sets of actions depending on a Boolean condition. The syntax of the **if** statement is given by the following diagrams

S47 if_statement

$$\rightarrow \text{"if"} \rightarrow \text{condition} \rightarrow \text{"then"} \rightarrow \text{sequence\_of\_statements}$$
$$\rightarrow \text{"elsif"} \rightarrow \text{condition} \rightarrow \text{"then"} \rightarrow \text{sequence\_of\_statements}$$
$$\rightarrow \text{"else"} \rightarrow \text{sequence\_of\_statements}$$
$$\rightarrow \text{"end"} \rightarrow \text{"if"} \rightarrow \text{";"} \longrightarrow$$

S48 condition

———————————————→   expr   —————————————————————————→

Ignoring the **elsif** part for the moment, the basic form of an **if** statement is illustrated by the following example

```
if  X > 0 then
    Y := 1;
else
    Y := -1;
end if;
```

It contains a conditional expression, that is, one returning a Boolean result and two nested statement sequences. When control reaches the **if** statement, the condition is evaluated and if the result is true then the sequence of statements between the symbols **then** and **else** are executed, otherwise the sequence between the symbols **else** and **end** are executed. Thus, following the execution of the above **if** statement, Y will be 1 if X is positive otherwise Y will be -1.

If no **else** part is required then it may be omitted, as in, for example,

```
if  I < 0 then                    - - compute abs I
    I := -I;
end if;
```

This is exactly equivalent to

```
if  I < 0 then
    I := -I;
else
    null;
end if;
```

It should be noted that the **if** statement has the explicit closing keywords **end if**. This is a characteristic of all Ada compound statements. It enables them to be nested within each other whilst retaining good program readability. Also, the use of distinct closing keywords for each kind of compound statement enables the compiler to give better diagnostic information when syntax errors occur. However, in the case of the **if** statement, the explicit closing keyword is cumbersome when further **if** statements are nested within the **else** part. For example, consider the statement

```
if  B1 then
    S1;
else
    if  B2 then
        S2;
```

```
    else
        if  B3 then
            S3;
        end if;              - - closing keywords
    end if;                  - - for nested if
end if;                      - - statements
```

To simplify this kind of structure, Ada allows an **elsif** part as an abbreviation of *"*else if .... end if*"*. Using this facility the above becomes

```
if  B1 then
    S1;
elsif  B2 then
    S2;
elsif  B3 then
    S3;
end if;
```

which is clearly more readable and succinct.

4.6 CASE STATEMENTS

The **case** statement is used to select one of a number of alternative statement sequences depending on the value of an expression (which must be a discrete type). The syntax of the **case** statement is given by the following diagrams

S49 case_statement

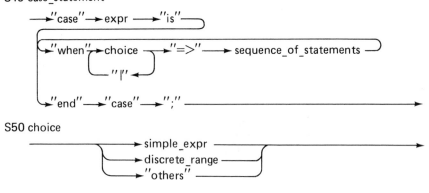

S50 choice

Each alternative statement sequence in the **case** statement is prefixed by one of more choices. A choice may be either a single static expression (that is, an expression whose value can be computed at compile time) or a static discrete range. For example, in

```
case TODAY is
    when MON         => RECEIVE_ORDERS;
    when TUE .. THU  => MAKE_ORDERS;
    when FRI         => SEND_GOODS;
    when SAT | SUN   => REST;
end case;
```

where TODAY is of type DAY (given in section 3.2), RECEIVE_ORDERS is executed if TODAY=MON, MAKE_ORDERS is executed if TODAY=TUE or WED or THU, SEND_GOODS is executed if TODAY=FRI and REST is executed if TODAY=SAT or SUN.

Notice that the syntax of the choice part is extremely flexible. Suppose that VAL is a variable of sub-type UP_TO_20 as defined by

```
subtype UP_TO_20 is INTEGER range 1 .. 20;
```

and it is required to take some specific action only if VAL is a prime number. The following case statement would do this in which the choice for DO_PRIME is constructed from a range and several single choices

```
case VAL is
    when 1 .. 3 | 5 | 7 | 11 | 13 | 17 | 19 =>
        DO_PRIME;
    when others =>
        null;
end case;
```

This example also illustrates the use of the choice **others**. If this choice is included in a case statement, then it must be given last and stands for all those possible values of the case expression which have not been given previously as explicit choices. Hence, the statement sequence prefixed by **others** denotes a default action.

Finally, note than when **others** is not given, every possible value of the case expression must be included in one of the choices. Also, the same choice may not occur in more than one position within the same case statement. Hence, the following example contains two errors

```
case VAL is
    when -1   => VAL := +1;
    when +1   => VAL := -1;
    when 0 | 1 => COUNT := COUNT + 1;
end case;
```

as the choice VAL=1 occurs twice and not all possible values of VAL are represented.

4.7 LOOP STATEMENTS

Loop statements are used to denote the repeated execution of a sequence of statements. Ada provides just one loop construct, with three variations for representing different kinds of loop. The syntax of the **loop** statement is given by the following diagrams

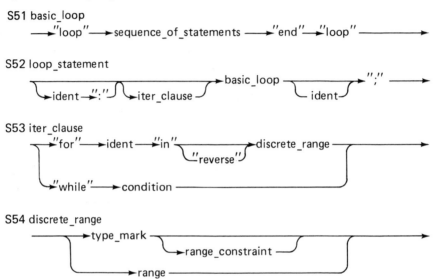

S51 basic_loop

S52 loop_statement

S53 iter_clause

S54 discrete_range

As can be seen from these, a **loop** statement consists of a basic loop optionally preceded by an iteration clause. An example of the basic loop is

```
loop
    A := A + B;
    COUNT := COUNT - 1;
end loop;
```

This statement specifies that the sequence of statements within the loop are to be repeated indefinitely. Although such infinite loops have little use in sequential programs, they are commonly used to denote the activity of a cyclic task in multi-task programs.

The number of repetitions to be performed by a loop can be controlled by prefixing it with an iteration clause. The **for** clause allows a loop to be executed a pre-determined number of times. For example, factorial N may be computed by

```
FACT := 1;
for I in 2 .. N loop
    FACT := FACT*I;
end loop;
```

In this example, I is called the loop parameter. It is a read-only variable (that is, it cannot be assigned to) which is declared implicitly on entry to the loop and ceases to exist when the loop is exited. The loop is executed once for each value in the specified discrete range with I taking successive values in the range each time around the loop. Thus, in the example, I will take the successive values 2,3,4,5, ... N. The range can be null (that is, N<2 in the example) in which case the statements within the **for** loop are skipped. Hence, in the example, if N is 0 or 1 the range is null and the statement "FACT := FACT*I" will be skipped. Notice from the syntax diagrams that the range of values to be taken by the loop parameter can be specified by giving a type or sub-type name with an optional constraint as an alternative to just giving the range bounds. Hence, the above example could have been written as

```
FACT := 1;
for I in INTEGER range 2 . . N loop
    FACT :– FACT*I,
end loop;
```

When a type name is not given, then the type of the loop parameter must be inferred from the types of the range bounds. Hence, in the first 'FACT' example, the type of I would be the same as that of N. Where both bounds are integer literals, the loop parameter is assumed to be of type INTEGER. Finally, note that the values of the **for** loop range may be assigned to the loop parameter in descending order by including the symbol **reverse**. For example,

```
for TODAY in reverse DAY loop
    - - TODAY takes the successive values
    - - SUN,SAT,FRI,THU, . . . ,MON
    - - each time around the loop
end loop;
```

The **for** iteration clause allows a sequence of statements to be repeated a predetermined number of times. In contrast, the **while** iteration clause allows a sequence of statements to be repeated whilst a specified condition remains true. For example,

```
C := 0;
while B>0 loop
    C := C+A;
    B := B-1;
end loop;
```

computes C := A*B by repeated addition. Before each cycle of the **while** loop, the condition B>0 is evaluated and if it is true the loop statements are executed otherwise the loop is terminated and control passes to the next statement.

In addition to the above two methods of controlling the execution of a
loop statement, Ada provides a further termination mechanism in the form of
the **exit** statement. The syntax diagram for this statement is as follows

S55 exit_statement

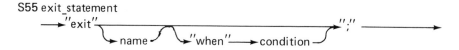

Execution of the unconditional form of **exit** statement, that is,

> **exit**;

causes the enclosing loop to be terminated immediately. Execution of the
conditional form, that is,

> **exit when** CONDITION;

causes the enclosing loop to be terminated only if the specified condition
evaluates to true, otherwise the **exit** statement has no effect.

The use of the **exit** statement can simplify certain forms of loop construct
by allowing the terminating condition to be computed at some intermediate
point within the loop. For example, consider again the body of the procedure
PRINT_BRACKETS given in Chapter 1,

```
TEXT_IO.GET(CH);
while CH /= '.' loop
    if CH='(' or CH=')' then
        TEXT_IO.PUT(CH);
    end if;
    TEXT_IO.GET(CH);
end loop;
```

This can be rewritten more succinctly using an **exit** statement as

```
loop
    TEXT_IO.GET(CH);
    exit when CH='.';
    if CH='(' or CH=')' then
        TEXT_IO.PUT(CH);
    end if;
end loop;
```

The **exit** statement can also be used to terminate several nested loop statements. To do this, the outermost loop to be terminated must be given a name
which is then specified in the **exit** statement. For example, in

```
OUTER: loop
          - -;
          - -;
       loop
            - -;
          exit OUTER when DONE;
            - -;
       end loop;
          - -;
          - -;
     end loop OUTER;
```

the outermost loop is given the name OUTER. Notice that this name must be given both at the beginning and end of the loop. When DONE evaluates to true, both the inner loop and the named OUTER loop are terminated.

4.8 EXAMPLE — IMPLEMENTING A CALENDAR

Suppose that the following type declarations are given

```
type DAY is new INTEGER range 1 . . 31;
type MONTH is (JAN,FEB,MAR,APR,MAY,JUN,
               JUL,AUG,SEP,OCT,NOV,DEC);
type YEAR is new INTEGER range 1901 . . 1999;
```

then write a sequence of statements to increment the current date denoted by the variables D, M and Y of type DAY, MONTH and YEAR, respectively, by one day.

In order to solve this problem, two special cases need to be handled in addition to the normal case where D is not the last day of the month, that is, the case where D is the last day of the month and the case where D is the last day of the year. The following solution increments the date using an **if** statement to distinguish the three cases. In order to simplify the 'end of the month' test, an intermediate value DAYS_IN_MONTH is computed using a **case** statement:

```
case M is                        - - compute days in the month
   when APR|JUN|SEP|NOV =>
       DAYS_IN_MONTH := 30;
   when FEB =>
       if Y mod 4 = 0 then
         DAYS_IN_MONTH := 29;
       else
         DAYS_IN_MONTH := 28;
       end if;
   when others =>
       DAYS_IN_MONTH := 31;
end case;
```

```
if D = DAYS_IN_MONTH then          - - increment date
   D := 1;
   if M = DEC then
      M := JAN;
      Y := Y+1;                    - - increment year
   else
      M := MONTH'SUCC(M);          - - or increment month
   end if;
else
   D := D+1;                       - - or increment day
end if;
```

4.9 EXAMPLE – TESTING FOR PRIMALITY

Given a non-negative integer number denoted by VAL, write statements to determine whether VAL is prime. Record the result in the Boolean variable PRIME.

This example is introduced mainly to illustrate some of the alternative forms of loop structure which can be used in Ada. Hence, only a very simple (and rather inefficient) solution will be presented. Three sequential tests will be made on VAL

   (1) if VAL <= 3 then VAL is prime
   (2) if VAL is even then VAL is not prime
   (3) if VAL is exactly divisible by FACTOR where FACTOR = 3,5,7,9, . . .
        SQRT(VAL) then VAL is not prime

The following solution is a straightforward implementation of these three tests using an **if** statement and a nested **while** loop for test 3.

```
- - Test for Primality / solution 1
if VAL<=3 then                     - - Test 1
   PRIME := TRUE;
elsif VAL mod 2 = 0 then           - - Test 2
   PRIME := FALSE;
else                               - - Test 3
   PRIME := TRUE; FACTOR := 3;
   while FACTOR**2 <= VAL and PRIME loop
      PRIME := VAL mod FACTOR /= 0;
      FACTOR := FACTOR + 2;
   end loop;
end if;
```

The interesting part of this solution is the construction of the loop required to implement test 3. The provision in Ada of the **exit** statement allows the loop to be expressed in several different ways. For example, the loop can be exited immediately that a valid factor is discovered,

```
- - Test 3 / version 2
PRIME := TRUE; FACTOR := 3;
while FACTOR**2 <= VAL loop
    if VAL mod FACTOR = 0 then
      PRIME := FALSE;
      exit;
    end if;
    FACTOR := FACTOR + 2;
end loop;
```

Alternatively, a conditional **exit** can be used to replace the nested **if** statement as in

```
- - Test 3 / version 3
FACTOR := 3;
while FACTOR**2 <= VAL loop
    PRIME := FALSE;
    exit when VAL mod FACTOR = 0;
    PRIME := TRUE;
    FACTOR := FACTOR + 2;
end loop;
```

The **while** loop itself can be replaced by a conditional **exit** as in

```
- - Test 3 / version 4
FACTOR := 3;
loop
    PRIME := TRUE;
    exit when FACTOR**2 > VAL;
    PRIME := FALSE;
    exit when VAL mod FACTOR = 0;
    FACTOR := FACTOR + 2;
end loop;
```

These are just a few of the several possible variations on the original solution. As there is little to choose between them on efficiency grounds, the original solution is considered marginally superior simply because it avoids using the **exit** statement altogether. The point to emphasise is that when an **exit** statement is used within a **while** or **for** loop or where more than one **exit** statement appears in the same loop, then the loop becomes *unstructured* in the sense that it breaks the structured programming rule that all control constructs should have a single entry point and a single exit point. Thus, whilst the use of the **exit** statement may sometimes lead to simpler and more efficient programs in certain cases, it should be used with care.

4.10 EXERCISES

(4.1) The time of day is represented by the variables HOURS, MINS and SECS using the 24-hour clock. Define suitable types for these variables and write a sequence of statements to increment the time of day by 1 second.

(4.2) Write a sequence of statements to print out the following pattern assuming that the statement

    SPACES(N);

causes N spaces to be output,

    PUT(CH);

causes the character CH to be output and

    NEW_LINE;

starts a new line.

A

ABA

ABCBA

ABCDCBA

ABCDEDCBA

.

.

.

ABCDEFGHIJKLMNOPQRSTUVWXYZYXWVUTSRQPONMLKJIHGFEDCBA

(4.3) Given that FACTORIAL(N)=FACT_N, write a sequence of statements to compute N given FACT_N.

(4.4) Given three integer numbers stored in variables VAL1, VAL2 and VAL3, write a sequence of statements to compute the middle value of the three numbers. It may be assumed that no two numbers are equal.

(4.5) Write a sequence of statements to print out an integer number in octal (that is, base 8) using the statement PUT(CH) to output each digit.

5

Declarations and Blocks

5.1 BLOCK STRUCTURE

An Ada program is built using three kinds of program unit: packages, subprograms and tasks. At the outermost level of a program, its structure consists of a sequence of separate program units (cf. the examples in Chapter 1). Because each of these units can be compiled separately, they are called *compilation units* (Note: tasks cannot be compilation units). Within each compilation unit there may be many more program units nested within each other. Each program unit may contain a set of declarations and a sequence of statements and this combination of declarations and statements is called a block. The basic structure of a block is

```
<HEADING>          - - depends on kind of block
        - - declarative part
begin
        - - statement part
end;
```

The declarative part will typically contain type, number and object declarations and may also contain the declarations of further (that is, nested) program units. The statement part contains the sequence of statements which define the actions to be taken by the block when it is executed. It may also contain some special statements which are to be executed when errors occur. These latter statements are called *exception handlers* and are described in Chapter 13.

The aim of this chapter is to introduce the basic principles of block structure and also to describe the facilities for declaring numbers, types and objects within a block.

In addition to program units, a block may also be introduced by a declare statement. This statement will be used to illustrate the main features of block structure before going on to describe subprograms, packages and tasks in later chapters.

5.2 DECLARATIONS

The declarative part of a block is described by the following syntax diagrams

S56 declarative_part

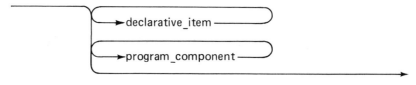

S57 declarative_item

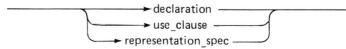

S58 declaration

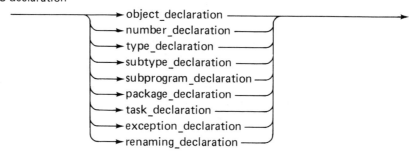

S59 program_component

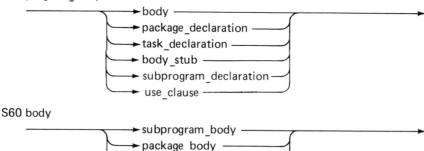

S60 body

The reader may well at this point be somewhat alarmed by the apparent complexity of the above diagrams. Ada provides a rich set of language features and as a result a large number of different kinds of declaration are needed. Ada recognises two classes of declaration:

(i) Declarative items — types, objects, program unit declarations, etc., and representation specifications which specify how types are represented in memory, etc.
(ii) Program units — package, task and subprogram declarations and their bodies.

In practice, representation specifications are only used in special and rather rare circumstances and may be forgotten for now. As a general rule, the simplest approach to organising declarations is

(a) Declare types, objects, numbers, exceptions first.
(b) Declare tasks, packages and subprograms second.

One further rule which must be adhered to at all times is that all identifiers must be declared before they are used. Note, however, that program unit specifications can be included in (a) where this becomes a problem.

Type and sub-type declarations were introduced in Chapter 3. The next two sections cover object and number declarations. All the other declarations mentioned above will be dealt with in later chapters.

5.3 OBJECT DECLARATIONS

Many examples of object declarations have already been given but only the basic form has been used so far, that is,

x:T;

which means "declare an object of type T with the name x". In fact, the full syntax of an object declaration is as follows

S61 object_declaration

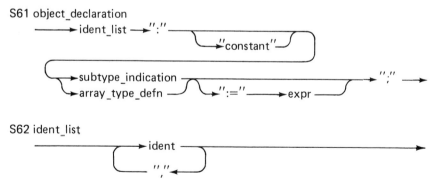

S62 ident_list

The first point to note is that the type of an object must normally be given explicitly in terms of a type or sub-type name. For example,

SW:(ON,OFF);

is illegal. Instead, an explicit type name must be introduced, that is,

> **type** SWITCH **is** (ON,OFF);
> SW:SWITCH;

This is required even if SW is the one and only instance of an object of type SWITCH occurring in the whole program. The one exception to this rule is that array objects can be introduced directly (see Chapter 8).

The second point to note is that an object may be given an initial value. For example,

> INDEX:INTEGER **range** 0 .. MAX := 0;

declares an object of type INTEGER with initial value zero. Notice that several objects may be declared in the same object declaration. If an initial value is specified in such cases then it is given to each of the named objects. Thus:

> I,J,K:SMALL_INT := 1;

initialises each of I, J and K to the value 1. The initial value need not be a simple literal value as in the above examples but can be any expression yielding a value of the required type. Furthermore, this expression may include components whose value can only be computed at run time. For example,

> L:LENGTH := (ASIZE + BSIZE)/2;

where ASIZE and BSIZE are variables is quite legal.

Finally, an object may be declared as being **constant**. For example,

> MAXIMUM:**constant** INTEGER := 100;

declares an object of type INTEGER which has an initial value of 100. The keyword **constant** prohibits any operation being applied to MAXIMUM which might change its value. Apart from this restriction, the object MAXIMUM has all the properties of a normal integer variable. In particular, the initialising expression (which can never be omitted) may be computed at run time when the block in which the declaration occurs is entered. In many respects, therefore, it is more appropriate to consider such objects as read-only variables rather than as constants.

5.4 NUMBER DECLARATIONS

Number declarations are used to give a name to a constant numeric value. The syntax of a number declaration is

S63 number_declaration
$$\longrightarrow \text{ident\_list} \longrightarrow ":" \longrightarrow "constant" \longrightarrow ":=" \longrightarrow \text{expr} \longrightarrow ";" \longrightarrow$$

and examples of number declarations are

PI   : **constant** := 3.14159;
LIMIT : **constant** := 1000;
ZERO : **constant** := 0;
SIZE   : **constant** := LIMIT*2;

Number declarations serve a similar purpose to constant object declarations but there are 3 important differences

(a) Number declarations are limited to integer and real values. Hence:

STAR: **constant** := '*';

is not allowed (a constant object declaration must be used instead).

(b) The expression denoting the value of a number declaration must be static (that is, computable at compile time).

(c) Numbers introduced by number declarations have a *universal* type. If the value of the defining expression is real (for example, PI above) then the type of the number is *universal_real*, otherwise its type is *universal_integer* (for example, LIMIT, ZERO and SIZE above). The consequence of this is that a number can be used anywhere that a literal value could be used. For example, suppose that the following are given in addition to the above examples

LIMIT2: **constant** INTEGER := 1000;
VAL1: INTEGER;
VAL2: MY_INT;

where MY_INT is a derived integer type then

VAL1 := LIMIT2;

and

VAL1 := LIMIT;

are both legal and have an equivalent effect. However,

VAL2 := LIMIT2;

is not legal because the types do not match, whereas

VAL2 := LIMIT;

is legal since the type of LIMIT is *universal_integer*, which is assignment compatible with any integer type.

5.5 DECLARE STATEMENTS

Having described how objects and numbers are declared, attention will now be focused on blocks. The simplest way of introducing a block into an Ada program is by using a declare statement, whose syntax is given by the following diagram

S64 declare_statement

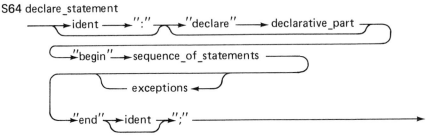

The 'exceptions' part of a block is optional and will not be discussed here (see Chapter 13). The remaining parts are illustrated by the following example, which uses a declare statement to swap the values of two integer variables I and J.

        - - statements preceding block give appropriate values
        - - to I and J. TEMP is not accessible here.

    SWAP: **declare**
                TEMP:INTEGER;
            begin
                TEMP := I;
                I := J;
                J := TEMP;
            end SWAP;

        - - statements following block.
        - - TEMP is not accessible here

The block called SWAP introduces the local variable TEMP which is needed in order to swap the values of I and J. This variable is created when the block is entered and disappears when the block is left. Thus, it is only accessible within the block itself. The execution of a block therefore consists of two parts

   (i)   elaborate any declarations within the block;
   (ii) execute the sequence of statements within the block;

In practice, declare statements are not widely used since it is usually preferable to introduce a subprogram to perform the required actions. They are, however, useful in the following special circumstances

(a) When a very large data structure is needed at just one point in a program. In this case, the structure can be declared in a block, used and then disposed of by leaving the block. Thus, memory space is tied-up only temporarily, while the structure is actually being used.
(b) Ada allows data structures to be declared whose size is computed at run time. Sometimes a few calculations must be performed before the size of

such a structure can be determined. Hence, the structure cannot be declared immediately within the program unit that uses it. A declare block can be used to circumvent this problem.

(c) A small group of statements can be placed in a declare block to enable an exception handler to be introduced. In this case, the block may not need any local declarations and the **declare** symbol can be omitted.

Despite the rather minor importance of the declare statement, it serves as a suitable example for illustrating some of the main features of block structure in preparation for the discussion of subprograms given in the next chapter.

As noted in the SWAP example above, the entities declared within a block are local to it and are inaccessible outside. Entities declared in enclosing blocks are, however, accessible within the block (cf. I and J in the example). Hence, a block serves as a one-way *membrane*. The region over which an entity is accessible is called its scope. In the example, the scope of TEMP extends from the point of its declaration to the end of the block in which it is declared. Thus, if further blocks were declared within SWAP, TEMP would be accessible within these too. To illustrate this further, consider the following example,

```
OUTER: declare
          I,J:INTEGER;
       begin
          - - I,J:INTEGER directly accessible here
          - -
  INNER: declare
            I:MY_INT;
         begin
            - - I:MY_INT and J:INTEGER directly
            - - accessible here.
            - - I:INTEGER is indirectly accessible here.
         end INNER;
         - - I,J:INTEGER directly accessible here
         - - I:MY_INT not accessible here
       end OUTER;
```

This example consists of a block called INNER nested within another block called OUTER. OUTER contains declarations for two INTEGER variables called I and J. The scope of these variables extends over the whole of the OUTER block and therefore includes the INNER block. Within INNER, however, a third variable also called I is declared. This second declaration of I *hides* the outer declaration of I so that within INNER, I (INTEGER) is no longer directly accessible. How then can I (INTEGER) be referred to within INNER? The answer is that the full name of any entity X declared within a block B is B.X. This is called the *selected component notation*, that is, X is a selected component of B. When a name is directly accessible the prefix 'B.' can be omitted and this is the normal case. Thus, within INNER, the value of I (INTEGER) can be assigned to J by

$$\text{OUTER.J} := \text{OUTER.I}$$

or

J := OUTER.I;   – – J is directly accessible

but not

J := I;   – – type mismatch, I now refers
                 – – I:MY_INT

To summarise, a block introduces a new scope for names. Any name introduced within a block is accessible from its point of declaration through to the end of the block, including any nested blocks. If a name is used again within an inner block then the outer use of the name is hidden but it is still accessible by using the selected component notation. Within any one block, a name can only be used once (unless it is the name of a subprogram – see next chapter).

Finally, note that in the case of blocks introduced by a declare statement, the name of the block can be omitted. The block is then anonymous and any names hidden within nested blocks are inaccessible.

5.6 EXAMPLE – TESTING FOR PRIMALITY

As a simple example of using declare statements, the test for primality given in section 4.8 could be written as follows

```
declare
    VAL:INTEGER range 0 .. INTEGER'LAST;
    PRIME:BOOLEAN;
begin
    – – compute value for VAL
    – –
    FIND_PRIME:
    declare
        FACTOR:INTEGER range 0 .. VAL;
    begin
        if VAL <= 3 then
            PRIME := TRUE;
        elsif VAL mod 2 = 0 then
            PRIME := FALSE;
        else
            PRIME := TRUE; FACTOR := 3;
            while FACTOR**2 <= VAL and PRIME loop
```

PRME := VAL **mod** FACTOR /= 0;

FACTOR := FACTOR + 2;

      end loop;

     end if;

    end FIND_PRIME;

   - -

   - - PRIME now valid indication of primality of VAL

   - -

  end;

An interesting point about this example is that FACTOR is declared to be constrained to the range 0 to VAL. This shows that a range constraint need not be static but the bounds can be computed at run-time. In this case, the dynamic constraint on FACTOR means that an error in the algorithm which allows FACTOR to be incremented indefinitely will be detected more quickly than if the alternative static constraint

FACTOR:INTEGER **range** 0 . . INTEGER'LAST;

had been used.

It must be emphasised, however, that the use of dynamic range constraints in the above example has been included mainly to illustrate that it is possible. In practice, dynamic constraints will normally carry a higher run-time overhead and so should be avoided where possible. Their main use is, in fact, in the specification of index variables for dynamic arrays where the run-time range checking on the index variable saves having to check the index bounds on array accesses (see Chapter 8).

5.7 EXERCISES

(5.1) Rewrite the solution to exercise 4.2 in the form of a declare statement with the required local data objects declared appropriately.

(5.2) In the following, state which assignment statements are illegal and explain why.

DS1: **declare**

    I,J:INTEGER;

    COUNT:POS_INT;

    A:BOOLEAN;

begin

    DS2:

    declare

        K:INTEGER;

        I:INDEX;

        A:CHARACTER;

        ON:BOOLEAN;

```
begin
    I:=J; COUNT:=INTEGER(I); J:=K;
    DS1.I:=J; A:=ON; J:=DS3.L;
end DS2;
DS3:
declare
    L:INTEGER;
begin
    L:=I; L:=K; L:=DS2.K;
end DS3;
I:=DS1.J; I:=DS2.K; I:=DS3.L;
end DS1;
```

where POS_INT and INDEX are derived integer types.

6

Subprograms

Subprograms are one of the three kinds of program unit provided by Ada; the others being *packages* and *tasks* which are described later. Subprograms may either be compiled separately as individual units or they can be declared within the declarative part of any other program unit or block.

A subprogram denotes a set of logically related actions grouped together into a single unit and given a name. These actions may then be invoked anywhere that they are required by a subprogram call. The use of subprograms provides two main benefits. First and foremost, they allow the various actions required in a program to be divided up into small manageable chunks. This makes programs easier to design and easier to understand. In particular, it facilitates the design of a program by a process known as stepwise refinement. This technique is illustrated by the example given at the end of this chapter and developed further in later chapters once packages have been introduced. Second, the use of subprograms makes it possible to avoid having to duplicate code when a given action must be performed at several different places in a program. Instead, the code is written just once as a subprogram, and each time that the action is required, the subprogram is called.

In Ada, there are two kinds of subprogram: *procedures* and *functions*. The actions of a procedure are invoked by writing a procedure call statement. Functions, on the other hand, are invoked by writing their names as components of expressions and are executed to compute values. The versatility of subprograms is greatly increased by allowing parameters to be specified for them. When the subprogram is called, the actual parameters supplied in the call are operated on by the subprogram as input values and, in the case of procedures, may also be used to return results.

6.1 SUBPROGRAM BODIES

A subprogram is defined by writing a subprogram body, with the syntax denoted by the following diagrams

S65 subprogram_body

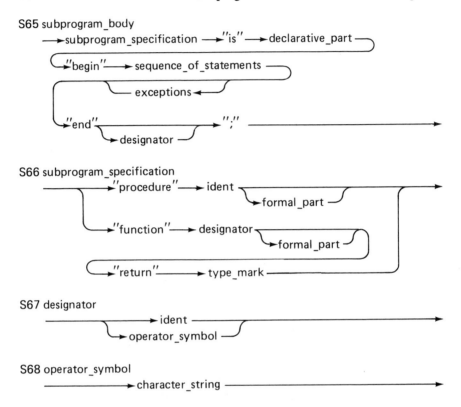

S66 subprogram_specification

S67 designator

S68 operator_symbol

As can be seen from the above diagrams, subprograms have a block structure similar to that described for the declare statement in the preceding chapter. Ignoring formal parts for the moment, the structure of a procedure is illustrated by the following example

```
procedure WRITE_ALPHABET is
    LETTERS_PER_LINE:constant := 10;
    COUNT:INTEGER range 0 .. LETTERS_PER_LINE := 0;
begin
    for LETTER in CHARACTER range 'A' .. 'Z' loop
        PUT(LETTER);
        COUNT := (COUNT+1) mod LETTERS_PER_LINE;
        if COUNT=0 then
            NEW_LINE;
        else
            PUT(' ');
        end if;
    end loop;
end WRITE_ALPHABET;
```

The symbol **procedure** is immediately followed by the name of the procedure, that is, WRITE_ALPHABET, followed by the symbol **is**. The remainder of the procedure has the structure of a block, that is, local declarations followed by a sequence of statements between the symbols **begin** and **end**. The name of the procedure is repeated after the **end**. This is optional, but it is good practice to include it since it is an additional aid to readability. The actions of this procedure may be invoked by writing a procedure call statement, that is,

WRITE_ALPHABET;

whose effect in this case is to write out the alphabet, that is,

```
A B C D E F G H I J
K L M N O P Q R S T
U V W X Y Z
```

Functions are written in a similar way to procedures except that the type of the value computed by the function must be included in the specification part. As an example, the following function generates a pseudo-random integer in the range 0 to 4095 each time it is called

```
function RAND return INTEGER is
begin
    RAND_VAL := (259*RAND_VAL) mod 4096;
    return RAND_VAL;
end RAND;
```

RAND_VAL is assumed to be a global integer variable whose value is unchanged between calls to RAND (in practice RAND_VAL and RAND would be encapsulated within a package — see next chapter). The actual value returned by RAND is given by the value of an expression given in the **return** statement which has the following syntax

S69 return_statement

As can be seen, this statement consists of the single symbol **return** optionally followed by an expression. Within a function, this expression must be included and the type of its value must match that given in the function specification. Execution of the **return** statement in this case has two effects. Firstly, the function result is given the value denoted by the expression and secondly, the function is terminated. **Return** statements may also be used in procedures (and **accept** statements — see Chapter 12). In this case, an expression must not be given and the effect of the statement is just to terminate the procedure. Thus, **return** statements mark the logical end of a subprogram, and there may be several in the same subprogram denoting alternative exit points. In a procedure without **return** statements (as in WRITE_ALPHABET above) then execution terminates when the physical end of the procedure is reached.

6.2 PARAMETERS

A subprogram may have parameters declared in the formal part of its specification with the syntax given by the following diagrams

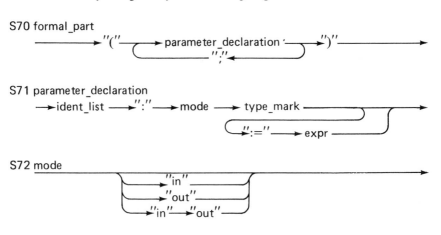

S70 formal_part

S71 parameter_declaration

S72 mode

Each parameter declaration names one or more formal parameters with a given mode and type and may also indicate a default initial value.

The mode of a parameter determines how the parameter is used:

in   The parameter acts like a local constant whose value is given by the value of the actual parameter supplied with the call.

out   The parameter acts like a local variable whose value is assigned to the actual parameter supplied in the call when the subprogram terminates.

in out The parameter acts like a local variable and permits access and assignment to the corresponding actual parameter supplied in the call.

Thus, in essence, the **in** mode is used to input values, the **out** mode is used to output values and the **in out** mode is used to update variables. A function must only have parameters of the **in** mode emphasising the fact that functions should not, in general, modify their environment. If the mode indication is omitted in a parameter specification, then the **in** mode is assumed by default.

As an example, in a signal processing application a long sequence of sample values must be organised into blocks with 256 individual samples in each block. Thus, each individual sample is denoted by an address consisting of a block number 0,1,2,3, ... etc., and an offset within the block in the range 0 to 255. A set of subprograms are required to manipulate sample addresses. The first of these is a procedure to increment an address to point to the next sample in the input sequence

  procedure NEXT(BLK:**in out** BLOCK; OFF:**in out** OFFSET) **is**
  begin
   OFF := (OFF + 1) **mod** 256;
   if OFF = 0 **then**
    BLK := BLK + 1;
   end if;
  end NEXT;

where

  subtype BLOCK is INTEGER range 0 . . MAX_BLOCK;
  subtype OFFSET is INTEGER **range** 0 . . 255;

  The procedure NEXT takes two parameters, a block and an offset, of mode **in out**. This mode is required because both parameters are given an updated value based on their previous values. Subprogram calls are dealt with in detail in the next section but it will be helpful here to illustrate how the procedures work by showing some examples of their use. Consider,

  B1 := 1; 01 := 254;
  NEXT(B1,01);   - - call NEXT
  - - B1=1 and 01=255
  NEXT(B1,01);   - - call NEXT again
  - - B1=2 and 01=0

Each time NEXT is called the following occurs:

(1) the values of the actual parameters B1 and 01 are assigned to the formal parameters BLK and OFF, respectively.
(2) the statements of NEXT are executed
(3) the final values of BLK and OFF are assigned to B1 and 01, respectively.

Thus, parameter passing in **in out** mode is achieved by a copy-in and a copy-out.
  (Note: when parameters are structured types, then the language allows alternative parameter passing mechanisms to be used, such as call-by-reference. This applies to the **in** and **out** modes also.)
  Consider now a procedure to compute the absolute position of a sample in the input data sequence

  procedure POSITION(BLK:**in** BLOCK; OFF:**in** OFFSET;
          POS:**out** INTEGER) **is**
  begin
   POS := BLK*256 + OFF;
  end POSITION;

In this case BLK and OFF are input values only and so the **in** mode is specified. The POS parameter is only used to return a value and so the **out** mode is used. Hence, the call

    POSITION(2,16,P1);

would assign the value 528 to P1. In detail, the execution of POSITION involves the following steps

(1) the values of the actual **in** mode parameters are assigned to BLK and OFF.
(2) the statement POS := BLK∗256 + OFF is executed
(3) the value of POS is assigned to the corresponding actual parameter P1

Thus, **in** mode parameter passing involves a copy-in and **out** mode parameter passing involves a copy-out.

Note that the actual parameters corresponding to **in** mode parameters need not be variables but can be any expression yielding a value of the required type. Actual parameters corresponding to **out** or **in out** modes must be variables of the same type. Note also that **in** mode formal parameters may not be assigned to within the procedure but those of the other modes may. Hence, POSITION could have been written as

    procedure POSITION(BLK:in BLOCK; OFF:in OFFSET;
                                  POS:out INTEGER) **is**
    begin
         POS := BLK∗256;
         POS := POS + OFF;
    end POSITION;

The POSITION procedure could equally well be written as a function as follows

    function POSITION(BLK:BLOCK; OFF:OFFSET) **return** INTEGER **is**
    begin
         return BLK∗256 + OFF;
    end POSITION;

and the corresponding call would be

    P1 := POSITION(2,16);

In the functional form of POSITION, the **in** mode has not been stated explicitly. For functions, an explicit indication of mode is unnecessary since only the **in** mode is allowed. For procedures, however, it is good practice to always specify the mode explicitly.

6.3 SUBPROGRAM CALLS

Examples of subprogram calls have already been given; in this section they will be described in more detail. The syntax of a subprogram call is given by the following diagrams

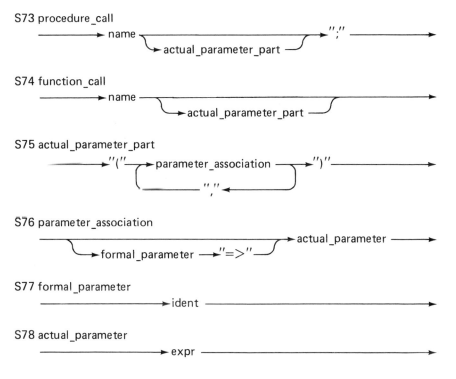

S73 procedure_call

S74 function_call

S75 actual_parameter_part

S76 parameter_association

S77 formal_parameter

S78 actual_parameter

A subprogram call consists of the name of the subprogram followed by a list of the actual parameters, if any. As stated earlier, the actual parameter corresponding to an **in** mode formal parameter may be any expression yielding a value of the appropriate type, whereas the actual parameters corresponding to other modes must be variables.

In the case of a parameterless procedure only the name is given in the call, for example,

        WRITE_ALPHABET;

The same applies to parameterless function calls, for example,

        I := RAND;

When a subprogram has parameters, then the call must give the actual parameters and state their association with the corresponding formal parameters. Ada allows this association to be denoted in two ways. Firstly, the simple positional order of the actual parameters can be used as has been done in all previous examples of subprogram calls. Hence, in the call

POSITION(2,16,P1);

the 2 is associated with the first formal parameter (that is, BLK), the 16 is associated with the second formal parameter (that is, OFF) and P1 is associated with the third formal parameter (that is, POS). Ada also allows parameter associations to be stated explicitly without regard to order. For example,

POSITION(BLK => 2, OFF => 16, POS => P1);
POSITION(OFF => 16, BLK => 2, POS => P1);
POSITION(POS => P1, BLK => 2, OFF => 16);

are all equivalent. These named associations obviously require more effort in writing but they considerably improve readability when the subprogram call is textually remote from the corresponding subprogram specification. Furthermore, when long lists of parameters of similar types are involved it is easy to make mistakes using the positional notation. For example, writing

POSITION(16,2,P1);

instead of the above would be an error which might require considerable effort to locate during program testing.

Positional and named parameters can be mixed in a call provided that positional parameters occur first. Hence, for example,

POSITION(2, POS => P1, OFF => 16);

is also equivalent to the previous calls.

6.4 DEFAULT PARAMETER VALUES

As mentioned in section 6.2, the formal parameters of a subprogram may be given default initial values provided that they are of **in** mode. As an example, suppose that a more general version of NEXT was required, called STEP, in which a sample address could be incremented by any number of samples:

```
procedure STEP(BLK:in out BLOCK; OFF:in out OFFSET;
               INC:in INTEGER := 1) is
     NEW_POSITION:INTEGER;
begin
     NEW_POSITION := POSITION(BLK,OFF) + INC;
     BLK := NEW_POSITION / 256;
     OFF := NEW_POSITION mod 256;
end STEP;
```

In this case, the number of samples to be stepped through is denoted by the **in** mode parameter INC, and this has a default initial value of 1. A normal call to STEP might be

STEP(B1,01,10);

However, if the number of samples to be incremented was just 1 then the actual parameter corresponding to INC may be omitted, that is,

STEP(B1,01);

is equivalent to writing

STEP(B1,01,1);

In this example, the default parameter was given last and so positional notation could be used. When a parameter is omitted any subsequent parameters must be given in named notation. Hence, if the specification for STEP gave the parameter INC first, that is,

procedure STEP(INC:**in** INTEGER := 1; BLK:**in out** BLOCK;
                OFF:**in out** OFFSET) **is** . . .

then the call

STEP(B1,01);

would be illegal. Instead the named notation must be used, that is,

STEP(BLK => B1, OFF => 01);

6.5 SUBPROGRAM SPECIFICATIONS

Referring back to syntax diagrams S65 and S66, it can be seen that the first line of a subprogram definition is called its *specification*. This specification defines the kind of subprogram, that is, procedure or function; its name; its parameters, if any; and its result type, if it is a function. A major aspect of Ada is the ability to separate the implementation of a program unit from its specification. Subprograms are no exception to this, and subprograms may be declared in advance of their implementation. In fact, the syntax diagram for a subprogram declaration is as follows where it can be seen that only the specification of a subprogram is required to declare it:

S79 subprogram_declaration

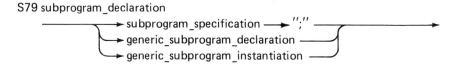

(The generic forms of subprogram declarations are covered later in Chapter 14.)

As an example, the full declaration and implementation of NEXT would be

procedure NEXT(BLK:**in out** BLOCK; OFF:**in out** OFFSET);

- - other declarations

procedure NEXT(BLK:**in out** BLOCK; OFF:**in out** OFFSET) **is**
begin
    OFF := (OFF + 1) **mod** 256;
    if OFF = 0 **then**
      BLK := BLK + 1;
    end if;
end NEXT;

Where the specification and implementation of a procedure are textually close together, then the specification can be omitted and the implementation (that is, body) serves as both declaration and definition. This has been done in all of the examples in preceding sections and is, in fact, the normal practice in Ada.

There are, however, two cases where a separate subprogram specification is mandatory. Firstly, when the subprogram is a visible component of a package, then the package specification must include the subprogram specification. Examples of this case were given in section 1.3 (see also the next chapter). Secondly, where two or more subprograms call each other, then the declaration-before-use rule means that the subprograms must be declared before they can be defined. For example, suppose that procedure A calls procedure B, and procedure B calls procedure A. Then A and B can be declared and defined as follows

      procedure A;   - - declare A

      procedure B;   - - declare B

      procedure A **is**
      begin
        - -
        B;   - - call B
        - -
      end A;

      procedure B **is**
      begin
        - -
        A;   - - call A
        - -
      end B;

The procedures A and B are said to be *mutually recursive*. Mutually recursive procedures often arise in recursive descent syntax analysers and other similar applications but otherwise they are quite rare.

6.6 OVERLOADING AND QUALIFIED EXPRESSIONS

In section 3.2, it was stated that the same enumeration literal could appear in several different enumeration declarations within the same declarative part. Such literals are said to be overloaded. When they are used, context information must be applied to identify the type of the overloaded literal. In the same way, subprogram names can be overloaded.

Consider, for example, the following subprogram declarations

procedure SET(THIS_DAY:**in** DAY);   - - (a)

procedure SET(TINT:**in** COLOUR);   - - (b)

procedure SET(STATE:**in** ALARM_STATE);   - - (c)

The procedure SET is overloaded, the same name being used to denote three different procedures. When a call to SET is made, it must be possible to determine from the context which procedure is meant. For example,

SET(MON);

must be a call to (a) because the actual parameter MON is of type DAY. However, the call

SET(YELLOW);

is ambiguous because the enumeration literal YELLOW is itself overloaded. This call as it stands is therefore illegal. In order to resolve the ambiguity the type of the literal YELLOW must be stated explicitly. This is done using a qualified expression

S80 qualified_expr

Ignoring the aggregate part which refers to structured types, it can be seen that a qualified expression has the same form as a type conversion except that an extra " ' " mark has been added. Hence, legal calls to SET can now be written as follows

SET(COLOUR'(YELLOW));   - - that is, SET (b)

or

SET(ALARM_STATE'(YELLOW));   - - that is, SET (c)

Having introduced the idea of overloading, the rules for overloading subprograms will now be given. Two subprogram specifications with the same name are equivalent if

(a) they have the same number of parameters

(b) each corresponding parameter has the same base type.

Parameter names, modes, subtypes and default values, if any, are not taken into account when determining the equivalence of two subprogram specifications.

When a subprogram is declared which is equivalent to an existing subprogram defined in an outer block, then the new definition hides the existing definition in the same way that object names may be hidden by re-using the name in an inner block. In such cases, the hidden subprogram may be accessed using the selected component notation described in section 5.5. Equivalent subprogram declarations may not occur in the same program part. Normally, however, subprogram definitions with the same name are not equivalent and then the subprogram is said to be overloaded. The newer definition does not hide the existing definition but simply overloads it. Overloaded subprogram definitions may occur in the same declarative part.

When an overloaded subprogram is called, then the context is used to determine which definition is to be used as described above. It should be emphasised, however, that this selection of the correct definition is made at compile time. Overloading does not carry any run-time overhead.

6.7 OPERATORS

Although Ada does not allow new operators to be defined, it does allow the existing pre-defined operators to be overloaded. An operator may be overloaded by writing a function definition with the operator symbol written as a string constant in place of the function name.

As a simple example, suppose that the following type is declared

type DIRECTION **is** (N,NE,E,SE,S,SW,W,NW);

The relational operators are automatically provided for this type (that is, $=$, $/=$, $<$, $>$, $<=$, $>=$, **in, not in**) and the basic discrete type attribute enquiries are available. However, if further operations are required then they must be supplied by the user. Suppose that an addition operator is required such that

D + M

denotes the direction obtained by starting in direction D and turning through M octants clockwise, for example,

$$
\begin{aligned}
N + 1 &= NE \\
N + 4 &= S \\
N + 13 &= SW \\
N + (-1) &= NW \text{ etc}
\end{aligned}
$$

This adding operator can be defined as follows

> **function** $"+"$(D:DIRECTION; M:INTEGER) **return** DIRECTION **is**
> **begin**
>   **return** DIRECTION'VAL((DIRECTION'POS(D) + M) **mod** 8);
> **end** $"+"$;

The function $"+"$ has two parameters. The first parameter D corresponds to the left operand and the second parameter M corresponds to the right operand. Hence, given

> D1,D2:DIRECTION;

then the effect of writing

> D2 := D1 + 3;

is to execute the function $"+"$ defined above with D => D1 and M => 3, the function result being assigned to D2.

In general, a programmer should ensure that the commonly assumed properties of the built-in operators are preserved for new overloaded definitions. This is not a language rule, but simply good programming sense. For example, the $"+"$ operator is normally commutative, and hence a second overloading should also be defined

> **function** $"+"$(M:INTEGER; D:DIRECTION) **return** DIRECTION **is**
> **begin**
>   **return** DIRECTION'VAL((DIRECTION'POS(D) + M) **mod** 8);
> **end** $"+"$;

that is, the same as before but with the operand order reversed.

There are two major restrictions on overloading. Firstly, the membership operators **in** and **not in** and the short circuit logical operators **and then** and **or else** may not be overloaded. Secondly, the equality operator $"="$ may only be overloaded if the operands are *limited private* (see next chapter). Even then, the result returned by $"="$ must always be of type **BOOLEAN** and $"/="$ may never be overloaded but always automatically gives the complementary result to $"="$.

Operators are usually defined in packages along with the definition of the data type on which they operate. They are a useful feature of the language for developing libraries (especially of numerical algorithms) but care needs to be exercised if they are used as a general programming tool. For example, with the definitions for $"+"$ given above, what is the meaning of

> D2 := D1 + 3 + 2;

where the second $"+"$ could be either the normal arithmetic $"+"$ or the overloaded $"+"$ depending on the order of evaluation, that is, either

$$D2 := (D1 + 3) + 2;$$

or

$$D2 := D1 + (3 + 2);$$

In fact, operators of equal precedence are applied in left to right order, so the first interpretation is correct. Nevertheless, it should be clear that confusions could easily arise. With the definitions for "+" given, the two alternatives given are equivalent and so there is no real problem here. However, it is easy to construct examples where this is not the case.

6.8 EXAMPLE – PASCAL'S TRIANGLE

Design a procedure with the following specification

procedure PASCALS_TRIANGLE(LAST_ROW:**in** INDEX);

such that a call to PASCALS_TRIANGLE(N) will print out the 0th through to the Nth row of Pascal's Triangle, for example, PASCALS_TRIANGLE(4) would give

```
            1                  - - row 0
          1   1                - - row 1
        1   2   1              - - row 2
      1   3   3   1            - - row 3
    1   4   6   4   1          - - row 4
```

Assume that the procedures NEW_LINE and SPACES are available as in Exercise 4.2, and that a call to PUT(I,F) will print out the number I in a fieldwidth of F characters. Assume further that the following declarations are given

FIELD_WIDTH:**constant** := 6;
MAX_ROW_NUMBER:**constant** := 10;
subtype INDEX **is** INTEGER **range** 0 . . MAX_ROW_NUMBER;

where FIELD_WIDTH gives the number of characters allocated for the printing out of each individual value in the triangle.

The design of PASCALS_TRIANGLE involves two stages of refinement:

Stage I:
For each row in the triangle there are two basic actions to be performed:
(a) output a new line and then output the required number of leading spaces to give a symmetrical pattern, that is, ALIGN_OUTPUT;
(b) print the values of the current row allowing FIELD_WIDTH characters per value, that is, PRINT_VALUES.

Hence, PASCALS_TRIANGLE may be described at the first level of refinement as a single **for** loop, namely:

```
for ROW in 0 . . LAST_ROW loop
    ALIGN_OUTPUT(ROW);
    PRINT_VALUES(ROW);
end loop;
```

Stage II:

At the second level of refinement the procedures ALIGN_OUTPUT and PRINT_VALUES must be defined.

ALIGN_OUTPUT starts a new line and then outputs the correct number of spaces to make the printing of the triangle symmetrical. Consider the case where LAST_ROW equals MAX_ROW_NUMBER: the number of leading spaces required for the last row of the triangle would be 0. The row immediately above this would require FIELD_WIDTH/2 leading spaces, the row before that 2*(FIELD_WIDTH/2) spaces and so on. Hence, for the ROWth row of the triangle

Number of leading spaces =
$$(MAX\_ROW\_NUMBER-ROW)*(FIELD\_WIDTH/2)$$

Thus, the body of ALIGN_OUTPUT is just

```
NEW_LINE;
SPACES((MAX_ROW_NUMBER-ROW)*(FIELD_WIDTH/2));
```

PRINT_VALUES prints the ROW+1 values of the current row where each value in the row is computed from the previous value, that is, the sequence is

$$\frac{1}{1} \quad \frac{n}{1} \quad \frac{n.(n-1)}{1 \quad 2} \quad \frac{n.(n-1).(n-2)}{1 \quad 2 \quad 3} \quad \cdots etc.$$

where n=ROW. Hence, the body of PRINT_VALUES can be implemented by

```
PUT(VAL,FIELD_WIDTH);
for COLUMN in 1 . . ROW loop
    VAL := (VAL*(ROW-COLUMN+1))/COLUMN;
    PUT(VAL,FIELD_WIDTH);
end loop;
```

where VAL is initially set equal to 1.

Putting the above pieces together, the required procedure PASCALS_TRIANGLE may be written as follows where the procedures ALIGN_OUTPUT and PRINT_VALUES are declared locally within it

```
procedure PASCALS_TRIANGLE(LAST_ROW:in INDEX) is
  procedure ALIGN_OUTPUT(ROW:in INDEX) is
  begin
      NEW_LINE;
      SPACES((MAX_ROW_NUMBER-ROW)*(FIELD_WIDTH/2));
  end ALIGN_OUTPUT;
  procedure PRINT_VALUES(ROW:in INDEX) is
      VAL:INTEGER := 1;
  begin
      PUT(VAL,FIELD_WIDTH);
      for COLUMN in 1 .. ROW loop
          VAL := (VAL*(ROW-COLUMN+1))/COLUMN;
          PUT(VAL,FIELD_WIDTH);
      end loop;
  end PRINT_VALUES;
begin
    for ROW in 0 .. LAST_ROW loop
        ALIGN_OUTPUT(ROW);
        PRINT_VALUES(ROW);
    end loop;
end PASCALS_TRIANGLE;
```

As a final comment on this example, it is worth noting that the technique of successive refinement using procedures is the normal approach taken when using traditional languages such as Pascal. To some extent, this methodology is forced, because the procedure is often the only unit of modularisation provided by these languages. Ada, however, provides a much more powerful construct for modularisation in the form of the package (see Chapter 1 and Chapter 7). Packages allow programs to be designed by the successive refinement of abstract resources (in particular, abstract data types) and this is a much better technique, especially for very large programs. Later examples of program design in this book will concentrate on this latter approach.

6.9 EXERCISES

(6.1) Write a procedure to read in a sequence of characters denoting an integer number with the syntax

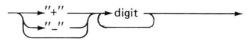

and compute the value of the number. Assume that characters are read by the call GET(CH), where CH is of type CHARACTER and the specification of the procedure is

procedure READ_INT(VAL:**out** INTEGER);

(6.2) Write a procedure to perform the inverse operation to READ_INT using the call PUT(CH) to output a character. The specification of the procedure is

procedure WRITE_INT(VAL:**in** INTEGER);

(6.3) Define a function with the specification

function UPPER_CASE(CH:CHARACTER) **return** CHARACTER;

which returns the value of its argument unchanged unless that value is a lower-case letter, in which case, the corresponding upper-case letter is returned.

(6.4) Write a function called MIDDLE_VALUE which takes three integer values as arguments and returns the middle value as result. For example, MIDDLE VALUE(5,2,9) returns 5 (See Question 4.4.)

(6.5) Write a procedure to solve the Towers of Hanoi problem with the specification

procedure HANOI(NO_OF_DISKS:**in** NATURAL);

This problem is described as follows. There are three wooden poles named left(L), right(R) and middle(M). A stack of n disks of decreasing size is held on pole L which passes through a hole in the centre of each disk (n=NO_OF_DISKS). The object is to move all the disks from pole L to pole R according to the following rules

(a) only one disk may be moved at a time
(b) a disk must never be placed on top of a smaller one
(c) at any time, each of the disks must be on one of the three poles
The output from the procedure should be in the form of a sequence of moves

L > R
M > R etc.

(use PUT(CH) and NEW_LINE for output). Hence, for example, the call HANOI(3) would generate

L > R
L > M
R > M
L > R
M > L
M > R
L > R

(Hint: a recursive solution is the simplest.)

7

Packages

As mentioned previously, the primary building block in Ada programs is the package. A package encapsulates a set of logically related entities and provides facilities to explicitly control access to those entities from outside of the package. A package consists of two parts: a specification in the form of a package declaration and an implementation in the form of a package body. Packages are one of the three kinds of program unit in Ada — the others are subprograms and tasks.

7.1 PACKAGE SPECIFICATIONS

The syntax of a package specification is given by the following diagrams

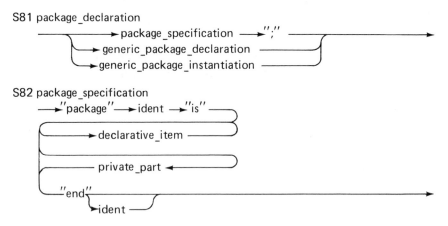

S81 package_declaration

S82 package_specification

Generic package declarations are described in Chapter 14. Private parts are dealt with later in the chapter.

As can be seen, a package specification consists of a sequence of declarative items enclosed between the symbols **is** and **end**, preceded by the symbol **package** and the name of the package. The package name may also be optionally given at the end of the package specification. As with subprograms, this practice is recommended as it improves program readability. As a simple example, the random number generator given in section 6.1 could be declared within a package as follows

package RAND OM **is**
    function RAND **return** INTEGER;
end RANDOM;

This package specification declares a single entity as being visible to the outside world, that is, the function RAND. The implementation of RAND and any other entities needed to support it will be hidden in the corresponding package body and are inaccessible to the user of the package (see next section).

The package RANDOM defines a resource which may be used by other program components which lie within the scope of the above declaration. Packages may be declared at the outermost level of a program as compilation units. In this case, the package specification and the corresponding package body may be compiled separately from each other (and from the rest of the program) and will be globally accessible from then on. When a package is declared within another program unit, then the corresponding body must be given in the same declarative part. The scope of the package in this case extends from the point of its declaration to the end of the enclosing program unit.

An entity declared within a package specification may be referenced from outside of the package using the selected component notation, for example,

    I := RANDOM.RAND;

is a call to the function RAND declared within the package RANDOM.

In general, a package specification will include constants, variables, types and the specifications of program units (mainly subprograms but sometimes tasks and packages). The implementation details of these program units will be given in the corresponding package body. Sometimes, however, a package is used simply to group together data items, in which case, no corresponding package body is required. For example, a package may declare a set of global constants and types as in

package SYSTEM_GLOBALS **is**

    subtype POSINT **is** INTEGER **range** 0 . . INTEGER'LAST;

    NO_OF_CHANNELS:**constant** := 16;
    subtype CHANNEL_NUM **is**
                INTEGER **range** 0 . . NO_OF_CHANNELS-1;
    MAX_VAL:**constant** := 2047;
    subtype SAMPLE_VAL **is** INTEGER **range** 0 . . MAX_VAL;

    type CHANNEL_COMMAND **is** (OPEN, CLOSE, RESET);

end SYSTEM_GLOBALS;

Here, the package SYSTEM_GLOBALS defines some constants and subtypes which are required throughout a program. There will be no corresponding package body because there are no unspecified implementation details needing to be defined.

7.2 PACKAGE BODIES

A package body has the same basic block structure as the subprogram body (and the declare statement). Its syntax is given by the following diagram

S83 package_body

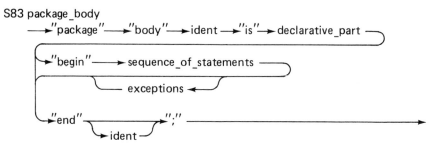

The sequence of statements in a package body is executed when the package is elaborated. This sequence is optional, and if included, is intended to perform any initialisation operations required by the package. If the package is declared in the outermost level of a program, then this initialisation will occur just once when the program is first started. If the package is declared within another program unit, then the initialisation will occur each time that the enclosing program unit is elaborated. Hence, if a package is declared within a subprogram, then its initialisation statements will be executed each time that the subprogram is called.

As an example, the body of RANDOM specified above could be defined as follows

```
package body RANDOM is

    RAND_VAL:INTEGER range 0 . . 4095;

    function RAND return INTEGER is
    begin
        RAND_VAL := (259*RAND_VAL) mod 4096;
        return RAND_VAL;
    end RAND;

begin
    RAND_VAL := 999;
end RANDOM;
```

The variable RAND_VAL is private to the package and is inaccessible to users of the package. When the package declaration is elaborated then the initialisation statement is executed setting RAND_VAL to 999. From then on, the package is entirely passive. All subsequent changes to RAND_VAL occur only as a result of calls to the function RAND.

In practice, the inclusion of explicit initialisation statements are quite rare. Firstly, many packages require no initialisation. Secondly, variables may be initialised directly at the point of their declaration. Thus, for example, the body of RANDOM could be coded more simply as

package body RANDOM **is**

RAND_VAL:INTEGER **range** 0 . . 4095 := 999;

function RAND **return** INTEGER **is**
begin
    RAND_VAL := (259*RAND_VAL) **mod** 4096;
    return RAND_VAL;
end RAND;

end RANDOM;

Notice that the **begin** symbol is omitted when there are no initialisation statements.

At this point, it may be helpful to review the differences between a package and a subprogram to dispel any confusions which may have arisen. Consider the following subprogram outline

procedure EXAMPLE **is**

    procedure SUB;   – – procedure spec

    package X **is**   – – package spec
        procedure XSUB;
    end X;

    procedure SUB **is**   – – procedure body
        I:INTEGER := 0;

    begin
        – – statements of SUB
    end SUB;
    package body X **is**   – – package body
        C:CHARACTER;

        procedure XSUB **is**
        begin
            – – body of XSUB
        end XSUB;
    begin
        – – initialise C
    end X;

```
begin
    - - use procedure SUB and package X
end EXAMPLE;
```

The procedure EXAMPLE contains two declarative items — a procedure and a package. When EXAMPLE is called, these declarations are elaborated. The effect of this elaboration is

(a) define X as the name of a package
(b) define SUB as the name of a procedure
(c) elaborate all declarations within the package X, that is, XSUB and C
(d) execute the initialisation statements of X

Notice that I is a local variable of SUB and C is a local variable of X, but C is elaborated whereas I is not. The essential difference is that SUB is an active component whereas X is a passive component. Within the statement body of EXAMPLE, SUB may be called but X may not (although, of course, XSUB may be called). Each time that SUB is called, then, and only then, is the local variable I elaborated. A consequence of this is that C exists throughout the lifetime of EXAMPLE, whereas I only exists whilst SUB is actually being executed.

In fact, the package has no significance at run-time at all. It is a compile time facility, used only to structure and control access to program entities. The procedure EXAMPLE may be rewritten by removing the package X without changing the meaning of the procedure at all, namely,

```
procedure EXAMPLE is

    procedure SUB;

    procedure XSUB;

    C:CHARACTER;

    procedure SUB is
        I:INTEGER := 0;
    begin
        - - statements of SUB
    end SUB;

    procedure XSUB is
    begin
        - - body of XSUB
    end XSUB;

begin
    - - initialise C
    - - use procedure SUB and XSUB
end EXAMPLE;
```

The only difference now is that the variable C is accessible within the statement body of EXAMPLE, whereas before it was hidden within the package.

Thus, packages are purely program structuring devices which carry no run time overheads. They are vital to the construction of large well-engineered programs because

(a) they allow the interface to a resource to be specified separately from the actual definition of how the resource is implemented
(b) they prevent the user of a resource from accessing (and hence corrupting) the data objects and program units needed to implement the resource
(c) they provide an extremely useful construct for the specification of separately compiled modules.

Or, to put it another way, packages allow programs to be designed, constructed and tested using the principle of data abstraction. Chapter 1 gave a simple example of how Ada programs can be built using this methodology. Later chapters include further and less trivial examples.

7.3 THE USE CLAUSE

As noted previously, the entities declared within a package are referenced externally by using the selected component notation. Thus, for example, to use the entities declared in the package SYSTEM_GLOBALS given earlier, considerable writing is required, for example,

> MY_CHANNEL:SYSTEM_GLOBALS . CHANNEL_NUM;
> THIS_SAMPLE:SYSTEM_GLOBALS . SAMPLE_VAL;

To alleviate this problem, Ada provides a **use** clause whose syntax is given by the following diagram

S84 use_clause

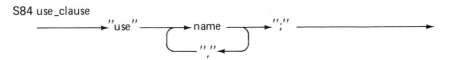

where *name* must be the name of a package.

A **use** clause can be written anywhere that a declarative item may be written. Its effect is to make the entities declared within the named packages directly visible so that the selected component notation can be dispensed with. Hence, to use the SYSTEM_GLOBALS package as above, the following could be written

> **use** SYSTEM_GLOBALS;
>
> MY_CHANNEL:CHANNEL_NUM;
> THIS_SAMPLE:SAMPLE_VAL;

It should be noted, however, that if the effect of a **use** clause is to make two entities with the same names (from different packages) become directly visible, then the selected component notation must still be used. Otherwise, the compiler could not tell which entity was being referred to.

7.4 PRIVATE TYPES

A major use of packages is to define a data type and the set of operations which may be applied to that data type. As an example, suppose that in a file management system, an i/o channel must be associated with a file before it can be read or written to. If the i/o channels are numbered 0 to 15 then care must be taken that

(a) an attempt is not made to associate a file with a channel number outside of the range 0 to 15
(b) an attempt is not made to associate a file with a channel which is already in use

A suitable way of avoiding any potential problems of this nature is to define a data type IOCHAN and two procedures GRAB and FREE to obtain and release a channel, respectively. Clearly, these entities should be declared within a package thus

> **package** IO_CHANNEL_MANAGER **is**
>
>   **type** IOCHAN **is range** 0 .. 15;
>
>   **procedure** GRAB(CHN:**out** IOCHAN);
>   **procedure** FREE(CHN:**in** IOCHAN);
>
>   **end** IO_CHANNEL_MANAGER;

where the case that all channels are in use when GRAB is called is being ignored for simplicity. The corresponding package body will include definitions for GRAB and FREE and a private data structure to record which channels are in use. The details of the body will not be given here as they are not relevant to the discussion.

Given this package, an i/o channel can be set up as follows

> **procedure** DO_IO **is**
>   **use** IO_CHANNEL_MANAGER;
>   MY_CHANNEL:IOCHAN;
>
> **begin**
>   GRAB(MY_CHANNEL);
>
>   - - use MY_CHANNEL
>
>   FREE(MY_CHANNEL);
> **end** DO_IO;

So far, the package IO_CHANNEL_MANAGER effectively separates the problem of allocating channels from that of using them. It is, however, deficient in certain other respects. It defines the type IOCHAN but also indicates how the type is implemented, that is, an integer in the range 0 to 15. This information is irrelevant to the user of the package, who is not (or should not be) concerned with what a channel number is, but only how to get one. More seriously, this knowledge of the representation for the type IOCHAN allows the IO_CHANNEL_MANAGER to be by-passed altogether. For example, there is nothing to prevent a direct assignment to MY_CHANNEL as in

MY_CHANNEL := 6;

thus ignoring the possibility that channel 6 is already in use.

It should be remembered here that the construction of secure systems is a primary concern of Ada. When a system is written by a team of programmers, an individual who writes a package such as IO_CHANNEL_MANAGER needs to be sure that his package cannot be inadvertently misused or bypassed by other members of the team. Also, of course, the IO_CHANNEL_MANAGER could be a pre-defined library package, in which case naive users need to be protected against inadvertent misuse of the filing system.

To solve the above deficiencies in the formulation of the IO_CHANNEL_MANAGER, Ada allows a type to be declared within a package specification as *private*. The syntax of a private type declaration is given by the following diagram

S85 private_type_defn

Hence, IOCHAN may now be declared as

type IOCHAN is private;

When a type is declared in a package specification as private, its full type declaration must be given in a private part of the specification. The syntax of this private part is given by the following diagram

S86 private_part

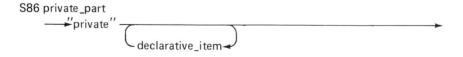

Thus, the package IO_CHANNEL_MANAGER may now be re-formulated as follows

```
package IO_CHANNEL_MANAGER is

    type IOCHAN is private;

    procedure GRAB(CHN:out IOCHAN);
    procedure FREE(CHN:in IOCHAN);

private

    type IOCHAN is range 0 .. 15;

end IO_CHANNEL_MANAGER;
```

The effect of declaring IOCHAN as *private* is to exclude the user of the type from applying any operations to objects of the type other than those operations defined within the same package specification, that is, GRAB and FREE. The only exceptions to this rule are that assignment and the tests for equality and inequality are available for private types. However, because the actual representation of a private type is (conceptually) unknown to the user of the type, literal values of the type cannot be assumed. Hence, assignments such as

```
MY_CHANNEL := 6;
```

are now illegal because 6 is not a literal of type IOCHAN (except within the package body where the representation of IOCHAN is known).

The security offered by the IO_CHANNEL_MANAGER is now more acceptable. However, it may be noted that it is still possible to duplicate channel numbers by copying, for example,

```
MY_CHANNEL, YOUR_CHANNEL:IOCHAN;

    --

GRAB(MY_CHANNEL);
YOUR_CHANNEL := MY_CHANNEL;

--associate MY_FILE with MY_CHANNEL
--associate YOUR_FILE with YOUR_CHANNEL but same channel!
```

This possibility can be excluded by specifying IOCHAN as not just *private* but *limited private*, that is,

```
type IOCHAN is limited private;
```

In this case, the only operations which may be applied to objects of type IOCHAN are those defined explicitly by the package, that is, GRAB and FREE. The inclusion of the keyword **limited** makes assignment and the tests for equality no longer automatically available.

(Note: the solution to the IO_CHANNEL_MANAGER package is actually still incomplete, since the question of initialising objects of type IOCHAN has been carefully avoided! The complete solution is given in section 8.10.)

The above description of private and limited private types has been presented in terms of a mechanism for increasing the security of package operations. The key point, however, is that making a type private immediately makes it an abstract type. From the point of view of the user of the package, the type is abstract because he does not know anything about its internal structure and there are no literals which he can assign to objects of the type. All that is known is the name of the type and the operations that can be applied to it. This may seem restrictive but, in fact, it is beneficial. Firstly, it frees him from worrying about the details of manipulating objects of the type, and allows him to concentrate on the higher level design. Secondly, by restricting any actual manipulations of a type to within one package, subsequent modification and maintenance is much easier. The examples in subsequent chapters will demonstrate how to design programs using abstract data types.

Before leaving the subject of private types, it is worthwhile emphasising what can and what cannot be done with a private type outside its defining package. The user of a private type can declare objects of the type, assign one object to another, test whether two objects are equal or unequal and apply any of the operations supplied within the defining package to these objects. He cannot apply any other operations to them even if he knows that they are compatible with the way in which the type is actually represented. If a type is limited private, then the further restriction is placed that assignment and the tests for equality and inequality are prohibited. Note, however, that these operations can be supplied if required by the defining package. The implications of no assignment are more far-reaching than may at first be apparent. For example,

(a) A declaration of a variable of a limited private type cannot include an explicit initialisation.

(b) Parameters of a limited private type may not have default values.

(c) No constant of a limited private type can be declared outside the defining package.

Furthermore, these rules apply not just to a limited private type itself but also to any other type which has a component of a limited private type.

Finally, it should be noted that it is possible to declare constants of a private type in the visible part of a package. This is done by omitting the actual value of the constant in the visible part and then repeating the constant declaration in full in the private part. Such constants are called *deferred constants*. For example, in the COUNTER package given in Chapter 1, the need for an explicit INIT procedure and the IS_ZERO test could be avoided by declaring a constant of type TOTAL called ZERO, that is,

        package COUNTER **is**

            type TOTAL **is private**;

ZERO: constant TOTAL;

procedure INCREMENT(X: in out TOTAL);
procedure DECREMENT(X: in out TOTAL);

private

type TOTAL is new INTEGER range 0 .. INTEGER'LAST;
ZERO: constant TOTAL :=0;

end COUNTER;

Given this revised version of the COUNTER package, an object can be declared of type TOTAL and initialised using the constant value zero, for example,

use COUNTER;
T1: TOTAL := ZERO;

and subsequently tested for equality to zero by

if T1 = ZERO then ....

Note, however, that tests such as

if T1 > ZERO then ....

are not allowed. The type TOTAL is being thought of as a scalar type and although, in fact, it is, no such assumption is justified: TOTAL is just a private type.

In summary, the ability to define private types in Ada allows the abstract properties of a type to be specified so that the user of a type need not be concerned with how the type is actually implemented. The use of these abstract data types enables programs to be designed top-down by successive refinement of data types and allows relatively secure systems to be built.

7.5 DERIVED TYPES AND PACKAGES

Every type in Ada is characterised by the set of literals which denote the values of the type, the set of attributes defined for the type and the set of operations which may be applied to the type. The set of operations may be in the form of operators, functions or procedures.

As noted in Chapter 3, the facility to derive new types from existing types is a powerful tool for enhancing program security. When a type is derived from an existing (parent) type then it automatically inherits all the literals and attributes of that type. If the parent type is a predefined type, then all of the predefined operators for that type are also inherited. However, any further operators which may have been defined by the user are not inherited. For example, suppose that the following function is declared

function BLOB(B:INTEGER) **return** INTEGER;

then the set of operations for INTEGER types (that is, +, -, *, etc.) is augmented by the BLOB operation. If, however, a new type is subsequently derived from INTEGER such as in

type NUMBER **is new** INTEGER;

then the type NUMBER only inherits the predefined operations of INTEGER. It does not inherit BLOB so that if BLOB for NUMBERs is required it must be explicitly re-declared.

In practice, of course, a large program may have several hundred subprograms declared which involve predefined types such as INTEGER and it would clearly be ridiculous to allow derived types to inherit all these subprograms. When a type is declared within a package, however, the situation is rather different since usually the subprograms declared within that same package are considered to be the operators for that type. Hence, when a type is derived from a parent type which is defined within a package, then the derived type inherits all of the subprograms which have been provided as operators for that type within the same package. In this context, a subprogram is considered to be an operator of a given type T if it has at least one parameter which is of type T or if it is a function returning a result of type T. As an example, consider the following declarations

> **package** GONG_TYPE **is**
>
>   **type** GONG **is** . . .
>
>   **procedure** MAKE(G:**in out** GONG);
>   **function** WEIGHT(G:GONG) **return** POUNDS;
>
> **end** GONG_TYPE;
>
> **use** GONG_TYPE;
>
> **function** COLOUR(G:GONG) **return** TINT;
>
> **type** MEDAL **is new** GONG;
>
> M:MEDAL; G:GONG; T:TINT; W:POUNDS;

The package GONG_TYPE defines a type GONG (Note: this need not be a private type) and two subprograms MAKE and WEIGHT. These subprograms are considered to be the operations defined for the type GONG and are therefore inherited by any type derived from GONG. Hence in the above, the type MEDAL inherits MAKE and WEIGHT but it does not inherit COLOUR. Thus, the subsequent statements

> MAKE(G); MAKE(M);
> W:=WEIGHT(G); W:=WEIGHT(M);
> T:=COLOUR(G);

are all legal but the call

     T:=COLOUR(M);

is not since COLOUR is not inherited by the type MEDAL.

7.6 EXAMPLE – AN ERROR REPORTING PACKAGE FOR A COMPILER

As a straightforward but nevertheless practical example of the use of a package, a simple error reporting facility for a compiler will be described. This package provides two procedures as shown

     package ERROR_REPORTER **is**

       procedure ERROR(ERROR_NUMBER:**in** NATURAL);
       procedure TOTAL_ERRORS;

     end ERROR_REPORTER;

The procedure ERROR will output the given error number and an appropriate message to the output stream each time it is called. The procedure TOTAL_ERRORS is called at the end of the compilation to output the total number of errors detected. Input/output in Ada is covered fully in Chapter 15; here it is sufficient to assume that the following output operations are available

     NEW_LINE;   – – start a new line
     PUT("String");   – – output the given string
     PUT(N);   – – output the given integer value

The package body for ERROR_REPORTER is as follows

     package body ERROR_REPORTER **is**

       ERROR_COUNT:INTEGER **range** 0 . . INTEGER'LAST := 0;

       procedure ERROR(ERROR_NUMBER:**in** NATURAL) **is**
       begin
          NEW_LINE;
          PUT("**** Error ");
          PUT(ERROR_NUMBER);
          PUT(" ");
          case ERROR_NUMBER **is**
             when 1 => PUT("Undeclared Identifier");
             when 2 => PUT("Closing Bracket Expected");
             – –
             – – etc
             when others => PUT("Undefined Error!");
          end case;
          ERROR_COUNT := ERROR_COUNT + 1;
       end ERROR;

```
procedure TOTAL_ERRORS is
begin
    NEW_LINE;
    if ERROR_COUNT = 0 then
        PUT("No");

    else
        PUT(ERROR_COUNT);
    end if;
    PUT(" Error");
    if ERROR_COUNT /= 1 then
        PUT("s");
    end if;
    PUT(" Detected");
  end TOTAL_ERRORS;
end ERROR REPORTER;
```

7.7 EXERCISES

(7.1) A VDU screen consists of 24 rows (numbered 0 to 23 from top to bottom) of 80 characters per row (numbered 0 to 79 from left to right). A character may be written to any position on the screen by calling OUT_CH and the screen may be cleared by calling CLEAR_SCREEN. Both of these procedures are defined in the package SCREEN defined as

```
package SCREEN is
    subtype ORDINATE is INTEGER range 0 .. 23;
    subtype ABSCISSA is INTEGER range 0 .. 79;
    procedure OUT_CH (CH:in CHARACTER;
                    X: in ABSCISSA;
                    Y: in ORDINATE);
    procedure CLEAR_SCREEN;
end SCREEN;
```

Design a package to allow the user to draw horizontal and vertical lines on the screen using a character of his choice.

(7.2) Write a procedure to read a sequence of 20 integer numbers from the input stream (using GET(N)) and display their values as a histogram on the VDU screen using the package designed in exercise 1 above. The range of each number is 0 to 100 and the histogram should be sideways, for example,

```
 1 | *****
 2 | ************
 3 | **
 4 | ***********
 5 | ******
   ..
   ..
19 | ******
20 | ****
   - - - - - - - - - - - - - - - - - - - - - - - - - - - - - - - - - - -
   0                                                          100
```

8

Structured data types

So far the facilities for describing data have been restricted to simple discrete types such as numbers and characters. In this chapter, structured data types are described, that is, those which are a composite of other simpler data types. Ada provides just two data structuring mechanisms – the array and the record.

8.1 ARRAY TYPES

An array is a collection of components all of which have the same type. An individual component of an array is referenced by specifying one or more index values which may be of any discrete type. The syntax of an array definition is given by the following diagrams

S87 array_type_defn

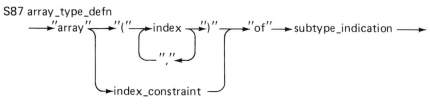

S88 index

Ignoring index constraints for the moment, the basic form of an array type declaration is illustrated by the following examples

        type VECTOR **is array** (INTEGER **range** <>) **of** INTEGER;

        type MATRIX **is array** (INTEGER **range** <>,
                             INTEGER **range** <>) **of** INTEGER;

        type DAY_SET **is array** (DAY **range** <>) **of** BOOLEAN;

The type VECTOR denotes an array of integer components indexed by an integer value. The type MATRIX is a two dimensional array of integer components indexed by a pair of integer values. The type DAY_SET is an array of Boolean components indexed by values of type DAY. In each case, the symbol <> is called a *box* and indicates that the range of values which are allowed for each index has been left unspecified. Thus, each of these array types is characterised by the type of its components and the types of its indices but not by its dimensions. The general array type declaration therefore defines a template for declaring array objects of varying sizes.

When an array object is declared, its size must be specified by giving an index constraint

S89 index_constraint

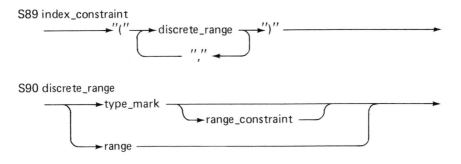

S90 discrete_range

Thus, for example

IVEC:VECTOR(0 .. 9);

declares an array object IVEC with 10 integer elements indexed by the values 0 to 9. Similarly,

IMAT:MATRIX(1 .. 2, 1 .. 2);

declares a 2 by 2 matrix of integer elements.

When several objects of an array type are required all with the same upper and lower index bounds, then an array sub-type can be introduced to avoid having to specify an explicit index constraint with each object declaration. For example,

subtype WORK_DAY_SET **is** DAY_SET(MON .. FRI);

defines an array sub-type with fixed index bounds MON to FRI. Objects of sub-type WORK_DAY_SET can now be declared directly, for example,

JOHNS_ATTENDANCE:WORK_DAY_SET;
FREDS_ATTENDANCE:WORK_DAY_SET;

The above describes the basic array type mechanism in Ada. The key feature is that the actual index bounds of an array type are not specified directly by the type, but are imposed in the form of an index constraint when an object of the type is actually declared. This mechanism allows great flexibility in the use of arrays. In particular, it allows procedures to be written which can accept actual array parameters of varying size. An example of this is given later.

Although the general array type mechanism is very flexible, it is rather long-winded when only a single sub-type of the array is actually ever required. To remedy this, Ada allows an index constraint to be specified directly in an array type declaration (see syntax diagram S87). For example,

> **type** ALARM_SET **is array** (ALARM_CODE) **of** ALARM_STATE;
> **type** SMALL_VEC **is array** (0 .. 6) **of** INTEGER;

declare array types ALARM_SET and SMALL_VEC whose index bounds are fixed. Objects of these types may be declared directly without specifying an index constraint, for example,

> ALARMS:ALARM_SET;
> FACTORS:SMALL_VEC;

Technically, the general form of an array type with unspecified index bounds is called an *unconstrained array type*. Objects declared of an unconstrained array type must include an index constraint, or an array sub-type can be introduced. The form of an array type in which the index bounds are fixed is called a *constrained array type*. It is not possible to declare sub-types of a constrained array type and no index constraint should be given when declaring an object of the type. In fact, a constrained array type declaration of the form

> **type** A **is array** (INDEX) **of** T;

is exactly equivalent to the following sequence of declarations

> **type** *** **is array** (INDEX **range** <>) **of** T;
> **subtype** A **is** *** (INDEX);

where *** denotes an anonymous identifier distinct from all other identifiers used in the program.

Normally, the index bounds specified in an index constraint will be static expressions. Thus, in

> IVEC:VECTOR(0 .. 9);

the size of IVEC is fixed at compile time. Ada does not, however, insist that index bounds be static. When they are not, the resulting array is called a dynamic array and its actual size is not known until run time. For example, consider the following

```
GET(N);               - - read a value for N
declare
     DYN_VEC:VECTOR(0 .. N);
begin
     - - DYN_VEC is a dynamic array
end
```

In this example, the size of DYN_VEC can be different every time that the declare statement is executed. Dynamic arrays are useful in some contexts (such as string handling) but they should in general be used with some restraint, since they lead to significant run time overheads.

Finally, it may be noted that array objects can be declared directly in the form

ARRAY_NAME:**array**(INDEX) **of** COMPONENT_TYPE;

(see syntax diagram S61 in section 5.3). This is useful when only one object of a given array type is required, but note that in this case the type of the array object ARRAY_NAME is anonymous. The implication of this is that if a second array was declared as in

ARRAY_NAME2:**array**(INDEX) **of** COMPONENT_TYPE;

then the assignment

ARRAY_NAME := ARRAY_NAME2;   - - type mismatch

would be illegal, since the types of the two array objects are not the same. Note, also, that even if the two arrays had been declared in the same array object declaration, for example, as in

ARRAY_NAME,ARRAY_NAME2:**array**(INDEX) **of** COMPONENT_TYPE;

then the above assignment would still be illegal.

8.2 ARRAY AGGREGATES

An array aggregate is used to denote a whole array value. The syntax of an aggregate is given by the following diagrams

S91 aggregate

S92 component_assoc

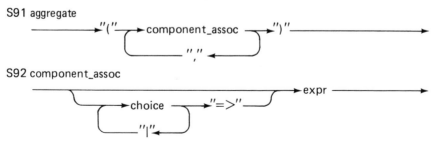

The basic idea of an aggregate is to specify a value for each and every component of the array. The association between a value and a particular component can be made using either positional or named notation, as in the case for subprogram call parameters. For example, using positional notation

FACTORS := (0,1,1,1,3,0,0);

assigns a value to the array FACTORS such that the first component (that is, index position 0) is set to 0, the next is set to 1 and so on. Using the named notation, the above could be written in any of the following ways

FACTORS := (0=>0, 1|2|3=>1, 4=>3, 5|6=>0);
FACTORS := (1 .. 3=>1, 0|5|6=>0, 4=>3);
ГACTORS := SMALL_VEC'(1 .. 3=>1, 4=>3, **others** =>0);

In each case, the choice of components to be given a specific value is denoted in exactly the same way as was described for the case statement in section 4.5. The choice **others** means all those components which have not already been named. When the choice **others** is used, it must always be given as the last item in the list of component associations and the sub-type of the aggregate must be specified explicitly using the notation of a qualified expression (see section 6.6). An exception to this rule is when the aggregate is used in a subprogram call as an actual parameter which corresponds to a formal parameter of a constrained array type, or when it appears in a return statement and the corresponding function result is a constrained array type.

Aggregate values for n-dimensional arrays are written as a one-dimensional aggregate of components that are themselves (n-1)-dimensional array values. Each component at the outermost level corresponds to the first index, each component at the first level of nesting corresponds to the second index, and so on. For example, if in the matrix IMAT given above, the first index is interpreted as the row number and the second as the column number, then the assignment

IMAT := ((1,2), (3,4));

sets the first row to (1,2) and the second row to (3,4), that is, the value of row 1 column 1 is 1, row 1 column 2 is 2, row 2 column 1 is 3 and row 2 column 2 is 4.

Finally, it may be noted that when a constant array object is declared of an unconstrained array type, then the index constraint can be omitted, with the bounds being fixed instead by those of the initial value, for example,

FULL_TIME:**constant** DAY_SET := (MON .. FRI => TRUE);

where FULL_TIME denotes a constant array object of 5 components each of which is TRUE.

8.3 USING ARRAYS

In order to use arrays, it is necessary to assign and access both whole array values and individual array components. Whole array assignment is straightforward. For example, given

V1,V2:VECTOR(0 . . 9);

then

V1 := V2;

assigns the value of V2 to V1, that is, every component value of V2 is assigned to the corresponding component value of V1. Array objects with different index bounds may be assigned to each other, for example, given

V3:VECTOR(1 . . 10);

then

V3 := V1;

is also a legal assignment, since the types of V3 and V1 are the same. In this case, each component of V1 is assigned to the component of V3 in the corresponding position from the beginning of the array. Index values are not relevant to whole array assignments. However, if V4 is declared as follows

V4:VECTOR(0 . . 10);

then the assignment

V4 := V1;

is not legal, since V4 and V1 are not the same size. Thus, two array values are assignment compatible if they have the same type name and are of the same size.

Individual components of an array are denoted by indexing the component, as described by the following syntax diagram

S93 indexed_component

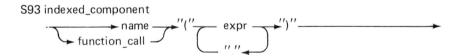

where each expression within the parentheses denotes the value of the corresponding index. For example,

V3(1) := V4(0);

assigns the first component of V4 to the first component of V3,

> **for** I **in** 0 . . 9 **loop**
>   V1(I) := V1(I) + V2(I);
> **end loop**;

adds the vector V2 to the vector V1 and finally

IMAT(1,1) := 1;	IMAT(2,1) := 3;
IMAT(1,2) := 2;	IMAT(2,2) := 4;

is equivalent to the aggregate assignment given in the previous section.

Note also here that a component of an array object returned by a function call can also be accessed using an index (S93), as can slices (below) and record components (section 5.9).

An indexed component of an array can itself be an array In such cases, the indexing operation needs to be repeated to access the ultimate constituents of the array. For example, suppose that the following array object is declared

ATTENDANCE_TABLE:**array**(1 . . NO_OF_EMPLOYEES)
                                                of WORK_DAY_SET;

then,

       ATTENDANCE_TABLE(1)

denotes the first component of ATTENDANCE_TABLE which is an array of subtype WORK_DAY_SET and

       ATTENDANCE_TABLE(1)(MON)

denotes the first component of this sub-array which is of type BOOLEAN. Note that an array of arrays is not the same as a two-dimensional array. For example, an alternative way of defining ATTENDANCE_TABLE might be

ATTENDANCE_TABLE:**array**(1 . . NO_OF_EMPLOYEES,MON . . FRI) **of**
                                                        BOOLEAN;

but in this case the notation for denoting the BOOLEAN value corresponding to the Monday attendance of employee 1 is

       ATTENDANCE_TABLE(1,MON)

The key point about this second definition of ATTENDANCE_TABLE is that the original two-level hierarchy of types has been removed. As a result, it is not now possible to extract the WORK_DAY_SET of a single employee and manipulate it as a single array object.

As well as the individual components of an array, Ada also provides a notation for denoting a slice of an array

S94 slice

A slice is a contiguous sequence of components within a one-dimensional array. For example, the slice

V1(0 .. 4)

denotes the first five components of the array V1. Slices of arrays may be assigned to each other and to other arrays provided that the types and sizes are the same. Hence, for example,

V1(0 .. 4) := V2(5 .. 9);

assigns the last five components of V2 to the first five components of V1. The last five components of V1 are unaffected. In,

V4(0 .. 9) := V1;

the whole of the array V1 is assigned to the first 10 components of V4. Note finally that a slice of one component is not the same as an indexed component. For example,

V1(1 .. 1)

denotes an array value of type VECTOR whereas

V1(1)

denotes an array component value of type INTEGER.

In addition to the assignment operation, the relational operators $'='$ and $'/='$ may be applied to any two arrays of the same type and size. The two arrays are equal if each pair of corresponding array components are equal. Again, *corresponding* means the same position in the array, counting from the beginning, regardless of the actual index values.

For one-dimensional arrays, a number of further operations are defined:

> <= > >= apply to two arrays of the same type with discrete components but not necessarily the same size. The result of the test corresponds to lexicographic ordering

and or xor apply to two arrays of the same type and size and which have Boolean component types. The specified logical operation is applied between each pair of corresponding components

& applies to two arrays of the same type but not necessarily the same size. The result is the catenation of the two arrays. Either the left or the right operand may be a value of the component type in place of one of the arrays

not applies to a single array with Boolean components. Each component of the array is complemented.

Given the following declarations

W1:WORK_DAY_SET := (TRUE,FALSE,TRUE,TRUE,FALSE);
W2:WORK_DAY_SET := (FALSE,FALSE,TRUE,FALSE,TRUE);
A:VECTOR(0 .. 2) := (1,1,3);
B:VECTOR(1 .. 2) := (2,1);
C:VECTOR(6 .. 8) := (1,1,2);

then the following are examples of the above operations

W1 **and** W2	- - (FALSE,FALSE,TRUE,FALSE,FALSE)
W1 **or** W2	- - (TRUE,FALSE,TRUE,TRUE,TRUE)
not W1	- - (FALSE,TRUE,FALSE,FALSE,TRUE)
W1 − W2	- - FALSE
A < B	- - TRUE
A < C	- - FALSE
A & B	- - (1,1,3,2,1)
A & 4	- - (1,1,3,4)
4 & A	- - (4,1,1,3)

8.4 STRINGS

Ada provides a pre-defined array type called **STRING** defined within the package STANDARD as follows

subtype POSITIVE **is** INTEGER **range** 1 .. INTEGER'LAST;
type STRING **is array** (POSITIVE **range** <>) **of** CHARACTER;

There are no operations which are specific to strings but the relational operators and the catenation operator ('&') defined above are particularly useful for working with **STRING** types. String aggregates may be denoted by character string literals as a convenient alternative to the normal notation, that is,

"ABC"   is equivalent to   ('A','B','C')

8.5 ARRAY ATTRIBUTES

Ada provides a set of attributes for determining certain properties of arrays

A'FIRST(N)	- - lower bound of N'th index
A'LAST(N)	- - upper bound of N'th index
A'LENGTH(N)	- - size of N'th dimension
A'RANGE(N)	- - the subtype defined by the range A'FIRST(N) .. A'LAST(N)

In each case, A may be an array object name or the type mark of a constrained array type. If N is 1 then it can be omitted, for example,

    V1'FIRST

gives the lower index bound of the array object V1.

These array attributes provide a convenient way of writing procedures which operate on arrays of varying sizes. The formal parameters of a subprogram may be of an unconstrained array type. Within the subprogram, the bounds of the formal array parameter are constrained by the actual array object supplied with the call. Hence, for example, vector addition could be defined by overloading the '+' operator as follows

```
        function "+" (V1,V2:VECTOR) return VECTOR is
            V3:VECTOR(V1'RANGE);
            V2_IDX:V2'RANGE := V2'FIRST;
        begin
            if V1'LENGTH /= V2'LENGTH then
                - - take error action - V1 and V2 are
                - - not the same size!
            else
                for V_IDX in V1'RANGE loop
                    V3(V_IDX) := V1(V_IDX) + V2(V2_IDX);
                    V2_IDX := V2_IDX + 1;
                end loop;
                return V3;
            end if;
        end "+";
```

Note in this example that only the sizes of the actual array parameters corresponding to V1 and V2 need be the same: the index bounds need not match.

8.6 ARRAY TYPE CONVERSIONS

In section 3.7, the concept of a type conversion was described. Type conversions may be applied to array types provided that both corresponding index types and corresponding component types are the same or are derived from each other. The basic form of an array type conversion is

    ARRAY_TYPE(ARRAY_VALUE)

If the ARRAY_TYPE is a constrained type then the size of the constrained type must be the same as the size of the ARRAY_VALUE. The index bounds of the result are then the same as those of the ARRAY_TYPE. If the ARRAY_TYPE is an unconstrained type then the bounds of the result are the same as the ARRAY _VALUE. For example, given

```
type TITLE is array(1 .. 5) of CHARACTER;
HEADING:TITLE;
NAME:STRING(1 .. 10);
```

then

STRING(HEADING)

gives an array value of type STRING with bounds determined by HEADING, that is, 1 .. 5 whereas

TITLE(NAME(6 .. 10))

gives an array of type TITLE with bounds determined by TITLE, that is, 1 .. 5.

8.7 RECORD TYPES

The record is the second mechanism provided in Ada for structuring data. A record is a collection of components of possibly differing types. Each component is denoted by a component name. Hence, records differ from arrays in two major respects. Firstly, all components of an array must have the same type whereas in records they may be different. Secondly, the selection of an array component can be made dynamically at run time by evaluating an expression denoting the index value. The selection of a record component is always static and determinable at compile time.

The syntax of a record type definition is given by the following diagrams

S95 record_type_defn

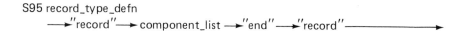

S96 component_list

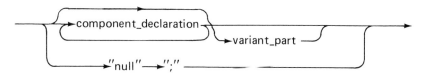

S97 component_declaration

Variant parts and the use of null components are described later in Chapter 10.

The form of record type declarations is illustrated by the following two examples. First,

```
type TANK_LEVEL is
    record
        HI_LIMIT,LO_LIMIT:INTEGER:
        LEVEL:INTEGER;
        STATUS:ALARM_STATE;
    end record;
```

here TANK_LEVEL is the name of a record type with four components. HI_LIMIT, LO_LIMIT and LEVEL are components of type INTEGER and STATUS is a component of type ALARM_STATE. Second,

```
type NAME is
    record
        VAL:STRING(1 .. MAX_SIZE);
        SIZE:INTEGER range 0 .. MAX_SIZE;
    end record;
```

here NAME is an example of a record containing a component which is itself a structured type. Thus, VAL is an array of characters and SIZE is an integer denoting the actual number of characters stored in VAL.

8.8 RECORD AGGREGATES

A record aggregate denotes a record value, that is, a value for each and every component of the record. The syntax used for record aggregates is the same as for array aggregates, as given in syntax diagrams S91 and S92. As with arrays, either positional or named notations may be used to specify the association between a component and its value. For example, given

```
TL1:TANK_LEVEL;
```

then

```
TL1 := (100, -100, 0, GREEN);
```

and

```
TL1 := (HI_LIMIT  => 100,
        LEVEL     => 0,
        LO_LIMIT  => -100,
        STATUS    => GREEN);
```

are equivalent.

The only restrictions on the use of the aggregate notation in the case of records are that the choice notation

    A .. B => ...

is meaningless and therefore not allowed; and that where several components are named in a single choice, as in

    A | B | C => ...

then each component must be of the same type.

8.9 USING RECORDS

The assignment operation and the comparison operations '=' and '/=' are provided for copying and testing whole record values. The individual components of a record are denoted using the selected component notation mentioned previously in connection with referencing the named components of blocks and program units. The syntax of the selected component notation is given by the following diagram

S98 selected_component

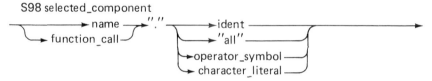

where operator_symbol refers only to the components of blocks and program units, and where **all** is used only in connection with access types (see Chapter 11). In the case of records, *name* is the name of the record object and *ident* is the name of the selected component of that record. Thus,

    TL1 . HI_LIMIT

denotes the HI_LIMIT component of the record object TL1.

As an example of using records, the following procedure takes a TANK_LEVEL object as parameter and sets its STATUS component accordingly:

```
procedure SET_STATUS(TL:in out TANK_LEVEL) is
    MARGIN:constant := 5;
begin
    if  TL . LEVEL<TL . LO_LIMIT
                        or TL . LEVEL>TL . HI_LIMIT then
        TL . STATUS := RED;
    elsif  TL . LEVEL < TL . LO_LIMIT+MARGIN  or
           TL . LEVEL > TL . HI_LIMIT-MARGIN   then
        TL . STATUS := YELLOW;
```

```
    else
        TL . STATUS := GREEN;
    end if;
end SET_STATUS;
```

This procedure first checks whether the current tank level is outside the pre-
scribed limits, in which case STATUS is set to RED. Otherwise it checks to see
if the level is within MARGIN points of either limit, in which case the STATUS
is set to YELLOW as a warning. Otherwise the normal situation is denoted by
setting STATUS to GREEN.

As well as illustrating the way that records can be used, the SET_STATUS
example also shows that the selected component notation can be tedious to use
when repeated references to the same record component must be made. Ada
provides a limited form of abbreviation to be used in such cases, in the form of
a *renaming* facility. As shown by the following diagram, renaming can be applied
to a variety of Ada program entities. Here, however, only the renaming of record
and array components will be described, as denoted by the first option in the
syntax diagram

S99 renaming_declaration

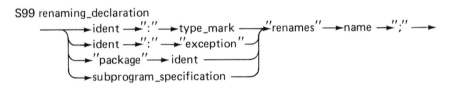

To illustrate the use of renaming as an abbreviatory device, the procedure
SET_STATUS given above could be rewritten as follows

```
procedure SET_STATUS(TL:in out TANK_LEVEL) is
    MARGIN:constant := 5;
    L:INTEGER renames TL . LEVEL;
    HI:INTEGER renames TL . HI_LIMIT;
    LO:INTEGER renames TL . LO_LIMIT;
    S:ALARM_STATUS renames TL . STATUS;
begin
    if L<LO or L>HI then
        S := RED;
    elsif L < LO+MARGIN or L > HI-MARGIN then
        S := YELLOW;
    else
        S := GREEN;
    end if;
end SET_STATUS;
```

In this case, the saving in writing is rather marginal, although in larger procedures it can be worthwhile. However, care must always be taken not to overdo abbreviations, since loss of program clarity may result.

Renaming can also be used to force the partial evaluation of a name. For example, suppose that an array of tank levels was declared as in

TANKS: **array**(1 . . 100)**of** TANK_LEVEL;

and it was required to increment the level of each tank by one and set the status accordingly, that is,

for I **in** 1 . . 100 **loop**
    TANKS(I) . LEVEL := TANKS(I) . LEVEL + 1;
    SET_STATUS(TANKS(I));
end loop;

In this solution, the record component selected by I is computed three times, which is quite unnecessary. Renaming can be used to avoid this, as in

for I **in** 1 . . 100 **loop**
    declare
        TL:TANK_LEVEL **renames** TANKS(I);
    begin
        TL . LEVEL := TL . LEVEL + 1;
        SET_STATUS(TL);
    end;
end loop;

where the Ith component of TANKS is now computed once only, during the elaboration of the declarative part of the declare block. From then on it is referred to by the local name TL.

8.10 DEFAULT INITIAL VALUES

Record type declarations have the unique property that a default initial value can be specified for one or more components (see syntax diagram S97). For example, the type NAME declared in section 8.7 could be re-written as

type NAME **is**
    record
        VAL:STRING(1 . . MAX_SIZE);
        SIZE:INTEGER **range** 0 . . MAX_SIZE := 0;
    end record;

Giving the SIZE component a default initial value ensures that every object of type NAME introduced into a program will be consistent from the moment it is declared. For example,

N1:NAME;

declares an object N1 which by default holds a string of zero length. Default initial values can be overridden by an explicit initial value, for example,

```
N2:NAME := ("FRED    ",4);
N3:NAME := ("GEORGE",6);
```

where it is assumed that MAX_SIZE=6.

The ability to specify default initial values is particularly useful in the implementation of abstract data types. It enables the designer of a package to guarantee that objects of an abstract type cannot be declared and used without assigning an initial value to them. For example, in section 7.4, the use of a limited private type was illustrated by considering a mechanism for the secure allocation of input/output channel numbers. As noted, the solution presented was not complete. A user of the package IO_CHANNEL_MANAGER could still declare an object of type IOCHAN and use it without first calling GRAB. If the uninitialised value of such an object happened to be a legal channel number, then he could still corrupt the system. Furthermore, there was no way that the IO_CHANNEL_MANAGER could ensure that users were calling GRAB and FREE in the correct order. These loop-holes can be plugged by redefining the type of IOCHAN to be a record containing a flag to indicate whether each object of type IOCHAN is valid. A default initial value of FALSE is specified for this flag so that the user must call GRAB before he can use an input/output channel. The revised package specification is as follows

```
package IO_CHANNEL_MANAGER is

    type IOCHAN is limited private;

    procedure GRAB(CHN:in out IOCHAN);
    procedure FREE(CHN:in out IOCHAN);

private
    type IOCHAN is
        record
            N:INTEGER range 0 .. 15;
            VALID:BOOLEAN := FALSE;
        end record;

end IO_CHANNEL_MANAGER;
```

This package now represents a secure solution to the problem. A user may declare an object as in

```
MY_CHANNEL:IOCHAN;
```

and the VALID component will automatically be set FALSE. The only way that VALID can be set true is to call GRAB, which is precisely what the designer of the IO_CHANNEL_MANAGER intends. Hence, all uses of MY_CHANNEL can be checked for validity and the user cannot interfere with the input/output systems operation.

8.11 EXAMPLE – A NETWORK MANAGER PACKAGE

A digital communications system consists of a set of nodes linked together to form a network. Each node is linked to at most 8 other nodes in the network and a maximum of 100 nodes is allowed.

As part of a simulation program to investigate network performance, a package is required to maintain a record of the network structure at any time. It must provide facilities to insert and remove nodes, insert and remove the links between nodes and allow the current network structure to be interrogated.

The actual data structure used to represent the network will be hidden within the package body. The only access to this structure is therefore via the procedures and functions defined within the package specification. Hence, the integrity of the network representation can be guaranteed against corruption by users of the package. In the design that follows, checks are applied to ensure that all operations performed by the user of the package are consistent (for example, he is not allowed to make a link to a non-existent node). However, when an error is detected, no action is taken. Suitable procedures for handling errors must await the discussion of exception handlers given in Chapter 13. Here the emphasis is on manipulating data structures, so the error handling aspects of the problem can be ignored for the present.

The package specification for the network manager is given as follows

```
package NETWORK_MANAGER is

    MAX_NODE:constant := 100;
    MAX_LINK:constant := 8;

    type NODE_ID is range 1 .. MAX_NODE;
    type LINK_NUM is range 0 .. MAX_LINK;
    subtype LINK_INDEX is LINK_NUM range 1 .. MAX_LINK;
    type LINK_VEC is array (LINK_INDEX) of NODE_ID;
    type LINK_SET is
        record
            USED:LINK_NUM := 0;
            LINK:LINK_VEC;
        end record;

    - - Network Operations
    procedure INSERT(NODE:in NODE_ID);
    procedure REMOVE(NODE:in NODE_ID);
    procedure CONNECT(A_NODE,B_NODE:in NODE_ID);
    procedure DISCONNECT(A_NODE,B_NODE:in NODE_ID);

    - - Interrogation of Current Network Structure
    function NODE_INSERTED(NODE:NODE_ID) return BOOLEAN;
    function GET_LINKS(NODE:NODE_ID) return LINK_SET;

end NETWORK_MANAGER;
```

Each node in the network is identified by a unique integer number in the range 1 to 100 (type NODE_ID). The nodes connected to a given node are returned by the function GET_LINKS in the form of a record of type LINK_SET. This record contains a component called USED which denotes the number of nodes connected to the given node and an array called LINK whose first USED components contain the identifiers of those nodes.

As an example of the use of this package, the following operations would build the network shown in Fig. 8.1:

```
INSERT(1);        INSERT(2);
INSERT(7);        INSERT(20);
CONNECT(1,2);     CONNECT(1,20);
CONNECT(2,20);    CONNECT(2,7);
```

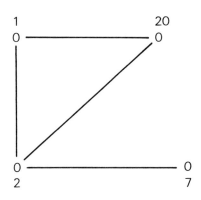

Fig. 8.1 – A Network with 4 Nodes

Given this network, its state could be interrogated as follows

```
for I in NODE_ID loop
    if NODE_INSERTED(I) then
        PRINT(I);
        PRINT(GET_LINKS(I));
    end if;
end loop;
```

where the two print procedures are assumed to print out the node identifier and the list of node connections in a suitable format, for example,

NODE	LINKS		
1	2	20	
2	1	7	20
7	2		
20	1	2	

Having defined the package specification of the NETWORK_MANAGER, attention can now be turned to the implementation of the package body. The first step is to design the data structure needed to represent the network. A simple approach, and the one to be taken here, is to represent the network as an array, that is,

NETWORK:array(NODE_ID)of NODE_REC;

where NODE_REC is a data structure containing information to record whether or not the given node has been inserted into the network and if so which nodes it is connected to. Thus, the NETWORK array has a component for every potential node in the network, regardless of whether or not it has actually been inserted by the user (Note: a more elegant approach is possible using dynamic data structures – see Chapter 11).

At this point the NODE_REC itself could be defined, but instead this decision will be deferred, by letting NODE_REC be an abstract data type defined by a further package as follows

```
package NODE_MANAGER is

    type NODE_REC is private;

    procedure INSERT(N:in out NODE_REC);
    procedure REMOVE(N:in out NODE_REC);
    procedure ADD_LINK(N:in out NODE_REC);
                    LINK_NODE: in NODE_ID);
    procedure REM_LINK(N:in out NODE_REC);
                    LINK_NODE: in NODE_ID);

    function INSERTED(N:NODE_REC) return BOOLEAN;
    function GET_LINKS(N:NODE_REC) return LINK_SET;
private
    type NODE_REC is . . . . . ;

end NODE_MANAGER;
```

Given this abstract type with the operations specified, the implementation of the NETWORK_MANAGER is quite straightforward

```
package body NETWORK_MANAGER is

    package NODE_MANAGER is          - - define abstract
        . . .                        - - type NODE_REC
    end NODE_MANAGER;

    use NODE_MANAGER;      - - make it directly accessible

    NETWORK:array(NODE_ID)of NODE_REC; - - the data structure

    procedure INSERT(NODE:in NODE_ID) is
```

```
begin
    INSERT(NETWORK(NODE));
end INSERT;

procedure REMOVE(NODE:in NODE_ID) is
    LSET:LINK_SET := GET_LINKS(NETWORK(NODE));
begin
    for I in LINK_NUM range 1 .. LSET . USED loop
        REM_LINK(NETWORK(LSET . LINK(I)),NODE);
    end loop;
    REMOVE(NETWORK(NODE));
end REMOVE;
procedure CONNECT(A_NODE,B_NODE:in NODE_ID) is
begin
    ADD_LINK(NETWORK(B_NODE),A_NODE);
    ADD_LINK(NETWORK(A_NODE),B_NODE);
end CONNECT;

procedure DISCONNECT(A_NODE,B_NODE:in NODE_ID) is
begin
    REM_LINK(NETWORK(B_NODE),A_NODE);
    REM_LINK(NETWORK(A_NODE),B_NODE);
end DISCONNECT;

function NODE_INSERTED(NODE:NODE_ID) return BOOLEAN is
begin
    return INSERTED(NETWORK(NODE));
end NODE_INSERTED;

function GET_LINKS(NODE:NODE_ID) return LINK_SET is
begin
    return GET_LINKS(NETWORK(NODE));
end GET_LINKS;

end NETWORK_MANAGER;
```

The formulation of the abstract type NODE_REC has made the implementation of the above higher level network operations almost trivial. The only points to note are that, firstly, all node connections are two way, that is, if node A is connected to node B then node B is connected to node A (see the procedures CONNECT and DISCONNECT). Secondly, when a node is removed then all links to the removed node recorded in any other node must be erased (see the REMOVE procedure). Finally, note that the procedure names INSERT and REMOVE are overloaded, being defined both by the NETWORK_MANAGER and by the NODE_MANAGER. This is a legal overloading, since the types of the parameters are different in the two cases.

The above description of the NETWORK_MANAGER body constitutes the first level of refinement of the solution. The second level of refinement now consists of defining the abstract type NODE_REC. First of all, the type NODE_REC must be defined and then its operations must be implemented. For each node it is necessary only to record whether or not the node has been inserted into the network and if so, the set of connections (links) to other nodes. Hence, a suitable data structure is a record as follows

```
type NODE_REC is
    record
        INSERTED:BOOLEAN := FALSE;
        CONNECTIONS:LINK_SET;
    end record;
```

This type definition must be placed in the private part of the NODE_MANAGER package specification given above.

Notice in the definition of NODE_REC that the INSERTED flag has a default value attached to it. Notice also that the connections are recorded using the LINK_SET type, which is defined in the NETWORK_MANAGER package specification. It should be stressed that this is not absolutely necessary, since the interface subprograms could map the user's representation of links (that is, LINK_SET) into any other suitable representation. However, in this case, the form of the LINK_SET structure is judged to be quite adequate, so there is little to be gained by mapping it into some other structure.

The full text of the NODE_MANAGER package body is given below. A fair amount of checking is performed to ensure that all operations on a node are consistent. The actual error handling is described later in Chapter 13. Examination of the code for each subprogram should make it clear how each operation is implemented. Notice the use of the renaming facility in the procedures ADD_LINK and REM_LINK to abbreviate the component names of nested records, that is,

C . USED   rather than   N . CONNECTIONS . USED

Although abbreviations are not generally encouraged in Ada, local abbreviations such as these, extending over only a few lines of code, can aid clarity by reducing the clutter caused by repeated use of long names.

```
package body NODE_MANAGER is
    procedure CHECK_INSERTED(N:in NODE_REC) is
    begin
        if not N . INSERTED then
            - - error: operation attempted on
            - -        non-existent node
        end if;
    end CHECK_INSERTED;
```

```
procedure INSERT(N:in out NODE_REC) is
begin
    if N . INSERTED then
        - - error: attempt to insert an
        - -         existing node
    else
        N . INSERTED := TRUE;
    end if;
end INSERT;

procedure REMOVE(N:in out NODE_REC) is
begin
    CHECK_INSERTED(N);
    N . INSERTED := FALSE;
    N . CONNECTIONS . USED := 0;
end REMOVE;

procedure ADD_LINK(N:in out NODE_REC;
                   LINK_NODE: in NODE_ID) is
    C:LINK_SET renames N . CONNECTIONS;
begin
    CHECK_INSERTED(N);
    if C . USED < MAX_LINK then
      C . USED := C . USED + 1;
      C . LINK(C . USED) := LINK_NODE;
    else
    - - error: all links to this node
    - -         have been used
    end if;
end ADD_LINK;

procedure REM_LINK(N:in out NODE_REC;
                   LINK_NODE: in NODE_ID) is

    C:LINK_SET renames N . CONNECTIONS;
    LINK_FOUND:BOOLEAN := FALSE;
begin
    CHECK_INSERTED(N);
    for I in 1 . . C . USED loop
        LINK_FOUND := C . LINK(I) = LINK_NODE;
        if LINK_FOUND then
            C . USED := C . USED - 1;
            C . LINK(I . . C . USED)    - - slice assignment
                := C . LINK(I+1 . . C . USED+1);
            exit;
        end if;
```

```
        end loop;
        if not LINK_FOUND then
            - - error: attempt to remove a
            - -         non-existent link
        end if;
    end REM_LINK;

    function INSERTED(N:NODE_REC) return BOOLEAN is
    begin
        return N . INSERTED;
    end INSERTED;

    function GET_LINKS(N:NODE_REC) return LINK_SET is
    begin
        CHECK_INSERTED(N);
        return N . CONNECTIONS;
    end GET_LINKS;

end NODE_MANAGER;
```

The above design of the NETWORK_MANAGER package illustrates how packages and the concept of data abstraction can be used to program operations on complex data structures. In this example, the network is represented by the following hierarchical data structure:

```
NETWORK: array(NODE_ID) of NODE_REC;
```

where

```
type NODE_REC is
    record
        INSERTED:BOOLEAN := FALSE;
        CONNECTIONS:LINK_SET;
    end record;
```

where in turn

```
type LINK_SET is
    record
        USED:LINK_NUM := 0;
        LINK: LINK_VEC;
    end record;
```

and

```
type LINK_VEC is array (LINK_INDEX) of NODE_ID;
```

Although the structure of NETWORK is not very complicated, its direct manipulation in terms of its detailed component structure would require careful thought and would be prone to error. To avoid this, the complexity of manipulating the NETWORK structure was broken down by separating the representation and manipulation of the network from that of the individual nodes themselves. This was done by treating nodes as objects of an abstract data type. This is clearly a powerful technique, since it effectively allows a data structure whose components are themselves data structures to be manipulated without having to consider the detail of how to handle the nested structures themselves. This technique can be applied to structures of arbitrary complexity by repeating the process. Thus if, for example, NODE_REC had itself been very complex, then it could have been defined in terms of further abstract data types, these in turn could have been defined in terms of still further abstract data types, and so on.

8.12 EXERCISES

(8.1) Design and implement a package called INTEGER_STACK which allows up to 100 integer numbers to be stored in a last-in/first-out buffer. The package specification should be

```
package INTEGER_STACK is
    procedure PUSH(X:in INTEGER);
    procedure POP(X:out INTEGER);
end INTEGER_STACK;
```

Ignore the possibility of stack underflow/overflow.

(8.2) Reformulate the package designed in (8.1) to provide an abstract data type called STACK so that a user of the package can declare and use any number of STACK objects.

(8.3) Define a record type TIME to represent the time of day in hours, minutes and seconds using the 24 hour clock. Write a procedure to increment a time by one second. Show how the type TIME could be defined by a package as an abstract data type. What other procedures would be needed to manipulate TIME objects? (see (4.1) section 4.10.)

(8.4) Implement a package body for the revised IO_CHANNEL_MANAGER described in section 8.10.

9

Program structure revisited

In Chapter 1, the main features of Ada program structure were illustrated by a few examples. This chapter describes program structure in more detail. The facilities for separate compilation are presented and the scope and visibility rules are reviewed.

9.1 COMPILATION UNITS

The text of an Ada program is submitted to the compiler in one or more compilations. Each compilation is a succession of one or more compilation units

S100 compilation

Thus, if for example a program consists of four compilation units, it can be submitted as a single compilation containing all four units, as two or three compilations each containing between one and three units, or as four compilations each containing a single unit. The decision as to how many compilation units to include in a single compilation is based entirely on convenience. Normally, the number of units placed within a separate compilation should be kept small, to make subsequent modification easier. When a change is made to a program, then only the unit altered and any other units which may be affected by the change need to be recompiled. It should be stressed, however, that the use of separate compilation in Ada does not in any way compromise security. The compiler checks all program unit interface specifications fully, regardless of whether or not the units involved have been compiled separately.

Compilation units are divided into two classes: library units and subunits. Library units are either packages or subprograms which have been declared at the outermost level of the program. Subunits are separately compiled program unit bodies and are described later. The syntax of a comilation unit is given by the following diagram

S101 compilation_unit

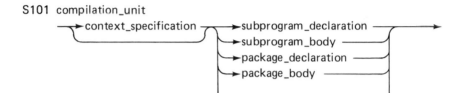

It is important not to be misled by the term library unit. In traditional programming languages, library programs are usually built in a different way to user programs. In Ada, pre-defined packages and subprograms are no different to user-defined packages and subprograms. Hence, any unit which occurs at the outermost level of the program, whatever its origin, is called a library unit.

Conceptually, program development in Ada can be viewed as building a *database* of library units. Initially, the database consists only of those units pre-defined by the implementation (for example, TEXT_IO) and are needed by the program. The user then adds his own library units to the database until his program is fully defined. Of course, very often previous software projects will have generated collections of useful packages and routines. Therefore, an established Ada user will rarely start from scratch, but will instead start by loading a number of existing library units into his database.

In fact, the designer of Ada, J. D. Ichbiah, has stated the belief that Ada will promote the development of an entirely new 'software components' industry. In the same way that present-day hardware designers build systems from components selected from hardware manufacturers' catalogs, the software designer of the future will select software components from the catalogs published by software manufacturers. All that he will then be required to do is provide the 'glue' to join these components together to make the required working system. It is interesting to note that this development is feasible only because of the facilities offered by the Ada package mechanism, viz.

(1) The specification of a package and its body, both of which may be compiled separately, are kept apart;

(2) The package specification provides the basis of a 'contract' between the customer and the vendor, being a detailed account of the facilities offered by that component;

(3) The package body hides the details of the method of implementation (thereby protecting the vendor's investment in research and development);

(4) The package body protects the inner workings of the package from external interference by the customer (allowing the vendor to offer a guarantee on the correct operation of the package);

(5) The Ada language will have an international standard and this standard will be rigorously enforced. (This fact, combined with the inbuilt features for

writing portable programs, should make it feasible to sell software components for a wide variety of different implementations, without portability
problems.)

Whether or not a 'software components' industry becomes a reality, it is
certain that the facilities listed above will make software project management
easier and more effective, and program development should involve far fewer
instances of 're-inventing the wheel' that seem to occur so often with existing
language systems.

9.2 CONTEXT SPECIFICATIONS

Every compilation unit which depends upon (that is, references entities within)
another unit must be prefixed by a context specification, with the syntax given
by the following diagrams

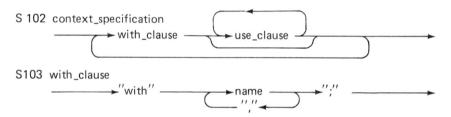

where the names given in the **with** clause must be the names of previously
defined program units. The effect of the **with** clause is to make all the named
units accessible to the compilation unit which follows it. When the name of a
package occurs in a **with** clause, then the same name may appear in a following
use clause (see section 7.3), to enable the entities defined by the package to be
named directly (that is, without having to use the selected component notation).
    To see how the separate compilation mechanism works, consider the follow-
ing program outline

```
        procedure MAIN is
            type COLOUR is (RED,BLUE,GREEN,YELLOW);
            package SETS is
                type CSET is private;
                procedure INSERT(C:in COLOUR; CS:in out CSET);
                - -
                - - other set operations
            private
                type CSET is array (COLOUR) of BOOLEAN;
            end SETS;
```

```
use SETS;
A,B:CSET;
package body SETS is
      procedure INSERT(C:in COLOUR; CS:in out CSET) is
         - -

         - -

      end INSERT;
         - -
      - - other set operations
         - -
   end SETS;
begin     - - MAIN
      - -

   INSERT(RED,A);
      - -

      - -
end MAIN;
```

The procedure MAIN represents a complete Ada program. It contains the declaration of a type COLOUR and a package called SETS which defines an abstract
type CSET for manipulating sets of colours.

As it stands, the procedure MAIN must be compiled as a single unit. The
package SETS is declared within MAIN and so cannot immediately be compiled
separately as a library unit (library units must be declared at the outermost level
of a program). If SETS did not depend on any other declarations within MAIN,
then it would be straightforward to move it to the outermost program level and
then compile it separately. Unfortunately, however, this is not the case here
since SETS depends on the type COLOUR. This kind of situation is quite
common in Ada programs, and the solution is to group all global constants and
types into a separate package, in advance of the main program and the packages
that depend on them. With the use of this technique, the program represented
by MAIN could be recoded as follows, where the broken lines indicate the
divisions between compilation units:

```
package GLOBALS is
   type COLOUR is (RED,BLUE,GREEN,YELLOW);
end GLOBALS;
- - - - - - - - - - - - - - - - - - - - - - - - - - - - - - - - - - - - - - - -
with GLOBALS; use GLOBALS;
package SETS is
   type CSET is private;
   procedure INSERT(C:in COLOUR; CS:in out CSET);
```

```
        - -
        - - other set operations
    private
        type CSET is array (COLOUR) of BOOLEAN;
    end SETS;
- - - - - - - - - - - - - - - - - - - - - - - - - - - - - - - - - - - - -
    package body SETS is
        procedure INSERT(C:in COLOUR; CS:in out CSET) is
            - -

            - -
        end INSERT;
        - -
        - - other set operations
        - -
    end SETS;
- - - - - - - - - - - - - - - - - - - - - - - - - - - - - - - - - - - - -
    with GLOBALS,SETS; use GLOBALS,SETS;
    procedure MAIN is
        A,B:CSET;
    begin
        - -
        INSERT(RED,A);
        - -

        - -
    end MAIN;
```

The program now consists of four compilation units which may, if required, be separately compiled. The package GLOBALS does not depend on any other packages, and so has no preceding context specification. The package SETS depends on GLOBALS and hence must name GLOBALS in its **with** clause. Finally, the procedure MAIN depends on both GLOBALS and SETS, so it must name both in its context specification.

When using separate compilation and **with/use** clauses, three points should be noted:

(1) The **with** clause prefixing a package should name only those packages on which it directly depends. For example, if the package SETS depended on a further package BASIC_OPS, then the context of MAIN would still not change. It should not and must not name BASIC_OPS in its context specification, because it depends on it not directly, but indirectly via the package SETS.

(2) If a **use** clause immediately follows a **with** clause, as in the above examples, then it makes the entities within the named package directly visible everywhere throughout the following program unit. Although it is common

practice, it is not necessary to place the **use** clause in this position. For example, the package SETS could equally well be written as

```
with GLOBALS;
package SETS is
    type CSET is private;
    use GLOBALS;
    procedure INSERT(C:in COLOUR; CS:in out CSET);
    - -
    - - other set operations
private
    type CSET is array (COLOUR) of BOOLEAN;
end SETS;
```

Placing the **use** clause within the unit gives the opportunity for finer control over the region of the unit over which the used package names are directly visible. The only time that the **use** clause must immediately follow the **with** clause is when the following unit is a subprogram whose parameter specifications include direct references to types declared within the used package.

(3) When a **with** clause prefixes a package specification, the region over which it applies extends to cover the corresponding package body as well as the specification part itself. Hence, there is no need to repeat the **with** clause in front of the body (cf. the package SETS above). This also applies to the effects of the use clause which, if given in the specification part of a package, also extends to cover the corresponding body.

9.3 SUB UNITS

The library unit mechanism described above allows a program to be built from the bottom-up, with the packages implementing the lower level details of a program occurring first, followed by those dealing with the higher level abstractions. Ada also allows separate compilation to be applied to the top-down construction of programs via its subunit facility.

The basic idea of subunits is that when a program unit B is declared within some other program unit A, then only the specification part of B is actually required to compile A. Hence, Ada allows the body of the program unit B to be detached and compiled separately as a subunit. The place in A where the body of B would have been is denoted by a *body stub*. The syntax of subunits and stubs is given by the following diagrams:

S104 subunit

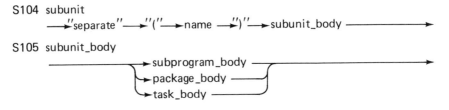

S105 subunit_body

S106 body_stub

```
   ┌──►subprogram_specification ──────┬─►"is"──►"separate"──►";"──────────►
   ├──►"package"──►"body"──►ident ─┤
   └──►"task"──────────►"body"──►ident ┘
```

A subunit is identified by the keyword **separate** followed by the name of the program unit from which it has been separated. The unit body then follows as normal. (Note: although a task body can be separately compiled as a subunit, a task cannot be a library unit.)

To illustrate the mechanism, consider the original version of the procedure MAIN given earlier. Instead of creating a new package GLOBALS and then coding the package SETS as a library unit, the structure of MAIN can be left unaltered and the body of SETS compiled separately as a subunit as follows

> **procedure** MAIN **is**
>
> > **type** COLOUR **is** (RED,BLUE,GREEN,YELLOW);
> >
> > **package** SETS **is**
> >
> > > – –
> > > – – as before
> > > – –
> >
> > **end** SETS;
> >
> > **use** SETS;
> >
> > A,B:CSET;
> >
> > **package body** SETS **is separate**;   – – the stub
>
> **begin**   – – MAIN
>
> > – –
> > INSERT(RED,A);
> > – –
> > – –
>
> **end** MAIN;
>
> –
>
> **separate**(MAIN)   – – subunit
> **package body** SETS **is**
>
> > **procedure** INSERT(C:**in** COLOUR; CS:**in out** CSET) **is**
> >
> > > – –
> > > – –
> >
> > **end** INSERT;
> >
> > – –
> > – – other set operations
> > – –
>
> **end** SETS:

This procedure can be taken even further. The procedures within the body of SETS can themselves be separately compiled, that is, the subunit SETS becomes

    separate(MAIN)
    package body SETS **is**
        procedure INSERT(C:**in** COLOUR; CS:**in out** CSET) **is separate**;
        – –
        – – other set operations – possibly also separate
        – –
    end SETS;
    -
    separate (MAIN . SETS)   – – subunit of SETS
    procedure INSERT(C:**in** COLOUR; CS:**in out** CSET) **is**
    begin
        – –
        – –
    end INSERT;

Notice here that the name of the program unit from which a subunit has been separated must be given in full, using the selected component notation. In other words, the first identifier in the name (for example, MAIN in the case of the subunit INSERT) must always be the name of a library unit.

The only rule which must be obeyed when using the subunit mechanism is that the corresponding stub must occur in the outermost declarative part of a compilation unit, that is, not within a nested program unit. Thus, in the above case, if the body of the package SETS had not been separately compiled, then INSERT could not have been separated from it as a subunit.

Finally, it should be emphasised that the names visible to a subunit are exactly those visible at the point where its corresponding stub is written. Hence the use of the subunit mechanism does not restrict the separated body's access to entities declared in enclosing program units. Note, however, that a subunit may have a context specification (that is, a **with** clause) in the same way as any other compilation unit. As a result, closer control over name visibility is possible. For example, consider the following two outlines of the package body Q:

(1)   **with** TEXT_IO;
    package body Q **is**
        procedure A **is**   – – doesn't use TEXT_IO
        – –
        – –
        end A;
        procedure B **is**   – – does use TEXT_IO
        – –
        – –
        end B;
    end Q;

(2)   **package body** Q **is**
      procedure A **is**

         - -

         - -

      end A;
      procedure B **is separate**;
    end Q;

----

    with TEXT_IO;
    separate(Q)
    procedure B **is**

       - -

       - -

    end B;

In the first version, the package TEXT_IO is visible throughout the package Q even though only procedure B needs to use it. In the second version, where the body of B has been separated, access to the TEXT_IO package is limited to B only.

9.4 ORDER OF COMPILATIONS

The universal rule in Ada that all names must be declared before they can be used applies equally well to compilation units. Hence, the order in which units are submitted to the Ada compiler must obey the following rules

(1) A unit may not be compiled before any of the units listed in its **with** clause.
(2) A subprogram or package body may never precede its corresponding specification.
(3) A subunit may never precede the unit from which it has been separated.

When a unit is re-compiled after a modification, then all those units which may potentially be affected by the change must also be re-compiled. The user should not, however, be concerned with this, since all such required re-compilations will normally be determined automatically by the compiler.

9.5 THE SCOPE AND VISIBILITY OF NAMES

The preceding description of separate compilation completes the picture of how Ada programs are built. At the outermost level there is a sequence of one or more compilation units, each compilation unit being a package, subprogram or subunit of some preceding compilation unit. Within each compilation unit various entities will be declared, such as constants, types, variables and further nested program units. Within each of these nested program units, further nested units can be declared, and this process of nesting declarations may continue to any depth.

A key property of block structured languages is that entities may be introduced locally to a block. Outside the block such entities are inaccessible, so that the language can safely allow the same name to be used to refer to several different entities at different points in the program. This is extremely useful to the programmer, since it frees him from having to invent large numbers of unique names and avoids possible errors by limiting the set of names which are accessible at any one point in the program. Technically, the association of a name with a particular program entity is effected by means of a declaration, and the region of text over which this association holds is called the *scope* of the declaration.

The ideas of scope and block structure were informally introduced in Chapter 5 in the discussion of declare statements. Since Ada is somewhat unconventional in its approach to block structure, it is worth reviewing the main features of the Ada scope rules and establishing some terminology before presenting the Ada scope rules in detail.

Consider the following program outline

```
procedure X is
    A:INTEGER;
    procedure Y is
        A:BOOLEAN;
    begin
        - - X . A is the integer object
        - - Y . A is a Boolean object
        - - A here means Y . A
    end Y;
begin
    - - only X . A is in scope here
    - - A here means X . A
end X;
```

Procedure Y is an example of a block nested within another block (procedure X). The scope of a name declared within the declarative part of a block extends from the point of its declaration to the end of the block. Thus, the declaration "A:INTEGER" has an effect throughout the rest of procedure X, including the nested procedure Y. The name A is used again within procedure Y to declare a Boolean variable. In other programming languages (for example, Algol, Pascal, etc.), the re-use of the name A in the declaration "A:BOOLEAN" would have the effect of excluding the procedure Y from the scope of "A:INTEGER". In Ada this is NOT the case: the scope of a name declaration is never affected by any re-use of the name, and so scopes involving different uses of the same name may overlap. Hence, within procedure Y, the name A is associated with both the outer integer variable and the local Boolean variable.

In order to resolve potential ambiguities caused by overlapping scopes, Ada has a separate concept called *visibility*. At any point in a program within the scope of an entity whose name is N, that entity is either *directly visible* or *hidden*. When it is directly visible, it can be referred to immediately by the name N. When it is hidden, it must be referred to explicitly using the selected component notation. For example, in the above, "A:INTEGER" is directly visible within procedure X but within Y it is hidden by the declaration "A:BOOLEAN". Within Y, therefore, the name A refers to Y . A, that is, the local Boolean object. In order to refer to integer A within Y, the selected component notation must be used, that is, X . A.

Having established the ideas of scope and visibility, the detailed rules for them can be given. These depend both on what kind of entity a name denotes and on where in the program it is declared. In formulating these rules, it is helpful to distinguish between two classes of name

(a)   those declared explicitly as the subject of a declaration
(b)   those declared implicitly as a side-effect of a declaration

For example, the purpose of the declaration

> **type** POINT **is**
> **record**
>   X,Y:INTEGER;
> **end record**;

is principally to declare a record type and give it the name POINT. As a side-effect of the declaration, the names X and Y are also introduced as the names of record components.

The scope and visibility of names in class (a) depends only on the place at which they are declared. The scope and visibility of names in class (b) depends on what the name refers to.

The following tables summarise the scope and visibility rules of Ada:

Table 9.1   Names in class (a)

Place of Declaration	Region of Scope	Region of Direct Visibility
Names of library units declared in outermost level of the program	The library unit itself (both spec and body), any subunits belonging to that unit and any other unit listing the name in a with clause	Entire scope

Table 9.1 (*continued*)

Place of Declaration	Region of Scope	Region of Direct Visibility
Within the declarative part of a block, that is, declare statement, subprogram, package or task body	Point of declaration to the end of the block	Entire scope
Within the visible part of a package or task specification	Point of declaration to end of the scope of package or task declaration itself. This includes the corresponding body	Point of declaration to end of specification part plus the corresponding body
Within the private part of a package specification	Point of declaration to end of specification plus the corresponding body	Entire scope

Table 9.2 Names in class (b)

Kind of Name	Region of Scope	Region of Direct Visibility
Record component or discriminant occurring within the declaration of type T	Point of declaration to end of the scope of type T	Point of declaration to end of the declaration of type T
Enumeration literal occurring within the declaration of type T	Point of declaration to end of the scope of type T	Entire scope
Loop parameter name	Point of occurrence in iteration clause to the end of the loop body	Entire scope
Formal parameter name occurring within the specification of a program unit P	Point of occurrence to the end of the scope of P	Point of occurrence to the end of the specification part plus the body of P. Also directly visible within a named association occurring within a call to P

In the above rules covering direct visibility, an entity may be hidden within an inner construct which contains a declaration using the same name.

9.6 ACCESSING ENTITIES WHOSE NAMES ARE HIDDEN

The name of an entity declared immediately (that is, not within a nested program unit) within a subprogram, package or task can always be written as a selected component of that unit. For example, in the previous section, the name of the integer object A can always be written as

X . A

anywhere within the scope of A regardless of whether or not A is hidden. When A is directly visible, as in the procedure X, then the procedure name prefix can be omitted, that is, just

A

is sufficient and this is the normal case. Wherever A is hidden, as in the procedure Y, then the full selected component notation must be used.

The name of an entity declared immediately within a declare statement or a loop parameter named in a for iteration clause can be written using the selected component notation if the block or loop is named. Again, the selected component notation is necessary only if the name is hidden within another nested construct. If the block or loop is unnamed, then throughout any inner region where the name is hidden, the object to which it refers is inaccessible.

Entities named within the visible part of a package are not directly visible outside the package. Such entities can be named using the selected component notation. In addition, package entities can be made directly visible by means of the **use** clause (see section 7.3). The effect of a **use** clause is conceptually similar to re-declaring all the entities specified within the named packages at the point where the **use** clause is written. However, if this effect would be to contravene the rules concerning the uniqueness of names (see next section) then any affected name is omitted from the set of names made directly visible by the **use** clause. For example, in the following

```
package ALPHA is
    type T1 is . . . . ;
    type T2 is . . . . ;
end ALPHA;

package BETA is
    type T1 is . . . . ;
    type T3 is . . . . ;
end BETA;
procedure GAMMA is
    use ALPHA,BETA;
    - - T2 and T3 directly visible here
    - - T1 still hidden. ALPHA . T1 or BETA . T1 must
    - - be used as appropriate
end GAMMA;
```

the names T2 and T3 are unique and can be made directly visible without ambiguity. T1 is defined in both ALPHA and BETA, however, so the **use** clause does not make them directly visible and the full selected component notation must still be used.

Entries named within the visible part of a task (see Chapter 12) are not directly visible outside the task. Such entities can be named using the selected component notation. A **use** clause cannot be used to make entry names directly visible.

Finally, a renaming declaration can be used to associate another new name with an entity. Renaming was first mentioned in section 8.9 as a mechanism for accessing the components of data structures. A renaming declaration can also be used to give a directly visible name to any data or task object, package, subprogram or exception name. It can also be used to rename a task entry as a procedure. For example, within the declarative part of procedure Y given in section 9.5, the renaming declaration

YA:INTEGER **renames** X . A;

would allow the integer A to be referenced directly by YA within the body of procedure Y. Note, however, that renaming does not hide the existing name so that X . A would still have a valid meaning within Y. Type names cannot be renamed but a subtype declaration can be used to give the same effect. For example, in procedure GAMMA above, two new subtypes could be declared

subtype A1 **is** ALPHA . T1;
subtype B1 **is** BETA . T1;

so that within GAMMA, A1 is effectively a rename for ALPHA . T1 and B1 is effectively a rename of BETA . T1.

9.7 OVERLOADING AND THE UNIQUENESS OF NAMES

Wherever a name is used in a program it must be possible to associate that name with a unique entity. For this to be possible, certain rules must be obeyed when choosing names within declarations.

(a) Within any program unit or declare statement, the identifiers used to denote all explicitly declared names must be distinct. The one exception to this rule is that the same identifier can be used to denote the names of several subprograms, provided that no two subprograms with the same name have equivalent specifications (see section 6.6). Such identifiers are said to be overloaded.

(b) The identifiers used to name the values of an enumeration type must all be distinct but can be the same as those used within other enumeration type declarations. Such identifiers are said to be overloaded.

(c) The identifiers used to denote the components (and discriminants, if any) of a record type must all be distinct.

Note that with regard to overloading, it is good practice to overload only when the names have a natural meaning in all relevant contexts in the problem area (for example, overload MAX(A) but not F(A)).

9.8 EXERCISES

(9.1) Discuss the relative merits of splitting a program into separate compilation units

   (a) Using library units
   (b) Using subunits
   (c) As a mixture of library units and subunits

(9.2) Show how the NETWORK_MANAGER package designed in section 8.11 could be compiled

   (a) as separate library units
   (b) as two library units plus a subunit for the body of the NODE_MANAGER

Note that in case (a), the NODE_MANAGER package cannot be extracted immediately from the NETWORK_MANAGER as it depends on declarations within the latter.

(9.3) Consider the following program outline

```
procedure ONE is
    type POINT is
      record
          X,Y:INTEGER;
      end record;
    P:POINT;
    procedure TWO is
        X:INTEGER;
    begin
        - -
        P . X := 0; P . Y := 1;
        - -
    end TWO;
begin
    - -
end ONE;
```

Are the assignments to the components of P within procedure TWO affected by the local declaration of X? Could any further local declarations in TWO be added which would affect the meanings of these assignments, and if so what are they?

(9.4) In the following declarations state which identifiers are being used illegally

```
DECS:
declare
    type SWITCH is (ON,OFF);
    type DEVICE_STATUS is (ON,CONNECTED,OFF_LINE);

    X,Y:INTEGER;
    CONNECTED:BOOLEAN;
    ON:SWITCH;

    procedure SWAP(X,Y:in out INTEGER);
    procedure SWAP(X,Y:in out DEVICE_STATUS);
    function ON(S:SWITCH) return BOOLEAN;
begin
    - -

    - -
end DECS;
```

10

Discriminated types

In Chapter 8, the record data type was described as a collection of named components. In its basic form the number of components, their names and their types are fixed by the type declaration. Ada, however, allows a more flexible record type to be declared which enables certain features of the structure of the type to be parametrised. Such types are called *discriminated types* and the corresponding parameters are called *discriminants*. Two distinct parametrisations are provided. Firstly, a record may have variant parts in which certain components are present only for certain values of the discriminant. Secondly, a record may have array components whose bounds are fixed by the values of discriminants.

10.1 VARIANT RECORDS

The ideas of variant records are best introduced by means of an example. Suppose that a manufacturer of motor cars wishes to maintain certain information on each car that he produces. The following record type could be defined to hold this information

```
type CAR is
    record
        SERIAL_NO:INTEGER;
        MODEL:MODEL_NAME;
        PAINT:COLOUR;
        STYLE:CAR_STYLE;
    end record;
```

Suppose also that the same manufacturer produced a range of vans. He might then need similar information to be stored for these, for example,

```
type VAN is
    record
        SERIAL_NO:INTEGER;
        MODEL:MODEL_NAME;
        PAINT:COLOUR;
        CAPACITY:CUBIC_METRES;
        LOAD:TONNES;
    end record;
```

Notice that some of the information stored for vans and cars is the same whereas some of the information is peculiar to each class of vehicle.

For many kinds of processing application, the separation of these two sets of information into separate types would be a severe limitation. For example, all common operations such as "given the SERIAL_NO find the MODEL" would have to be coded twice, once for cars and once for vans. A more natural solution is to represent the data for vans and cars using a single record type with optional components for storing the data peculiar to each class of vehicle. To do this in Ada, a record can be defined with a fixed common part and a number of variant parts. In the example, the information on vehicles could be combined into a single variant record as follows

```
type VEHICLE_KIND is (CAR,VAN);

type VEHICLE(KIND:VEHICLE_KIND) is
    record
        SERIAL_NO:INTEGER;
        MODEL:MODEL_NAME;
        PAINT:COLOUR;
        case KIND is
            when CAR =>
                STYLE:CAR_STYLE;
            when VAN =>
                CAPACITY:CUBIC_METRES;
                LOAD:TONNES;
        end case;
    end record;
```

The identifier KIND names the discriminant of the VEHICLE record. This discriminant may have one of two values, either CAR or VAN, and is stored as the first component of the record. Following the discriminant there are three fixed components: SERIAL_NO, MODEL and PAINT. The remaining components of the record then depend on the value of the discriminant. If it is CAR, then the record has one more component called STYLE; otherwise it has two more components called CAPACITY and LOAD. Thus, an object of type VEHICLE will have one of the two structures depicted by the diagrams in Fig. 10.1 below

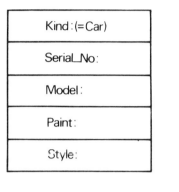
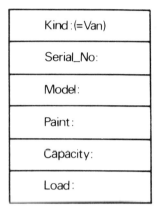

Fig. 10.1 – Variants of the VEHICLE Record

Given an object V of type VEHICLE, its components can be accessed in the normal way. For example, to set the CAPACITY and LOAD fields of V the following could be written

V . CAPACITY := 8;
V . LOAD   := 5;

This assumes, of course, that V . KIND=VAN. If this was not the case, then an error would occur when these assignments were executed. A safer way of accessing the variant fields of a record is by using a case statement, for example,

case V . KIND **is**
   when VAN => V . CAPACITY := 8;
                  V . LOAD   := 5;
   when CAR => PUT("V is not a van!");
end case;

Although the discriminant KIND may be read, it cannot be assigned to directly, since this could leave the structure of V in an inconsistent state. Ada has strict rules about the way that discriminated types are used to ensure that inconsistencies do not arise. More will be said about this later.

Returning now to the declaration of variant records, the syntax diagrams for discriminants and variant record parts are:

S107 discriminant_part

S108 discriminant_declaration

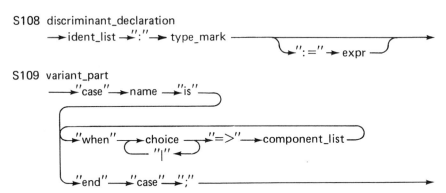

S109 variant_part

[Note: these diagrams should be read in conjunction with S14 in section 3.1 and S95 to S97 in section 8.7]

The form of a variant part is similar to that of the case statement. The discriminant must be a discrete type (usually an enumeration) and all possible values of the discriminant must be represented within the list of choices. Each option starting with the keyword **when** denotes a variant. Only one variant from the list of possible variants may be present in the record at any one time, and this variant is that for which the current value of the discriminant is given in the associated set of choices. The same flexibility in the specification of the choices is provided as for case statements, that is, a selection of alternative single values and ranges of values. As with the case statement, each specified choice value must be statically determinable at compile time. The choice **others** is allowed but it may only be associated with the last variant in the list.

If no variant components are required for a particular value of the discriminant then the component list cannot simply be omitted; instead, the keyword **null** must be used. Thus, for example, if in the VEHICLE type given above, no specific information relating to cars was required, then a null variant would be specified, as follows:

```
type VEHICLE(KIND:VEHICLE_KIND) is
    record
        SERIAL_NO:INTEGER;
        MODEL:MODEL_NAME;
        PAINT:COLOUR;
        case KIND is
            when CAR => null;
            when VAN =>
                CAPACITY:CUBIC_METRES;
                LOAD:TONNES;
        end case;
    end record;
```

The component list associated with any variant may itself contain variants. Thus, a hierarchy of variant parts can be built. In such cases, there must be a discriminant part for each variant although several variant parts may depend on the same discriminant. Hierarchical data structures involving discriminated types are discussed further in section 10.4.

10.2 VARIABLE LENGTH ARRAYS

If a record contains a component of an unconstrained array type, then each bound of the required index constraint may be specified by the value of a discriminant. For example, a record for holding variable length text strings could be defined as

```
subtype INDEX is INTEGER range 0 . . MAXIMUM;

type TEXT(MAX_LENGTH:INDEX)is
    record
        CURRENT_LENGTH:INDEX .= 0;
        VALUE:STRING(1 . . MAX_LENGTH);
    end record;
```

The record type TEXT allows objects to be created which contain a string of variable length. The maximum length of string which can be stored is set by the value of the discriminant, and the current length is recorded within CURRENT_LENGTH. Section 10.6 describes the use of this record type in more detail.

As another example, consider the following where MATRIX is the unconstrained array type defined in section 8.1

```
type SQUARE_MATRIX(SIDE:INTEGER)is
    record
        DATA:MATRIX(1 . . SIDE,1 . . SIDE);
    end record;
```

In this case, the discriminant value is used twice. In general, any number of discriminants can be defined to fix any number of index bounds, and variable length arrays can appear in a record with variant parts. The only rule limiting the use of discriminants in fixing index bounds is that the discriminant name must appear by itself and not as a component of an expression. Thus, for example,

```
type DYNVEC(SIZE:INTEGER)is
    record
        VALUE:VECTOR(0 . . SIZE-1);
    end record;
```

is illegal, since "SIZE-1" is an expression. This rule applies not just to the use of discriminants in fixing index bounds, but to any use of a discriminant within a record.

10.3 DISCRIMINANT CONSTRAINTS

Conceptually, a discriminated type can be thought of as introducing a set of record values, each value in the set having a different structure. In the same way that a range constraint can be used to restrict the value set of a discrete type, a discriminant constraint can be applied to restrict the value set of a discriminated type. In the case of discriminant constraints, however, the constraint must always restrict the value set to a single discriminant value.

The syntax of a discriminant constraint is given by the following diagrams

S110 discriminant_constraint

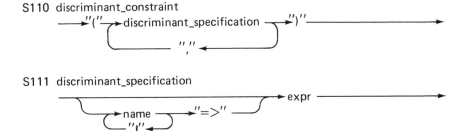

S111 discriminant_specification

A discriminant constraint specifies fixed values for each of the discriminants of a discriminated type. It is written immediately after the type name (see S17 and S18 in section 3.1) and must specify a value for every discriminant of that type. Discriminant values can be denoted either using positional or named notation (cf. the analogy with procedure parameters).

To illustrate the basic idea of discriminant constraints, consider an object declared of type VEHICLE, for example,

MACHINE:VEHICLE;

(actually this declaration is illegal but that does not matter for now — see next section). The record object MACHINE can hold information pertaining to cars or vans and by changing the discriminant at run-time the structure of MACHINE can change. MACHINE therefore represents a general object for storing vehicle information. Very often, however, objects of type VEHICLE will only ever be required to hold information pertaining to either cars or vans but never both. In such cases, the discriminant can be fixed to the required value by a discriminant constraint. For example, the declaration

C:VEHICLE(KIND => CAR);

introduces an object of type VEHICLE called C whose discriminant is constrained to the value CAR. Once fixed by a constraint, the discriminant can never be changed and effectively becomes a constant component of the record initialised to the specified value.

Where several objects need to be declared with the same discriminant constraint, then a subtype can be introduced, for example,

subtype VAN_INFO **is** VEHICLE(KIND=>VAN);

defines a record subtype VAN_INFO so that subsequent object declarations such as

V:VAN_INFO;

are equivalent to

V:VEHICLE(KIND => VAN);

Discriminant constraints can also be applied to records containing variable length arrays. For example,

SMALL_SQUARE:SQUARE_MATRIX(3);

introduces a record object called SMALL_SQUARE containing a fixed size 3 by 3 matrix.

When applying discriminant constraints, it should be noted that where a record type contains several discriminants then all must be constrained. It is not possible to have a record with some discriminants constrained and others unconstrained. Also, it is occasionally useful to be able to determine whether or not an object of a discriminated type is constrained or not. This can be determined via the Boolean attribute CONSTRAINED. For example,

MACHINE'CONSTRAINED   =   FALSE

SMALL_SQUARE'CONSTRAINED   =   TRUE

Wherever it is appropriate to apply a constraint to a discriminated type then it is generally good practice to do so (in fact it is mandatory under certain circumstances – see next section). Firstly, constraints improve program readability since they give valuable information on the type of data to be found in the various objects of a discriminated type. Secondly, they allow the compiler to optimise both the use of memory space and the amount of check code needed to ensure that accesses to variant records and variable length arrays are legal.

10.4 USING DISCRIMINATED TYPES

In order that discriminated types can be used properly and securely, it is clearly imperative to ensure that the value of a discriminant is always consistent with the current structure of the corresponding record. To guarantee that this is always the case, Ada insists that the following rules be obeyed:

(1) Within a record type definition, a discriminant may only be used as a bound in an index constraint, as the discriminant name in a variant part, as part of

a default expression in a record component or as a discriminant value in a discriminant constraint. In each case, the discriminant name must appear by itself, and not as a component of some larger expression.

(2) If default initial values are not supplied for the discriminants of a type, then a discriminant constraint must be applied to every object declared of that type (either directly by specifying discriminant constraints in the object declaration, or indirectly by specifying a subtype which incorporates such constraints).

(3) The discriminant of an unconstrained record object may never be assigned to as an individual component of the record. It can only be altered by making a whole record assignment.

(4) The discriminant of a constrained record object can never be changed.

The remainder of this section will now explore some of the consequences of these rules.

Consider first the case of variant records and the VEHICLE type given earlier. As the definition of this type stands, all objects of the type must be constrained, since there is no default initial value specified for the discriminant. To allow unconstrained objects to be declared, the type VEHICLE must be rewritten as

        type VEHICLE(KIND:VEHICLE_KIND:=CAR) is
            record
                - - as before
            end record;

When an object of type VEHICLE is declared now as in

        MACHINE:VEHICLE;

then the discriminant of MACHINE is set by default to CAR. Subsequent assignments could then set the remaining components of MACHINE, for example,

        MACHINE . SERIAL NUMBER := 10759;
        MACHINE . MODEL := SUPERIOR;
        MACHINE . PAINT := STARDUST;
        MACHINE . STYLE := HATCHBACK;

If MACHINE is subsequently required to hold data on a van, then a whole record assignment must be used, as in

```
MACHINE := (KIND         => VAN,
            SERIAL_NO => 10111,
            MODEL        => UTILITY,
            PAINT        => BLACK,
            CAPACITY  => 8,
            LOAD         => 4  );
```

Of course, a record aggregate could also have been used to assign the initial car data to **MACHINE**.

Variant records are usually implemented by the compiler in such a way that the variant parts share the same storage locations in memory so that if all the possible variants are of similar size, then little memory is wasted by declaring unconstrained record objects. The memory allocated for each is that required to accommodate the largest variant. In the case of the VEHICLE type it would not be unduly wasteful to implement a simple data base of vehicle information as an array of VEHICLE records, that is,

type V_DATA **is array** (1 .. MAX_VEHICLES) **of** VEHICLE;

If, however, the van variant was significantly larger than the CAR variant, it might be better to separate the two, for example,

type VAN_DATA **is array**(1 .. MAX_VAN) **of** VEHICLE(VAN);
type CAR_DATA **is array**(1 .. MAX_CAR) **of** VEHICLE(CAR);

In this case, the components of the two arrays are constrained record types and the compiler will allocate just enough storage to hold each respective variant. This explains why a discriminant can never be changed once it has been fixed by a constraint. If, for example, the VAN variant is larger than the CAR variant then an attempt to write

CAR_DATA(I) := VAN_DATA(J);

must fail because physically there is insufficient storage available in each component of **CAR_DATA** to hold a **VAN** record. Such an assignment would, therefore, result in a constraint error.

The use of variable length arrays within discriminated types is rather different to that of variant records. Consider the following type definition

```
subtype LINE_SIZE is INTEGER range 0 .. 100;
type LINE(SIZE: LINE_SIZE := 10) is
    record
        VAL: STRING(1 .. SIZE);
    end record;
```

If an unconstrained object of type LINE is declared as in

L:LINE;

then the record L will contain a string of 10 characters. However, although the logical size of L.VAL is 10 characters long, the compiler must allow for a subsequent change of the discriminant SIZE upto a maximum value of 100, for example,

$$L := (SIZE => 100, VAL => (1 .. 100 => ' '));$$

Thus, the actual size of string allocated by the compiler within L will always be 100 characters long regardless of the value of SIZE. There is, therefore, little point in using a discriminated type in such cases. A simple record type would be just as satisfactory, that is,

```
type LINE2 is
   record
      SIZE: LINE_SIZE;
      VAL: STRING(1 .. 100);
   end record;
```

Objects of type LINE2 would be just as useful as those of type LINE and furthermore could often be used more efficiently, since the value of SIZE could be assigned to directly without the need to re-initialise the string at the same time.

In fact, discriminated variable arrays are provided principally to give more power to private types defined within packages where the intention is to allow the user of the private type the ability to declare variable sized (and therefore constrained) record objects — see next section.

Discriminated types may have components which are themselves discriminated types. However, the rules given earlier imply that a certain amount of care must be taken in the design of such hierarchical data structures. As an illustration, suppose that in a communications system, each data transmission is either a variable length data packet or a control packet. The following type declarations describe a data structure which could be used for this

```
type PACKET_KIND is (DATA, CONTROL);

type PACKET (KIND:PACKET_KIND := CONTROL) is
   record
      case KIND is
         when CONTROL =>
            CP: CONTROL_PACKET;
         when DATA =>
            DP: DATA_PACKET;
      end case;
   end record;
```

where the CONTROL_PACKET type might be a simple enumeration such as

```
type CONTROL_PACKET is (ACK, NAK, STX, ETX);
```

Notice, here that the discriminant of the PACKET type has been given an initial value to allow unconstrained PACKET objects to be declared.

The interesting point about this example is that the DP component of the PACKET type will itself be a discriminated type, that is

```
subtype INDEX is INTEGER range 0 .. MAX;

type BYTE_VEC is array (INDEX range <>) of BYTE;

type DATA_PACKET (SIZE: INDEX := MAX) is
    record
        VAL: BYTE_VEC(1 .. SIZE);
    end record;
```

Hence, when objects of type PACKET are declared, as in for example

```
P: PACKET (KIND -> DATA);
```

then the internal DP component will be unconstrained and, therefore, the compiler must always reserve sufficient space to store the maximum length data packet allowed. If the size of a data packet is known in advance then this may be unacceptably inefficient. It can, of course, be avoided by applying a constraint to the DP component as each packet is declared, the problem then though is how to obtain a value for the constraint. The answer is that the only safe way is to make the constraint depend on a second discriminant of the PACKET type a as in

```
type PACKET(KIND:PACKET_KIND; DPSIZE: INDEX) is
    record
        case KIND is
            when CONTROL =>
                CP:CONTROL_PACKET;
            when DATA =>
                DP:DATA_PACKET(DPSIZE);
        end case;
    end record;
```

where now the constraint for the nested DATA_PACKET is supplied as a discriminant constraint in the declaration of PACKET objects.

10.5 DISCRIMINATED PRIVATE TYPES

As mentioned in the previous section, a private type defined within a package may be implemented as a discriminated type. When this is the case, then the discriminants of the private type are made visible to the user of the package.

This facility is particularly useful for record types which include variable length arrays. As an example, consider the following

```
package DISCR_PRIVATE_TYPE is
    subtype INDEX is INTEGER range 0 . . 100;
    type FLEX(SIZE:INDEX) is private;
    procedure INIT(F: in out FLEX);
    - - other operations
private
    type SOME_ARRAY is array (INDEX range <>) of SOME_TYPE;
    type FLEX(SIZE:INDEX) is
        record
            AY: SOME_ARRAY (1 . . SIZE);
            - - other components
        end record;
end DISCR_PRIVATE_TYPE;
```

The type FLEX is a private type whose internal structure is hidden from the user of the package, but the discriminant SIZE is visible and has no default initial value. A user of the package may declare objects of type FLEX but he must specify a discriminant constraint with each, for example,

```
F1: FLEX(SIZE => 10);
F2: FLEX(SIZE => 20); etc.
```

Thus, objects of type FLEX may be declared with sizes chosen to meet the users' individual requirements. A practical example of this is given in the next section. Variant records may, of course, be defined as private types in a similar way.

In addition, it may be noted that discriminants can be declared for a record which are never referred to within the record itself. This gives the capability for defining private record types which are only partially hidden. For example, in

```
package PARTIAL_HIDING is
    type X(A,B,C:INTEGER := 0) is private;
    - - operations for X
private
    type X(A,B,C:INTEGER := 0) is
        record
            D,E,F:INTEGER := 0;
        end record;
end PARTIAL_HIDING;
```

then for any object declared of type X, the user can access components A, B and C, but not D, E or F since these are hidden within the package. Note, however, that the rules prohibiting assignment to individual discriminant components still apply, even though there are no dependencies on the discriminants within the record.

Finally, when designing packages which export discriminated private types, the rules concerning the usage of discriminants must be remembered. In particular, if a default initial value is given for the discriminant, then unconstrained objects of the type may be declared. However, the discriminant can only be changed directly by the user by assigning the value of another object of the same type to it. An aggregate cannot be used because the internal structure of the type is unknown outside of the package. Of course, if the type is limited private then no assignment is allowed anyway.

10.6 EXAMPLE – A TEXT HANDLING PACKAGE

The direct use of the pre-defined STRING type is restricted by the necessity to ensure that the lengths of string values are always the same. For example, given

　　　S:STRING(1 . . 10);

then to assign a string constant to S denoting the name of a person, say, blanks must be inserted to pad out the name to the required length, for example,

　　　S := "FRED　　　　";

or

　　　S := "GEORGE　　　";

and so on. In section 10.3, a discriminated record type called TEXT was introduced for holding variable length strings. In this section, it will be shown how this type can be incorporated into a package to give a useful text handling facility which avoids the difficulties inherent in working directly with STRING types.

The specification of the package will be given first, followed by an example of its use. The implementation of the package will then be described.

The package specification is as follows

　　　package TEXT_HANDLING **is**

　　　　MAXIMUM:**constant** := 512;

　　　　subtype INDEX **is** INTEGER **range** 0 . . MAXIMUM;

　　　　type TEXT(MAX_LENGTH:INDEX) **is limited private**;

　　　　- - functions to give the length and value of a
　　　　- - TEXT object T

```
        function LENGTH(T:TEXT)return INDEX;
        function STR(T:TEXT)return STRING;

        - - function to find a substring within a TEXT object
        - - T. Value returned is index position of first
        - - character in substring (=0 if not found)

        function POSITION(SUBSTR:TEXT;     T:TEXT)return INDEX;
        function POSITION(SUBSTR:STRING;  T:TEXT)return INDEX;
        - - function to extract a substring COUNT characters
        - - long starting at position POS from a TEXT object T

        function SUBSTR(T:TEXT;POS,COUNT:INDEX)return TEXT;

        - - concatenation operation

        function "&" (LEFT:TEXT;     RIGHT:TEXT)return TEXT;
        function "&" (LEFT:STRING;  RIGHT:TEXT)return TEXT;
        function "&" (LEFT:TEXT;  RIGHT:STRING)return TEXT;

        - - copy SOURCE to TARGET

        procedure COPY(SOURCE:in STRING; TARGET:out TEXT);
        procedure COPY(SOURCE:in TEXT;     TARGET:out TEXT);

        - - delete COUNT characters from TEXT object T
        - - starting at position POS

        procedure DELETE(T:in out TEXT; POS,COUNT:in INDEX);

        - - insert the given substring into TEXT object T
        - - starting at position POS

        procedure INSERT(T:in out TEXT; POS:in INDEX;
                            SUBSTR:in STRING);
        procedure INSERT(T:in out TEXT; POS:in INDEX;
                            SUBSTR:in TEXT);
    private
        type TEXT(MAX_LENGTH:INDEX) is
            record
                CURRENT_LENGTH:INDEX:=0;
                VALUE:STRING(1 .. MAX_LENGTH);
            end record;

    end TEXT_HANDLING;
```

The TEXT_HANDLING package provides an abstract data type called TEXT for holding variable length strings and a set of operations for manipulating them. To use this package, objects of type TEXT are declared with the required maximum string length specified by a discriminant constraint. For example, the TEXT object MY_TEXT declared as

```
        MY_TEXT:TEXT(80);
```

can hold text strings with lengths varying from 0 to 80 characters. The TEXT_
HANDLING package sets an upper limit on the maximum length string of 512
but this is arbitrary.

Before illustrating how this package can be used, three points of importance
should be noted. Firstly, the type TEXT is **limited private**. Thus, no operations
are available for the type except for those provided by the package. In particular,
it is not possible to directly assign one text object to another. This restriction is
imposed to avoid potential discriminant constraint errors. For example, if
OTHER_TEXT was declared by

OTHER_TEXT:TEXT(100);

then even though the assignment

OTHER_TEXT:=MY_TEXT;

is logically valid, in practice it is illegal: the objects are of different sizes and so a
constraint error would occur. To protect users against this, the type is limited
and the supplied COPY operation must be used instead, that is,

COPY(MY_TEXT,OTHER_TEXT);

would have the desired effect. Another rather more subtle reason for making
TEXT limited is that it allows the implementation of the package to be changed
without affecting its users. For example, if at some later date it was decided that
dynamic storage should be used (see next chapter) whereby the TEXT record
became a pointer into a 'string pool', then the semantics of the assignment
operation for TEXT objects would be completely different. As the TEXT_
HANDLING package is intended to be a general library facility, it is clearly
prudent to avoid such potential problems by making TEXT limited.

Secondly, several of the operations are overloaded for both STRING and
TEXT arguments. This allows string literals to be used to denote constant TEXT
objects. For example,

COPY("This is text string",OTHER_TEXT);

would initialise OTHER_TEXT to the given string value.

Thirdly, the package provides a catenation operation for text strings. Since
the semantics of this operation are identical to the pre-defined "&" operator,
this operator has been overloaded in preference to using a regular function.

To illustrate the use of this package, suppose that in an operating system,
file names are written with the following syntax

[<DEV> :] [<NAME> [. <EXT>]]

where <DEV> denotes a physical device name, <NAME> denotes the name of
the file, and <EXT> denotes an optional extension. If a device name is given
alone, then it denotes a physical device, for example, "TTY:" might denote the

terminal. If a <NAME> is given then it denotes a disc file, and if either <DEV> or <EXT> are omitted then suitable default names must be appended. Finally, the user is allowed to specify names of any length but these are truncated by the system to 3 characters for <DEV>, 6 characters for <NAME> and 3 characters for <EXT>. A suitable function for formatting user supplied file names can be specified as follows

function FORMATTED_FNAME(NAME,DEF_DEV,DEF_EXT:STRING)**return**
                                                                    STRING;

where NAME is the user supplied file name and DEF_DEV and DEF_EXT are the default device and extension names, respectively. Examples of the mappings performed by this function are

"DK1:TEST . PAS"	=>	"DK1:TEST . PAS"
"TEST"	=>	"DK0:TEST . DAT"
"A:SORT"	=>	"A:SORT . DAT"
"LONGNAME . EXTENSION"	=>	"DK0:LONGNA . EXT"
"TTYUSER:"	=>	"TTY:"

where DEF_DEV="DK0" and DEF_EXT="DAT".

The function FORMATTED_FNAME may be implemented using the TEXT_HANDLING package as follows

```
with TEXT_HANDLING; use TEXT_HANDLING;

function FORMATTED_FNAME(NAME,DEF_DEV,DEF_EXT:
                                  STRING) return STRING is
    MAX_DEV_LEN:constant INDEX := 3;
    MAX_NAM_LEN:constant INDEX := 6;
    MAX_EXT_LEN:constant INDEX := 3;

    COLON_POS:INDEX;
    FILE_NAME:TEXT(80);

    procedure TRUNCATE_DEV_NAME(FN:in out TEXT) is
        DEV_LEN:INDEX;
    begin
        DEV_LEN:=POSITION(":",FN)-1;
        if DEV_LEN>MAX_DEV_LEN then - - truncate device name
            DELETE(FN,MAX_DEV_LEN+1,
                                  DEV_LEN-MAX_DEV_LEN);
        end if;
    end TRUNCATE_DEV_NAME;

    procedure TRUNCATE_FILE_NAME(FN:in out TEXT) is
        NAM_LEN,EXT_LEN:INDEX;
        COLON_POS,DOT_POS:INDEX;
```

```
begin
    COLON_POS:=POSITION(":",FN);
    DOT_POS    :=POSITION(".",FN);
    EXT_LEN   :=LENGTH(FN)-DOT_POS;
    NAM_LEN  :=DOT_POS-COLON_POS-1;
    if EXT_LEN>MAX_EXT_LEN then - - truncate extension
        DELETE(FN,DOT_POS+MAX_EXT_LEN+1,
                EXT_LEN-MAX_EXT_LEN);
    end if;
    if NAM_LEN>MAX_NAM_LEN then - - truncate name
        DELETE(FN,COLON_POS+MAX_NAM_LEN+1,
                NAM_LEN-MAX_NAM_LEN);
    end if;
end TRUNCATE_FILE_NAME;

begin
    - - convert to TEXT
    COPY(NAME,FILE_NAME);

    COLON_POS:=POSITION(":",FILE_NAME);

    if COLON_POS<>LENGTH(FILE_NAME) then

        - - a name and extension are needed

        if COLON_POS=0 then
            - - add default device name
            COPY(DEF_DEV & ":" & FILE_NAME,FILE_NAME);
        end if;

        if POSITION(".",FILE_NAME)=0 then
            - - add default extension
            COPY(FILE_NAME & "." & DEF_EXT,FILE_NAME);
        end if;

        TRUNCATE_FILE_NAME(FILE_NAME);

    end if;

    TRUNCATE_DEV_NAME(FILE_NAME);
    return STR(FILE_NAME);

end FORMATTED_FNAME;
```

The implementation of the TEXT_HANDLING package is given below. Most of the operations are quite straightforward; however, to simplify matters no error checking has been included. This would, of course, be needed in a practical implementation, and would probably make use of the exception handling facilities provided by Ada (see Chapter 13). Notice also the frequent use of slice assignments, and the way that the overloaded operations are defined in detail just once, and the remaining overloadings implemented as calls to the basic definition with appropriate parameter conversions. This approach leads to compact code, but carries some execution time overheads in the extra subprogram calls needed. If speed was important then each overloading could be coded individually.

```
package body TEXT_HANDLING is
    function LENGTH(T:TEXT)return INDEX is
    begin
        return T . CURRENT_LENGTH;
    end LENGTH;

    function STR(T:TEXT)return STRING is
    begin
        return T . VALUE(1 . . T . CURRENT_LENGTH);
    end STR;

    function POSITION(SUBSTR:STRING; T:TEXT)return INDEX is
        SIZE :constant INDEX := SUBSTR'LENGTH;
        LIMIT:constant INDEX := T . CURRENT_LENGTH-SIZE+1;
        IDX :INDEX := 1;
    begin
        loop
            if IDX>LIMIT then
                return 0;
            end if;
            if SUBSTR=T . VALUE(IDX . . IDX+SIZE-1) then
                return IDX;
            else
                IDX := IDX+1;
            end if;
        end loop;
    end POSITION;

    function POSITION(SUBSTR:TEXT; T:TEXT)return INDEX is
    begin
        return POSITION(STR(SUBSTR),T);
    end POSITION;

    function SUBSTR(T:TEXT; POS,COUNT:INDEX)return TEXT is
        RESULT:TEXT(COUNT);
    begin
        RESULT . CURRENT_LENGTH:=COUNT;
        RESULT . VALUE:=T . VALUE(POS . . POS+COUNT-1);
        return RESULT;
    end SUBSTR;
```

```
function CONCAT(LEFT,RIGHT:STRING)returnTEXT is
    RESULT:TEXT(LEFT'LENGTH+RIGHT'LENGTH);
begin
    RESULT . CURRENT_LENGTH:=RESULT . MAX_LENGTH;
    RESULT . VALUE:=LEFT & RIGHT;
    return RESULT;
end CONCAT;

function "&" (LEFT:TEXT;  RIGHT:TEXT)return TEXT is
begin
    return CONCAT(STR(LEFT),STR(RIGHT));
end "&";

function "&" (LEFT:STRING;  RIGHT:TEXT)return TEXT is
begin
    return CONCAT(LEFT,STR(RIGHT));
end "&";

function "&" (LEFT:TEXT;  RIGHT:STRING)return TEXT is
begin
    return CONCAT(STR(LEFT),RIGHT);
end "&";

procedure COPY(SOURCE:in STRING;TARGET:out TEXT) is
    SIZE:constant INDEX := SOURCE'LENGTH;
begin
    TARGET . CURRENT_LENGTH:=SIZE;
    TARGET . VALUE(1 . . SIZE):=SOURCE;
end COPY;

procedure COPY(SOURCE:in TEXT;  TARGET:out TEXT) is
begin
    COPY(STR(SOURCE),TARGET);
end COPY;

procedure DELETE(T:in out TEXT; POS,COUNT:in INDEX) is
    NEW_LENGTH:constant INDEX := T . CURRENT_LENGTH
                                               -COUNT;
begin
    T . VALUE(POS . . NEW_LENGTH) :=
        T . VALUE(POS+COUNT . . T . CURRENT_LENGTH);
    T . CURRENT_LENGTH:=NEW_LENGTH;
end DELETE;

procedure INSERT(T:in out TEXT; POS:in INDEX;
                  SUBSTR:in STRING) is
    INSERT_SIZE:constant INDEX := LENGTH'SUBSTR;
    NEW_LENGTH :constant INDEX := T . CURRENT_LENGTH
                                            +INSERT_SIZE;
```

```
begin
     T . VALUE(POS+INSERT_SIZE . . NEW_LENGTH) :=
          T . VALUE(POS . . T . CURRENT_LENGTH);
     T . VALUE(POS . . POS+INSERT_SIZE-1) := SUBSTR;
     T . CURRENT_LENGTH:=NEW_LENGTH;
end INSERT;

procedure INSERT(T:in out TEXT; POS:in INDEX;
                    SUBSTR:in TEXT) is
begin
     INSERT(T,POS,STR(SUBSTR));
end INSERT;

end TEXT_HANDLING;
```

10.7 EXERCISES

(10.1) Define a variant record type which enables the co-ordinates of a point to be stored either as a pair of cartesian co-ordinates X and Y of type ABSCISSA and ORDINATE, respectively, or as a pair of polar co-ordinates R and THETA of type RADIUS and ANGLE, respectively.

(10.2) In a government records office, certain data must be stored on all persons living within the country. For each person, a name, sex, and date of birth must be recorded. In addition, if the person is a national then his/her place of birth must be stored otherwise the person is assumed to be a visiting alien and his/her country of origin and date of entry must be stored. Define a suitable variant record type for storing the above information on a single person.

 Suppose further that aliens are further classified into visitors and temporary residents. For the latter class only, amend the record type to include whether or not a work permit has been issued and if so its number and expiry date. It may be assumed that the types PERSON_ NAME, DATE, PLACE_NAME, SEX, COUNTRY and PERMIT_NUMBER are already defined.

(10.3) In a graphics system, a picture is built-up from a matrix of 512×512 elements. Each element is called a pixel and consists of three dots arranged in a triangle coloured red, green and blue. Each colour has an intensity in the range 0 to 63. Define a data type to represent the graphics screen.

 In this system, a picture can be built by super-imposing a number of sub-pictures onto a given background. If each sub-picture consists of an $m \times n$ matrix of pixels, define a data type for representing a sub-picture.

Design a procedure with the specification

procedure SUPER_IMPOSE(SCREEN:**in out** GRAPHICS_SCREEN;
                                         SUB_PIC:**in** SUB_PICTURE;
                                         X, Y:**in** SCREEN_INDEX);

which superimposes the given SUB_PIC onto the given graphics SCREEN such that the top left corner of the SUB_PIC is located at co-ordinates X, Y of the screen. For each affected pixel p in the SCREEN, then if the corresponding pixel in the SUB_PIC s is black (that is, all intensities = 0) then p is unchanged otherwise p is replaced by s.

11

Access types

11.1 STATIC AND DYNAMIC ALLOCATION OF DATA OBJECTS

When a data object is declared in the declarative part of some program unit (or declare statement), storage space for that object is allocated within the data area of that unit. Once allocated, both the location and the size of this storage space is fixed for the lifetime of the object. Such an object is, therefore, said to be static, and because it is static it can be referenced simply by giving it a name. Hence, for example, in

```
procedure P is
    X:T;
begin
    - -
end P;
```

when procedure P is called the declaration "X:T" is elaborated. The type T specifies (amongst other things) the amount of storage space needed to accommodate the object X. This amount of storage is therefore allocated for X within the data area belonging to P. Because the compiler can determine in advance where X will be located within P's data area, it can always translate subsequent references to X into references to the corresponding locations in memory.

For most programming applications, statically allocated data objects are quite satisfactory. However, there are circumstances where static allocation causes difficulties. Firstly, the size of a static data object must be fixed before it is allocated. Thus, in applications where an unknown amount of data must be input and then stored, an upper bound on the amount of data which can be accepted must be decided on in advance. This is unsatisfactory, because if the amount of data is much less than expected then a lot of storage space is wasted, while conversely, if the amount of data exceeds expectations, then the program will fail. Secondly, static data objects have a fixed structure. Even in the most complex structured data type, the relationships between each of the individual components are fixed. For example, if an array is used to store a list of values then the ordering of the values in that list, as determined by the corresponding index values, is fixed. The only way that the ordering can be changed is to copy the values into different components of the array. In the TEXT_HANDLING package given at the end of the last section, insertion and deletion of characters within a text string is effected by copying substrings from one slice of the array to another. In this case, the components of the array are simple discrete types and so copying is not unduly expensive. However, if each component of the array was itself a large data structure, then clearly copying would be a very inefficient method of re-ordering the components.

As an alternative to statically allocated data, Ada provides a mechanism for allocating data objects dynamically during program execution. Unlike the case for static data objects, the storage locations used for dynamic objects cannot be predicted in advance. Therefore, they cannot be referenced by a name but must instead be referenced indirectly via a so-called *access type*. An access type gives access to a dynamically allocated data object.

The dynamic data allocation facilities provided by Ada allow both of the difficulties for static data noted above to be avoided. Unknown amounts of data can be handled by dynamically allocating a data object to contain each new datum as and when it is received. Complex data structures can be built whose components are allocated dynamically and the relationships between them denoted by access types. These relationships can be modified at run-time by manipulating access values, and great flexibility is thereby obtained.

11.2 BASIC IDEAS OF ACCESS TYPES

To introduce the basic mechanisms involved in the use of access types, and to establish some necessary terminology, a simple example of a dynamic data structure will be developed. Later sections will then cover the more detailed aspects of using access types.

Suppose that a file containing a list of persons' names is given, and the number of names in this list is unknown. The type used to represent each name is defined as

type PERSON_NAME **is new** STRING(1 .. 6);

and a procedure is provided to read names from the file

procedure NEXT(NAME:**out** PERSON_NAME; DONE:**out** BOOLEAN);

such that each call to NEXT returns the next name from the file. The parameter DONE is set *true* when the file is exhausted.

A program is required to read the given file and construct a list of persons' names. Since the file is of unknown length, the use of an array to store the names is inappropriate, and so a linear list structure will be used. Each item in the list will be allocated dynamically as each name is read from the file, and each item in the list will be linked to its predecessor by an access value.

Let each dynamically allocated list item be of type ITEM. An access type can then be declared, as follows:

type ITEM_POINTER **is access** ITEM;

The access type ITEM_POINTER denotes a set of access values which allow dynamically allocated objects of type ITEM to be referenced. Technically, the type ITEM is said to be the *base type* of the access type ITEM_POINTER, and values of this access type are said to *designate* objects of type ITEM.

When an access type is first declared, the set of access values that it denotes contains a single value called **null**. **Null** is a value of every access type, and it designates no object at all. Each time that an object of the base type is allocated, the access value which designates it is added to the set of values denoted by the access type. For example, suppose that the following objects are declared

IP1,IP2:ITEM_POINTER;

IP1 and IP2 are access variables. By default, an access variable declared without an explicit initial value is given the value **null**. Thus, in the above case, IP1 and IP2 both have the value **null**. At the moment, the set of values denoted by the access type ITEM_POINTER only contains the value **null** and so this is the only possible value which can be given to IP1 and IP2. Hence, the assignments

IP1 := IP2;
IP2 := **null**;

are both legal but achieve nothing!

A dynamic object can be created by means of an *allocator*. An allocator is like a function call with side-effects. The side-effect is to allocate a data object dynamically, and the function result is an access value designating this object. For example,

IP1 := **new** ITEM;   - - "**new** ITEM" is an allocator

creates a new object of type ITEM and assigns its access value to IP1. At this stage, a diagram may be helpful. The following represents the current situation, where data objects (both static and dynamic) are shown as boxes and access values are represented by arrows:

IP 1

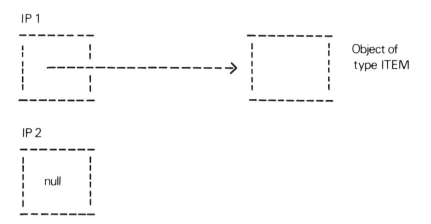

It can be seen from this that access values are nothing more than pointers to dynamically created objects (at the level of the implementation, an access value is just the address in memory of a dynamically allocated storage unit).

The set of values denoted by the type ITEM_POINTER has now been augmented by the newly created access value. Hence, some further assignments can be made. For example,

>   IP2 := IP1;

assigns the access value held by IP1 to IP2. This means that both IP1 and IP2 now designate the same object, that is, pictorially

IP 1

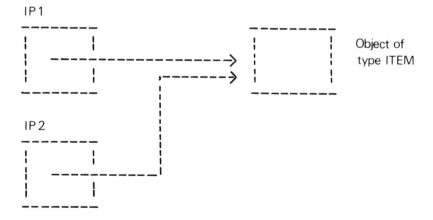

There are now two ways of designating the ITEM object. Suppose, however, that instead

>   IP1 := IP2;

had been written. This would result in

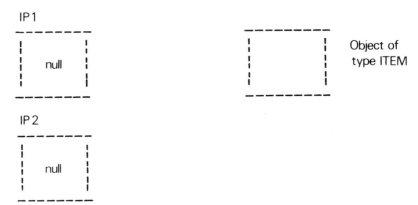

Now no access variables designate the ITEM object and so it is effectively lost. It may continue to exist, but it can never be accessed by the program. Some implementations of Ada might reclaim the storage space that it is using, whereas others may leave it as it is (see section 11.7). The main point, however, is that the object is lost to the program forever. Therefore care needs to be taken in using access types, so that situations such as these only happen deliberately and not by accident.

Returning to the problem at hand, the type of ITEM needs to be defined before any further progress is possible. Each item object must hold firstly a name and secondly an access value designating the next item in the list. A suitable type, therefore, is a record, as follows:

```
type ITEM is
    record
        NAME:PERSON_NAME;
        NEXT:ITEM_POINTER;
    end record;
```

Before showing how objects of type ITEM can be used to construct a list, it is necessary to explain how values of an access type are distinguished from those of the object that it designates.

When the name of an access type is used on its own, then it always refers to the access object itself. Thus, in

```
IP1 := IP2;
```

the access value held by IP2 is assigned to IP1. In order to denote the base object designated by an access object, the name of the access object is followed by ″.all″. For example,

```
IP1.all := (NAME => "GEORGE", NEXT => null);
```

assigns the given record value to the object designated by IP1. Where the base type of an access type is structured (and this is the usual case), the individual components are denoted as though the name of the access object was the name of the base object itself. For example,

IP1 . NAME := "RUPERT";

would assign the name "RUPERT" to the NAME component of the object designated by IPI. Note that in this case there is no need to distinguish between the access variable and the object that it designates, because only the latter can possibly have a component (access types are not structured types).

Enough information on using access types has now been given to allow a procedure to be designed which will build the required list of names read from the input file. This procedure will be called BUILD_LIST, and its code is as follows

```
procedure BUILD_LIST is

            - - assume types PERSON_NAME,ITEM,ITEM_POINTER
            - - and procedure NEXT are previously defined

            HEAD:ITEM_POINTER;        - - designates 1st item in list
            TAIL:ITEM_POINTER;        - - designates last item in list
            TEMP:ITEM_POINTER;        - - general access variable

            NEW_NAME:PERSON_NAME;
            INPUT_EXHAUSTED:BOOLEAN;

begin
            NEXT(NEW_NAME,INPUT_EXHAUSTED);
            while not INPUT_EXHAUSTED loop

                        - - allocate a new list item
                        TEMP := new ITEM;

                        - - initialise it
                        TEMP . all := (NEW_NAME,null);

                        - - add new item to tail of list
                        if HEAD = null then
                                    - - list is empty
                                    HEAD :=TEMP;TAIL := TEMP;
                        else
                                    - - normal case
                                    TAIL . NEXT := TEMP;
                                    TAIL := TEMP;
                        end if;

                        NEXT(NEW_NAME,INPUT_EXHAUSTED);
            end loop;
end BUILD_LIST;
```

This program utilises three access variables TEMP, HEAD and TAIL. TEMP is used as a general purpose variable to give temporary access to each newly created item before it is appended to the list. HEAD always designates the first item in the list and TAIL always designates the last item in the list. Initially, when the list is empty both of these have the value **null**.

To understand the operation of the program, suppose that the input file contained three names "GEORGE", "FRED " and "RITA   ". On the first iteration round the loop, an item is created holding the name "GEORGE", accessible initially only via TEMP. When the **if** statement is executed, HEAD is **null** since the list is empty, and so HEAD and TAIL are set equal to TEMP. Hence, at the end of the first iteration both HEAD and TAIL designate the same object. Pictorially, the situation is as follows

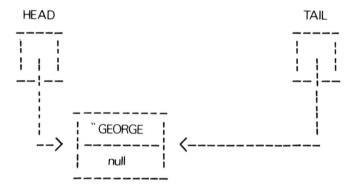

On the second iteration, a second item is created holding the name "FRED   ". Before the execution of the **if** statement, the situation is as follows

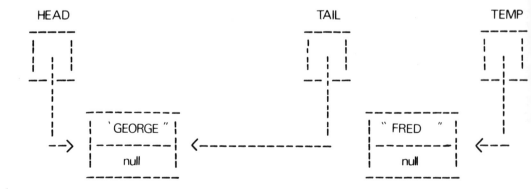

This time HEAD is not **null** and so the **else** part of the **if** statement is executed. After

TAIL.NEXT := TEMP;

the situation is

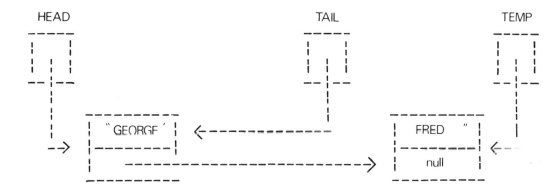

and after

TAIL := TEMP;

the situation is

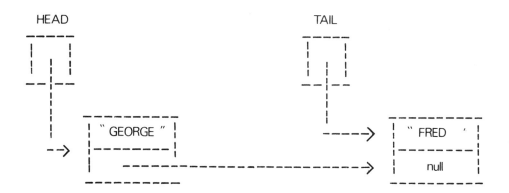

The object holding the name "FRED   " is now linked into the list and the invariant condition that TAIL designates the last item in the list is re-established (note that TEMP is not shown in the last picture because it is only relevant within the loop). The third and final iteration round the loop proceeds in the same way as the second, to give the final list structure as follows

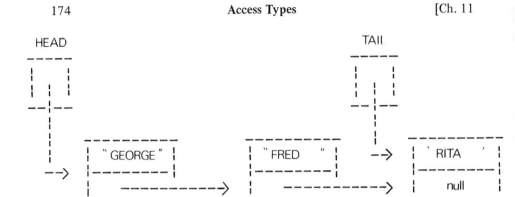

This simple example of building a dynamic data structure illustrates both the way that access types are used and their great flexibility. The size of the list can be increased at will (until storage space is exhausted) and it can be manipulated simply and efficiently. To demonstrate this last point, suppose that it is required to move the first item in the list to the end of the list. This can be simply achieved by manipulating access values, for example,

        TEMP := HEAD;
        HEAD := HEAD .NEXT;
        TAIL .NEXT := TEMP;
        TAIL := TEMP;

Notice that no copying of the actual data in the list is required.

The main ideas of access types having been introduced, the following sections describe their use in more detail.

11.3 ACCESS TYPE DECLARATIONS AND NAMES

An access type declaration introduces the name of a type denoting a potential set of access values for designating dynamically created objects of the specified base type. The syntax diagram for an access type declaration is as follows

S112 access_type_defn

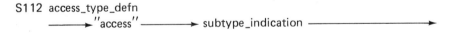

The subtype indication names the base type of the access type. Variables of the access type may hold values which designate objects of this type and this type only. Any type may serve as a base type, but record types are most commonly used in practice. If the base type is a discriminated type or an unconstrained array type, then a discriminant or index constraint may be specified in the subtype indication (see section 11.6). These are the only kinds of constraint allowed in access type definitions.

Note that because each access type may designate only one type of dynamic base object, the strong typing rules are just as strict for dynamic data as for normal statically allocated data.

In the example given in section 11.2, a potential difficulty in the declaration of access types was carefully overlooked. The declaration of the type ITEM uses the name ITEM_POINTER and the declaration of the type ITEM_POINTER uses the name ITEM. Ada, however, insists that all names be declared before they are used. This difficulty is resolved by using a so-called *incomplete type declaration*. Referring back to syntax diagram S14 (section 3.1), it can be seen that the actual specification of a type can be omitted, and just the name of the type given. This feature is used to allow mutually recursive type declarations to be written. For example, the types ITEM and ITEM_POINTER would be properly declared in Ada by

```
type ITEM;           - - incomplete declaration of base type

type ITEM_POINTER is access ITEM;        -  access type

type ITEM is              - - full declaration of base type
    record
        NAME:PERSON_NAME;
        NEXT:ITEM_POINTER;
    end record;
```

An incomplete type declaration introduces the name of a type prior to its full definition so that an access type can use that type name as the name of its base type. The full definition of the base type must always follow in the same declarative part.

As noted previously, the name of an access object written on its own refers to the access object itself. When the name appears within a selected component or an indexed component, then the component referred to is that of the base object currently designated by the named access value. When the name appears suffixed by .all then it denotes that whole base object currently designated by the named access value. The following examples illustrate these naming conventions

```
type ARRAY_BASE is array(1 .. 10)of INTEGER;

type RECORD_BASE is
    record
        I:INTEGER;
        C:CHARACTER;
    end record;

type AB_PTR is access ARRAY_BASE;
type RB_PTR is access RECORD_BASE;

A:AB_PTR;   R:RB_PTR;
```

```
- - assume A and R designate dynamically created
- - base objects. Then  ...
```

A . **all** := (1 .. 10 => 0);	- - whole array assignment
A(1 .. 5) := A(6 .. 10);	- - array slice assignment
A(K) := 100;	- - array component assignment
A := **null**;	- - access type assignment
R . **all** := (I=>0,C=>'A');	- - whole record assignment
R . I := 12;	- - record component assignment
R := **null**;	- - access type assignment
R := A;	- - illegal — type error
R . I := A(4);	- - legal assignment of integers

11.4 ALLOCATORS

An allocator is used to create a new dynamic data object. The syntax of an allocator is as follows

S113 allocator

An allocator is written as a component of an expression. It consists of the reserved word **new** followed by either a subtype indication or a qualified expression. The former is used to define just the type of the object to be allocated and possibly an index or discriminant constraint (see section 11.6). The latter is used to allocate an object with a specific initial value.

The execution of an allocator has the following effect:

(1) the initial value (qualified expression), if any, is evaluated;
(2) a new dynamic object of the specified type is created;
(3) if the type has any default initial values, the newly created object is initialised accordingly;
(4) if an explicit initial value has been given, this value is assigned to the created object;
(5) an access value designating the object is returned as result.

For example, the elaboration of the declaration

        PTR:ITEM_POINTER := **new** ITEM ' ("GEORGE", **null**);

would result in the introduction of an access variable called PTR of type ITEM_
POINTER and the creation of a new dynamic object of type ITEM initialised to
the value (''GEORGE'', **null**). Further, the value PTR is initialised with an access
value designating the newly created object.

11.5 ACCESS CONSTANTS

As with any other object declared in an Ada program, an access object can be
defined to be constant. Such an object must be given an initial value either by
an allocator or by a previously established access value. For example, in

> CP1:**constant** ITEM_POINTER := **new** ITEM'('' ''', **null**);
> CP2:**constant** ITEM_POINTER := CP1;

both CP1 and CP2 are declared as access constants. The elaboration of CP1
creates a dynamic object of type ITEM with a blank name component, and CP1
is initialised to designate this object. CP2 is then initialised to designate the
same object.

The value of an access constant may never be subsequently changed. For
example,

> CP1 := **null**;
> CP2 := PTR;

are both illegal. However, the value of the object designated by an access constant
can be changed. For example,

> CP1 . NAME := ''******'';

is legal (note that this assignment also changes the value of CP2 . NAME!). Hence,
an access constant always designates the same dynamic object, but the value of
that object may be changed.

11.6 DISCRIMINATED AND UNCONSTRAINED ARRAY BASE TYPES

The base type of an access type can be any type including discriminated record
types and unconstrained array types. However, in these two cases, Ada imposes
the restriction that actual dynamic objects of these types must be constrained.
Thus, it is not possible to dynamically allocate a variant record or a record
containing a variable length array and then subsequently change the variant or
array size during program execution.

The necessary index or discriminant constraints can be applied by specifying
the constraint explicitly in the allocator or implicitly via an initial value. For
example, suppose that the type VPTR is declared as

> **type** VPTR **is access** VEHICLE;

where VEHICLE is the variant record type defined in section 10.1, then

V1:VPTR := **new** VEHICLE(KIND => CAR);

and

```
V2:VPTR := new VEHICLE'(KIND        => VAN,
                        SERIAL_NO   => 1032,
                        MODEL       => HEAVY_DUTY,
                        PAINT       => RED,
                        CAPACITY    => 20,
                        LOAD        => 10 );
```

are both legal object declarations; however,

V_BAD:VPTR := **new** VEHICLE;

is illegal, since an attempt is being made to allocate dynamically an unconstrained discriminated record.

The first two examples illustrate the two different ways of providing a constraint. V1 designates an object whose discriminant has been explicitly constrained to the value CAR by means of a discriminant constraint. The remaining components have no initial value. V2, however, designates an object in which all components have been initialised by means of a record aggregate. In this case, the value given to the discriminant (that is, VAN) also serves as an implicit discriminant constraint. Note that this is not the same as for static objects of type VEHICLE, where an initial value does not preclude the possibility of subsequent changes to the discriminant.

A discriminant constraint applied to a dynamically allocated object only constrains that object and not the access object which initially designates it. For example, the assignment

V1 := V2;

is quite legal. The fact that V1 was initialised to point to an object with the discriminant constraint CAR does not prevent it from being changed to designate an object with the discriminant constraint VAN. However, it is possible to specify such a constraint if desired. For example, in

V3:VPTR(KIND => CAR);

the access variable V3 is constrained to point to objects of type VEHICLE whose discriminant must be CAR. Thus, assuming the initial values specified for V1 and V2 given at the beginning of this section, then

V3 := V1;

is legal, whereas

V3 := V2;

would raise a constraint error because the discriminant value of the object designated by V2 does not satisfy the constraint applied to V3.

11.7 CONTROL OF STORAGE ALLOCATION AND RECLAMATION

When a dynamic data object is created by an allocator, it continues to exist for at least as long as there is an access path to it (that is, there is some means of referring to it). This implies that the maximum lifetime of a dynamic object is the same as the lifetime of the program unit (or block) in which the associated access type is declared. This follows because, once the scope of the access type declaration has been left, no access paths can exist, since there will no longer be any access objects in existence to provide them.

A consequence of this is that the control of storage allocation and subsequent reclamation in Ada is closely tied to access type declarations. Each access type declaration is considered to introduce a set of potential access values and thereby implies a potential *collection* of dynamically allocated objects. Each actual member of this collection is created when needed by an allocator, but it may then continue to exist until the entire collection is reclaimed when the corresponding access type goes out of scope. To clarify this, consider the following program outline

```
procedure DYN_STORAGE_EXAMPLE is

   type INT_PTR is access INTEGER;

   IP_GLOBAL:INT_PTR;
   IP_ZERO    :constant INT_PTR := new INTEGER'(0);
                   - - create object 0

   procedure LOCAL_GENERATOR is
       IP_LOCAL:INT_PTR;
   begin
       IP_LOCAL := new INTEGER'(1);  - - create object 1
       IP_GLOBAL := IP_LOCAL;
       IP_LOCAL := new INTEGER'(2);  - - create object 2
   end LOCAL_GENERATOR;

begin
   - -
   LOCAL_GENERATOR;
   - -
   IP_GLOBAL := null;
   - -
end DYN_STORAGE_EXAMPLE;
```

When DYN_STORAGE_EXAMPLE is called, the type declaration for INT_PTR is elaborated and this establishes an associated potential collection of dynamic objects. When DYN_STORAGE_EXAMPLE terminates, this collection ceases to exist and the Ada run-time support system will reclaim the memory used by any objects which have actually been allocated to the collection.

Notice first that apart from the lifetime of the collection being tied to the scope of the associated access type, the lifetime of any individual object created is not related to the static scope of the program text. For example, two objects are created locally within LOCAL_GENERATOR, but these may continue to exist even after LOCAL_GENERATOR has terminated.

The lifetime of the collection to which a dynamic object belongs only fixes an upper limit on the life expectancy of that object. As stated at the start of this section, once no access path can be found to a dynamic object, then that object can be disposed of and the memory that it used reclaimed. For example, in the above, two objects are created within LOCAL_GENERATOR, but after its termination there is only an access path to the first (via IP_GLOBAL). The second object created is only ever designated by IP_LOCAL, and this access variable ceases to exist when LOCAL_GENERATOR terminates. Ada allows such objects to be disposed of immediately that they become inaccessible. This kind of automatic storage reclamation is called *Garbage Collection*. It has the advantage that optimal use is made of available memory, but has the disadvantage that it carries high run-time execution overheads. If garbage collection was operating in the above example, then when LOCAL_GENERATOR terminates the storage used by object 2 could be reclaimed immediately. When, a few statements later in the body of DYN_STORAGE_EXAMPLE, the access value held by IP_GLOBAL designating object 1 is over-written, then (assuming no other copies of that access value exist) the storage that it used could also be reclaimed.

It is important to realise that the rules concerning the use of access types in Ada have been carefully formulated to allow a variety of underlying implementation strategies to be adopted. Ada is designed to be useful for a wide range of applications, not only those in the real time area. Thus, the rules allow a garbage collector to be provided, even though such a device can rarely be tolerated in a real time program. This is not only because garbage collection is slow, but also because it is unpredictable. In fact, garbage collectors do not in practice attempt to reclaim dynamic objects immediately that they become eligible for disposal, but instead wait until memory is exhausted and then collect garbage in one go. This means that a program can suddenly and unpredictably 'stop' for a few seconds whilst the garbage is collected. This topic is discussed further at the end of the section.

To ensure that garbage collection does not operate even if it is provided, a pragma called CONTROLLED can be issued. The form of this pragma is

    pragma CONTROLLED(access_type);

where access_type is used to identify the collection whose storage allocation and reclamation is to be controlled. Hence, a garbage collector can be selectively suppressed. As an example, writing the pragma

pragma CONTROLLED(INT_PTR);

within the declarative part of DYN_STORAGE_EXAMPLE would ensure that each of the three objects allocated during its execution would be disposed of when and only when it had terminated.

It is sometimes useful to be able to program explicitly the disposal of a dynamic data object, especially when garbage collection is not provided. This can be done by instantiating a generic procedure called UNCHECKED_DEALLO-CATION. Generic procedures are described in Chapter 14. For now it is sufficient to understand that a generic procedure serves as a template for creating actual instances of a procedure for which certain aspects of the procedure's definition have been parameterised (for example, the types of formal parameters). To create a disposal procedure called DISPOSE for dynamic objects of type BASE_TYPE designated by an access type ACCESS_TYPE, the following should be written

procedure DISPOSE **is new**
UNCHECKED_DEALLOCATION(BASE_TYPE,ACCESS_TYPE);

[Note that the name UNCHECKED_DEALLOCATION must appear in the context specification of the enclosing compilation unit before it can be used in this way.] For example, a DISPOSE procedure for the ITEM records introduced in section 11.2 would be declared as

procedure DISPOSE **is new**
UNCHECKED_DEALLOCATION(ITEM,ITEM_POINTER);

A call to DISPOSE takes a single parameter which must be a variable of type ACCESS_TYPE. For example, if AVAR is such a variable, then when the call

DISPOSE(AVAR);

is executed the dynamic object designated by AVAR is disposed of and AVAR is set equal to **null**. If AVAR was **null** originally, then the call would have no effect. As a concrete example, the following procedure removes the first ITEM in the list constructed by BUILD_LIST (section 11.2) and then deallocates it:

```
procedure REMOVE_HEAD(HEAD_OF_LIST:in out ITEM_POINTER) is
    TEMP: ITEM_POINTER;
begin
    if HEAD_OF_LIST /= null then
        TEMP := HEAD_OF_LIST;
        HEAD_OF_LIST := HEAD_OF_LIST.NEXT;
        DISPOSE(TEMP);
    end if;
end REMOVE_HEAD;
```

The problem with this mechanism is that it is insecure. It introduces the classic difficulty in dynamic storage systems of the 'dangling pointer'. For example, suppose that a disposal procedure was instantiated for the DYN_STORAGE_EXAMPLE procedure, that is,

procedure DISPOSE **is new**
            UNCHECKED_DEALLOCATION(INTEGER,INT_PTR);

Normally, an attempt to access a null object simply raises a constraint error and no serious damage is done. Thus, if the statements

            IP_LOCAL := **new** INTEGER'(1);
            IP_GLOBAL := IP_LOCAL;

were followed by

            DISPOSE(IP_LOCAL);

then a subsequent erroneous assignment such as

            IP_LOCAL.**all** := 10;

would be detected, since the call to DISPOSE sets IP_LOCAL equal to **null**. Such an error could be handled at run-time (see Chapter 13) and the program could then continue. Consider now, however, the subsequent assignment

            IP_GLOBAL.**all** := 10;

In this case, IP_GLOBAL does not hold the value **null** but an access value designating a non-existent object (IP_GLOBAL is said to be a *dangling pointer*). This erroneous assignment cannot be detected, and so the result would be a 'wild' store into the memory which would very probably cause the program to malfunction. Great care, therefore, needs to be exercised when using the UN-CHECKED_DEALLOCATION mechanism. In fact, it is usually better to program the management of dynamic data explicitly by keeping a *free-list* of dynamic objects which are not currently in use. When an object needs to be disposed of it is just added to the free-list. When a new object needs to be allocated, the free-list is examined and if it is not empty the required object is taken from it; otherwise an allocator is executed to create it.

As an example of the use of this technique, suppose that objects of type ITEM (section 11.2) need to be allocated and disposed of within the scope of the declaration for ITEM_POINTER. The following package would provide such a facility.

            package ITEM_MANAGER **is**

                function CREATE **return** ITEM_POINTER;
                procedure DISPOSE(P: **in out** ITEM_POINTER);

            end ITEM_MANAGER;

```
package body ITEM_MANAGER is
    FREE_LIST:ITEM_POINTER;
    function CREATE return ITEM_POINTER is
        NEW_ITEM:ITEM_POINTER;
    begin
        if FREE_LIST=null then
            - - free list is empty so allocate
            - - a new object in the normal way
            NEW_ITEM := new ITEM;
        else
            - - take first ITEM off of the free list
            NEW_ITEM := FREE_LIST;
            FREE_LIST := FREE_LIST.NEXT;
            - - make sure that NEXT component of new
            - - object is null
            NEW_ITEM.NEXT .= null;
        end;
        return NEW_ITEM;
    end CREATE;
    procedure DISPOSE(P:in out ITEM_POINTER) is
    begin
        - - if P is not null then add the object that
        - - it designates to the free-list
        if P /= null then
            P.NEXT := FREE_LIST;
            FREE_LIST := P;
            - - return P as null
            P := null;
        end if;
    end DISPOSE;
end ITEM_MANAGER;
```

Now a new ITEM object can be allocated by calling the function CREATE rather than by using an allocator directly. ITEM objects which are no longer needed can be disposed of by calling the procedure DISPOSE. Note that although the use of the ITEM_MANAGER package does not prevent dangling pointers from arising, they are no longer as dangerous, because 'wild' stores only corrupt existing ITEM objects in the free-list and not unknown areas of memory.

Finally, it should be noted that Ada allows the total amount of storage required to accommodate a collection of dynamically allocated objects to be specified explicitly. The mechanism for doing this is described in Chapter 17 and the subject will not be pursued further here. However, it is worth considering why such a specification should be allowed. At the beginning of this chapter it was stated that one of the great advantages of dynamic data is that it allows data structures to be built whose size is not fixed in advance. If, however, the size of a collection is specified explicitly, then clearly this advantage is lost. The design of Ada access types had to take two factors into account. Firstly, the mechanism had to be secure, and secondly, it had to be efficient enough to use in real time applications. The first requirement meant that an explicit deallocation procedure should not be the central means of disposal for dynamically created objects. So instead, the concept of a *collection* was introduced to allow safe disposal when the access type goes out of scope. The concept of a collection also provides a solution to the second requirement. In a general dynamic data allocation scheme, the storage required for each collection would be taken from a central reservoir called a *heap*. Any one collection could then grow indefinitely, until this heap was exhausted. Such a scheme is very flexible but (even without garbage collection) also carries high run-time overheads. The individual objects of each collection are scattered throughout the heap and so the disposal of a collection is non-trivial. An alternative is to allocate the storage needed for each collection within the workspace of the program unit that declares it. Explicit deallocation of a collection is then unnecessary, since the entire workspace of a program unit is recovered automatically when that unit terminates. To use this alternative, however, the size of the collection must be known. Hence, Ada gives the programmer two alternatives

(a) a general dynamic data facility with significant run-time overheads – no size specified for each collection
(b) a restricted dynamic data facility with virtually zero run-time overheads – size specified for each collection in advance

Alternative (b) is useful for time critical applications where although the advantage of 'expandable storage' is lost, the other and probably more important advantage of dynamic data is still retained, namely flexible manipulation of data structures.

11.8 EXAMPLE – A CROSS REFERENCE GENERATOR FOR ADA SOURCE TEXTS

In this section an example of the use of access types will be presented. A program is required which reads an Ada source text and prints out the text with line numbers followed by a cross reference list of identifier usage. As an example, when applied to the program given in section 1.2, the output would be as follows

```
1       with TEXT_IO;
2       procedure MAIN is
3          CH:CHARACTER;
4       begin
5          TEXT_IO.GET(CH);
```

```
 6              while CH /= '.' loop
 7                  if CH = '(' or CH =')' then
 8                      TEXT_IO . PUT(CH);
 9                  end if;
10                  TEXT_IO . GET(CH);
11              end loop;
12          end MAIN;
```

BEGIN	4				
CH	3	5	6	7	7	8
	10				
CHARACTER	3				
END	9	11	12		
GET	5	10			
IF	7	9			
IS	2				
LOOP	6	11			
MAIN	2	12			
OR	7				
PROCEDURE	2				
PUT	8				
TEXT_IO	1	5	8	10	
THEN	7				
WHILE	6				
WITH	1				

Each identifier used in the program is listed in alphabetical order followed by the line numbers of the lines in which it appears. Lower and upper case letters are not distinguished: all are treated as upper case. As well as demonstrating a realistic use of access types, this example also serves as a good illustration of design by data abstraction.

As the first stage of the design process, two abstract resources are proposed. Firstly, an input/output interface is defined by the following package

```
package IO_INTERFACE is
    type LINE_NUM is private;
    type IDENT is private;
    NULL_IDENT: constant IDENT;

    procedure GET_ID(ID: out IDENT; LN: out LINE_NUM;
                     DONE: out BOOLEAN);
  . procedure PRINT(ID: in IDENT);
    procedure PRINT(LN: in LINE_NUM);

    function ">"(ID1,ID2:IDENT)return BOOLEAN;
```

```
private
   - - to be defined
end IO_INTERFACE;
```

This package defines two abstract data types: IDENT for representing identifiers and LINE_NUM for representing line numbers. The procedure GET_ID scans the input source text and returns successive identifiers. For each identifier returned its line number is also returned, and when the source text is exhausted, DONE returns TRUE. It will be assumed also that GET_ID takes care of the production of the line numbered listing. Printing of the cross reference listing is performed using the two PRINT procedures. The first of these prints an identifier starting on a new line, left justified in a fixed field width, and the second prints a line number, right justified in a fixed field width. The function $">"$ allows two identifiers to be compared in order to determine the required alphabetic ordering of the output. Finally, a deferred constant NULL_IDENT is defined which is used to print a blank identifier field for the purpose of continuation lines (see CH in the example listing above).

The second package defines the resource used to store identifiers and their line numbers. The term *identifier bag* will be used to describe the resource offered by this package. Its specification is

```
with IO_INTERFACE; use IO_INTERFACE;

package IDENT_BAG is

   procedure STORE(ID: in IDENT; LN: in LINE_NUM);
   procedure TABULATE;

end IDENT_BAG;
```

The procedure STORE is called to store each identifier encountered in the input text in the bag along with its associated line number. The procedure TABULATE is called when the bag has been filled, to produce the tabulated output. This procedure will use the PRINT procedures defined by the IO_INTERFACE package. The term *identifier bag* is used to emphasise that at this level of the design there is no concern for how identifiers are actually stored. It may be a list structure, a tree structure or something else, but at this level such details are irrelevant.

Given the above two abstract resources, the design of the cross-reference program is almost trivial

```
with IO_INTERFACE, IDENT_BAG;
use IO_INTERFACE, IDENT_BAG;

procedure CROSS_REFERENCE is
   ID: IDENT;
   LN: LINE_NUM;
   DONE: BOOLEAN;
```

```
begin
   loop              - - fill identifier bag
      GET_ID(ID,LN,DONE);
      exit when DONE;
      STORE(ID,LN);
   end loop;
   TABULATE;    - - list contents of bag
end CROSS_REFERENCE;
```

The first stage of the design is now complete. The second stage involves the refinement of the abstract resources proposed in the first stage. Since the implementation of the IO_INTERFACE requires detailed knowledge of the Ada input/output facilities, the implementation of this package will not be pursued here (see Chapter 15). It may be noted, however, that a simple but adequate definition for the private part of the package specification might be

```
private              - - of IO_INTERFACE

   MAX_ID_SIZE: constant := 16;
   MAX_LINE_NUM: constant := 10 000;

   type LINE_NUM is range 0 . . MAX_LINE_NUM;
   type IDENT is new STRING(1 . . MAX_ID_SIZE);

   NULL_IDENT: constant IDENT := (1 . . MAX_ID_SIZE=>' ');

end IO_INTERFACE;
```

The remainder of this section will, therefore, concentrate on the design of the identifier bag.

The identifier bag must store identifiers in alphabetical order and associated with each identifier there will be a list of line numbers. In order to simplify the design at this level, it is convenient to defer consideration of how to store line numbers by introducing another abstract data type:

```
package LINE_LIST_TYPE is

   type LINE_LIST is private;

   function NEW_LIST(FIRST_LN: LINE_NUM) return LINE_LIST;

   procedure ADD_TO_LIST(NEW_LN: in LINE_NUM;
                         LIST: in out LINE_LIST);
   procedure PRINT_LIST(LIST: in LINE_LIST);

private
   - - to be defined
end LINE_LIST_TYPE;
```

The abstract type LINE_LIST can be used to store a list of line numbers of unknown length. The function NEW_LIST creates a new line list and initialises it to contain the single line number given as its argument. The procedure ADD_ TO_LIST is used to add further line numbers to an existing list, and finally PRINT_LIST is used to print out a given list of numbers.

Given this abstract type, the identifier bag can be designed without worrying how line numbers are stored. Only the storage of identifiers needs to be considered. Since these must be stored in alphabetical order, a reasonable choice of data structure is a simple binary tree built using access types, that is,

```
type NODE;

type LINK is access NODE;

type NODE is
    record
        KEY:IDENT;
        LINES:LINE_LIST;
        LEFT,RIGHT:LINK;
    end record;
```

Each node in the tree holds an identifier, a line list, and two access values designating adjacent left and right subtrees. The nodes are linked together such that if L is an access variable designating any node in the tree, then

$$\text{if } L.RIGHT \mathrel{/=} \textbf{null then } L.RIGHT.KEY > L.KEY$$

and

$$\text{if } L.LEFT \mathrel{/=} \textbf{null then } L.KEY > L.LEFT.KEY$$

The package body for the identifier bag is as follows

```
with LINE_LIST_TYPE; use LINE_LIST_TYPE;

package body IDENT_BAG is

    type NODE;

    type LINK is access NODE;

    type NODE is
        record
            KEY:IDENT;
            LINES:LINE_LIST;
            LEFT,RIGHT:LINK;
        end record;

    ROOT:LINK;      -- root of the tree
                    -- initialised to null by default

    procedure STORE(ID:in IDENT; LN:in LINE_NUM) is

        procedure INSERT(HERE:in out LINK) is
```

```
            begin
                if  HERE=null then
                    HERE := new NODE'(KEY=>ID,
                                        LINES=>NEW_LIST(LN),
                                        LEFT | RIGHT=>null);

                elsif HERE . KEY>ID then
                    INSERT(HERE . LEFT);
                elsif ID>HERE . KEY then
                    INSERT(HERE . RIGHT);
                else
                    ADD_TO_LIST(LN,HERE . LINES);
                end if;
            end INSERT;

        begin
            INSERT(ROOT);
        end STORE;

        procedure TABULATE is

            procedure PRINT_SUBTREE(HERE: in LINK) is
            begin
                if  HERE/=null then
                    PRINT_SUBTREE(HERE . LEFT);
                    PRINT(ID=>HERE . KEY);
                    PRINT_LIST(LIST=>HERE . LINES);
                    PRINT_SUBTREE(HERE . RIGHT);
                end if;
            end PRINT_SUBTREE;

        begin
            PRINT_SUBTREE(ROOT);
        end TABULATE;

    end IDENT_BAG;
```

The procedure STORE is implemented using the recursive procedure INSERT which attempts to insert the given identifier and line number at the current node designated by HERE. If HERE is **null**, then the end of a branch has been reached, and a new cell is created and attached to that branch. Otherwise, the KEY of the current node is compared with the new ID to be inserted. Depending on the result of this comparison, INSERT is called recursively to insert the new ID in either the left or right subtrees as appropriate. If the new ID is the same as the current KEY, then the identifier must have been stored previously in the tree and so ADD_TO_LIST is called to append the new line number to the list of line numbers already stored for that identifier.

The procedure TABULATE prints out the contents of the tree again, using a recursive procedure PRINT_SUBTREE which performs a standard left to right traversal of the nodes. At each node visited, the actual identifier is printed using the IO_INTERFACE procedure PRINT, and then the corresponding list of lines is printed using the LINE_LIST_TYPE procedure PRINT_LIST. Note that the IO_INTERFACE package does not need to be named in the context specification preceding the IDENT_BAG body, since it has already been made available for the corresponding package specification.

The third stage of the design process is to implement the packages introduced at the second stage. In this case, this involves implementing the LINE_LIST_TYPE package. Since the number of line numbers which may be associated with any identifier is potentially unbounded, again some form of dynamic data structure will be needed. Unlike the case of the identifiers, however, line numbers are also encountered in increasing order so that a simple linear list structure of the sort described in section 11.2 is quite adequate. The private part of the LINE_LIST_ TYPE package specification may therefore define a linear list data structure as follows

```
        private                 - - part of LINE_LIST_TYPE
            type CELL;
            type LINK is access CELL;
            type CELL is
                record
                    LN:LINE_NUM;
                    NEXT:LINK;
                end record;
            type LINE_LIST is
                record
                    HEAD,TAIL:LINK;
                end record;
        end LINE_LIST_TYPE;
```

where the actual LINE_LIST type is a record containing two access types designating the head and the tail of the list. The body of the LINE_LIST_TYPE package is given as follows:

```
        package body LINE_LIST_TYPE is
            function NEW_LIST(FIRST_LN:LINE_NUM)
                                return LINE_LIST is
                LL:LINE_LIST;
```

```
          begin
              LL.HEAD := new CELL'(LN=>FIRST_LN,
                                        NEXT=>null);
              LL.TAIL := LL.HEAD;
              return LL;
          end NEW_LIST;

          procedure ADD_TO_LIST(NEW_LN:in LINE_NUM;
                                    LIST:in out LINE_LIST) is
          begin
              LIST.TAIL.NEXT := new CELL'(LN=>NEW_LN,
                                              NEXT=>null);
              LIST.TAIL := LIST.TAIL.NEXT;
          end ADD_TO_LIST;

          procedure PRINT_LIST(LIST:in LINE_LIST) is
              NUMS_PER LINE:constant INTEGER :- 6;
              THIS:LINK := LIST.HEAD;
              COUNT:INTEGER := 0;
          begin
              while THIS/=null loop
                  if COUNT=NUMS_PER_LINE then       - - start continu-
                      PRINT(NULL_IDENT);            - - ation line
                      COUNT:=0;
                  end if;
                  PRINT(THIS.LN);
                  THIS := THIS.NEXT;
                  COUNT := COUNT+1;
              end loop;
          end PRINT_LIST;
      end LINE_LIST_TYPE;
```

The above implementation of the LINE_LIST_TYPE package completes the design of the cross reference program, since there are no further packages remaining to be defined.

At this point it is useful to review what has been achieved. The structure of the program consists of a main procedure and several packages where each package represents an abstract resource. Pictorially, this structure may be depicted as shown in Fig. 11.1 where it is assumed that the IO_INTERFACE package makes use of the pre-defined library package TEXT_IO

This diagram shows the hierarchical structure of the program and indicates the main dependencies of one program unit on another. These dependencies have consequences both for the order in which program units may be compiled, and for the order in which they can be tested. In order to see these dependencies in

more detail, the above diagram can be redrawn to show the package specification
and bodies as separate units. This is shown in Fig. 11.2.

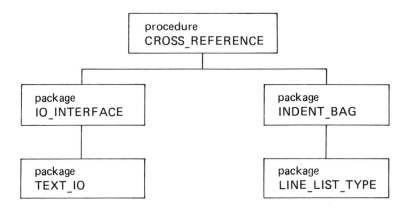

Fig. 11.1 – Structure of Cross Reference Program

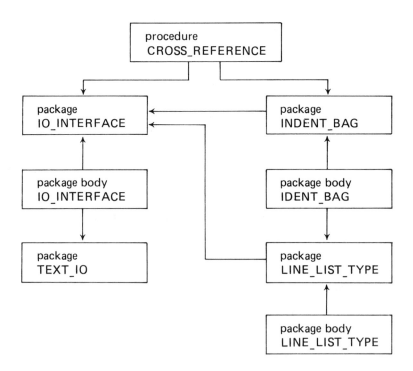

Fig. 11.2 – Detailed Structure of Cross Reference Program

The arrows in this revised diagram now correspond to the dependencies of one unit on another arising out of the implicit dependencies of a package body on its corresponding specification and the explicit dependencies introduced by **with** clauses.

The rules stated in section 9.4 concerning compilation order may now be fully appreciated. In order to compile any unit, all units on which it depends must have already been compiled. Thus, for example, the specification of LINE_ LIST_TYPE depends on the specification of IO_INTERFACE but on no others. Therefore, this unit can be compiled at any time after the specification of IO_INTERFACE. Taking this required partial ordering into account, a sensible order of compilation might be

1.   IO_INTERFACE   (spec)
2.   IO_INTERFACE   (body)
3.   LINE LIST_TYPE   (spec)
4.   LINE_LIST_TYPE   (body)
5.   IDENT_BAG   (spec)
6.   IDENT_BAG   (body)
7.   CROSS_REFERENCE

The same partial ordering rules also determine the order in which program components should be tested. A great advantage of the package concept is that it allows programs to be tested and built incrementally. Thus, the components of the above program should be tested and installed in the following order

1.   IO_INTERFACE
2.   LINE_LIST_TYPE
3.   IDENT_BAG
4.   CROSS_REFERENCE

At each stage, a test program is written to exercise the component currently being commissioned. When that component is working satisfactorily, it can be installed and used by subsequent components. The protection offered by packages to their inner components ensures that when a fault is detected at any stage, then the fault must lie in the component currently being tested. No matter how erroneous a component is, it cannot corrupt the operation of previously tested and installed components. Hence, the package construct of Ada is not only a powerful design tool, but also a vital requirement for methodical program testing.

Finally, it should be noted again that well-structured Ada programs are textually much longer than might be the case in other languages. For example, the cross reference program given here could be condensed by removing all the packages and implementing everything using procedures nested within the main procedure. This would, however, severely limit the use of the design methodology of data abstraction and the capability for incremental testing. For the construction of large programs both of these are considered vital and so the apparent verbosity of Ada is entirely justified.

11.9 EXERCISES

(11.1) The following package specification defines a buffer for storing messages

> **with** MESSAGE_TYPE; **use** MESSAGE_TYPE;
>
> **package** BUFFER **is**
>> **subtype** PRIORITY **is** INTEGER **range** 0 . . 6;
>>
>> **procedure** SEND(M: **in** MESSAGE; P: **in** PRIORITY);
>> **procedure** RECEIVE(M: **out** MESSAGE);
>
> **end** BUFFER;

Each message is placed in the buffer by a call to SEND and messages are extracted from the buffer by calls to RECEIVE. Each message placed in the buffer has a priority in the range 0 (lowest) to 6 (highest). Messages of the same priority are stored in a first-in first-out order with messages of a higher priority stored ahead of those with lower priority. Thus the sequence of messages MA to ME, sent in the order

MA(1)   MB(1)   MC(2)   MD(1)   ME(2)

with the priorities shown in brackets, would be received in the order

MC   ME   MA   MB   MD

with the higher priority messages 'jumping the queue' above the lower priority messages.
Implement the body of the package BUFFER.

(11.2) Redesign the body of the NETWORK_MANAGER package given in section 8.11 so that each node is represented by a dynamically allocated record with inter-node links represented by access types.

(11.3) In a natural language processing system, the syntactic structure of an input sentence is represented by a *phrase marker*. This is a multi-way tree structure with each node of the tree containing a syntactic symbol denoting the syntactic category of the phrase which it dominates, that is,

> **type** SYN_CAT **is** (SENTENCE,CLAUSE,ADJECTIVE,NOUN,
>   VERB,AUX,DET,NOUN_PHRASE,VERB_PHRASE, ...);

Any node of the tree may have any number of branches, so a typical structure might be

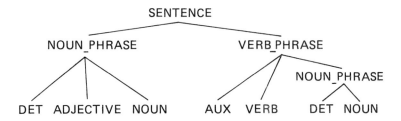

which corresponds to sentences such as 'The brown fox is eating the chicken'. Design a data structure for representing such a parse tree using access types.

12

Tasks

12.1 THE CONCEPT OF CONCURRENCY

Most traditional programming languages such as Fortran, Algol, Pascal, etc., allow only purely sequential programs to be written. In a sequential program, each statement is executed in sequence one-by-one. If a snapshot of such a program is taken at any point in its execution, there will be one and only one statement currently being executed. Technically it may be stated that there is a single *thread of control*.

. In many applications, especially in the real time area, the ability to create several threads of control is extremely useful. Each individual thread then represents a sequence of activities which is being executed concurrently (that is, in parallel) with each of the other threads. A program which contains more than one thread of control is called a *concurrent program*. If a snapshot of such a program is taken at any point in its execution, there may be several statements being executed simultaneously (though as a special case, there may be just one).

In Ada, each additional thread in a concurrent program is introduced by a special kind of program unit called a task. Before describing tasks in detail, a simple example will be developed to illustrate the differences between a sequential program and a concurrent program and to demonstrate the usefulness of concurrency in certain kinds of application.

Suppose that a computer is connected to a number of terminals numbered 1,2,3,... etc. When a user presses a key on the keyboard of any terminal, he expects to see the character that he types reflected on the screen. In practice, the keyboard and screen of a terminal are not connected directly together. Hence when the computer receives a character from the keyboard, it must immediately send it back to the terminal to display it on the screen (note that the advantage of this system is that the user is given confirmation that the character he typed was actually received by the computer). Suppose therefore that a program is to be written to perform this task of reflecting characters typed at each terminal. If the read and write operations are denoted by procedure calls, characters may be reflected for a single terminal, say terminal 1, using a simple loop, that is,

```
     procedure REFLECT1 is
        CH:CHARACTER;
     begin
        loop
            READ(1,CH);          - - read keyboard of terminal 1
            WRITE(1,CH);         - - write char back to screen 1
        end loop;
     end REFLECT;
```

It is assumed here that when the call to READ is made, the program will wait until the user of terminal 1 actually presses a key. This is important, because if the program is now extended to service several terminals, a problem arises. It is not known, in advance, the order in which users will press the keys on their terminals. So what order should the READ requests be issued? Certainly the following will not work:

```
     procedure REFLECT2 is
        CH:CHARACTER;
     begin
        loop
            READ(1,CH);          - - read keyboard of terminal 1
            WRITE(1,CH);         - - write char back to screen 1
            - -
            READ(2,CH);          - - read keyboard of terminal 2
            WRITE(2,CH);         - - write char back to screen 2
            - -
            - - etc.
            - -
        end loop;
     end REFLECT2;
```

When the user of terminal 2 presses a key, he must wait for the user of terminal 1 to press a key before his character can be read and then reflected. But what if terminal 1 is not being used? If that was the case then terminal 2 could not be used either, in fact, neither could any of the other terminals. Clearly, the program is useless!

In order to overcome the problem of not knowing the order in which keys will be pressed on the terminals and still retain a purely sequential program structure, a Boolean function READY(N) is needed to test whether or not a key has been pressed on terminal N. Given this function, a workable program can be constructed as follows

```
procedure REFLECT3 is
   CH:CHARACTER;
begin
   loop
       if READY(1) then      - - ok to read terminal 1
          READ(1,CH);
          WRITE(1,CH);
       end if;
       if READY(2) then      - - ok to read terminal 2
          READ(2,CH);
          WRITE(2,CH);
       end if;
       - -
       - - etc.
       - -
   end loop;
end REFLECT3;
```

This form of the REFLECT program uses a method called *polling*. Each terminal is polled in turn, to see whether or not it has a character waiting to be read before the program actually commits itself to reading a character from that terminal. Polling is the only option open in purely sequential programs for handling asynchronous events such as keys being pressed in a random order on a number of terminals. It is, however, a very limited technique for all but the most trivial of applications. Firstly, it wastes a great deal of processing power, since most of the time is spent polling (that is, calling READY in the above example) rather than doing useful work. Secondly, as programs get larger their overall structure becomes distorted by the control statements needed to sequence each of the distinct activities.

In fact, the necessity for polling only arises because a single sequential program is being used to respond to several different asynchronous and un-related events. In Ada, therefore, a much more appropriate solution to the above problem is possible by using tasks. A distinct task is created to service each individual terminal, independently of what is happening to the other terminals. In outline, the Ada solution would be

```
task TERMINAL1;

task body TERMINAL1 is
   CH:CHARACTER;
begin
   loop
       READ(1,CH);WRITE(1,CH);
   end loop;
end TERMINAL1;
```

```
task TERMINAL2;
task body TERMINAL2 is
    CH:CHARACTER;
begin
    loop
        READ(2,CH); WRITE(2,CH);
    end loop;
end TERMINAL2;

-- etc.
```

Each task represents a separate thread of control. The sequence of statements in each task body are executed concurrently with those of the other tasks. If there is nobody using terminal 1, for example, then the TERMINAL1 task will simply wait at the READ procedure indefinitely. The user of terminal 2, however, is now unaffected by this, since his terminal is being serviced by a separate and distinct task (TERMINAL2) which executes its statements independently of all other tasks.

The operation of the two approaches to the solution of the terminals problem is illustrated pictorially in Fig. 12.1. The sequential version consists of a single thread of control, whereas the concurrent version consists of several threads of control.

(a) Sequential

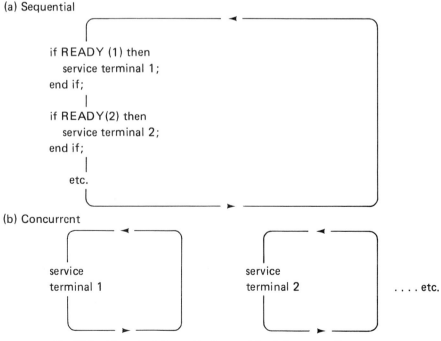

(b) Concurrent

Fig. 12.1 – Threads of Control in Sequential and Concurrent Programs

The above simple example, whilst not being particularly realistic, is nevertheless indicative of the types of problem which must be faced in real time programming. When any computer system is interfaced to the real world in such a way that it must respond to a variety of unpredictable external events, then the simplest and most natural solution to the design of its software is to represent the various distinct functions to be performed as tasks. Thus, concurrent programs are an essential feature of real time programming (and also many systems programming areas such as operating systems). Although Ada was designed specifically to support real time programming, its tasking facilities are not limited to this area. Many experts now believe that there are many other areas where the concurrent approach to program design can be usefully employed. For example, many data processing functions can be performed by constructing a *pipeline* of tasks where each task performs a single transformation of the input. By this means, complex operations can be broken down into a sequence of very simple operations. An extra bonus of this approach is that programs written in this way will be able to take full advantage of future multi-processor computing hardware without a radical redesign of the software.

Having mentioned multi-processors, it may be as well to make some comments on how tasks are implemented. Most current computing systems only have a single processor. On such systems, tasks are implemented by time-sharing the processor amongst each of the tasks. Thus, tasks do not actually execute in parallel, but instead their execution is interleaved. Of course, if several processors are available then tasks can be executed truly in parallel. The important point, however, is that regardless of the underlying implementation, tasks are always conceptually executed in parallel. The correctness of a concurrent program must never depend on any assumptions being made about the implementation.

The 'terminals' example given above is very simple and unrealistic in the sense that in practical programs tasks rarely operate in total isolation of each other, but interact both to synchronise their activities and to communicate with each other. Furthermore, it is often useful to be able to create and dispose of tasks dynamically as a program proceeds. The remaining sections of this chapter explain how this is done in Ada by examining its tasking facilities in some detail.

12.2 TASK DECLARATIONS

A task must be declared within the declarative part of some enclosing program unit or block, that is, within a package, subprogram, declare statement or another task. Tasks may not be declared at the outermost level of a program, that is, tasks cannot be compilation units.

The structure of a task is very similar to that of a package. There is a specification part and a corresponding body as shown by the following syntax diagrams:

S114 task_declaration

————————————————▶ task_specification ————————————————▶

S115 task_specification

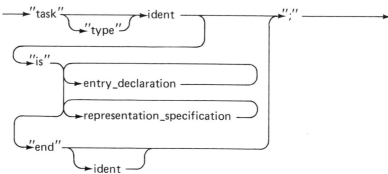

S116 task_body

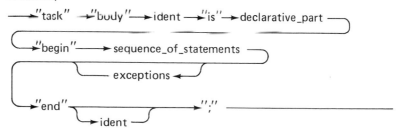

The task specification names the task and optionally declares one or more entries for that task (for the time being, ignore the optional keyword **type**). An entry is a special kind of procedure call which is used to program interactions between tasks. They are described in later sections. A task specification may also contain representation specifications, but these will not be discussed here but are left until Chapter 17. The body of a task has the same form as that of a package. Following the heading is a declarative part in which local entities needed by the task can be declared, followed by a statement part which defines the actions to be performed by the task.

As a very simple example of using a task, suppose that a procedure is required to calculate the sum and difference of two integer vectors defined by

type VECTOR **is array**(1 .. 1000)**of** INTEGER;

The procedure could be designed to use a task to calculate the difference while it calculated the sum in parallel, that is,

procedure SUMDIF(A,B: **in** VECTOR; SUM: **out** VECTOR;
                                    DIF: **out** VECTOR) **is**

    task MINUS;

    task body MINUS **is**

```
begin
    for I in 1 . . 1000 loop
        DIFF(I) := A(I) - B(I);
    end loop;
end MINUS;

begin
    for I in 1 . . 1000 loop
        SUM(I) := A(I) + B(I);
    end loop;
end SUMDIF;
```

This formulation of SUMDIF could (if implemented on multi-processor hardware) execute faster than a purely sequential version, since the sums and differences are computed in parallel. The point of this example, however, is not to demonstrate the potential speed advantages of multi-processing, but to illustrate the main ideas of task creation and termination.

When the procedure SUMDIF is called, its local declarations are elaborated. The elaboration of the task specification simply establishes the name MINUS as denoting a task. The elaboration of the task body involves first of all elaborating any local declarations of the task (in this case there are none) and then establishing the statement part of the task as being the definition of what it does. At some point between elaborating the task and executing the first statement of SUMDIF, the task starts executing. The wording is important here. What it means is that if SUMDIF had declared several tasks, then the order in which they would start executing is not defined. It is guaranteed, however, that on completing the elaboration of SUMDIF's declarative part, all tasks within it will have started executing.

A call to SUMDIF, therefore, generates an additional thread of control. Whilst the statement body of SUMDIF is being executed, the statement body of MINUS is executed in parallel.

A subprogram, task or declare statement which declares one or more tasks in its declarative part is called a *parent* and the tasks that it declares are its *offspring*. Thus, in the above, SUMDIF is a parent and MINUS is its offspring. A task terminates normally when it reaches the end of its statement sequence. In order for a parent to terminate, however, all of its offspring must have terminated. If a parent reaches the end of its own statement sequence before all of its offspring have terminated, then it will wait until they have. Hence in the example, it does not matter whether SUMDIF or MINUS completes its statement sequence first. SUMDIF will only terminate and return to its caller when it has reached its end and MINUS has terminated.

These rules on the creation and termination of tasks ensure that the number of threads of control active before the execution of a subprogram, declare statement or task is always the same after it terminates.

When a task is declared within a package, however, the situation is rather different. A package cannot be a parent. If the package is declared within a subprogram, declare statement or task, then that unit or block is considered to be the parent and the normal rules of termination then apply. The reason for this rule is that packages are essentially passive constructs used for program structuring. It would not be reasonable to prevent a package body from terminating until any tasks that it had declared had terminated. As an example, consider the following program outline,

```
procedure P is
    package Q is
        - -
    end Q;
    package body Q is
        task T;
        task body T is
            - -
        end T;
    begin
        - - initialise Q
    end Q;
begin
    - -
end P;
```

When the body of package Q is elaborated, the task T starts executing and the initialisation statements of Q are executed. When the latter are completed, control transfers to the body of P whether or not task T has terminated, because P is the parent of T not Q. Before P can terminate, however, the task T must have terminated. Note here that nested package declarations do not affect the relation between a task and its parent. For example, if the previous program outline was rewritten with the task T declared in a package R declared within Q, that is,

```
procedure P is
    package Q is
        - -
    end Q;
    package body Q is
        package R is
            - -
        end R;
```

```
package body R is
    task T;
    task body T is
        - -
    end T;
end R;
begin
    - - initialise Q
end Q;
begin
    - -
end P;
```

then the procedure P is still the parent of task T. In other words, the parent of any task is the innermost enclosing subprogram, task or declare statement, regardless of any intervening packages.

All tasks which have a parent are said to be *dependent* tasks. When a program in which all tasks are dependent is first started, there is just one thread of control. Additional threads are then created as and when further task declarations are elaborated. However, no matter how many new threads of control are created, the rules on termination ensure that before the main program can terminate there will be just one thread of control left, that is, the main program itself. Thus, if a concurrent program is being written which is designed to have a finite execution time (for example, a compiler, a file transfer program, etc.), then all tasks should be dependent to ensure an orderly termination.

It is also possible to declare tasks immediately within library packages. Such tasks, therefore, are *independent* since clearly they have no parent. The language rules do not state how a program which includes independent tasks terminates. Hence, a program which has a finite execution time should, if possible, avoid declaring independent tasks, since the termination of such a program will depend on individual Ada implementations and may involve something as crude as just switching off the power. Independent tasks are of most use in non-stop real time systems, where the program is expected to run continuously for days, weeks or even years. In such applications, termination is an abnormal rather than normal event and so it can be justifiably treated as an error case and the failure/abort operations used if necessary (see section 12.12).

12.3 TASK COMMUNICATION AND THE RENDEZVOUS

In the example given in the previous section, the task MINUS communicated with its parent by reading and writing to the parameters of SUMDIF directly. This form of communication via *shared variables* is not a generally useful technique. In the case of SUMDIF, it works only because neither SUMDIF nor

MINUS attempt to change the data that the other is reading. To see why communication between tasks using shared variables is not generally useful, consider a very simple example.

Suppose that there are two tasks, one called PRODUCER and one called CONSUMER. The PRODUCER generates a stream of characters which are passed one-by-one to the CONSUMER. For example, the PRODUCER may be reading a text file stored on disc, and the CONSUMER may be formatting it and printing it on a line printer. The exact functions of the PRODUCER and CONSUMER are not relevant here; the only concern is the method by which information can be transferred between them. At first sight, it may appear that the transmission of characters from the PRODUCER to the CONSUMER can be simply achieved by using a shared variable, that is,

```
SHARED_CH:CHARACTER;     - - Shared Variable

- -

task PRODUCER;                   - - Producer Specification
task body PRODUCER is            - - Producer Body
    C:CHARACTER;
begin
    loop
        PRODUCE(C);              - - produce a character and then
        SHARED_CH:=C;            - - write it into shared variable
    end loop;
end PRODUCER;

- -

task CONSUMER;                   - - Consumer Specification
task body CONSUMER is            - - Consumer Body
    C:CHARACTER;
begin
    loop
        C:=SHARED_CH;            - - read in character from shared
        CONSUME(C);              - - variable and then consume it
    end loop;
end CONSUMER;
```

where the procedures PRODUCE and CONSUME represent the actions of producing and consuming a character, respectively. This outline program will not work satisfactorily for two reasons. Firstly, the relative execution speeds of the two tasks are not known, so it is not possible to guarantee that the CONSUMER will read the shared variable SHARED_CH at the same rate that the PRODUCER writes to it. For example, if CONSUMER is faster than the PRODUCER, it may read the same character several times before the PRODUCER updates it with a new value. Conversely, if the CONSUMER is slower than the PRODUCER then it may miss out characters and only, for example, read every third one. This problem is called the *synchronisation problem*. Secondly, the PRODUCER may attempt to write a new value into CH at exactly the same time as the CONSUMER is reading it, with unpredictable results. This is called the *mutual exclusion problem*. Concurrently executing tasks must only access shared data in a mutually exclusive fashion otherwise the integrity of the shared data cannot be guaranteed.

These problems of synchronisation and mutual exclusion are well known to the designers of concurrent programs, and over the years a number of solutions have been developed. Ada has a very novel approach to the problem, which combines synchronisation and mutual exclusion into a single mechanism called a *rendezvous*. The basic idea of the rendezvous will now be described.

In Ada, the proper way for two tasks to exchange information with each other is not by reading and writing to shared memory areas, but by performing a rendezvous. This involves one task which is named the *caller* calling an *entry* defined by some other task which is called the *server*. An entry is similar to a procedure, but has certain special properties. The server task need not respond to an entry call immediately (in which case the caller is made to wait), but eventually it will acknowledge it by executing an **accept** statement. An **accept** statement is similar to a procedure body and defines what actions are to be performed as a result of the entry call. When the caller has made the entry call and the server has accepted the call by starting the execution of the corresponding **accept** statement, then both tasks are synchronised together. It is at this point that the rendezvous begins. Data may be transferred from the caller to the server tasks via parameters which may be included in the entry call. This data may be processed by the statements within the body of the **accept** statement and, where appropriate, results computed and returned to the caller, again via the entry parameters. Whilst the **accept** statement is being executed by the server, the caller task just waits. When the execution of the **accept** statement is completed, then the rendezvous is broken and both tasks proceed again independently of each other.

Thus the rendezvous mechanism allows data to be transferred between two tasks safely by ensuring that both tasks are locked together before the transfer can take place. It therefore provides both task synchronisation and, because a server can only rendezvous with one caller at a time, mutual exclusion.

The structure of a server task is similar to a package. Its specification includes the declarations for all the entries which it provides, and its body contains **accept** statements which define what those entries do.

In order to illustrate how the rendezvous works in practice, consider again the producer/consumer problem. A safe way to transfer characters between the two tasks is to introduce a third task which implements a simple single character buffer. The specification of this task is as follows

```
task BUFFER is
    entry PUT(C: in CHARACTER);
    entry GET(C: out CHARACTER);
end BUFFER;
```

This specification says that the task BUFFER provides two entries. PUT may be called to put a character into the buffer, and GET may be called to get a character from the buffer. Notice that the entry parameters are specified in the same way as procedures. Given this buffering task, the PRODUCER and CONSUMER tasks can now be rewritten as follows

```
task PRODUCER;

task body PRODUCER is
    C:CHARACTER;
begin
    loop
        PRODUCE(C);
        BUFFER . PUT(C);
    end loop;
end PRODUCER;


task CONSUMER;

task body CONSUMER is
    C:CHARACTER;
begin
    loop
        BUFFER . GET(C);
        CONSUME(C);
    end loop;
end CONSUMER;
```

Thus the PRODUCER and CONSUMER tasks cycle endlessly, calling the entries PUT and GET within the BUFFER task. The implementation of the BUFFER task ensures that calls to PUT and GET are accepted in mutual exclusion (that is, one at a time) and strictly in sequence (PUT, GET, PUT, GET, ... etc.). In fact, the body of BUFFER is as follows

```
task body BUFFER is
    BUF:CHARACTER;
begin
    loop
        accept PUT(C: in CHARACTER) do
            BUF := C;
        end PUT;
```

```
            accept GET(C: out CHARACTER) do
               C := BUF;
            end GET;
         end loop;
      end BUFFER;
```

The variable BUF serves as a single character buffer. The statement part of the task consists of a single loop containing two **accept** statements in sequence.

The BUFFER task works in the following way. When it is first started, it immediately encounters the **accept** PUT statement. At this point it must wait until the PRODUCER calls the entry PUT to initiate a rendezvous. When this occurs, the actual parameter supplied by the entry call is copied into the corresponding formal parameter of the **accept** statement, and then the body of the **accept** statement is executed. This has the effect of copying the input character into the BUF variable. On completion of the **accept** statement, both the PRODUCER and the BUFFER proceed again independently. In this case, the latter immediately encounters the **accept** GET statement. It therefore waits until the CONSUMER calls the GET entry to initiate another rendezvous. This time the entry parameter is of mode **out**, so the body of the **accept** is executed immediately. This has the effect of copying the value of BUF into the formal parameter C. On completion of the rendezvous, the value of C is copied into the corresponding actual parameter, that is, its value is returned to the CONSUMER. Finally, the rendezvous is broken and both tasks proceed again independently.

It is important to realise that two events are necessary to initiate a rendezvous. Firstly, the caller must call the relevant entry, and secondly, the server must reach the corresponding **accept** statement. It does not, however, matter which event happens first. If the entry call occurs first, then the caller is made to wait until the server reaches the **accept** statement. If, on the other hand, the server reaches the **accept** statement first, then it is made to wait until the corresponding entry is called. Hence, in the producer/consumer example, the task BUFFER repeatedly executes an **accept** PUT statement followed by an **accept** GET statement. If the PRODUCER executes BUFFER.PUT before the BUFFER has reached the corresponding **accept** PUT statement, then the PRODUCER has to wait. Alternatively, if the BUFFER reaches the **accept** statement before the PRODUCER calls BUFFER.PUT, then the BUFFER has to wait; and similarly for the CONSUMER task. Thus, the BUFFER task uses the rendezvous mechanism to synchronise calls from the PRODUCER and CONSUMER tasks by alternately accepting the PUT entry followed by the GET entry. Because a rendezvous can only occur with one caller at a time, all accesses to the buffer variable BUF are guaranteed to be mutually exclusive. Therefore, data is transferred between the PRODUCER and CONSUMER safely and correctly.

12.4 ENTRIES AND ACCEPT STATEMENTS
The basic principle of the rendezvous mechanism having been explained, this

section gives the syntax diagrams relating to entries and **accept** statements and discusses the mechanism in more detail. Firstly, the syntax diagrams are as follows

S117 entry_declaration

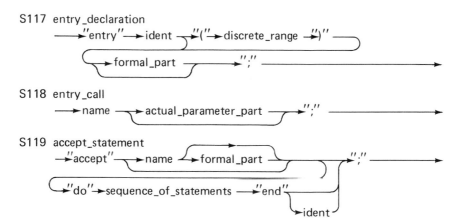

S118 entry_call

S119 accept_statement

An entry declaration may occur only in the specification part of a task. It consists of the keyword **entry** followed by the name of the entry. This is normally followed by a list of formal entry parameters. For example, the task specification for BUFFER given in the previous section, that is,

>   **task** BUFFER **is**
>   **entry** PUT(C: **in** CHARACTER);
>   **entry** GET(C: **out** CHARACTER);
>   **end** BUFFER;

declares two entries called PUT and GET each with a single parameter called C of type CHARACTER, but with modes **in** and **out**, respectively. Entry parameters may have the same modes as procedure parameters, that is, **in, out** or **in out** and exactly the same rules for parameter passing and the association of actual and formal parameters apply. Note at this point that a task specification may only include entry declarations. It may not include subprograms, types, constants, variables, etc., in the same way that a package can. Thus, apart from possible accesses to non-local shared variables, tasks may only communicate by making entry calls.

Accept statements have the form of a procedure body without a declarative part. The keyword **accept** is followed by the name of the entry to be accepted and the formal parameters, if any. The specification of the latter must match those given in the corresponding entry declaration exactly. Between the **do** and **end** of the **accept** statement are placed the statements to be executed during the rendezvous. If no actions are to be taken during the rendezvous then these statements can be omitted, that is,

> **accept** E;

is equivalent to

> **accept** E **do**
>   **null**;
> **end** E;

Accept statements may only appear in task bodies. There must be at least one **accept** statement corresponding to each entry declared for the task but there may be more.

The syntax of an entry call is the same as for a procedure call, for example,

> BUFFER.PUT('A');

is an entry call to store the character 'A' in the single character buffer provided by BUFFER. Named associations can be used as for subprograms, for example,

> BUFFER.PUT(C => 'A');

has the same effect as the previous call. The selected component notation is used to name the entry of a task in the same way that it is used to name the entities declared within the visible part of a package. However, the **use** clause cannot be used to make task entries directly visible. The only way to avoid having to give the full name of an entry is by renaming it as a procedure. For example, if within the PRODUCER task given previously, the renaming declaration

> **procedure** SEND(C: **in** CHARACTER) **renames** BUFFER.PUT;

was written, then a subsequent call

> SEND(CH);

would have the effect of calling the entry PUT in BUFFER just as though BUFFER.PUT(CH) had been written. It must be emphasised that, even though SEND is declared as a procedure, any call to SEND is an entry call and not a procedure call. Thus, renaming an entry does no more than introduce a synonym for the entry name. It should be noted also that entries may be overloaded, both with each other and with procedures with the same identifier.

The actual parameters supplied in an entry call are evaluated before entering the rendezvous. This means that entry parameters are not evaluated in mutual exclusion. Normally this makes no difference, but care needs to be taken if a variable which is shared between two tasks is named by both tasks simultaneously in the same entry call. For example, consider the following

> COUNT:INTEGER **range** 0 .. INTEGER'LAST := 0;

> **task** INC **is**
>   **entry** UPDATE(C: **in out** INTEGER);
> **end** INC;

```
task body INC is
begin
    loop
        accept UPDATE(C: in out INTEGER) do
            C := C+1;
        end UPDATE;
    end loop;
end INC;

--

task ONE; task TWO;

task body ONE is
begin
    loop
        --
        INC . UPDATE(COUNT);
        --
    end loop;
end ONE;

task body TWO is
begin
    loop
        --
        INC . UPDATE(COUNT);
        --
    end loop;
end TWO;
```

The shared variable COUNT is used to count the total number of cycles performed by a group of tasks represented in this case by ONE and TWO. The
server task INC is intended to ensure that COUNT is always updated in mutual
exclusion. In fact, however, the program does not work properly. To see why,
suppose that both ONE and TWO call UPDATE simultaneously. The actual
parameters supplied in each case are evaluated immediately, that is, the current
value of COUNT is computed, say this is 4. Suppose that task ONE is then
allowed to proceed to rendezvous with INC. This will have the effect of updating
COUNT to 5, as intended. However, when task TWO subsequently performs its
rendezvous with INC, it still believes that the current value of COUNT is 4 so
COUNT gets updated to 5 again. Of course, COUNT should by this time be
equal to 6. This is another case where the use of shared variables leads to problems. A much better approach is to make COUNT local to the task INC instead
of being passed into it as a parameter, that is,

```
task INC is
    entry UPDATE;
end INC;

task body INC is
    COUNT:INTEGER range 0 .. INTEGER'LAST := 0;
begin
    loop
        accept UPDATE do
            COUNT := COUNT+1;
        end UPDATE;
    end loop;
end INC;
```

The variable COUNT is now protected within the task INC, and all calls to UPDATE are registered properly. One slight disadvantage of this second solution is that it provides a single counter only, unlike the first where any number of count variables could be declared. In fact this is easy to rectify, since Ada allows the task INC to be replicated as many times as required (see section 12.9).

Another point illustrated by this example is that several tasks may call the same entry simultaneously. Associated with every entry declared within a server task is a queue. When several tasks call the same entry, each entry call is placed in its associated queue and the calling task is suspended. Each time that the server task reaches an **accept** statement, then a pending call is removed from the entry queue, and a rendezvous occurs with the task that made the call.

As another example of where the ability is required to queue several tasks all calling the same entry, suppose that in a particular program a number of tasks need to share the use of a line-printer. In order to ensure that the outputs from each task are not mixed-up, it is necessary to provide some mechanism which allows a task to gain exclusive access to the line-printer. Such a mechanism can be provided by a task with the following specification

```
task LP_CONTROL is
    entry SECURE;
    entry RELEASE;
end LP_CONTROL;
```

This task allows users of the line-printer to ensure that they get mutually exclusive access to it, by bracketing their output operations with calls to SECURE and RELEASE, for example,

```
- - body of user task
- -
LP_CONTROL . SECURE;
- -
- - output information to
- - line printer
```

```
- -
LP_CONTROL.RELEASE;
- -
- - line printer now available
- - other users
- -
```

The body of LP_CONTROL is a simple loop just like the BUFFER task given earlier, that is,

```
task body LP_CONTROL is
begin
    loop
        accept SECURE;
        accept RELEASE;
    end loop;
end LP_CONTROL;
```

Notice first that the entries SECURE and RELEASE are parameterless. They are called simply for their synchronising effect. Hence the corresponding **accept** statements in the task body have no statement bodies.

To understand how LP_CONTROL works, suppose that initially three tasks simultaneously call SECURE to gain exclusive access to the line-printer. Only one of these calls will succeed immediately, and the remaining two tasks will be placed in the queue associated with the SECURE entry. Following the execution of the **accept** SECURE statement, the LP_CONTROL task proceeds immediately to the **accept** RELEASE statement. Here it must now wait until the task that is currently using the line-printer releases its exclusive access by calling RELEASE. When it does this, LP_CONTROL will loop back to execute the **accept** SECURE statement again, taking the first task waiting in the entry queue for SECURE as its partner in the rendezvous. That task can then proceed to use the line-printer as before and so the process continues. If at any time the entry queue for SECURE becomes empty then the LP_CONTROL task will be left waiting at the **accept** SECURE statement until a new task comes along to call SECURE.

There are three further points to note about this example. Firstly, LP_CONTROL relies entirely on the cooperation of its users for properly controlling accesses to the line-printer. If any task chooses to disobey the established protocol, that is, that each call to SECURE must be followed by a call to RELEASE, then the mechanism fails. Also, there is no way of checking that the task which calls RELEASE is the one which previously called SECURE. For example, an unscrupulous task could execute

```
LP_CONTROL.RELEASE;
LP_CONTROL.SECURE;
- -
- - use line-printer illegally
```

to gain premature access to the line-printer or even, of course, simply ignore SECURE and RELEASE altogether.

Secondly, once created, LP_CONTROL will execute forever. Therefore, any task which creates LP_CONTROL as one of its offspring will never be able to terminate. In fact, it is possible to abort a task and so get round this problem, but such extreme action is generally undesirable (see section 12.12). An alternative formulation of the LP_CONTROL task allows a more graceful termination, and this is explained later in section 12.6.

Thirdly, the language specifies that entry calls which have to be queued are serviced in the order in which they arrive (that is, entry queues are first-in/first-out). Thus, no special action needs to be taken to ensure that all tasks which request the use of the line-printer are treated fairly.

It should also be noted from syntax diagram S117 that an entry declaration can include a discrete range immediately after the entry name. This notation is used to denote a *family* of entries which may be thought of as a one-dimensional array of entries each with the identical parameter specifications. The use of families of entries is described later in section 12.8.

12.5 NON-DETERMINISM AND THE SELECT STATEMENT

In all of the examples of server tasks given so far the sequence in which **accept** statements are executed has been entirely deterministic. In both the BUFFER task and the LP_CONTROL task, entry calls are accepted in a predetermined order. Indeed, this sequencing of entry calls is a basic requirement of their operation. In many applications, however, a server task must accept entry calls in an order which depends on the order in which the calls are actually made.

As an example, suppose that a clock task wishes to keep a copy of the current time, in a variable which is accessible to all other tasks in the system. The clock task will update the value of this variable at regular intervals, and in between any number of other tasks may read the value of the variable to find out what time it is. As noted previously, the direct use of a shared variable leads to problems. In this case, there are no synchronisation constraints on the order in which read and writes to the variable are allowed, but all accesses should be made in mutual exclusion. One solution to the problem is to encapsulate the shared time variable in a task whose sole purpose is to ensure that accesses to it are made in mutual exclusion. The specification of such a task might be

> **task** PROTECTED_TIME **is**
>   **entry** READ(T: **out** TIME);
>   **entry** WRITE(T: **in** TIME);
> **end** PROTECTED_TIME;

The protected time variable may be written to by a call to WRITE and its value read by a call to READ. The function of PROTECTED_TIME is thus similar to

the BUFFER task given earlier, but with one important difference: the PRO-
TECTED_TIME task must not constrain the order in which calls to READ and
WRITE are accepted.

In order to implement the PROTECTED_TIME task, an extra mechanism
is needed which provides some means of selecting from a number of possible
accept statements, depending on which entry is actually called first. This mechanism is provided in Ada by the **select** statement, whose syntax is as follows

S120 select_statement

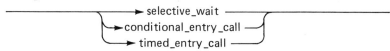

As can be seen there are three varieties of select statement. The selective wait
may only be used by server tasks, and the conditional and timed entry calls may
only be used by caller tasks. In this section only the selective wait will be considered. Its syntax is as follows

S121 selective_wait

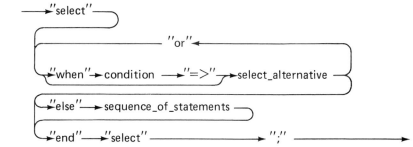

S122 select_alternative

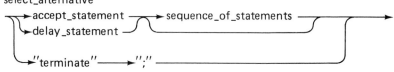

Inspection of these syntax diagrams shows that there are a variety of optional
forms that the selective wait statement may take. However, the basic form is

> **select**
>   **when** B1 => **accept** E1 ... ;
> **or**
>   **when** B2 => **accept** E2 ... ;
> **or**
>
>   . . .

or
    when Bn => **accept** En ... ;
end select;

The selective wait statement in this basic form consists of a sequence of alternative **accept** statements. Each accept is preceded by a **when** condition which is called a *guard*. The effect of executing the above statement is as follows:

(1) Each of the n guard conditions from B1 to Bn are evaluated. Each guard whose condition evaluates to TRUE is said to be *open*.

(2) From the set of open **accept** statements for which an entry call is pending, one **accept** statement is selected at random. This **accept** statement is executed in the normal way (that is, a rendezvous occurs with the calling task). When the execution of the **accept** statement is complete, then the selective wait statement terminates.

(3) If there are no entry calls pending for any of the open **accept** statements, then the task owning the selective wait statement simply waits until such a call does occur. Note that the guards in a selective wait statement are never re-evaluated. Hence, if a guard changes whilst the task is waiting within the selective wait statement, this will not affect the set of entry calls which may be accepted.

(4) If, when the guards are evaluated, all of them are found to be closed then a *program_error* occurs. This is a situation which the logic of the program must ensure will never arise.

The guard preceding any accept alternative may be omitted, in which case it is always considered to be open.

Given this basic form of the selective wait statement, the body of the PROTECTED_TIME task may be implemented as follows

```
        task body PROTECTED_TIME is
            TIME_NOW:TIME;
        begin
            loop
                select
                    accept READ(T: out TIME) do
                        T := TIME_NOW;
                    end READ;
                or
                    accept WRITE(T: in TIME) do
                        TIME_NOW := T;
                    end WRITE;
                end select;
            end loop;
        end PROTECTED_TIME;
```

Within the body of PROTECTED_TIME is a loop containing a single selective wait statement with two alternative permanently open **accept** statements. Each time this selective wait statement is executed, there are four possibilities to consider

(1) No calls are pending for either READ or WRITE
(2) A call is pending for WRITE but not READ
(3) A call is pending for READ but not WRITE
(4) Calls are pending for both READ and WRITE

For case (1), the PROTECTED_TIME task waits until a call is made to either READ or WRITE. For cases (2) and (3) the pending call is accepted by executing the appropriate select alternative. For case (4), one of the pending calls (that is, either READ or WRITE) is accepted by executing the appropriate select alternative. The decision as to which pending call to choose is taken at random. Hence, the PROTECTED_TIME task will accept entry calls without regard to their ordering, and its sole effect is to ensure that all accesses to TIME_NOW are mutually exclusive.

As mentioned in the previous section, a task body may contain several **accept** statements for the same entry. This possibility can be used to improve the design of the PROTECTED_TIME task, as follows:

```
task body PROTECTED_TIME is
    TIME_NOW:TIME;
begin
    accept WRITE(T:in TIME) do
        TIME_NOW := T;
    end WRITE;
    loop
        select
            accept READ(T:out TIME) do
                T := TIME_NOW;
            end READ;
        or
            accept WRITE(T:in TIME) do
                TIME_NOW := T;
            end WRITE;
        end select;
    end loop;
end PROTECTED_TIME;
```

Now the PROTECTED_TIME task must always start off by accepting a WRITE entry call. This ensures that no task can read the time before is has been initialised. Once the first call to WRITE has been accepted, however, subsequent calls can be accepted in any order. Note that, although a task may include local procedure declarations, it is not legal to include **accept** statements within them. **Accept** statements may only be given in the main body of the task which owns the corresponding entry. Hence in the above, the two identical **accept** WRITE statements must be written out in full each time. They cannot be replaced by a procedure call.

In order to illustrate the use of guards in the selective wait statement, the producer/consumer problem described earlier will be used again. In section 12.3, a single character BUFFER task was described to implement a communication channel between a PRODUCER task and a CONSUMER task. Although the single character buffer will work correctly, in many situations it is unsatisfactory because the speeds of the PRODUCER and CONSUMER are forced to be equal. Every time that the PRODUCER delivers a character to the buffer, it must wait for the CONSUMER to remove that character before it can deliver another. In most real applications, it is better to decouple the PRODUCER and CONSUMER tasks by providing a larger intervening buffer. Although the average speeds of the two tasks must still be equal, in the short term a larger buffer allows the instantaneous speeds of each task to fluctuate without affecting the other. For example, if the CONSUMER is printing lines of characters on a line-printer, it will be able to take characters rapidly from the buffer until the end of the line is reached, but would then have to pause whilst the line was printed. The buffer would prevent such pauses from slowing down the PRODUCER.

A suitable implementation of the required buffer uses a fixed length array called BUF as follows

```
BUF  : array(1 . . SIZE)of CHARACTER;
USED: INTEGER range 0 . . SIZE :=0;
INX,OUTX: INTEGER range 1 . . SIZE :=1;
```

The variable USED denotes the number of characters currently stored in the buffer. INX gives the index position of the next character to be inserted into the buffer, and OUTX gives the index position of the next character to be extracted from the buffer. After each insertion or extraction, the appropriate index is incremented by 1 modulo SIZE so that the array is effectively circular, for example, after inserting a character in BUF(SIZE) the next character would be inserted in BUF(1). This kind of buffer is usually referred to as a *bounded buffer*.

Using this bounded buffer, the task BUFFER may be re-formulated as follows

```
task body BUFFER is
     SIZE  :constant INTEGER := 64;
     BUF  : array(1 . . SIZE)of CHARACTER;
     USED: INTEGER range 0 . . SIZE :=0;
     INX,OUTX: INTEGER range 1 . . SIZE :=1;
```

```
begin
   loop
      select
         when USED<SIZE =>
            accept PUT(C:in CHARACTER) do
               BUF(INX) := C;
            end PUT;
            INX := (INX mod SIZE) + 1;
            USED := USED + 1;
      or
         when USED>0 =>
            accept GET(C:out CHARACTER) do
               C := BUF(OUTX);
            end GET;
            OUTX := (OUTX mod SIZE) + 1;
            USED := USED - 1;
      end select;
   end loop;
end BUFFER;
```

The local declarations within BUFFER declare the circular array and its associated index variables, initialised to denote an empty buffer. The statement body of BUFFER contains a single selective wait statement which is repeated indefinitely. This selective wait statement contains two guarded alternatives, one to accept calls to PUT and the other to accept entry calls to GET. Normally, the buffer is partially full and so both guards will be open. In this state, calls to both PUT and GET are accepted immediately. If, however, the buffer becomes empty (as is also the case initially) then the guard on GET is closed and so only a call to PUT will then be accepted. In other words, the CONSUMER is held up until the PRODUCER puts a character into the buffer. A similar mechanism operates when the buffer becomes full. This time the guard on PUT is closed so that only a call to GET will then be accepted and the PRODUCER is held up until the CONSUMER gets a character from the buffer.

As a final comment on this example, notice that when a GET or PUT rendezvous occurs, only the transfer of the entry call parameter to or from the appropriate component of BUF is actually performed within the body of the accept statement. The updating of USED and the relevant index variable is done immediately after the **accept** statement has terminated, that is, after the rendezvous has completed. Referring back to syntax diagram S122 it can be seen that this is quite legal. In general, it is good practice to minimise the extent of the rendezvous as far as possible. In this case, there is no need to hold up the calling task while the buffer indices are updated, so it is released immediately after the character has been transferred.

To close this section, the idea of a conditional rendezvous will be introduced. If syntax diagram S121 is inspected it can be seen that a selective wait statement may have an **else** part. Normally, when a selective wait statement is executed by a server task, that task is committing itself to performing a rendezvous. If at least one call is pending for an entry with an open guard, then that entry may be accepted immediately otherwise the server task must wait until such time as a call is made. This commitment to performing a rendezvous is not always convenient. The server task may wish to enter a rendezvous only if a caller is already waiting. To meet this need, the conditional form of the selective wait statement is provided in which an **else** part is included. If when a conditional selective wait statement is executed, no calls are currently pending to any of the accept alternatives with open guards, then the sequence of statements given in the **else** part is executed instead of a rendezvous. Note that, in the case of the conditional select statement, it is not an error to have all the guards closed. When such a situation arises, the statements of the **else** part are simply executed instead.

The conditional form of the selective wait statement allows a server task to test whether any callers are waiting to rendezvous without committing itself to a rendezvous if there are none. For example, if at some point in a server task an entry call to HELP should be accepted if and only if that call is pending, then a simple conditional selective wait statement can be used, that is,

```
select
    accept HELP  . . . .
      - -
    end HELP;
else
    null;
end select;
```

where the **else** part is a simple **null** statement.

In this section, the basic operation of the selective wait statement has been described. This statement is the major variant of the select statement. It is used only in server tasks, and allows entry calls to be accepted in a non-deterministic order. There are two additional facilities available with the selective wait statement which have not yet been described: a mechanism for programming timeouts, and a mechanism for terminating a server whose parent wishes to terminate. These are discussed in the next section. The other two variants of the select statement, that is, the conditional entry call and the timed entry call, are much less widely used and are only relevant to caller tasks. They are described in section 12.7.

12.6 DELAYS, TIME-OUTS AND TERMINATION

Any task can delay itself for a given period of time by executing a **delay** statement whose syntax is

```
S123  delay_statement
         ────►"delay"────► simple_expr ────► ";" ────────────────────►
```

The simple expression following the keyword **delay** must yield a value of the pre-defined fixed-point type DURATION, which denotes the duration of the required delay in seconds (see Chapter 16 for more information on fixed-point types). The actual range of values and the accuracy provided by the type DUR-ATION is implementation dependent, but the language description requires that at least a duration of one day (86400 seconds) must be representable.

As a simple example of the use of the delay statement, the following task will ring the bell of a terminal approximately once every minute:

```
        task RING_A_DING;

        task body RING_A_DING is
             PERIOD: constant DURATION := 60.0;
        begin
             loop
                  delay PERIOD;
                  RING_BELL;
             end loop;
        end RING_A_DING;
```

where the call to RING_BELL is assumed to ring the bell of a terminal.

The semantics of the **delay** statement are such that the actual delay will be at least that specified, but may be greater. Also, of course, the other statements in the loop take a finite time to execute. Thus, in the above formulation of RING_A_DING, the actual periods between successive calls to RING_BELL will vary, and will always be greater than the required one minute.

Although it is not possible to avoid these variations, it is possible to reduce them, and to avoid the accumulated error which occurs as a result. Every Ada implementation provides a pre-defined package called CALENDAR, whose specification is as follows:

```
        package CALENDAR is
             type TIME is private;

             subtype YEAR_NUMBER    is INTEGER    range 1901 .. 2099;
             subtype MONTH_NUMBER   is INTEGER    range 1 .. 12;
             subtype DAY_NUMBER     is INTEGER    range 1 .. 31;
             subtype DAY_DURATION   is DURATION   range 0.0 .. 86400.0;

             function CLOCK return TIME;
```

```
function YEAR      (DATE:TIME) return YEAR_NUMBER;
function MONTH     (DATE:TIME) return MONTH_NUMBER;
function DAY       (DATE:TIME) return DAY_NUMBER;
function SECONDS   (DATE:TIME) return DAY_DURATION;
-- rest of package defines conversions between a time and its external
-- YEAR, MONTH, DAY, SECONDS form and arithmetic and compare
-- operations for TIME objects.
```

end CALENDAR;

This package defines a type called TIME, some operations on TIME objects, and a function called CLOCK which can be used to find the current system time. Given this package, the task RING_A_DING can be reformulated so that in the long term it will average one ring per minute, that is, there will be no cumulative drift resulting from variations in each cycle delay:

```
task RING_A_DING;

task body RING_A_DING is
    PERIOD: constant DURATION := 60.0;
    use CALENDAR;
    NEXT_DUE:TIME := CLOCK+PERIOD;
begin
    loop
        delay NEXT_DUE - CLOCK;
        RING_BELL;
        NEXT_DUE := NEXT_DUE+PERIOD;
    end loop;
end RING_A_DING;
```

Each cycle around the loop, the period of delay actually needed is computed by subtracting the actual time as returned by the CLOCK function from the time when the next bell ring is due. Notice that, as well as eliminating any long term cumulative drift, this also compensates for the time taken to execute the other statements in the loop.

As shown by syntax diagram S122 given in the previous section, **delay** statements can also appear as select alternatives in a selective wait statement. This can be used to program time-outs on select operations. The basic form is

```
select
    accept E1 . . . .
or
    accept E2 . . . .
or
    delay T;
    sequence_of_statements
end select;
```

When the select statement is reached and there is at least one entry call pending for an open accept alternative, then a rendezvous takes place for that entry, as normal. If, however, there are no entry calls pending, and no calls arrive within the subsequent T seconds, then the delay alternative is selected. This causes the sequence of statements following the **delay** statement (if any) to be executed, and the execution of the selective wait statement is then terminated. If T is an expression, then its value is computed on entry to the selective wait at the same time as any guards are evaluated.

Thus the **delay** statement used in this way allows a server task to partially commit itself to making a rendezvous. On reaching the select statement, the server says that it is prepared to wait for upto T seconds for an entry call to occur. If one does occur in that period, then it is accepted as normal; if, however, the period expires, then the select statement is effectively aborted.

For example, suppose that a task called VITAL must signal that it is still operating normally by calling an entry OK at least once every 10 seconds. The entry OK could be declared in a task called WATCHDOG, as follows:

```
task WATCHDOG is
    entry OK;
end WATCHDOG;

task body WATCHDOG is
begin
    loop
        select
            accept OK;
        or
            delay 10.0;
            RING_BELL;
            PUT("VITAL is not Functioning");
        end select;
    end loop;
end WATCHDOG;
```

The task WATCHDOG repeatedly executes its selective wait statement. Each time that it does so, a call to OK must occur with 10 seconds otherwise the warning message following the **delay** statement is issued. Notice that, even after a time-out has occurred, the select statement is entered again and a new delay period begins. Thus, if the task VITAL is simply late in calling OK, the warning message will be given only once. If, on the other hand, VITAL has died, then WATCHDOG will issue a warning once every 10 seconds for as long as the program is allowed to run.

Finally, with regard to **delay** statements used as select alternatives, some rules should be noted. Firstly, any number of delay alternatives may be given in one selective wait statement; however, only the one with the shortest delay will have any effect, since this will time-out first. Secondly, a delay can be preceded by a guard in which case it is ignored if the guard is closed. Thirdly, a selective wait statement containing a delay alternative may not have an **else** part.

The one remaining feature shown in the syntax diagrams for the selective wait statement (S121 and S122 – section 12.5) which has yet to be described is the **terminate** alternative. Many of the server tasks described in preceding examples have consisted of endless loops. A typical example was the LP_CONTROL task described in section 12.4. As noted previously, non-terminating tasks cause difficulties in programs which need to terminate cleanly.

The **terminate** alternative allows a server task which operates in an endless cycle to terminate as soon as its parent reaches a position to terminate. For example, suppose that the following outline selective wait statement appears in the body of a task T whose parent P is a block, subprogram or task:

```
select
    accept X ...
or
    accept Y ...
or
    terminate;
end select;
```

When this statement is executed, its effect depends on whether or not the parent P is waiting to terminate or not. If it is not then T will wait until a call to X or Y occurs, at which point a rendezvous will ensue as normal. If, however, P is waiting to terminate, that is, has reached its own end (or, if P is a task, a terminate alternative has been reached within its own body) then the task T will not accept any further entry calls but will terminate immediately. This assumes that T does not have any offspring of its own. If it does, then they must all have terminated. Also, if P has any further offspring besides T, then they must also either have already terminated or be waiting at a selective wait statement containing a terminate alternative.

A **terminate** alternative may not occur within the same selective wait statement as a **delay** statement or an **else** part, nor may it be used within independent tasks, that is, one which has no parent (see section 12.2). A **terminate** alternative may be preceded by a guard in which case it is ignored if the guard is closed.

As a first example of the use of the terminate alternative, consider again the LP_CONTROL task. In order to let this task terminate when its parent wishes to terminate, the structure of the task must be altered to allow the inclusion of a selective wait statement. This can be done by replacing the previous deterministic sequencing of **accept** SECURE and **accept** RELEASE with a non-deterministic selective wait statement which uses a guard to ensure that SECURE is accepted only when the printer is free, that is,

```
task body LP_CONTROL is
    FREE: BOOLEAN := TRUE;
begin
    loop
        select
            when FREE =>
                accept SECURE;
                FREE:=FALSE;
        or
                accept RELEASE;
                FREE:=TRUE;
        or
            when FREE =>
                terminate;
        end select;
    end loop;
end LP_CONTROL;
```

This latest version of LP_CONTROL uses a Boolean flag to ensure that it will accept a call to SECURE only if the line printer is FREE. No guard is placed on RELEASE, since it does no harm to accept this call at any time. When the parent of LP_CONTROL wishes to terminate, then the **terminate** alternative of the selective wait statement will be selected. Note, however, that this alternative is guarded, to ensure that the task is not terminated while some other task is still using the line printer.

As a second example, the BUFFER task given in section 12.5 can be modified to allow it to terminate gracefully. Again it is a useful safety precaution to guard the **terminate** alternative, to ensure that the buffer is empty before the task may be terminated, that is, the selective wait statement within BUFFER is modified as follows

```
select
    when USED<SIZE =>
        accept PUT  . . . .
or
    when USED>0 =>
        accept GET  . . . .
or
    when USED=0 =>
        terminate;
end select;
```

To illustrate how this task could be used in an actual application, the following program will copy a text file stored on a cartridge tape onto a line printer. End of lines in the input text are marked by linefeed characters, and the end of the file is marked by an ETX character. To simplify the input/output, it will be assumed that the procedure call INCH will read the next character from the input file and the call PRINTS will print a string of characters, terminated by a linefeed character, on the line printer. The complete text of the copy program is as follows, where the I/O routines are defined in a library package called SIMPLE_IO:

```
with SIMPLE_IO;
procedure COPY is
        EOF: constant CHARACTER := ASCII.ETX;
        EOL: constant CHARACTER := ASCII.LF;
        LINE_LENGTH: constant := 132;

        CH:CHARACTER;

        task PRINTER;

        task BUFFER is
            entry PUT(C: in CHARACTER);
            entry GET(C: out CHARACTER);
        end BUFFER;

        task body PRINTER is separate;
        task body BUFFER is separate;

begin
    loop
        SIMPLE_IO.INCH(CH);
        BUFFER.PUT(CH);
        exit when CH=EOF;
    end loop;
end COPY;
- - - - - - - - - - - - - - - - - - - - - - - - - - - - - - - - - - - -
separate(COPY)
task body PRINTER is
    subtype LINE_INDEX is INTEGER range 0 .. LINE_LENGTH;
    CH:CHARACTER;
    LINE:STRING(1 .. LINE_LENGTH);
    LINE_IDX:LINE_INDEX := 0;
begin
    loop
        BUFFER.GET(CH);
        exit when CH=EOF;
```

```
            LINE_IDX := LINE_IDX+1;
            LINE(LINE_IDX) := CH;
            - - print line if EOL character or a full line
            if CH=EOL or LINE_IDX=LINE_LENGTH then
               SIMPLE_IO . PRINTS(LINE);
               LINE_IDX := 0;
            end if;
         end loop;
         - - last line may not have an EOL character after it
         if LINE_IDX>0 then
            LINE(LINE_IDX+1) := EOL;
            SIMPLE_IO . PRINTS(LINE);
         end if;
      end PRINTER;
- - - - - - - - - - - - - -     - - - - - - - - - - - - - - - - - - - - - -
separate(COPY)
task body BUFFER is
      SIZE  : constant INTEGER := 256;
      BUF   : array(1 . . SIZE)of CHARACTER;
      USED: INTEGER range 0 . . SIZE := 0;
      INX,OUTX: INTEGER range 1 . . SIZE :=1;
begin
      loop
         select
            when USED<SIZE =>
               accept PUT(C: in CHARACTER) do
                  BUF(INX) := C;
               end PUT;
               INX := (INX mod SIZE) + 1;
               USED := USED + 1;
         or
            when USED>0 =>
               accept GET(C: out CHARACTER) do
                  C := BUF(OUTX);
               end GET;
               OUTX := (OUTX mod SIZE) + 1;
               USED := USED - 1;
         or
            when USED=0 =>
               terminate;
         end select;
      end loop;
end BUFFER;
```

This copy program is an example of the producer/consumer structure mentioned at the start of the chapter. It is built from three separately compiled units. The COPY procedure itself implements the producer task, and includes declarations for the BUFFER task and the PRINTER task (which is the consumer). The actual bodies of these last two tasks are compiled separately as sub-units (remember that a task can be a sub-unit even though it cannot be a library unit). The actual operation of the program is quite straightforward but what is of more interest here is the way that it terminates.

When COPY is called, the tasks BUFFER and PRINTER start executing and then COPY starts executing its statement sequence in parallel. COPY reaches its end as soon as it detects the EOF character. At this point, BUFFER and PRINTER will still be active, so COPY must then wait. The PRINTER then extracts the remaining characters from the buffer and after printing the last line, reaches its own end. At this point, the PRINTER task terminates immediately, since it has no offspring. Once the PRINTER task has terminated, the BUFFER task which has been waiting at its selective wait statement can also terminate by selecting the **terminate** alternative. Thus both dependent tasks have now terminated, and so the parent task, which in this case is the main program, also terminates. Note that in the design of the BUFFER task, the guard on the terminate alternative is merely a safety precaution. It does not imply that the BUFFER will terminate as soon as it becomes empty, but only that termination is not allowed when the buffer is not empty. Note also that BUFFER has to wait both for its *sister* task PRINTER to terminate as well as its parent to reach its end before it can itself select the **terminate** alternative.

Finally, the reader should understand why the above multi-task version of COPY may be preferred to the equivalent (and simpler) purely sequential version. The reason is that even on a single processor computer, the multi-task version will execute much faster even taking into account the additional overheads involved in time-sharing the processor amongst three tasks. This is quite simply because both reading from the input tape and printing the output are relatively slow operations. In the multi-task version they occur in parallel, that is, the main program can execute the call to INCH at the same time as the PRINTER task can call PRINTS. Hence both I/O devices are activated simultaneously. In a purely sequential version of COPY, calls to PRINTS can only be made between calls to INCH. Only one input/output device is ever active at a time and so the program executes considerably more slowly.

12.7 CONDITIONAL AND TIMED ENTRY CALLS

Once a server task reaches an **accept** statement, it commits itself to making a rendezvous with some other caller task. In the same way, when a caller task calls an entry, it too commits itself to making a rendezvous with the server task that owns the entry. In other words, in order to enter into a rendezvous, both partners must be prepared to wait for the other to arrive, no matter how long that might be. In the previous section it was shown that a server task can avoid committing itself to a rendezvous in two ways. In the conditional selective wait statement, the server task proceeds to execute an **accept** statement only if there is an entry call already pending, that is, a partner is already waiting. In the selective wait statement with a delay alternative, the server will wait for a partner to arrive, but only for a given period, after which time the selective wait statement is effectively aborted.

In an analogous manner to the above, a caller task may also avoid committing itself to a rendezvous. Firstly, it can issue a conditional entry call, whose syntax is

S124 conditional_entry_call

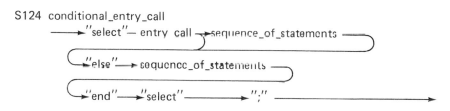

For example, the execution of the statement

```
select
      BUFFER.PUT(CH);
      BLOCKED:=FALSE;
else
      BLOCKED:=TRUE;
end select;
```

would result in an entry call being made to BUFFER.PUT only if BUFFER is ready to accept the call immediately. Following the entry call can appear a sequence of statements, which are executed only if the entry call was completed. In this case, there is a single statement to set to FALSE a Boolean flag called BLOCKED. If the entry call cannot be accepted immediately, then the statement sequence of the **else** part is executed instead. In this case, the effect would then be to set BLOCKED to TRUE.

The simplest (and perhaps most common) form of conditional entry call is where a task wishes to call an entry only if the server is waiting to accept it immediately, but otherwise wishes to do nothing. This is simply coded as

```
select
      SERVER.E;
else
      null;
end select;
```

where E is an entry defined by a task called SERVER.

The second way that a caller task can avoid committing itself to a rendezvous is by making a timed entry call. This is analogous to a server task executing a selective wait statement containing a delay alternative. The syntax of the timed entry call is

S125 timed_entry_call

For example, the effect of

> **select**
>> BUFFER . PUT(CH);
>> STATUS:=OK;
>
> **or**
>> **delay** T;
>> STATUS:=TIMED_OUT;
>
> **end select**;

would be to call the entry PUT in the task BUFFER. If the call is accepted within T seconds, then the rendezvous proceeds as normal and the STATUS variable would then subsequently be set to OK. If, however, the delay period T expires and the entry call has still not been accepted, then the entry call is cancelled and the STATUS variable is set to TIMED_OUT. As with the selective wait statement, the expression denoting T is evaluated prior to making the entry call.

12.8 FAMILIES OF ENTRIES

As noted at the end of section 12.4, it is possible to declare a family of entries where each entry in the family has the same formal parameter part. This is done by including a discrete range immediately after the name of the entry. For example,

> **entry** TRANSMIT(1 . . 6) (M: **in** MESSAGE);

declares a family of entries called TRANSMIT indexed by the integer values 1 to 6. An accept statement for TRANSMIT must include the index of the particular entry of the family which it wishes to accept. This may be specified by a constant, as in

> **accept** TRANSMIT(4) (M: **in** MESSAGE) **do** . . . .

or the index can be computed at run-time as in

> **accept** TRANSMIT(K) (M: **in** MESSAGE) **do** . . . .

where K is a variable. Similarly, entry calls to TRANSMIT must also include an index, for example,

> T . TRANSMIT(I)(SOME_MESSAGE);

is a call to the Ith TRANSMIT entry belonging to the task T.

Families of entries are commonly used to allow priorities to be applied to entry calls. For example, consider again the LP_CONTROL task given earlier. Suppose that tasks using the line-printer can request access to it with three levels of urgency: high, medium and low. The specification of the LP_CONTROL task could be altered to declare SECURE as a family of entries as follows

```
task LP_CONTROL is
    entry SECURE(PRIORITY);
    entry RELEASE;
end LP_CONTROL;
```

where

```
type PRIORITY is (HIGH, MEDIUM, LOW);
```

The essential point about a family of entries is that there is a separate entry queue associated with each member of the family. Hence, by examining each queue in turn, high urgency requests to secure the line-printer can be accepted before less urgent requests. A very simple formulation for the body of LP_CONTROL could be as follows

```
task body LP_CONTROL is
begin
    loop
        - - wait for a request for printer
        WAITING:
        loop
            for P in PRIORITY loop
                select
                    accept SECURE(P);
                    exit WAITING;
                else
                    null;
                end select;
            end loop;
        end loop WAITING;

        - - wait till line printer released
        accept RELEASE;
    end loop;
end LP_CONTROL;
```

Here the nested **for** loop contains a conditional selective wait statement. This contains an **accept** statement for SECURE(P), where P takes successively lower values of priority each time around the loop. When an entry call is finally accepted, then the outer loop WAITING is terminated and the task goes on to wait for the corresponding RELEASE entry to be called.

If many tasks are waiting to access the line printer then the design of LP_CONTROL given above is satisfactory. The **for** loop ensures that the queue associated with SECURE(HIGH) is always examined before that of SECURE-(MEDIUM) which in turn is always examined before that of SECURE(LOW). Hence, a call to SECURE(MEDIUM) will never be accepted as long as there are any tasks waiting in the queue for SECURE(HIGH). Similarly, a call to SECURE(LOW) will never be accepted as long as there are any tasks waiting in either of the other two queues. Thus the design above appears to meet the requirements of a priority-based resource allocation task.

Unfortunately, however, the design has a severe weakness. When there are no calls pending at any priority then the LP_CONTROL task cycles endlessly, executing the conditional selective wait statement. This so-called *busy waiting* is extremely wasteful of processor time and should always be avoided, since it can cause other tasks to be starved of processor time. Another problem with the above design is that there is no easy way to introduce a terminate alternative to allow a graceful close down when its parent no longer needs it.

To improve the design of LP_CONTROL, the servicing of entry calls which are already pending must be separated from the act of waiting for an entry call to arrive when all the queues are empty. The following revised version of LP_CONTROL avoids busy waiting, and includes a terminate alternative:

```
task body LP_CONTROL is
    FREE:BOOLEAN:=TRUE;
begin
    loop
        - - examine queues
        for P in PRIORITY loop
            select
                accept SECURE(P);
                FREE:=FALSE;
                exit;
            else
                null;
            end select;
        end loop;

        - - if queues empty then wait for next call
        - - to arrive or terminate
        if FREE then
```

```
            FREE:=FALSE;
            select
              accept SECURE(HIGH);
            or
              accept SECURE(MEDIUM);
            or
              accept SECURE(LOW);
            or
              terminate;
            end select;
          end if;

          - - SECURE now accepted so wait for RELEASE
          accept RELEASE;
          FREE:=TRUE;
        end loop;
    end LP_CONTROL;
```

12.9 TASK TYPES

In all of the preceding examples, tasks have been declared immediately as task objects, so that the elaboration of the task definition also implied its activation. In fact, this is a special case of a more general mechanism for activating tasks in Ada. Referring back to syntax diagram S115, it can be seen that, in a task specification, the keyword **task** may optionally be followed by the keyword **type**. When this is done, the task specification defines a *task type* rather than an actual task. The elaboration of the corresponding task body then simply defines what a task of that type does. It does not cause a task to be activated; instead, tasks are activated separately by declaring objects of the task type.

As an example, the LP_CONTROL task used in previous examples was introduced to schedule accesses to a line printer. The design of this task is equally applicable to any other resource. Hence, as an alternative to declaring a specific LP_CONTROL task, a general task type called RESOURCE can be declared as follows:

```
        task type RESOURCE is
            entry SECURE;
            entry RELEASE;
        end RESOURCE;

        task body RESOURCE is
            - -
            - - same as in LP_CONTROL task
            - -
        end RESOURCE;
```

An LP_CONTROL task can now be declared as an object of this type, that is,

        LP_CONTROL:RESOURCE;

and then used in exactly the same way as before. The great advantage of declaring a task type rather than a single task object is that it allows for task replication. For example, if a magnetic tape drive also requires a resource control task, then all that needs to be done is to declare another object of the task type RESOURCE with a suitable name, for example,

        MT_CONTROL:RESOURCE;

In general, a task type can be used anywhere that a normal abstract data type can be used. For example, if a system has ten disc drives requiring resource control, then an array of tasks can be declared, that is,

        DISC_CONTROL:**array**(1 .. 10)**of** RESOURCE;

thereby creating ten tasks to control access to the ten drives. The Ith disc drive is then secured by writing

        DISC_CONTROL(I).SECURE;

where the usual indexed component notation is used to select the required task in the array. If frequent access to an indexed task is needed, then renaming can be used to reduce the number of index calculations, for example,

        declare
            DI: RESOURCE **renames** DISC_CONTROL(I);
        begin
            DI.SECURE;
            - -
            - - access the Ith disc drive
            - -
            DI.RELEASE;
        end;

where DISC_CONTROL(I) is renamed as DI so that the indexing operation needs to be performed only once.

Task types may also appear as components of records. For example, if a vector of integers needs to be accessed by a group of tasks using direct reads and writes, rather than via the rendezvous mechanism, then the vector may be thought of as a shared resource. The following record type defines such a vector, and includes a task of type RESOURCE as one of its components:

        type SHARED_VECTOR(SIZE:INTEGER) **is**
            record
                DATA: VECTOR (1 .. SIZE);
                LOCK:RESOURCE;
            end record;

where VECTOR is the unconstrained array type defined in section 8.1.
Every object which is declared of this type will automatically have a task created
to control access to it. Hence, given

SPEECH_SIGNAL:SHARED_VECTOR(SIZE=>1024);

the actual data in SPEECH_SIGNAL would be accessed as in the following
example

```
procedure RECTIFY;
begin
    - - request exclusive access to speech signal
    SPEECH_SIGNAL . LOCK . SECURE;
    - - process the speech
    for I in 1 . . SPEECH_SIGNAL . SIZE loop
        declare
            DATUM·INTEGER renames SPEECH_SIGNAL . DATA(I);
        begin
            DATUM := abs DATUM;
        end;
    end loop;
    - - release exclusive access to speech signal
    SPEECH_SIGNAL . LOCK . RELEASE;
end RECTIFY;
```

[At this point it should be reiterated that using shared variables for task communication is not recommended practice and, in fact, programs which do use
them may not work properly. This is because an Ada compiler is allowed to
optimise store accesses under certain circumstances by keeping local copies of
global variables. The language rules relating to this area are rather complex and
will not be discussed further here except to note that they ensure that the
technique used in the SPEECH_SIGNAL example above does work properly.]

Finally, where very flexible manipulation of tasks is required, access types
can be used to designate dynamically created task objects. For example, given

type RESOURCE_ITEM is access RESOURCE;

then an object declaration such as

UNITO:RESOURCE_ITEM := new RESOURCE;

declares an access variable called UNITO, creates an instance of the task type
RESOURCE, and initialises the access variable to designate it. Subsequently,
the dynamically created task and its entries are named via the access variable,

for example, the entire task object is referred to as UNITO.**all** and its entries as UNITO.SECURE and UNITO.RELEASE.

When a task object is declared in terms of a task type, the parent of that task is the innermost enclosing subprogram, declare statement or task in which the object is declared regardless of where the corresponding task type is declared. In the case of dynamically created task objects, the parent is the innermost enclosing subprogram, declare statement or task in which the corresponding access type is declared. The place at which the task is actually allocated does not affect its parentage.

Task types behave like limited private types, and task objects behave like constants of a limited private type. Thus, neither assignment nor comparison for equality or inequality are available for a task type, and any formal parameter of a task type must be of **in** mode. Therefore, if assignment or comparison of task names or formal parameters of **out** or **in out** modes are required then access types must be used to designate the tasks. Finally, a task type may be used in the definition of an abstract type within the private part of a package specification, provided that the abstract type is limited private.

In summary, task types allow for the replication of task objects and facilitate their subsequent manipulation. They are a major feature of the Ada tasking system and contribute much to its power.

12.10 TASK PRIORITIES

Where the number of tasks declared in an Ada program exceeds the number of available physical processors, the underlying run-time system must time-share the available processing resources amongst the tasks. Normally, each task will be granted an approximately equal share of these resources. However, it is possible to specify a priority for some or all of the tasks in the system, by including a pragma in the specification part of a task of the form

pragma PRIORITY (P);

This pragma may also appear in the declarative part of a main program. P is a static expression denoting a value of subtype PRIORITY which is defined in the package SYSTEM (see section 17.4) as

subtype PRIORITY **is** INTEGER **range** LOW . . HIGH;

where LOW and HIGH are implementation dependent.

The effect of specifying priorities is to ensure that, where two tasks with different priorities are both eligible for execution, then it can never be the case that the task with the lower priority is executing whilst the other is not. Priorities are therefore used to specify the degree of urgency of a task, and are useful in certain time-critical applications. Priorities should never be used for task synchronisation. Note also that priorities are fixed at compile time and cannot be altered during execution.

12.11 TASK ATTRIBUTES

There are two attributes defined for any task object T. T'TERMINATED is a
Boolean attribute which is true only if task T has terminated. T'CALLABLE is a
Boolean attribute which is true if the task T has been activated but has not yet
terminated.

In addition to the above two attributes, the attribute E'COUNT can be
used to find out how many tasks are currently waiting in the queue associated
with entry E. However, this attribute should be used with caution, since the
actual number of tasks in any queue will often change even whilst E'COUNT
is being read. For example, the actual number may increase due to further entry
calls arriving, or decrease due to timed entry calls being removed after a time-
out. Note also that, within an **accept** statement for E, the value of E'COUNT
excludes the calling task engaged in the rendezvous (see question 12.2).

12.12 STOPPING FAULTY TASKS

Where possible a task should always be programmed to terminate by its own
actions, that is, by reaching its own end or by reaching a selective wait statement
with a delay alternative. There are occasions, however, where it is necessary for
one task to explicitly terminate the execution of another task, and this usually
arises when a task is known to be faulty.

The termination of a faulty task can be achieved using an **abort** statement.
The syntax of this statement is as follows

S126 abort_statement

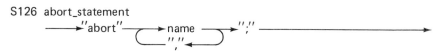

where each name in the list is the name of a task to be aborted.

Tasks terminated by the **abort** statement are said to be abnormally terminated. For example, the execution of

        abort LP_CONTROL , UNITO . all;

would force the abnormal termination of **LP_CONTROL** and of the task designated by the access variable UNITO.

Although the **abort** statement is very simple in concept, it must be emphasised that it has far-reaching and potentially dangerous consequences. Firstly,
the abnormal termination of a task also causes the abnormal termination of all
its offspring. Further, any task which is dependent on any subprogram (or
declare statement) which is being called by an abnormally terminated task is
also abnormally terminated. Thus a 'chain reaction' can take place, where each
task which is abnormally terminated leads to several more being abnormally
terminated and this effect may not always be obvious from examination of the
program text. Secondly, when a server task is abnormally terminated, then all
tasks which have entry calls pending for entries of that task, and any caller task

which is actually involved in a rendezvous with that task, have an exception called TASKING_ERROR raised in them. The nature of exceptions is explained in detail in the next chapter, but for now it is sufficient to note that the **abort** statement not only leads to the abnormal termination of tasks, but may also lead to errors occurring in a great many others. It should therefore be clear that the **abort** statement needs to be used with extreme care, and then only as a last resort.

12.13 EXAMPLE – A SERIAL COMMUNICATIONS INTERFACE

As an example of Ada's tasking facilities, the design of a simple serial communications interface will be developed. This interface can be used to connect two computers together allowing fixed length messages to be transmitted and received from one to the other. Each message is a sequence of 64 ASCII characters enclosed in a packet consisting of an STX character (start transmission), the message itself, a check sum character, and the ETX character (end of transmission). This is shown pictorially in Fig. 12.2.

| STX | 64 Character Message | CSUM | ETX |

Fig. 12.2 – Structure of a Serial Transmission Packet

Each received message is acknowledged by returning an ACK character if the message was received properly; otherwise a NAK character is returned. When the transmitting computer receives a NAK (or no reply at all within 3 seconds) then it retransmits the message. If after a total of 5 transmissions, an ACK has still not been received, then the attempt to transmit the message is abandoned.

To the user, the communications interface appears as a library package with the following specification

```
package COMMUNICATIONS_INTERFACE is

    MESSAGE_SIZE: constant INTEGER := 64;
    subtype MESSAGE is STRING(1 .. MESSAGE_SIZE);

    procedure TRANSMIT(M: in MESSAGE; OK: out BOOLEAN);

    procedure RECEIVE_P(M: out MESSAGE;
                READY: out BOOLEAN);
    procedure RECEIVE_W(M: out MESSAGE);

end COMMUNICATIONS_INTERFACE;
```

A message is transmitted by a call to TRANSMIT. On return from this procedure OK is set FALSE if a transmission failure occurred. Two procedures are provided for receiving messages. RECEIVE_P (read or proceed) returns a message if one is ready; otherwise READY is returned as FALSE. RECEIVE_W (read and wait) returns a message immediately if one is ready; otherwise the calling task is made to wait until a message is received.

In order to implement the body of COMMUNICATIONS_INTERFACE, a further package will be assumed which provides an interface to the actual serial line input/output hardware. The specification of this package is as follows:

```
package LINE_INTERFACE is
   procedure TX_OUT(CH: in CHARACTER);
   procedure RX_IN(CH: out CHARACTER);
end LINE_INTERFACE;
```

A call to TX_OUT transmits a character via the serial output line and a call to RX_IN receives a character from the serial input line. The body of this package depends on the actual underlying hardware, and so a discussion of its design is deferred until Chapter 17.

When considering the design of the COMMUNICATIONS_INTERFACE package, it becomes apparent that three distinct functions may be identified, and since these functions need to be performed concurrently they are best implemented as tasks.

Firstly, a task is needed to accept messages for transmission, format them into packets, transmit the packets character-by-character, and then await an acknowledgement. If a NAK acknowledgement is received, or if no acknowledgement at all is received within 3 seconds, then the packet is retransmitted. After 5 unsuccessful attempts, the task gives up. The specification of this task is:

```
task TX is
   entry TRANSMIT(M: in MESSAGE; TRANSMITTED: out BOOLEAN);
   entry ACKNOWLEDGED(OK: in BOOLEAN);
end TX;
```

The entry TRANSMIT is called to transmit a message M. The Boolean parameter TRANSMITTED is returned TRUE if the message was successfully transmitted; otherwise it is returned FALSE. The entry ACKNOWLEDGED is provided to allow the receipt of an acknowledgement to be signalled to the TX task.

The second task needed is to interpret the incoming character stream, which consists of a mixture of packets and acknowledgement characters. The processing of packets involves extracting the message, validating the checksum, and then sending the appropriate acknowledgement (that is, ACK or NAK). When an incoming ACK or NAK is received, the ACKNOWLEDGED entry of the TX task is called to signal the fact. The specification of this receiver task is

```
task RX is
   entry RECEIVE(M: out MESSAGE);
end RX;
```

The single entry RECEIVE is called to read a received message.

The third and final task is a simple resource control task to schedule accesses to the output line (that is, calls to LINE_INTERFACE.TX_OUT). This is necessary because both the TX and RX tasks need to transmit characters (packets and acknowledgements, respectively). The specification of this task is

> **task** TX_CONTROL **is**
>   **entry** SECURE;
>   **entry** RELEASE;
> **end** TX_CONTROL;

(cf. the LP_CONTROL task described in previous sections).

The above three tasks cooperate together to implement the required communications interface. The interactions between these tasks is shown pictorially in Fig. 12.3.

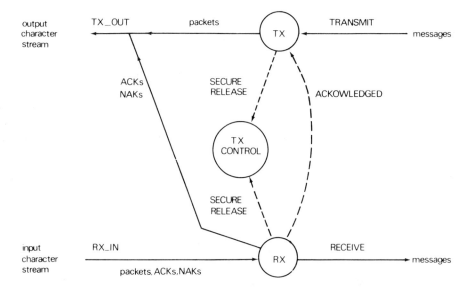

Fig. 12.3 – Task Interaction in the Communications Interface

To summarise, operation is as follows. When the TX task is asked to transmit a message, it calls SECURE to gain access to the output line and then transmits the message as a packet. When the transmission is completed, it calls RELEASE and then awaits an acknowledgement. This acknowledgement is detected on the input line by the RX task, which signals its occurrence by calling the ACKNOWLEDGED entry. If a NAK is received (or no reply at all) then the TX task repeats the process to re-transmit the message up to a total of 4 more times. When an input packet is received, the RX task extracts the message and then validates it by establishing that the check sum is correct. It then calls SECURE to gain access to the output line, transmits an acknowledgement, and finally calls RELEASE. If the message was received correctly, then it can be read by calling the RECEIVE entry.

Having established the basic operation of the communications interface, the package body can now be given as follows where the actual implementation of the tasks has been deferred by making their bodies into subunits:

```
package body COMMUNICATIONS_INTERFACE is
    task TX is
        entry TRANSMIT(M: in MESSAGE; TRANSMITTED: out
                                                        BOOLEAN);
        entry ACKNOWLEDGED(OK: in BOOLEAN);
    end TX;

    task RX is
        entry RECEIVE(M: out MESSAGE);
    end RX;

    task TX_CONTROL is
        entry SECURE;
        entry RELEASE;
    end TX_CONTROL;

    procedure TRANSMIT(M: in MESSAGE; OK: out BOOLEAN) is
    begin
        TX.TRANSMIT(M,OK);
    end TRANSMIT;

    procedure RECEIVE_P(M: out MESSAGE; READY: out
                                                        BOOLEAN) is
    begin
        select
            RX.RECEIVE(M);
            READY:=TRUE;
        else
            READY:=FALSE;
        end select;
    end RECEIVE_P;

    procedure RECEIVE_W(M: out MESSAGE) is
    begin
        RX.RECEIVE(M);
    end RECEIVE_W;

    task body TX is separate;
    task body RX is separate;
    task body TX_CONTROL is separate;
end COMMUNICATIONS_INTERFACE;
```

Notice the use in the above of the conditional entry call in RECEIVE_P to achieve the required read-or-proceed semantics.

Having established the overall systems structure, the remainder of the design concerns the implementation of each of the constituent tasks. The basic design of the TX task may be sketched out as follows

```
loop
    accept TRANSMIT(M: in MESSAGE; TRANSMITTED: out
                                                BOOLEAN) do
        SENT:=FALSE; TOTAL_TRIES:=0;

        while not SENT and TOTAL_TRIES<MAX_TRIES loop

            TRANSMIT MESSAGE M;      - - send the message
            UPDATE TOTAL_TRIES;

            select                           - - await the reply
                accept ACKNOWLEDGED(OK: in BOOLEAN) do
                    SENT:=OK;
                end;
            or
                delay TIME_OUT;
            end select;

        end loop;

        TRANSMITTED:=SENT;
    end TRANSMIT;
end loop;
```

The key feature of this design is that the entire processing is performed within the body of the **accept** TRANSMIT statement, so that the calling task is made to wait until either the transmission has been successfully completed or the attempt has been abandoned. The body of this accept statement is a loop containing the operations to transmit the message and then wait for the reply. The delay alternative in the selective wait statement is used to implement the required time-out. The loop is repeated until either the message is successfully transmitted or the maximum number of tries allowed has been reached. An interesting feature of this design is that the **accept** ACKNOWLEDGED statement is nested within the **accept** TRANSMIT statement. This is quite legal. It simply means that, during the time that the caller task is performing a rendezvous with the TX task, the latter also performs a rendezvous with the RX task.

It may be worth noting at this point that the necessity to hold the calling task in a rendezvous for the entire time that it takes to transmit a message may be unacceptable in some circumstances. This can be avoided, if required, in several ways. For example, the TRANSMIT entry could be split into two, so that the caller first loads the message to be transmitted and then returns some time later to check that the transmission was successful. Alternatively, the TRANSMITTED parameter could be abandoned altogether, so that the caller assumes that all transmissions succeed. In the event of a failure, the TX task could then signal the error by calling a suitable ERROR entry defined by the caller task. This alternative is rather limited, however, since it implies that all callers must leave their identity with the TX task when they deposit each message. This in turn restricts callers to dynamically allocated tasks whose identities are denoted by access types, since it is not possible to copy the name of a task directly.

Returning to the example, adding the appropriate details to the above outline of the TX task gives the final design as follows:

```
with LINE_INTERFACE; use LINE_INTERFACE;
separate(COMMUNICATIONS_INTERFACE)
task body TX is

    TIME_OUT: constant DURATION :=3.0;
    MAX_TRIES: constant INTEGER :=5;
    TOTAL_TRIES: INTEGER range 0 .. MAX_TRIES;
    SENT: BOOLEAN;

    procedure SEND(M: in MESSAGE) is
        CHECKSUM: INTEGER range 0 .. 127 := 0;
        CH: CHARACTER;
    begin
        TX_CONTROL.SECURE;              - - secure output line
        TX_OUT(ASCII.STX);             - - start of transmission
        for I in 1 .. MESSAGE_SIZE loop
            CH:=M(I);
            TX_OUT(CH);                 - - send message
            CHECKSUM:=(CHECKSUM+CHARACTER'POS(CH))
                                                mod 128;
        end loop;
        TX_OUT(CHARACTER'VAL(CHECKSUM)); - - send checksum
        TX_OUT(ASCII.ETX);             - - end of transmission
        TX_CONTROL.RELEASE;            - - release output line
    end SEND;

begin
    loop
        accept TRANSMIT(M: in MESSAGE;
                            TRANSMITTED: out BOOLEAN) do
            SENT:=FALSE; TOTAL_TRIES:=0;

            while not SENT and TOTAL_TRIES<MAX_TRIES loop

                SEND(M);                    - - send the message
```

```
                TOTAL_TRIES := TOTAL_TRIES+1;

                select                    - - await the reply
                    accept ACKNOWLEDGED(OK:in BOOLEAN) do
                        SENT:=OK;
                    end;
                or
                    delay TIME_OUT;
                end select;
            end loop;

            TRANSMITTED:=SENT;
        end TRANSMIT;
    end loop;
end TX;
```

In this final solution, the actual message transmission is performed by the procedure SEND. The control characters STX and ETX are defined within the ASCII package in STANDARD (see section 3.3). The checksum is a simple modulo sum of all the characters in the message.

The basic design of the RX task can be sketched out as follows

```
loop
    loop                          - - search for ACK, NAK or STX
        RX_IN(CH);
        if CH=ASCII.ACK or CH=ASCII.NAK then
            TX.ACKNOWLEDGED(CH=ASCII.ACK);
        elsif CH=ASCII.STX then
            exit;
        end if;
    end loop;

    RXM := INCOMING MESSAGE;       - - read packet
    CHECK MESSAGE IS VALID;

    if MESSAGE VALID then          - - send acknowledgement
        TRANSMIT(ASCII.ACK);
    else
        TRANSMIT(ASCII.NAK);
    end if;

    if MESSAGE VALID then          - - allow message to be read
        accept RECEIVE(M:out MESSAGE) do
            M := RXM;
        end;
    end if;
end loop;
```

The RX task operates in four phases. Firstly, ACK, NAK and STX input characters are intercepted, while all others are ignored. If an ACK or NAK is received, the TX task is signalled appropriately and the first stage restarted. The receipt of an STX character indicates the start of a packet transmission and causes the task to enter the second stage, in which the packet is received, the message extracted, and the checksum computed and verified. In the third stage, the appropriate acknowledgement is sent. Finally, in the fourth stage, the task accepts a RECEIVE entry to read the actual received message.

Although the above solution adequately expresses the main function of the RX task, it does not recognise any of the abnormal situations which may arise. The most obvious of these is where the input stream of characters is severely corrupted. For example, the end of a packet may be lost. In such a case, the task must not sit waiting for the rest of the packet to arrive, since in so doing it may miss subsequent acknowledgement characters or the start of a new packet. Here it will be assumed that control characters (such as ACK, NAK, etc.) are not allowed within messages. The receipt of any control character within a packet can therefore be used to abort any further processing of that packet.

A second and rather less obvious abnormal situation can arise when an acknowledgement is received very late. In such a case, the TX task may have already timed-out by the time that the RX task manages to call the ACKNOW-LEDGED entry. This would mean that the RX task would be suspended until the next message was transmitted by TX, at which time it would signal the wrong acknowledgement. To avoid this problem, the RX task must only call the ACKNOWLEDGED entry if the TX task is already waiting to accept it, that is, a conditional entry call must be used.

Taking these points into account and adding the necessary detail, the design of the RX task becomes:

```
with LINE_INTERFACE; use LINE_INTERFACE;
separate (COMMUNICATIONS_INTERFACE)
task body RX is

    CH:CHARACTER;
    RXM:MESSAGE;
    VALID:BOOLEAN;

    procedure READ_PACKET(M:out MESSAGE; OK:out
                                            BOOLEAN) is
        CHECKSUM:INTEGER range 0 .. 127 :=0;
    begin
        OK := FALSE;
        for I in 1 .. MESSAGE_SIZE loop      - - read message
            RX_IN(CH);
            if CH <' ' then
                return;
```

```
            end if;
            M(I) := CH;
            CHECKSUM:=(CHECKSUM+CHARACTER'POS(CH))
                                                    mod 128;
        end loop;
        RX_IN(CH);    - - compare received and computed c'sums
        if CHECKSUM /= CHARACTER'POS(CH) then
            return;
        end if;
        RX_IN(CH);    - - read ETX character
        OK := CH = ASCII.ETX;
    end READ_PACKET;
    procedure ACKNOWLEDGE(OK: in BOOLEAN) is
    begin
        TX_CONTROL.SECURE;
        if OK then
          TX_OUT(ASCII.ACK);
        else
          TX_OUT(ASCII.NAK);
        end if;
        TX_CONTROL.RELEASE;
    end ACKNOWLEDGE;

begin
    loop
        RX_IN(CH);

        loop                        - - search for ACK, NAK or STX
            if CH=ASCII.ACK or CH=ASCII.NAK then
                select
                    TX.ACKNOWLEDGED(CH=ASCII.ACK);
                else
                    null;
                end select;
            elsif CH=ASCII.STX then
                exit;
            else
                RX_IN(CH);
            end if;
        end loop;

        READ_PACKET(M=>RXM, OK=>VALID);

        ACKNOWLEDGE(OK => VALID);

        if VALID then                  - - allow message to be read
```

```
        accept RECEIVE(M: out MESSAGE) do
            M := RXM;
        end RECEIVE;
    end if;

  end loop;
end RX;
```

Notice that in this final solution if an error occurs within READ_PACKET, then the last input character received is left in the global variable CH. This ensures that if a packet is truncated in some way then a following ACK, NAK or STX character is not lost. Also it should be observed that a potential weakness of the above design is that the RX task must never be left waiting at the **accept** RECEIVE statement; otherwise subsequent incoming ACK's may not be relayed to the TX task before it times out. This problem can only be avoided by buffering incoming messages. The implementation of such a buffer is, however, straightforward and is left as an exercise to the reader.

The final task to be designed is the TX_CONTROL task. Since all tasks in the COMMUNICATIONS_INTERFACE package are non-stop independent tasks, the very basic form of resource control task given in section 12.4 is quite adequate, that is,

```
        separate(COMMUNICATIONS_INTERFACE)
        task body TX_CONTROL is
        begin
            loop
                accept SECURE;
                accept RELEASE;
            end loop;
        end TX_CONTROL;
```

This completes the design of the COMMUNICATIONS_INTERFACE package. As noted at the start of the section, the LINE_INTERFACE package is described in Chapter 17, when Ada's low level programming facilities have been explained.

12.14 EXERCISES

(12.1) Design a task with the following specification

```
        task SQUASHER is
            entry PUT(C: in CHARACTER);
            entry GET(C: out CHARACTER);
        end SQUASHER;
```

The function of this task is to accept a stream of characters from a producer task via calls to PUT, and relay the stream to a consumer process via calls to GET, in such a way that any occurrences of two consecutive asterisks (that is, **) are replaced by a single vertical bar (that is, |).

(12.2) In section 12.8, a version of the LP_CONTROL task was given which allows a priority to be associated with each call to SECURE. In fact, a simpler version of this task is possible using a single selective wait statement, in which each alternative accepts one member of the SECURE entry family. The required priority for accepting calls to these entries is achieved by guarding each alternative such that it is open only if the queues for all those entries with a higher priority are empty (this can be determined using the COUNT attribute). Redesign the priority version of the LP_CONTROL task using this technique.

(12.3) In section 7.4, an input/output channel manager package was described. Design a task to perform a similar function for a community of user tasks with the following specification

> **task** IO_CHANNEL_MANAGER **is**
>   **entry** GRAB(CHN: **out** IOCHAN);
>   **entry** FREE(CHN: **in** IOCHAN);
> **end** IO_CHANNEL_MANAGER;

A call to the entry GRAB immediately returns an unused input/output channel number if one is available; otherwise the calling task is made to wait until one becomes free. The type IOCHAN defined as

> **type** IOCHAN **is range** 0 . . 15;

may be assumed to be visible, and the security aspects discussed in section 7.4 may be disregarded.

(12.4) The PROTECTED_TIME task given in section 12.5 allows a number of tasks to read and write to a variable in such a way that all accesses to it are performed in mutual exclusion. In fact, it is unnecessarily restrictive to force each read operation to be performed in mutual exclusion of all other read operations. It is quite safe to allow any number of tasks to read the protected variable concurrently, provided that no write operations are attempted at the same time. Redesign the PROTECTED_TIME task to allow any number of reader tasks to read the protected variable concurrently, while ensuring that they are locked-out when any write operation is being performed.

13

Exception handling

13.1 RUN-TIME ERRORS

Unlike most programming languages in common use, Ada admits the possibility that errors may occur during program execution, and therefore provides an explicit mechanism for responding and recovering from such errors. At first sight this may seem like a strange admission from a language designed to support rigorous well-engineered software construction. Why should Ada concern itself with errors?

The answer lies primarily in its intended area of use, that is, real time systems. Such systems must often function continuously even in the face of errors, whether these result from malfunction of external equipment or from undetected errors in the software design. This does not mean, however, that Ada's error handling facilities are irrelevant outside the real time area. All useful programs interact with their environment in some way, whether it be by reading from an analogue to digital convertor or by writing to a data file. The possibility of input/output errors occurring must be catered for in any robust software design. In traditional languages, the handling of abnormal cases such as these must be programmed explicitly in the same way as the normal expected case with the result that the error handling code can grossly distort the structure of the main program flow. In Ada, the actions to be taken when an error occurs are kept separate from the main program flow so that no such distortion takes place.

Before Ada's exception handling mechanism is described, it should be understood that there are two main classes of error which can occur during the execution of a program. Firstly, there are the errors that are detected by the implementation. These mainly arise from a violation of the language rules, such as an attempt to divide a number by zero or to access a non-existent component of an array. It is interesting to note that in most existing languages errors such as these are handled by simply issuing a warning message and then aborting the program. In Ada, the programmer can specify what actions should be taken and then continue program execution. The second class of errors are those which are detected through explicitly programmed actions. For example, if at some point a variable X should be positive, the programmer may write

if X<0 **then** ERROR ...

In Ada the only difference between these two classes of error is in the way that they are detected and signalled. Once the occurrence of an error has been signalled, it is handled from then on in the same way regardless of which class it belongs to.

Finally, it should be emphasised that the ability to recover from errors should not be taken as an excuse for sloppy design and testing. Rather it should be considered as a facility firstly for handling predictable errors (such as bad input data formats) in a structured way and secondly for providing a layer of fault tolerance against those errors which are largely unpredictable.

13.2 REPRESENTATION OF ERRORS BY EXCEPTIONS

The detection of an error in an Ada program is indicated by *raising an exception*. An exception is an event which causes normal program execution to be suspended and control transferred instead to the execution of special error handling code called an *exception handler*. In essence, an exception is like a program interrupt, caused by errors occurring during program execution.

There are three aspects to using exceptions: declaring exceptions, raising exceptions, and handling exceptions. The declaration of exceptions is described here. Raising and handling exceptions is treated in the next section.

All programmer-defined exceptions must be explicitly declared in an exception declaration whose syntax is given by the following diagram

S127 exception_declaration
           ⟶ ident_list ⟶ ":" ⟶ "exception" ⟶ ";" ⟶

For example,

         BUFFER_FULL,BUFFER_EMPTY: **exception**;

declares two exceptions called BUFFER_FULL and BUFFER_EMPTY. Anywhere within the scope of this declaration, the occurrence of a buffer full/empty error can be signalled by raising the appropriate exception.

In addition to those exceptions which are explicitly declared by the programmer, there are five predefined exceptions which are raised automatically to signal the occurrence of an implementation-detected error. These are

1.   CONSTRAINT_ERROR — raised as a result of a violation of a range, index or discriminant constraint, an attempt to access a non-existent component of an array or discriminated record, or an attempt to access the object designated by an access type whose value is **null**.

2. NUMERIC_ERROR — raised when the result of a numeric operation exceeds the implemented range of the type, for example, underflow, overflow, divide-by-zero, etc.

3. PROGRAM_ERROR — raised when a program is detected to be erroneous, in particular, raised when attempt is made to call a subprogram which has not yet been elaborated and when all alternatives in a select statement are closed (see section 12.5).

4. STORAGE_ERROR — raised when the storage allocated to a task is exceeded, or when the storage allocated for a collection is exhausted during the execution of an allocator.

5. TASKING_ERROR — raised when an error occurs during inter-task communication (see section 13.6).

These five exceptions are in scope throughout a program and may be raised anywhere.

Having established how exceptions are introduced, the basic mechanisms for raising and handling exceptions will now be described.

13.3 RAISING AND HANDLING EXCEPTIONS

The five predefined exceptions are raised automatically by the underlying runtime system when the errors which they denote occur. For example, if VEC is an integer array of 10 elements indexed from 1 to 10, then the execution of the statement

   VEC(I) := 0;

will result in the exception CONSTRAINT_ERROR being raised if I is less than 1 or greater than 10.

Programmer-defined exceptions are raised explicitly by the execution of a **raise** statement whose syntax diagram is

S128 raise_statement

where *name* must be the name of a previously declared exception. In certain cases, the name of the exception can be omitted. The effect of the **raise** statement is then to raise again the most recently raised exception. The significance of this is explained in section 13.5. As an example of the normal case, the execution of the following statement would cause the BUFFER_FULL exception to be raised if the value of USED is not less than BUFFER_SIZE:

   if USED >= BUFFER_SIZE **then**
        raise BUFFER_FULL;
   end if;

When an exception is raised, the execution of the program (or task) is suspended and control is transferred to a special sequence of statements called an *exception handler*. In effect, the statements of the handler replace those of the interrupted program unit or block. Before describing how exception handlers work in detail, a simple example will help to illustrate the basic idea.

Suppose that an integer multiply operation is required for which overflow errors cannot occur. If the product of the two operands exceeds the implemented range of integers, then instead of the operation failing, the value of INTEGER'FIRST or INTEGER'LAST is returned instead, for example,

$$\text{MULT}(20,40) \qquad = \qquad 800 \qquad \qquad \text{- - normal multiply}$$

but

$$\text{MULT}(2000,10000) \quad = \text{ INTEGER'LAST} \quad \text{- - integer overflow}$$
$$\text{MULT}(-2000,10000) \quad = \text{ INTEGER'FIRST} \quad \text{- - same but -ve}$$

The function MULT may be written using an exception handler, as follows:

```
function MULT(A,B:INTEGER) return INTEGER is
begin
    return A*B;
exception
    when NUMERIC_ERROR =>
        if (A<0 and B<0) or (A>0 and B>0) then
            return INTEGER'LAST;
        else
            return INTEGER'FIRST;
        end if;
end MULT;
```

When the product of A and B lies within the implemented range of the INTEGER type, then the function behaves normally, returning A*B. If, however, the product lies outside this range then the exception NUMERIC_ERROR is raised during the evaluation of A*B. This causes the execution of the statement 'return A*B' to be abandoned and control to be transferred to the exception handler following the keyword **exception**. In this case, the handler for NUMERIC_ ERROR consists of a single **if** statement, returning the value INTEGER'FIRST or INTEGER'LAST depending on the signs of A and B. When execution of the handler is completed, the function returns as normal to the calling program unit. It should be emphasised that, even when an error occurs in MULT, the calling program unit is never 'aware' of the fact. MULT is a *robust* multiplication routine which is able to handle and recover from internal numeric errors.

Thus the general idea of exception handling is that any program unit (or block) may contain handlers for any exceptions which may be expected to be raised within it. When an exception does occur, then the execution of the program unit is suspended and control passes instead to the corresponding handler. The statements of the handler then replace the remaining statements of the suspended unit. These statements have exactly the same capabilities as the statements that they replace. For example, within the handler of a subprogram they can include return statements and statements which access the subprogram parameters. When execution of the handler has completed, the program unit terminates in the normal way.

Any number of handlers may follow the keyword **exception** and each handler may service several different exceptions. The names of the exceptions for which each handler applies are listed in the **when** prefix. The full syntax for exception handlers is given by the following diagrams:

S129 exceptions

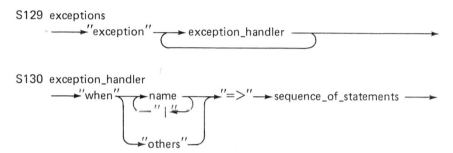

S130 exception_handler

The following outline illustrates the form of a procedure containing several exception handlers:

    procedure ERROR_HANDLING **is**
     E1,E2,E3 : **exception**;
    begin
      – –
      – – exceptions E1,E2,E3 and any of
      – – the pre-defined exceptions may
      – – be raised here.
      – –
    exception
     when E1 | E2 =>
      – – handler A
     when E3 =>
      – – handler B
     when others =>
      – – handler C
    end ERROR_HANDLING;

The procedure ERROR_HANDLING contains three exception handlers denoted A, B and C. If either exception E1 or exception E2 is raised within the body of the procedure then handler A is executed, and if E3 is raised then handler B is executed. The handler C is prefixed by the name **others**, which stands for any exceptions which have not been named in any of the preceding handlers. Thus the handler C is executed if any exception other than E1, E2 or E3 is raised within ERROR_HANDLING. (When a handler for **others** is given, then it must always be the last handler in the sequence.) Finally, note that no exception name may appear in the exceptions part of a given program unit (or block) more than once, although the same name may occur in several different program units − provided, of course, that it is in scope.

13.4 FINDING A HANDLER FOR A RAISED EXCEPTION

So far it has been assumed that when an exception is raised within a program unit (or block) then a corresponding handler for that exception exists in the same unit. In fact, this is not necessarily the case. Much of the power of Ada's exception handling mechanism stems from the fact that exceptions need not be handled locally within the unit in which they were first raised.

Consider first exceptions raised within subprograms. When an exception is raised in a subprogram and that subprogram does not contain a handler for it, then the subprogram is terminated and the same exception is raised at the point where the subprogram was called. If again no handler can be found for the exception, then the process is repeated. In other words, the exception propagates back along the chain of subprogram calls until a handler is found for it. This means that the association of handlers with exceptions occurs dynamically at run-time. There may be many handlers for a given raised exception, and the selection of which handler to execute will depend on the state of the computation at that point.

The following procedure outline illustrates a very simple case of dynamic handler selection:

```
procedure TOP is
    E: exception;
    procedure BOTTOM is
    begin
        - -
        raise E;
        - -
    end BOTTOM;
    procedure MIDDLE is
    begin
        - -
        BOTTOM;
        - -
```

```
        exception
            when E =>
                - - handler B
        end MIDDLE;
begin
    BOTTOM;
    MIDDLE;
    - -
    - -
exception
    when E =>
        - - handler A
end TOP;
```

The procedure TOP contains two nested procedures called MIDDLE and BOTTOM. When TOP is executed, the procedure BOTTOM will be called twice, once by TOP directly and once by MIDDLE. The exception E declared in TOP may be raised by BOTTOM, but BOTTOM does not contain a local handler for it. Hence, the handler selected to handle this exception will depend on which procedure it was that called BOTTOM. If E is raised during the first execution of BOTTOM, then BOTTOM is terminated and E is raised again in the calling procedure, that is, TOP, and is therefore handled by handler A. If E is raised during the second execution of BOTTOM, then similar action is taken except that this time the caller of BOTTOM is MIDDLE and therefore E is raised again in MIDDLE and so handled by handler B.

In effect, this means that it is possible to define regions of a computation over which a particular error is handled in a particular way. Each exception handler denotes a region over which its associated exception will be handled by that handler. This region includes the computation performed by the subprogram containing the handler, and any other subprograms called during its execution. However, it excludes any regions nested within it. In the example above, the regions associated with handlers A and B are illustrated pictorially in Fig. 13.1.

In this diagram, the solid vertical lines denote procedure execution and the dashed connecting lines represent calls and returns. The region of the computation covered by handler B is clearly shown nested within that of handler A. Notice from this diagram that, if handler B were removed, then both executions of BOTTOM would lie within the region covered by handler A. In this case, if E is raised during the second execution of BOTTOM, then the exception is first propagated back to MIDDLE and then from there back to TOP.

The extent of the region defined by a handler can range from the entire program down to a single statement. The former case corresponds to a handler placed in the body of the main program. The latter is achieved by enclosing the single statement within a declare block. For example, a statement involving the

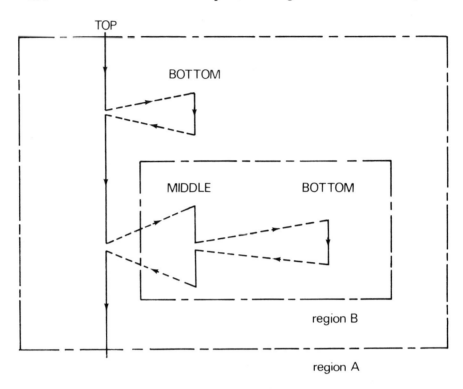

Fig. 13.1 – Error Handling Regions within Procedure TOP

use of an allocator can be given a local handler for the STORAGE_ERROR
exception as follows

```
    - -
    - -
begin
    P := new ITEM;
exception
    when STORAGE_ERROR =>
        P := null;
        PUT("Storage for ITEMS exhausted");
end;
    - -
    - -
```

Notice here that the declare part of the block has been omitted since no local
declarations are required. The only purpose of the block is to allow an exception
handler to be introduced.

The procedure TOP example illustrates the way that exceptions may propagate back along a chain of subprogram calls. Similar rules apply for exceptions which are raised in declare statements and which have no local handler. Execution of the declare statement is abandoned and the exception is raised again in the enclosing unit. For the cases of package and task bodies, however, the rules are slightly different. When an exception occurs within the body of a package and there is no local handler, then elaboration of the package body is terminated. If the package is declared within some other unit, then the exception is raised again within that unit. If the package is a library package, then the execution of the main program is abandoned. When an exception occurs in the body of a task (or the main program itself) and there is no local handler, then the task simply terminates and the exception propagates no further.

When an exception occurs in an exception handler itself, then execution of the handler is terminated and the exception is raised again in the enclosing environment. This rule is designed to avoid the possibility of inadvertently creating an infinite loop. For example, in

```
begin
    A := B/C;
exception
    when NUMERIC_ERROR =>
        A := B/C;
end;
```

if C is zero then the handler for NUMERIC_ERROR will be executed whereupon the same exception will inevitably be raised again. However, this does not cause the same handler to be executed. Instead the block is terminated and the exception raised again in the enclosing unit.

Finally, it may be noted that, as well as exceptions occurring during the execution of statements, they may also occur during the elaboration of the declarative part of a program unit or block. Whenever this occurs, the elaboration of the unit or block is abandoned and the exception is raised again, in the enclosing unit in the case of packages and declare statements, in the calling unit in the case of subprograms, and in the unit which caused its activation in the case of tasks.

13.5 ERROR HANDLING TECHNIQUES

The previous sections have outlined the mechanism involved in exception handling. This section will illustrate the way in which these mechanisms can be used.

In general, exceptions can be used in three ways. Firstly, they provide a simple and straightforward mechanism for error reporting. For example, suppose that a package is designed to maintain a table of symbols and their corresponding values, with operations to insert a symbol/value pair and to find the value of a given symbol. Two errors may obviously occur in the use of this package: the table may become full, or a request can be made for the value of a non-existent symbol. The specification of this package might be as follows, where the two errors are denoted by exceptions:

```
package SYMBOL_TABLE is

    procedure INSERT(S: in SYMBOL; V: in VALUE);
    function FIND(S:SYMBOL) return VALUE;

    TABLE_FULL, SYMBOL_ERR : exception;

end SYMBOL_TABLE;
```

Within the package body, these exceptions will be raised by raise statements whenever the associated error occurs. For example, within the body of INSERT would be written something like

```
if TABLE_USED >= TABLE_MAX then
    raise TABLE_FULL;
else
    - - insert new symbol
end if;
```

The user of the SYMBOL_TABLE package is free to deal with exceptions raised during calls to INSERT and FIND in any way that he chooses. For example, if the package were being used as part of an assembler (a program which translates assembly language into machine code) then the two errors would be treated differently. TABLE_FULL will be a fatal error leading to immediate termination of the program, whereas SYMBOL_ERR will be a non-fatal error arising every time that an undefined label is used in the assembly language program. Thus the handler for TABLE_FULL would be placed in the main program, so that if TABLE_FULL is raised anywhere within the program, the handler will be executed to issue an error message and the main program then terminated. The handler for SYMBOL_ERR, on the other hand, will be local to the procedure which substitutes the values of symbols into the output machine code file. Execution of this handler will also issue an error message; however, this time the program does not then terminate, but continues to process the remainder of the assembly language program.

The second use of exception handlers is to provide error recovery. The simplest way of recovering from an error occurring within a subprogram is to use a handler to provide sensible output values when the computation performed by the main body of the subprogram fails. One way of doing this is to design the handler in such a way that it recomputes the required output values by a different but much simpler algorithm. This will usually mean that the accuracy of the results returned by the handler will not be as good as are normally provided but will nevertheless be sufficient to allow the computation to proceed. Thus the subprogram's specification is effectively relaxed in exchange for a more robust operation. As an example, suppose that a procedure is required which takes as input an array of numbers representing fixed points along a segment of some unknown continuous function. The procedure must estimate the peak value of the function as accurately as possible. The main body of such a procedure could typically consist of a complex polynomial curve fitting algorithm. If an error occurs, however, the procedure is allowed to return a rough estimate of the peak value instead. A suitable outline for this procedure might be

```
procedure ESTIMATE_PEAK(X: in VECTOR; PEAK: out ORDINATE) is
begin
      - -
      - - compute PEAK from X using polynomial
      - - curve fitting technique – errors
      - - are possible here
      - -
exception
      when others =>
            PEAK := ORDINATE'FIRST;
            for I in X'RANGE loop
                  if PEAK < X(I) then
                        PEAK := X(I);
                  end if;
            end loop;
end ESTIMATE_PEAK;
```

where any exceptions raised within the main body of ESTIMATE_PEAK leads to the exception handler being executed. This handler estimates the peak value very crudely by finding the maximum value in the vector X. Though less accurate, the algorithm executed by the handler is so simple that the chances of an error occurring during its execution are minimal.

The third use of exceptions also relates to error recovery. As well as always trying to ensure that a subprogram returns useful results, error recovery also involves undoing any harmful effects caused by the error, before the damage can spread to other parts of the system. In this context, the idea of *layered error recovery* is important. This is where each subprogram in a system responds to the raising of an exception by first 'cleaning itself up' and then propagating the exception back to the caller. In other words, any subprogram in the sequence of calls leading to an error is allowed to express its 'last wishes' before being abnormally terminated. As an example of this, consider the following program outline, in which a file of data values is processed and some results computed. (The example includes file handling which has not been covered yet – see Chapter 15. Here it is sufficient to understand that the package DATAIO provides a type FILE_TYPE denoting a file of DATA items and operations to OPEN, READ and CLOSE the file.)

```
with DATAIO; use DATAIO;
procedure ANALYSE(FILE_NAME: in STRING;
                        RESULTS: out ANSWER) is
    procedure INIT(RESULTS: in out ANSWER) is
    begin
        - - initialise RESULTS
    end INIT;
    procedure UPDATE(CURRENT_DATUM: in DATA;
                        RESULTS: in out ANSWER) is
    begin
        - - process CURRENT_DATUM and update RESULTS
        - - exceptions may be raised during this operation
    end UPDATE;
    procedure PROCESS_FILE(FILE_NAME: in STRING;
                        RESULTS: out ANSWER) is
        F:FILE_TYPE;
        X:DATA;
    begin
        OPEN(F, IN_FILE,FILE_NAME);  - - open the file for reading
        INIT(RESULTS);
        while not END_OF_FILE(F) loop
            READ(F,X);
            UPDATE(X,RESULTS);
        end loop;
        CLOSE(F);                - - close the file
    exception
        when others =>
            CLOSE(F);            - - close file before abnormal
            raise;               - - termination
    end PROCESS_FILE;
begin
    - -
    - -
    PROCESS_FILE(FILE_NAME,RESULTS);
    - -
    - -
exception
    - - handlers for exceptions raised
    - - during analysis
end ANALYSE;
```

In normal operation, the procedure PROCESS_FILE opens the named file, processes the contents of the file one-by-one by calls to UPDATE, and then closes the file. The key point about this example concerns what happens if an exception is raised during the execution of UPDATE. The procedure PROCESS_FILE is not concerned with the actual computations involved in processing the file, but only with opening, reading and closing the file. Thus it is not appropriate to handle errors occurring in UPDATE within PROCESS_FILE; rather, they should be handled by the main procedure ANALYSE. However, if PROCESS_FILE contained no exception handlers at all, then when an error occurred in UPDATE it would be abnormally terminated, leaving the file F open. To avoid this, PROCESS_FILE is designed to intercept any exceptions propagated from UPDATE, and close the file F before propagating the exception back to the caller. This propagation of the unknown exception is achieved using the anonymous **raise** statement (that is, a **raise** statement without a name) which raises again the last raised exception. Thus the anonymous raise statement allows a subprogram such as PROCESS_FILE to perform its 'last wishes' before abnormally terminating, but still allows the offending exception to propagate further. (Note: an anonymous **raise** statement may only appear in an exception handler.)

From the above description of the three main uses of exceptions it should be clear that they allow very sophisticated strategies to be adopted when programming robust, fault-tolerant software. The general-purpose user may be content to treat exceptions as a very convenient method of error reporting, but for those involved in the design of non-stop real time systems they are a vital tool for the construction of highly reliable software.

13.6 EXCEPTIONS IN TASKS

As noted in section 13.4, exceptions do not normally propagate beyond a task. If an exception is raised in a task and not handled there, then the task simply terminates. There are some special cases, however, where an exception can be raised in one task as a result of an error occurring in another.

Firstly, an exception can occur during the execution of an **accept** statement, that is, during a rendezvous. If this occurs and the exception is not handled locally within the **accept** statement, then the same exception is also raised in the caller task at the place of the entry call. Secondly, if a server task is terminated abnormally while performing a rendezvous (for example, as the result of an **abort** statement) then the exception TASKING_ERROR is raised in the caller task at the place of the entry call. Note, however, that abnormal termination of a caller task does not cause any exceptions to be raised in the server task. If the entry call made by the caller has not yet been accepted, then the entry call is simply cancelled; otherwise, the rendezvous is allowed to complete normally and the server task is unaffected.

13.7 AN EXAMPLE – THE NETWORK MANAGER PACKAGE

In section 8.11, an example was given of the design of a network manager package. In that design, the reporting of errors to users of the package was omitted. Now that exceptions have been described, the design of this package can be completed. All that is required is to identify the different kinds of error that can occur within the package, declare an exception for each kind in the package specification, and then insert appropriate raise statements within the package body.

In the NETWORK_MANAGER there are four different kinds of errors, and therefore four different exceptions can be defined:

1.	NODE_ERR	– an attempt to perform an operation on a non-existent node
2.	INSERT_ERR	– attempt to insert an existing node
3.	LINK_ERR	– attempt to exceed the maximum number of links to a given node
4.	DISCONNECT_ERR	– attempt to disconnect a non-existent link

To make these exceptions visible to the user of the package, they must be declared in the package specification, which is therefore amended as follows:

```
package NETWORK_MANAGER is

    - - constant, type and subprogram
    - - declarations as before

    NODE_ERR,INSERT_ERR       : exception;
    LINK_ERR,DISCONNECT_ERR : exception;

end NETWORK_MANAGER;
```

In the design of the NETWORK_MANAGER as given in section 8.11, all error checking is, in fact, performed by the nested NODE_MANAGER package. This does not cause any problems, however, since the exceptions declared above are directly visible within this package. Hence, everywhere that an error is detected within the NODE_MANAGER package, a **raise** statement is placed. For example, the CHECK_INSERTED procedure becomes

```
procedure CHECK_INSERTED(N: in NODE_REC) is
begin
    if not N . INSERTED then
        raise NODE_ERR;
    end if;
end CHECK_INSERTED;
```

and so on for the procedures INSERT which raises INSERT_ERR, ADD_LINK which raises LINK_ERR and REM_LINK which raises DISCONNECT_ERR.

13.8 EXERCISES

(13.1) In question (8.1), the design of an INTEGER_STACK package was asked for. Extend the design of this package to include exceptions for reporting stack underflow and overflow errors.

(13.2) In question (9.2), it was suggested that the NODE_MANAGER package could be compiled separately from the NETWORK_MANAGER package. What impact would this have on the handling of errors?

14

Generic program units

14.1 PARAMETRISATION OF PROGRAM UNITS

One of the key ideas in Ada is that a program is built up from a number of separately compiled program units. Furthermore, many of these program units will have been selected from existing libraries of useful subprograms and packages. Thus, it is hoped that software development in Ada will be more productive because there should be far fewer instances of 'reinventing the wheel'.

An essential aspect of writing library units is to make them sufficiently general to be useful in a wide range of different applications. This generality can be achieved in Ada, as in most other languages, by using subprograms with appropriate parameters. When the subprogram is called, the actual parameters supplied in the call can be used to give that particular invocation of the subprogram the required characteristics. As an example, suppose that it is required to search a string of characters to find the first occurrence of the space character. A procedure could be written to do this, as follows

```
procedure SEARCH(S: in STRING; OK: out BOOLEAN;
                             IDX: out NATURAL) is
    CH: constant CHARACTER := ' ';
    FOUND: BOOLEAN;
begin
    for I in S'RANGE loop
        FOUND := S(I)=CH;
        if FOUND then
          IDX:=I;
          exit;
        end if;
    end loop;
    OK := FOUND;
end SEARCH;
```

where OK returns TRUE if a space character is found in the string S, and otherwise returns FALSE. The index position of the found character is returned in IDX.

Although this procedure may be useful in certain specific applications, it is not sufficiently general to warrant its inclusion in a library. Clearly some extra generality can be obtained by making the search character an input parameter, thereby enabling the routine to find any character in a string, not just a space, that is,

```
procedure SEARCH(S: in STRING; OK: out BOOLEAN;
               CH: in CHARACTER; IDX: out NATURAL) is
    FOUND: BOOLEAN;
begin
    - -
    - - as before
    - -
end SEARCH;
```

However, little more can be done to generalise the SEARCH procedure using the normal parameter mechanism. In particular, it is not possible to parametrise the type of the array searched so that the same procedure could be used to search for a given component of any one-dimensional array.

At this point it is important to emphasise that the substitution of actual parameters for formal parameters in subprogram calls occurs at run time. In order to make this substitution practical and efficient to implement, the forms of parametrisation allowed are restricted to values (**in** mode parameters) and objects (**out** and **in out** mode parameters). Types cannot be parametrised because implementation would be too costly. To overcome this restriction, Ada provides an entirely separate parametrisation facility called *generic program units*.

A generic program unit is not itself directly executable, but is a pattern or template for creating instances of that unit. This process of creating a particular instance of a generic unit is called *generic instantiation*. A generic unit may have parameters so that when a particular instance of the unit is created the actual parameters supplied in the instantiation determine the precise characteristics of that instance. The rules concerning generic program units are designed to allow all generic instantiations to be performed at compile time. This allows greater flexibility in the range of parametrisations provided, in particular, types may be parametrised.

As an example of using a generic program unit, the SEARCH procedure given above could be an instance of a general one-dimensional array search procedure, with specification as follows

```
generic
    type ITEM is private;
    type INDEX is (<>);
    type VECTOR is array (INDEX range <>) of ITEM;
    procedure ARRAY_SEARCH (VEC: in VECTOR; VALUE: in ITEM;
                           OK: out BOOLEAN; IDX: out INDEX);
```

The generic procedure ARRAY_SEARCH is a template for creating actual search procedures for use with different types of array. In this case, the parameters of the template are all types, that is, ITEM, INDEX and VECTOR (the details of the notation are described later) and these are listed immediately after the keyword **generic** before the actual procedure specification. Once a generic type parameter has been defined, it can be used from then on as if it were an actual type. In the above, generic types are used in the procedure specification. They can also be freely referenced within the corresponding body, which is

```
procedure ARRAY_SEARCH (VEC: in VECTOR; VALUE: in ITEM;
                         OK: out BOOLEAN; IDX: out INDEX) is
    FOUND: BOOLEAN;
begin
    for I in VEC'RANGE loop
        FOUND := VEC(I)=VALUE;
        if FOUND then
            IDX:=I;
            exit;
        end if;
    end loop;
    OK := FOUND;
end ARRAY_SEARCH;
```

To create an actual instance of the above template, a generic instantiation must be written. This instantiation gives the name of the new instance and supplies any necessary actual parameters. For example, writing

```
procedure SEARCH is new ARRAY_SEARCH(ITEM => CHARACTER,
                                      INDEX => POSITIVE,
                                      VECTOR => STRING);
```

would achieve exactly the same effect as writing down the complete definition for SEARCH given earlier. The instantiation creates a copy of the ARRAY_SEARCH procedure, with the name changed to SEARCH, and all occurrences of the identifiers ITEM, INDEX and VECTOR replaced by CHARACTER, POSITIVE and STRING, respectively.

As a second example, given

```
type PERSON is
    record
        AGE: AGETYPE;
        STATUS: MARITAL_STATUS;
        SEX: GENDER;
    end record;
type PEOPLE is array(ID_CODE range <>) of PERSON;
```

then the generic instantiation

> **procedure** FIND **is new** ARRAY_SEARCH (ITEM => PERSON,
>   INDEX => ID_CODE,
>   VECTOR => PEOPLE);

would create a procedure called FIND for searching an array of PERSON records. Thus, the generic procedure ARRAY_SEARCH allows any number of procedures to be created for searching arrays of quite different types.

This, then, is the basic idea of generic program units. The generic unit itself provides a template for creating actual copies of the unit. Each copy is made by writing a generic instantiation instead of a normal program unit declaration. The instantiation gives the name of the new copy, and supplies any actual parameters required. When the copy is made, these actual parameters are substituted for the formal parameters used in the template. This instantiation process can be performed entirely at compile time, and the final code produced is no different to that which would have occurred if the required instance had been written out in full. The main use of generics is in writing general purpose library subprograms and packages. However, they are not restricted to library units; a generic declaration can be written anywhere that a declaration is allowed.

Now that the principles of generic program units and the motivation for their use has been explained, they will be described in more detail.

14.2 GENERIC DECLARATIONS

A generic program unit must be a subprogram or a package. Generic tasks are not allowed. A generic program unit is written in exactly the same way as a normal unit except that its specification is preceded by the keyword **generic** followed by a list of generic parameters, if any. The syntax diagrams for generic program unit declarations are:

S131 generic_subprogram_declaration
    → generic_part ⟶ subprogram_specification ⟶ ";" ⟶

S132 generic_package_declaration
    → generic_part ⟶ package_specification ⟶ ";" ⟶

S133 generic_part
    → "generic" ⟶
                 ⟵ generic_formal_parameter ⟵

When a generic declaration is elaborated, each of the generic formal parameters are elaborated one by one in the order given. A generic parameter may refer to another generic parameter in the same generic part only if that parameter is a type. Any expressions occurring in the generic part are evaluated during its elaboration, except primaries involving generic types, whose evaluation is deferred until each instantiation.

Within the actual program unit specification and its corresponding body, the name of any generic parameter can be used anywhere that is consistent for that parameter's class (for example, value, type, etc.). All other identifiers used within a generic unit must either be declared locally within the unit or be visible at the point of its occurrence in the program.

The elaboration of a generic declaration is complete when its generic part has been fully elaborated. The following program unit specification is not elaborated, nor is the corresponding body; however, they are checked to be syntactically and semantically correct. Conceptually, the specification and body are simply established as being a template for forming instantiations of that unit.

A generic program unit can be declared anywhere that a normal program unit can be declared. If the specification part occurs in the declarative part of some other unit, then the corresponding body must follow in that same declarative part. If the specification occurs at the outermost level of the program, then it is a library unit and the body can be separately compiled (this is the usual case). Generic bodies can also be separately compiled as subunits. Finally, the name of any generic library unit must be mentioned in a **with** clause before copies of it can be instantiated.

Examples of generic declarations are given in section 14.4.

14.3 GENERIC INSTANTIATIONS

A generic instantiation may be written anywhere that a declaration is allowed. Its effect is to create a copy of the named generic unit, with the given name and with the given actual parameters substituted for the corresponding generic formal parameters. The syntax for a generic instantiation is given by the following diagrams:

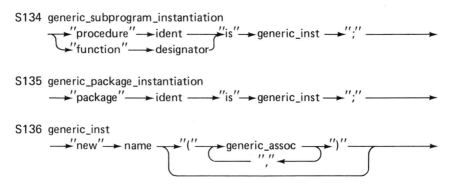

S134 generic_subprogram_instantiation

S135 generic_package_instantiation

S136 generic_inst

S137 generic_assoc

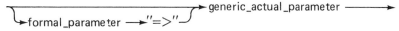

S138 generic_actual_parameter

The general form of a generic instantiation is shown by the examples given in section 14.1. The generic actual parameters may be associated with their corresponding formal parameters either by position or by name, just as is the case for subprogram calls.

The rules concerning actual generic parameters and further examples of generic instantiations are given in the next section.

14.4 GENERIC PARAMETERS

As shown by the following syntax diagram, there are three kinds of generic formal parameter: ordinary data values and objects, types, and subprograms:

S139 generic_formal_parameter

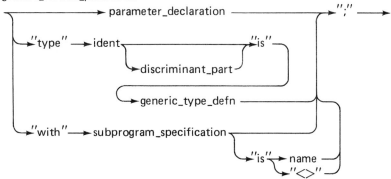

The first option in diagram S139 is an ordinary parameter declaration. This option is used to declare generic parameters which are data values and data objects, and the syntax used is exactly the same as for ordinary subprogram parameters. A parameter of **in** mode is used to denote a constant, whose value is specified by means of an expression at each instantiation. This mode is the default mode. A parameter of **in out** mode denotes a data object whose identity is determined at each instantiation. Parameters of **out** mode are not allowed.

As an example, suppose a ring counter is required which counts up to some specified value and then, on the next count, resets itself to zero. The following generic package provides this function:

```
generic
    PERIOD: in NATURAL;
package RING_COUNTER is
    function IS_ZERO return BOOLEAN;
    procedure INCREMENT;
end RING_COUNTER;

package body RING_COUNTER is

    COUNT: INTEGER range 0 .. PERIOD-1 := 0;

    function IS_ZERO return BOOLEAN is
    begin
        return COUNT=0;
    end IS_ZERO;

    procedure INCREMENT is
    begin
        COUNT := (COUNT+1) mod PERIOD;
    end INCREMENT;

end RING_COUNTER;
```

Given this package, a counter can be instantiated to count with any required period. For example, the following procedure prints out the contents of an array of integer values in tabular form with 6 values printed on each line:

```
procedure TABULATE(X: in INTEGER_VECTOR) is

    FIELD_WIDTH: constant := 10;

    package COUNTER is new RING_COUNTER(PERIOD => 6);
    use COUNTER;

begin
    for I in X'RANGE loop
        PUT(X(I),FIELD_WIDTH);
        INCREMENT;
        if IS_ZERO then
            NEW_LINE;
        end if;
    end loop;
end TABULATE;
```

where the call to PUT is assumed to print its first integer argument in the field-width specified by its second argument, and NEW_LINE just starts a new line (the next chapter explains input/output in detail).

The elaboration of the generic instantiation in the third line of this procedure creates a new copy of the RING_COUNTER package and calls it COUNTER, with a period of 6. The actual instantiated package is then elaborated as normal, so that the private variable COUNT is initialised to zero. Note here that conceptually this package is instantiated each time that the procedure TABULATE is called, but in practice it may be instantiated just once when TABULATE is compiled.

The second kind of generic parameter allowed is a type. Generic types are the key to the power of generics, since they greatly extend Ada's capabilities for creating abstract and highly generalised library units. Generic types were introduced in section 14.1. The basic idea is simply that a dummy type name is used within the generic unit, an actual type name then being supplied at instantiation. As a very simple example, suppose that a function is required called NEXT for discrete types which has a similar effect to the SUCC attribute described in section 3.2, except that asking for the successor of the last value of the type does not cause CONSTRAINT_ERROR to be raised, but instead returns the first value of the range. For example, given the DAY type defined in section 3.2 then NEXT(MON)=TUE, NEXT(SAT)=SUN, NEXT(SUN)=MON, etc. This subprogram can be defined as a generic function to allow instances to be created to operate on any discrete type. The specification of this function is

```
generic
    type DISCRETE is (<>);
function NEXT_OPERATION(X:DISCRETE) return DISCRETE;
```

Given this generic function, the required NEXT operation on the type DAY can be obtained by instantiation as follows

```
function NEXT is new NEXT_OPERATION(DAY);
```

Similarly, the NEXT operation can be instantiated for any other discrete type, for example,

```
function NEXT is new NEXT_OPERATION(BOOLEAN);
```

Notice that the same name can be used for both instantiations. This is possible under the normal overloading rules for subprograms.

The body of NEXT_OPERATION has the same form as any normal function except, of course, that it can refer to the type name DISCRETE as though it were an actual type:

```
function NEXT_OPERATION(X:DISCRETE) return DISCRETE is
begin
    if X=X'LAST then
        return X'FIRST;
    else
        return X'SUCC;
```

          end if;
       end NEXT_OPERATION;

Returning now to the declaration of NEXT_OPERATION, the generic type DISCRETE is declared as

       type DISCRETE **is** ($<>$);

where the box symbol $'<>'$ denotes any discrete type. It is important when using generics to understand that the language rules are designed to ensure that the legality of a generic unit can be established entirely at its point of declaration. No further checking then needs to be performed during instantiation. This is very important, since the user of a generic library unit should not be faced with the possibility of mysterious errors arising within a unit when he instantiates it. To make this checking possible, the class of type which may be supplied as an actual parameter must be restricted. In the above case, DISCRETE is restricted to any discrete type. Within the body of NEXT_OPERATION, all operations on objects of this type (that is, the parameter X) are known to be valid for any discrete type. Thus as long as the actual type supplied in the instantiation is a discrete type, then the new instance will work properly.

In all, a total of seven different classes of type are allowed for generic type parameters, as shown by the following syntax diagram

S140 generic_type_defn

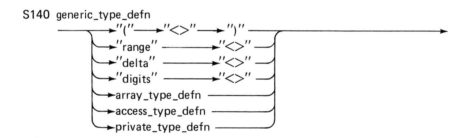

The first four of these correspond to the scalar types

      ($<>$)   – – denotes any discrete type
      range $<>$ – – denotes any integer type
      delta $<>$ – – denotes any fixed-point type
      digits $<>$ – – denotes any floating-point type

(fixed and floating point types are described in Chapter 16). For each of these classes of scalar type, all predefined operators and attributes are available within the generic unit. Notice that the generic type ($<>$) includes any integer type but excludes all the arithmetic operations that are specific to integers.

If a generic type is declared as an array type, then within the generic unit the usual operations on arrays are available, that is, indexing, slicing, assignment, etc. Note that the index and component types may be either actual types or previously declared generic types. This was illustrated in the ARRAY_SEARCH procedure given in section 14.1. The actual array parameter supplied in an instantiation must obey certain matching rules. Firstly, both the actual and formal arrays must have the same dimensions. Secondly, the index and component types must be the same. Thirdly, if the formal array type is unconstrained, then the actual type must also be unconstrained. Conversely, if the formal type is constrained then so must be the actual type.

If a generic type is declared as an access type, then within the generic unit the usual operations are available, including the use of allocators. Any actual access type parameter supplied in an instantiation must designate the same base type as the formal access type parameter. Of course, this base type could itself be a generic parameter.

Finally, if a generic type is declared as a private type, then within the generic unit the only operations available on objects of that type are assignment and tests for equality and inequality. Any actual type can be supplied for a formal private type, provided that these operations are available for that type. If a generic type is declared as **limited private** then no operations are available on objects of that type, and any actual type may be supplied for it. The only exception to these rules is that an actual type may not be an unconstrained array type.

One of the commonest uses of generic types is in parametrising packages which manage data structures. For example, the following package provides a first-in first-out buffer type similar to that used in the BUFFER task given in section 12.5. Here the type of the object buffered and the size of the buffer are generic parameters:

```
generic
     SIZE:NATURAL := 100;
     type OBJECT is private;
package FIFO is

     type FIFO_BUFFER is limited private;

     procedure STORE(B: in out FIFO_BUFFER; X: in OBJECT);
     procedure RETRIEVE(B: in out FIFO_BUFFER; X: out OBJECT);
     function EMPTY(B: FIFO_BUFFER) return BOOLEAN;
     function FULL(B: FIFO_BUFFER) return BOOLEAN;

     OVERFLOW, UNDERFLOW: exception;

private
     type SPACE is array (1 .. SIZE) of OBJECT;
     type FIFO_BUFFER is
```

```
        record
            BUF: SPACE;
            INX,OUTX:INTEGER range 1 . . SIZE := 1;
            USED:INTEGER range 0 . . SIZE := 0;
        end record;
end FIFO;

package body FIFO is
    procedure STORE(B: in out FIFO_BUFFER; X: in OBJECT) is
    begin
        if B . USED<SIZE then
            B . BUF(B . INX) := X;
            B . INX := (B . INX mod SIZE) + 1;
            B . USED := B . USED + 1;
        else
            raise OVERFLOW;
        end if;
    end STORE;

    procedure RETRIEVE(B: in out FIFO_BUFFER; X: out OBJECT) is
    begin
        if B . USED>0 then
            X := B . BUF(B . OUTX);
            B . OUTX := (B . OUTX mod SIZE) + 1;
            B . USED := B . USED - 1;
        else
            raise UNDERFLOW;
        end if;
    end RETRIEVE;

    function EMPTY(B:FIFO_BUFFER) return BOOLEAN is
    begin
        return B . USED=0;
    end EMPTY;

    function FULL(B:FIFO_BUFFER) return BOOLEAN is
    begin
        return B . USED=SIZE;
    end FULL;
end FIFO;
```

Each instantiation of the above package creates an abstract type representing a buffer of given size and component type. The user may then declare as many actual buffer objects of this type as he wishes. Notice the use of a default value for the SIZE parameter. This allows the user to omit the SIZE parameter in an instantiation if the default buffer size of 100 is required. For example,

```
package CHARACTER_BUFFER is
    new FIFO(OBJECT => CHARACTER);
```

is equivalent to writing

```
package CHARACTER_BUFFER is
    new FIFO(SIZE => 100, OBJECT => CHARACTER);
```

As an example of the use of the instantiated CHARACTER_BUFFER package, the body of the BUFFER task given in section 12.5 could be rewritten as follows:

```
task body BUFFER is
    use CHARACTER_BUFFER;
    B: FIFO_BUFFER;        - - declare buffer object
begin
    loop
        select
            when not FULL(B) =>
                accept PUT(C: in CHARACTER) do
                    STORE(B,C);
                end PUT;
        or
            when not EMPTY(B) =>
                accept GET(C: out CHARACTER) do
                    RETRIEVE(B,C);
                end GET;
        end select;
    end loop;
end BUFFER;
```

At this point it is worth noting that, although generic tasks are not allowed directly, a task can be declared in the specification part of a package. Therefore, a generic buffer task could be defined by a generic package to allow tasks to be created by instantiation with any required buffer size and object type. Alternatively, a task type could be included as part of the definition of the abstract buffer type (see next section).

The final kind of generic parameter allowed is the formal subprogram parameter. These are used to pass the names of subprograms to a generic unit, to augment the set of pre-defined operations provided for a generic type. As shown in syntax diagram S139, a subprogram parameter is introduced by the keyword **with** followed by the subprogram specification.

The basic idea of formal subprograms in generic units is illustrated by the following example. Suppose that a general purpose procedure is required to sort an array of objects into ascending order. In order to implement this procedure it will be necessary to compare array components to determine relative ordering. However, to keep the procedure entirely general, the component types of the array must be arbitrary. This means that the component type must be private, and hence no built-in comparison operators (that is, $>$, $<$, $>=$, etc.) can be assumed. The required compare operation must therefore be provided as a generic subprogram parameter.

One of the most efficient sorting algorithms known is 'quicksort' and this will be used here. The generic procedure specification is as follows

```
generic
     type ITEM is private;
     type INDEX is (<>);
     type VECTOR is array(INDEX range <>)of ITEM;
     with function "<"(X,Y:ITEM)return BOOLEAN;
procedure QUICKSORT(V:in out VECTOR);
```

Here the generic array type VECTOR is specified in exactly the same way as in the ARRAY_SEARCH procedure given in section 14.1; however, this time the type is augmented by the "$<$" operator supplied as a generic formal subprogram.

To use this generic procedure, each instantiation must supply three type names and the name of a Boolean function for the formal "$<$" operator. This last item can be either a built-in operator or a user-defined function. For example, a procedure to sort a string of characters could be instantiated by

```
procedure STRING_SORT is
     new QUICKSORT(CHARACTER, POSITIVE, STRING, "<");
```

where the actual subprogram argument is the name of a built-in operator. Given

```
MY_NAME:STRING(1 . . 5) := "STEVE";
```

then the call

```
STRING_SORT(MY_NAME);
```

would sort MY_NAME into ascending order. Suppose now, however, that a procedure is required to sort arrays of type PEOPLE, as defined in section 14.1, into ascending order of age. First of all a suitable compare function must be defined, for example,

```
function OLDER(A,B:PERSON)return BOOLEAN is
begin
     return A . AGE<B . AGE;
end OLDER;
```

The required sort procedure can then be instantiated as follows

```
procedure AGE_SORT is
     new QUICKSORT(PERSON, ID_CODE, PEOPLE, OLDER);
```

Notice here that it is quite legal to supply an ordinary function as actual parameter when the corresponding formal parameter is an operator. In general, an actual subprogram matches a formal subprogram if it has parameters in the same order, of the same mode and type, and with the same constraints. For functions, the result type and constraints must also be the same. Parameter names and the presence or absence of default values are ignored for this matching.

Referring back again to syntax diagram S139, it can be seen that a formal subprogram specification in a generic parameter can be followed by the keyword **is** and either a name or a box. These options are used to denote default subprograms. If a name is given after **is**, then the named subprogram will be used by default in any instantiation of the generic unit for which an actual subprogram is omitted. This named subprogram must be visible at the point of declaration of the generic unit. If a box is given after **is**, the effect is similar except that the default subprogram, if there is one, is the subprogram visible at the point of instantiation with both name and specification matching that of the generic formal parameter. If no such subprogram exists, then the actual subprogram parameter cannot be omitted. For example, if in the QUICKSORT procedure, the formal subprogram was declared with a box default, that is,

> **with function** $"<"(X,Y:ITEM)$ **return** BOOLEAN **is** <>;

then the instantiation of STRING_SORT could be written with the explicit naming of the built-in $"<"$ operator omitted, that is,

> **function** STRING_SORT **is**
> **new** QUICKSORT(CHARACTER, NATURAL, STRING);

Because of the default mechanism, this instantiation is exactly equivalent to the previous version. Note, however, that this parameter could not be omitted for the instantiation of AGE_SORT unless an overloading of the $"<"$ operator had been explicitly defined for operands of type PERSON.

Finally, for completeness, the body of QUICKSORT is given as follows:

> **procedure** QUICKSORT(V: **in out** VECTOR) **is**
>
>   **procedure** SORT(LEFT,RIGHT:INDEX) **is**
>   CENTRE_VALUE:ITEM := V((LEFT+RIGHT)/2);
>   LEFT_IDX:INDEX := LEFT;
>   RIGHT_IDX:INDEX := RIGHT;
>   **begin**
>   **loop**
>   **while** V(LEFT_IDX) < CENTRE_VALUE **loop**
>   LEFT_IDX := INDEX'SUCC(LEFT_IDX);
>   **end loop**;
>   **while** CENTRE_VALUE < V(RIGHT_IDX) **loop**
>   RIGHT_IDX := INDEX'PRED(RIGHT_IDX);
>   **end loop**;

```
            if LEFT_IDX <= RIGHT_IDX then
                declare
                    TEMP:ITEM := V(LEFT_IDX);
                begin
                    V(LEFT_IDX) := V(RIGHT_IDX);
                    V(RIGHT_IDX) := TEMP;
                end;
                LEFT_IDX := INDEX'SUCC(LEFT_IDX);
                RIGHT_IDX := INDEX'PRED(RIGHT_IDX);
            end if;
            exit when LEFT_IDX > RIGHT_IDX;
        end loop;
        if LEFT < RIGHT_IDX then
            SORT(LEFT,RIGHT_IDX);
        end if;
        if LEFT_IDX < RIGHT then
            SORT(LEFT_IDX,RIGHT);
        end if;
    end SORT;
begin
    SORT(V'FIRST,V'LAST);
end QUICKSORT;
```

14.5 EXAMPLE – A GENERIC BUFFER FOR TASK COMMUNICATION

In the previous section, a generic package called FIFO was presented and its use illustrated in the construction of a buffer task of the sort described in section 12.5. In this section, a package will be described which effectively provides a generic buffer for use between communicating tasks. In this case, however, the buffer is presented to the user as an abstract data type. The specification of the package is as follows

```
generic
    type OBJECT is private;
package BUFFER_TYPE is

    type BUFFER(SIZE:NATURAL)is limited private;

    procedure PUT(B:in out BUFFER; X:in OBJECT);
    procedure GET(B:in out BUFFER; X:out OBJECT);
    function FULL(B:BUFFER) return BOOLEAN;
    function EMPTY(B:BUFFER) return BOOLEAN;
    procedure INIT(B:in out BUFFER);
    procedure KILL(B:in out BUFFER);
```

private
> **task type** BUFFER_TASK **is**
>> **entry** SET_SIZE(BUFFER_SIZE: **in** NATURAL);
>> **entry** PUT(X: **in** OBJECT);
>> **entry** GET(X: **out** OBJECT);
>> **entry** CHECK_USED(COUNT: **out** NATURAL);
>> **entry** KILL;
> **end** BUFFER_TASK;
>
> **type** BUFFER(SIZE:NATURAL) **is**
>> **record**
>>> CONTROL:BUFFER_TASK;
>> **end record**;

end BUFFER_TYPE;

Ignoring the private part of this package specification for the moment, notice firstly that this approach to formulating a generic buffer is rather different to that used previously. Here the package provides an abstract BUFFER type in which the size of the buffer is specified via a discriminant rather than via a generic parameter. Secondly, notice that all buffer operations are defined by procedure calls. These procedures provide an interface between the user of the package and the task which actually controls buffer accesses.

To use this package for buffering characters, say, a copy would be instantiated as follows

> **package** CHARACTER_BUFFER **is**
>> **new** BUFFER_TYPE(OBJECT => CHARACTER);

and actual buffer objects declared as in

> **use** CHARACTER_BUFFER;
> MY_BUFFER, YOUR_BUFFER: BUFFER(SIZE => 64);

which declares two character buffers, each of which can hold up to 64 characters. Then, following a call to INIT to initialise each buffer, characters may be sent and received by procedure calls such as

> PUT(MY_BUFFER, 'A');
>
> GET(YOUR_BUFFER, NEXT_CHARACTER);

Finally, when the buffers are finished with, they can be explicitly destroyed by the calls KILL(MY_BUFFER) and KILL(YOUR_BUFFER), respectively. Otherwise, when the unit in which the buffers are declared terminates, then they will be destroyed automatically,

Turning now to the implementation of the BUFFER_TYPE, a buffer is actually a task, with an internal data structure for holding buffered objects, and entries for the required buffer operations. Hence, within the private part of the above package, a task type is declared called BUFFER_TASK. The actual BUFFER type is then a discriminated record with the buffer SIZE as discriminant and a single component called CONTROL which is a task of type BUFFER_ TYPE. Hence, every time that an object of type BUFFER is declared by the user, a task will be activated. The subsequent call to INIT then passes the required buffer size to this task via the entry call SET_SIZE. This allows storage space for the buffer to be declared, and the buffer operations may then commence.

In detail, the body of the BUFFER_TYPE package is

```
package body BUFFER_TYPE is

    task body BUFFER_TASK is
        SIZE:NATURAL;
    begin
        accept SET_SIZE(BUFFER_SIZE: in NATURAL) do
            SIZE:=BUFFER_SIZE;
        end SET_SIZE;
        - - Nested block to declare dynamic array
        - - of type OBJECT with SIZE components
        declare
            BUF: array(1 .. SIZE)of OBJECT;
            INX,OUTX:INTEGER range 1 .. SIZE := 1;
            USED:INTEGER range 0 .. SIZE := 0;
        begin
            BUFFER_OPERATIONS:
            loop
                select
                    when USED<SIZE =>
                        accept PUT(X: in OBJECT) do
                            BUF(INX) := X;
                        end PUT;
                        INX := INX mod SIZE + 1;
                        USED := USED + 1;
                or
                    when USED>0 =>
                        accept GET(X: out OBJECT) do
                            X := BUF(OUTX);
                        end GET;
                        OUTX := OUTX mod SIZE + 1;
                        USED := USED - 1;
                or
                    accept CHECK_USED(COUNT: out NATURAL) do
                        COUNT := USED;
                    end CHECK_USED;
```

```
            or
                accept KILL;
                exit BUFFER_OPERATIONS;
            or
                terminate;
            end select;

        end loop BUFFER_OPERATIONS;

    end;

end BUFFER_TASK;

- - Interface Procedures

procedure PUT(B: in out BUFFER; X: in OBJECT) is
begin
    B.CONTROL.PUT(X);
end PUT;

procedure GET(B: in out BUFFER;  X: out OBJECT) is
begin
    B.CONTROL.GET(X);
end GET;

function FULL(B:BUFFER) return BOOLEAN is
    COUNT:NATURAL;
begin
    B.CONTROL.CHECK_USED(COUNT);
    return COUNT=SIZE;
end FULL;

function EMPTY(B:BUFFER) return BOOLEAN is
    COUNT:NATURAL;
begin
    B.CONTROL.CHECK_USED(COUNT);
    return COUNT=0;
end EMPTY;

procedure INIT(B: in out BUFFER) is
begin
    B.CONTROL.SET_SIZE(B.SIZE);
end INIT;

procedure KILL(B: in out BUFFER) is
begin
    B.CONTROL.KILL;
end KILL;

end BUFFER_TYPE;
```

The above package provides one approach to implementing a general-purpose buffer facility for multi-task systems. A buffer is defined as an abstract type with the type of buffered object set by a generic parameter at each instantiation. The buffer size is then specified by a discriminant constraint at each object declaration. In the FIFO example of section 14.4, the buffer size was set by a generic parameter rather than a discriminant. Although both approaches are possible, the use of discriminants is usually preferable. To see why, suppose that several character buffers of different sizes were required. Then, firstly, each required buffer would need a separate package instantiation, which clutters the program text; and, secondly, each buffer type generated in this way would be a distinct type, and hence subprograms which implement common operations would have to be duplicated for each size of buffer.

14.6 EXERCISES

(14.1) Replace the generic function NEXT_OPERATION given in section 14.4 by a generic package which provides both the function NEXT_OPER-ATION and the inverse function PREVIOUS_OPERATION.

(14.2) Write a package called BLOCKING_BUFFER which defines a buffer task similar to that given in section 12.5 except that the size of the buffer and the type of the buffered objects are generic parameters.

(14.3) Reformulate the STACK package of question (8.1) Chapter 8 as a generic package in which the size and type of the stacked object are generic parameters. A similar effect can be gained by making only the type of stacked object generic and defining an abstract stack type with the required size as a discriminant. Show how this can be done, and compare the two approaches.

15

Input/Output

15.1 INPUT/OUTPUT IN ADA

In a general computing facility, a range of standard peripheral devices will usually be provided for transferring data to and from the computer. Typical examples are visual display units, printers, card readers, disc file stores, and so on. Because these devices are very common, the Ada language provides a set of built-in facilities for using them. These facilities are designed to be oriented towards the user and as far as possible are independent of the actual hardware used. For this reason they are called high level input/output facilities.

Ada, of course, is not only designed to support general purpose computing but also the production of real time software. A key characteristic of this latter area is the need to program special purpose input/output devices directly at the level of the machine. This is called low level input/output programming and Ada supports this activity also.

In this chapter, only high level input/output programming will be considered. Low level input/output programming is discussed later in Chapter 17.

The high level input/output facilities provided in Ada are not, as in many other languages, supplied in the form of additional language constructs but in the form of three predefined packages. These packages support two distinct types of input/output.

Firstly, programs often need to store data on backing store (e.g. disc, magnetic tape, etc.) so that it can be read back by the same or other programs later on. Because this data is written and read only by the computer and never needs to be examined directly by a human, it can be stored in the backing store in a compact machine-readable format. This kind of input/output is said to be unformatted and is supported in Ada by two generic packages called SEQUENTIAL_IO and DIRECT_IO.

Secondly, programs need to read in data generated by humans and write out data which can be read by humans. This human-readable input/output requires a conversion to be performed between the binary format used internally within the machine and the character format used by humans. This second kind of input/output is said to be formatted and is supported in Ada by a (non-generic) package called TEXT_IO. The specifications of each of these packages are given in Appendix D.

It is interesting to note how useful the package concept is in this context. The package specification gives a precise description of the input/output facilities provided, independent of the actual hardware being used. The package body then provides the interface between this machine independent specification and the machine itself. Thus, there can be just one package specification for all machines (and therefore for all Ada programs) even though a different package body will be needed for each different machine.

15.2 FILES

All high level input/output in Ada depends on the concept of a file. A file is an arbitrary sequence of data values of identical type. Externally, a file may be stored on a file structured device such as magnetic tape, magnetic disc or similar. However, the concept of a file is not restricted to file structured devices but extends to cover all input/output devices. Thus, a printer for example, is also considered to be a file. When a sequence of characters is transferred to a file on disc, it gets stored on the magnetic surface of the disc. When a sequence of characters is transferred to a printer it gets printed on the paper. From the point of view of the Ada programmer there is no difference between the two operations (except, of course, that certain operations which can be performed on a disc file such as reading cannot be performed on a printer!).

Internally, within an Ada program, files are represented by objects declared of type FILE_TYPE. This type is provided as a limited private type by each of the packages SEQUENTIAL_IO, DIRECT_IO and TEXT_IO along with a set of subprograms for manipulating objects of the type. A file object declared using the SEQUENTIAL_IO package is called a sequential file and a file object declared using the DIRECT_IO package is called a direct file. Both sequential and direct files consist of a sequence of elements all of the same type. The difference between the two is that the elements of a direct file can be accessed randomly whereas the elements of a sequential file cannot. There is no restriction on the element type of a sequential or direct file. In particular, it can be any user-defined structured type. In order to obtain a file for some given element type then an actual file handling package must first be obtained by instantiating the appropriate generic package, that is SEQUENTIAL_IO or DIRECT_IO, with the required element type as parameter. A file object declared using the TEXT_IO package is called a text file. This is a special kind of file consisting of a sequence of characters grouped into lines, and as sequence of lines grouped into pages. TEXT_IO is not generic so text files can be declared and operated on directly.

To perform any input or output operation in Ada, the following steps must be taken

(a) A file is declared of the appropriate file type.
(b) This file is then associated with an external file, e.g. printer, disc file, etc. This is called creating the file if the esternal file did not previously exist, otherwise it is called opening the file (a printer always exists but a disc file may not).
(c) The required input/output operations are performed on the file. If values are written to the file, the effect will be to transfer the values written to the associated external file. If values are read from the file, the effect will be to transfer values from the associated external file to the program.
(d) Finally, when no further input/output operations are needed, the association between the internal file and the external file is broken. This is called closing the file.

The following sections describe how to perform these steps in detail. The operations of declaring, opening and closing files are common to all file kinds and are described in the next section. Section 15.4 then covers the use of sequential files, section 15.5 deals with direct files and section 15.6 to 15.10 cover the use of text files. To conclude the chapter, section 15.11 completes the design of the cross-reference generator program given in Chapter 11 with an implementation of its IO_INTERFACE package.

15.3 DECLARING, OPENING AND CLOSING FILES

As noted above, each input/output package provides a limited private type called FILE_TYPE which can be used to declare file objects. The package TEXT_IO is non-generic and, hence, text file objects can be declared immediately, for example

LISTING : TEXT_IO.FILE_TYPE;

declares a text file object called LISTING. For the case of sequential and direct files, however, a suitable generic package must first be instantiated. For example, if a sequential file of integers was required than an instantiation of the package SEQUENTIAL_IO would be needed,

package INT_IO **is new**
SEQUENTIAL_IO(ELEMENT_TYPE=>INTEGER);

Having created this new package called INT_IO, actual files may then be declared in the normal way. For example,

SAMPLE_DATA : INT_IO.FILE_TYPE;

Once a file has been declared it must be associated with an external file before any input/output operations can be performed on it. Two procedures are provided for this purpose with specifications as follows

```
procedure CREATE (FILE: in out FILE_TYPE;
                  MODE: in FILE_MODE := default_mode;
                  NAME: in STRING := " ";
                  FORM: in STRING := " "
                  );

procedure OPEN   (FILE: in out FILE_TYPE;
                  MODE: in FILE_MODE;
                  NAME: in STRING;
                  FORM: in STRING := " "
                  );
```

The CREATE procedure is used to establish a new external file and associate it with the named FILE object. The OPEN procedure is used to associate the named FILE object with an existing external file. In both cases, the external file is denoted by a character string whose format is implementation dependent. Typically though it would have a format similar to that described in the example given in section 10.6 on the use of the TEXT_HANDLING package. In the case of the CREATE procedure, the external name can be omitted. The effect then is to create a temporary unnamed external file which is deleted as soon as the corresponding internal file is closed.

In addition to the external name of the file, each of these procedures may also specify a MODE and a FORM. The MODE of a file indicates what kind of operation is to be performed on the file, that is, reading or writing or both. The type FILE_MODE is defined as

```
type FILE_MODE is (IN_FILE, INOUT_FILE, OUT_FILE);
```

If the MODE of a file is set to IN_FILE then it can only be read, if it is set to OUT_FILE then it can only be written to. The MODE INOUT_FILE can only be specified for direct files and allows both reading and writing. When an explicit MODE is omitted in a call to CREATE then a default MODE applies which is OUT_FILE for sequential and text files and INOUT_FILE for direct files. The FORM of a file is a string which can be used by the programmer to control certain external characteristics of his files such as who is to have access to them. The format of these FORM strings is implementation dependent. Like the MODE of a file, it can be omitted in which case appropriate default characteristics are chosen by the implementation.

As an example of the use of the OPEN procedure, the call

```
OPEN(SAMPLE_DATA, IN_FILE, "DKO:SAMP1.DATA");
```

would associate SAMPLE_DATA with an external file called DKO:SAMP1.DATA (here DKO: denotes a physical disc and SAMP1.DATA is the name of a file which is already stored on that disc) and leave the file open for reading. Similarly, a LISTING file could be created by

CREATE(LISTING, NAME => "DKO: LIST.TEXT");

This call would create an external file LIST.TEXT on disc DKO: and associate it with the internal file LISTING. Following the call, the file LISTING is left open for writing since no MODE has been given and the default for text files is OUT_FILE. Remember here that the format of the external file names are only examples and will, in general, be different for each Ada installation.

Calls to OPEN and CREATE may, in practice, lead to exceptions being raised. An attempt to CREATE or OPEN a file which is already open will cause STATUS_ERROR to be raised. An attempt to OPEN an external file which does not exist or to which access is prohibited will cause NAME_ERROR to be raised. An attempt to CREATE an external file which already exists will also lead to NAME_ERROR being raised. Finally, calls to OPEN or CREATE which are logically inconsistent, such as attempting to open a printer for reading, will result in the exception USE_ERROR being raised.

These exceptions are particularly useful in an interactive environment where the user is allowed to specify which particular external files he wishes to operate on when the program executes. For example, the following outline demonstrates how a program can be written to ask the user to supply the name of his external source data file

```
loop
      - - ask user for name of an external file and read
      - - it into string S (input via user terminal)
      begin
          OPENED := TRUE;
          OPEN(SAMPLE_DATA, IN_FILE, S);
      exception
          when NAME_ERROR =>
              - - output message "File does not exist"
              - - to user terminal
              OPENED := FALSE;
      end;
      exit when OPENED;
end loop;
```

Here the loop is repeatedly executed until the user supplies an external file name which can be successfully opened. Complete examples of this technique both for opening and creating files can be found in the example in section 5.11.

When all processing of a file has been completed, it must be closed by a call to the CLOSE procedure which is specified as follows

procedure CLOSE(FILE: **in out** FILE_TYPE);

The effect of this procedure is to perform any termination operations necessary on the external file associated with FILE and then to sever the association between the two. Subsequently to this call, the closed file can be associated with another external file if required. Any attempt to close a file which is not already open leads to the exception STATUS_ERROR being raised. Unless the external file originally associated with FILE was unnamed, it is preserved after the CLOSE operation. If preservation of this file is not required, then instead of CLOSE, the procedure DELETE can be used

procedure DELETE(FILE: **in out** FILE_TYPE);

This has the same effect as CLOSE, but the associated external file is always deleted.

When a file is initially opened or created, it is initialised such that subsequent read or write operations will start from the beginning of the file. Such a file is said to be reset. A file can be explicitly reset at any time by using the RESET procedure

procedure RESET(FILE: **in out** FILE_TYPE);
procedure RESET(FILE: **in out** FILE_TYPE; MODE: **in** FILE_MODE);

As can be seen, there are two definitions of this procedure. The first is used to simply reset a file without changing its MODE whereas the second is used to reset a file and change its MODE. This latter form is particularly useful for reading back a file which has just been written. For example, suppose that a sequence of integer numbers must be created, stored on a file and then read back. The following outline shows how this would be done

```
with INT_IO;
procedure EXAMPLE is
     use INT_IO;              - - make INT_IO directly accessible
                              - - for convenience.
     TEMP : FILE_TYPE;        - - declare temporary file of integers
begin
     CREATE(TEMP);            - - create temp file using default
                              - - mode OUT_FILE and unnamed
                                   external file

     - - write data into file

     RESET(TEMP, IN_FILE);  - - reset the file and change mode

     - - read back data from file

     DELETE(TEMP);            - - finally close file and delete associ-
                              - - ated external file. Note that CLOSE
                              - - could have been used equally well
                              - - here.
end;
```

The RESET procedure must only be applied to open files otherwise the exception STATUS_ERROR is raised. Also, the exception USE_ERROR is raised if it is logically impossible to reset the file.

In addition to the above procedures, there are four functions which can be used to interrogate an open file. Firstly,

> **function** IS_OPEN(FILE: **in** FILE_TYPE) **return** BOOLEAN;

returns TRUE if the given FILE is open and the functions

> **function** NAME(FILE: **in** FILE_TYPE) **return** STRING;
> **function** FORM(FILE: **in** FILE_TYPE) **return** STRING;
> **function** MODE(FILE: **in** FILE_TYPE) **return** FILE_MODE;

return the NAME, FORM and MODE of the specified FILE. In these last three cases, the exception STATUS_ERROR is raised if the specified FILE is not already open.

15.4 SEQUENTIAL FILE MANIPULATION

Sequential files consist of a sequence of elements of the same type. The package SEQUENTIAL_IO provides all of the procedures described in the previous section for manipulating sequential files and in addition provides READ and WRITE procedures for accessing them.

When an existing sequential file is opened for reading, it will consist of a sequence of values of some type. Each of these values can be read by successive calls to the following procedure

> **procedure** READ(FILE: **in** FILE_TYPE; ITEM: **out** ELEMENT_TYPE);

where ELEMENT_TYPE denotes the type of each file element, whose value is specified as the actual generic parameter when the appropriate SEQUENTIAL_IO package is instantiated. In understanding sequential input/output, it may be helpful to imagine a pointer in the file which determines the next element of the file to be read. When the file is opened or reset, this pointer is set to point to the first element in the file. Each time that READ is called, the element pointed to in the file is copied into the ITEM parameter and then the pointer is moved to the next element in the file. Hence, successive calls to READ will return the values of each element in the file in sequence until the end of the file is reached. READ may only be applied to files of mode IN_FILE, any attempt to apply READ to a file of mode OUT_FILE will result in the exception MODE_ERROR being raised.

An attempt to read past the end of a file will cause the exception END_ERROR to be raised. To avoid this possibility, an explicit END_OF_FILE function is provided with specification as follows function END_OF_FILE(FILE: in FILE_TYPE) return BOOLEAN;

where the mode of the file must be IN_FILE. This function returns TRUE if there are no further elements in the file to read. Thus, each call to READ can be preceded by a call to END_OF_FILE to make sure that end of the file has not been reached. This is illustrated by the following example.

Suppose that the INT_IO package has been instantiated as in the previous section at the outermost level of the program. The following procedure will compute the sum of the sequence of integers stored in the file passed to it by its FILE parameter

```
with INT_IO; use INT_IO;
procedure SUM_FILE (FILE: in out FILE_TYPE; SUM: out INTEGER) is
    TOTAL: INTEGER := 0;
    VALUE: INTEGER;
begin
    RESET (FILE);
    while not END_OF_FILE (FILE) loop
        READ (FILE, VALUE);
        TOTAL := TOTAL + VALUE;
    end loop;
    SUM := TOTAL;
end SUM_FILE;
```

Here the READ operation is applied to the file repeatedly to read each integer value in the file in sequence and accumulate their sum. Each iteration of the while loop is preceded by a test for the end of file condition and when this occurs the loop is terminated.

When a sequential file is first created, it is initially empty. That is to say, it contains no elements. Subsequent calls to the following WRITE procedure will then write each value specified by the ITEM parameter sequentially into the file

procedure WRITE (FILE: in FILE_TYPE; ITEM: in ELEMENT_TYPE);

This process may, in principle, be continued indefinitely since there is no logical upper limit placed on the size that a file may grow to. However, in practice, the physical storage capacity of the external device will eventually be reached. When this happens, the exception USE_ERROR is raised.

One of the most straightforward examples of writing a file is in the duplication of an existing file. The following generic procedure may be instantiated to copy two files of any element type

```
generic
    ELEM is private;
procedure FILE_COPY (SOURCE, DESTINATION: in STRING);
```

```
with SEQUENTIAL_IO;
procedure FILE_COPY (SOURCE, DESTINATION: in STRING) is

    package IO is new SEQUENTIAL_IO (ELEMENT_TYPE => ELEM);
    use IO:

    INF, OUTF : FILE_TYPE;
    ITEM: ELEM;

begin
    - - Open Files
    OPEN (INF, IN_FILE, SOURCE);
    begin
        OPEN (OUTF, OUT_FILE, DESTINATION);
    exception
        when NAME_ERROR =>
            CREATE (OUTF, OUT_FILE, DESTINATION);
    end;

    - - Copy Source to Destination
    while not END_OF_FILE (INF) loop
        READ (INF, ITEM);
        WRITE (OUTF, ITEM);
    end loop;

    - - Close Files
    CLOSE (INF); CLOSE (OUTF);
end FILE_COPY;
```

The body of this procedure illustrates the three main phases in file processing. Firstly, the files are opened. Notice that the output file is initially assumed to already exist (i.e. the caller of the procedure wishes to overwrite an existing file or output to a permanent device such as a paper-tape punch). (Hence, the attempt is made to open the file first and if this raises NAME_ERROR then the file is created. The second phase is the actual copying of the files. Starting with the first element of each file, a value is read from the source and immediately written to the destination. When the end of the source file is reached, the copying is completed and the third phase then just consists of closing both files.

For simplicity, no explicit error handling has been included in the above design of FILE_COPY. Any exceptions raised during its execution will be immediately propagated back to the caller. Note that this is not entirely satisfactory as the names of all exceptions raised within FILE_COPY will be out of scope outside of it. Hence, the caller cannot distinguish the different kinds of exception which may be raised but must handle them all using 'others'.

In fact, a variety of different exceptions may be raised during the execution of FILE_COPY. NAME_ERROR may be raised during the file opening operations although STATUS_ERROR should not occur (see previous section). During any input/output operation, general errors are signalled by DEVICE_ERROR and USE_ERROR. DEVICE_ERROR is raised when a malfunction in the underlying hardware occurs. USE_ERROR is raised when an attempt is made to perform an operation which is incompatible with the currently opened external file. Also, a READ operation may raise the exception DATA_ERROR if the value read from the file is not of the required type.

The above describes the main principles involved in sequential file manipulation. The word 'sequential' as used in this context does not refer to the way that the external files are organised but to the way that they are accessed by the program. The SEQUENTIAL_IO package only allows the elements of a file to be written or read one after the other starting from the beginning of the file. For many data processing applications, this sequential file access is far too inefficient. Hence, Ada provides an alternative package for unformatted input/output called DIRECT_IO which allows the elements of a file to be accessed randomly.

15.5 RANDOM ACCESS FILE MANIPULATION

Like sequential files, direct files consist of a sequence of elements all of the same type. However, direct files have the additional property that each element of the file has a position denoted by an index value. Direct files can be though of as variable-length arrays in which the first element of the array always has the index value 1 and the last element of the array has an index value equal to the number of elements in the file. Associated with a direct file, there is a current index which denotes the element which will next be written or read. This current index can be changed by the programmer at will, thus allowing random access to the file. Furthermore, a direct file can have the mode INOUT_FILE which allows read and write operations to be mixed.

Direct file operations are provided by the package DIRECT_IO. This contains all the file management operations described in section 15.3 plus operations for reading, writing and manipulating the current index. The basic read and write operations for direct files are the same as those for sequential files. When a file is initially opened or created, the current index of the file is set to 1. Following each subsequent, read or write operation, the current index is always automatically incremented by one. Thus, the same sequential access mechanisms described in the previous section still apply to direct files. The extra power of direct files is gained by the provision of the following procedure which allows the current index to be altered

procedure SET_INDEX (FILE: **in** FILE_TYPE; TO: **in** POSITIVE_COUNT);

where POSITIVE_COUNT is defined by the following

```
type COUNT is range 0 . . implementation_defined;
subtype POSITIVE_COUNT is COUNT range 1 . . COUNT'LAST;
```

The procedure SET_INDEX allows any element of a direct file to be read randomly. For example, to read the Nth value of the file F all that is needed is

```
SET_INDEX(F,N);
READ(F,X);
```

Similarly, to write a value into the Nth element of the file F all that is needed is

```
SET_INDEX (F, N);
WRITE (F, X);
```

In fact, these two pairs of operations are so common that DIRECT_IO provides extended forms of READ and WRITE which allow the required index position to be specified directly, that is

```
procedure READ   (FILE: in FILE_TYPE;
                  ITEM: out ELEMENT_TYPE;
                  FROM: in POSITIVE_COUNT);

procedure WRITE  (FILE: in FILE_TYPE;
                  ITEM: in ELEMENT_TYPE;
                  TO: in POSITIVE_COUNT);
```

In both cases, the effect of these procedures is first to set the current index to the specified FROM or TO and then to apply the read or write operation as normal.

When reading a direct file, either sequentially or randomly, the exception END_ERROR will be raised if the current index denotes an element position beyond the end of the file. As with the SEQUENTIAL_IO package described previously, an END_OF_FILE function is provided by DIRECT_IO to explicitly test for this condition. In addition, the current index position and the current size of a direct file can be determined using the following two functions

function INDEX(FILE: **in** FILE_TYPE) **return** POSITIVE_COUNT;

function SIZE (FILE: **in** FILE_TYPE) **return** COUNT;

Two common examples of the uses of these functions when writing to a direct file are backspacing and appending. The call

```
WRITE (FILE, X, INDEX (FILE) − 1);
```

corresponds to a backspace operation in which the value X overwrites the previous value written to the file. Similarly, a value X can be appended to the end of a file by

```
WRITE (FILE, X, SIZE (FILE) + 1);
```

Finally, note that, unlike a sequential file, a direct file can have undefined elements. For example, consider the following

```
CREATE (FILE, INOUT_FILE);
WRITE (FILE, X, 10);
```

Here, the value of X is written into the 10th element of a newly created file, leaving elements 1 to 9 undefined. Subsequent attempts to read these undefined elements may result in the exception DATA_ERROR being raised but the language does not guarantee this; hence, care must be exercised to avoid such situations.

15.6 TEXT FILES

As noted at the start of this chapter, the input/output facilities provided by SEQUENTIAL_IO and DIRECT_IO are designed for transferring data in machine-readable format. The remaining sections of this chapter describe the use of the TEXT_IO package which allows input/output to be performed on data in human-readable format.

Unlike SEQUENTIAL_IO and DIRECT_IO, TEXT_IO is not generic but is an ordinary package (its full specification is given in Appendix D). Hence, to use TEXT_IO all that is needed is to mention it in an appropriate **with** clause. TEXT_IO does, however, contain generic packages within it. These provide for the input/output of integer, floating-point, fixed-point and enumeration types. Input/output for characters and strings is provided directly with no need for generic instantiation.

As well as operations for reading and writing the basic Ada types in text format, the TEXT_IO package also contains the file management operations described in section 15.3. Thus, text files are declared, opened and closed in the same way as sequential files. Hence, for example, the following procedure shows the general outline of the housekeeping operations which typically need to be performed in order to use text files (but see next section)

```
with TEXT_IO; use TEXT_IO;
procedure USE_TEXT_FILES is
    SOURCE, RESULT : FILE_TYPE;
begin
    - - open files
    OPEN (SOURCE, IN_FILE, "DATAFILE");
    CREATE (RESULT, OUT_FILE, "ANSWERFILE");

    - - use TEXT_IO operations on SOURCE and RESULT

    - - close files
    CLOSE (SOURCE) ;
```

                              CLOSE (RESULT);
                        end USE_TEXT_FILES;

A text file itself consists of a sequence of pages, each page consists of a sequence of lines and each line consists of a sequence of characters. Every character in a text file has a unique position which is denoted by a triple of indices: (column number, line numer, page number). The first character in any text file is always at column 1, line 1 and page 1. Every open text file has a current position associated with it which denotes the position in the file at which the next item will be written or read. When OPEN, CREATE and RESET are applied to a text file, the current position is reset to (1,1,1). Note here that the concept of a current position does not imply that TEXT_IO supports random access to text files. Subprograms exist to manipulate the current file position, but only to skip forwards, never backwards.

The ends of lines are marked by special *line marks* and the ends of pages are marked by special *page marks*. These are normally invisible to the user but subprograms are provided in TEXT_IO for writing them into output files and testing for their presence in input files. Within a text file used for output, an upper bound on the length of a line and on the size of a page can be fixed. Fixed length lines and pages are useful for dealing with tabulated data. The default for all text files is to leave line and page lengths unbounded.

TEXT_IO input/output operations are performed by two overloaded procedures called PUT and GET for writing and reading values, respectively. In both cases, the value is represented on the external file as a sequence of characters. The operation of both PUT and GET is in two stages

PUT: (a) Convert internal binary representation of value to be written into its equivalent external character representation, i.e. a sequence of characters.

        (b) Write character sequence to external file.

GET: (a) Read character sequence from external file.

        (b) Convert character sequence, i.e. the external character representation of the value, to its internal binary representation.

The actual external representation used for the various kinds of data type (integers, reals, etc.) is the same as that used to denote literals as described in Chapter 2.

Finally, as with unformatted files, it must be emphasised that the external file associated with a text file need not necessarily be a physical data file but can be any device capable of transferring ASCII characters between itself and the computer. In particular, in an interactive environment, the user's console keyboard is treated as a text file with mode IN_FILE and the user's console screen (or printer) is treated as a text file with mode OUT_FILE.

15.7 DEFAULT FILES

In the general case, all calls to a subprogram within TEXT_IO must supply the name of the text file to operate on as its first parameter. Hence, for example, the call

    PUT(F, X);

will output the value of X to the text file F. To make text input/output easier to use, however, the file parameter may be omitted in which case a default output file is used. For example, the call

    PUT(X);

causes the value of X to be output to the default output file. When an Ada program is first executed, the default files will be opened automatically. Typically, for an interactive system, they will be the console keyboard and screen. During execution, the program can change the default files by calls to SET_INPUT and SET_OUTPUT whose specifications are as follows

    procedure SET_INPUT (FILE: **in** FILE_TYPE);
    procedure SET_OUTPUT (FILE: **in** FILE_TYPE);

At any time, the current default files may be determined using the following two functions

    function CURRENT_INPUT **return** FILE_TYPE;
    function CURRENT_OUTPUT **return** FILE_TYPE;

Also, the original initial default files can be found using

    function STANDARD_INPUT **return** FILE_TYPE;
    function STANDARD_OUTPUT **return** FILE_TYPE;

As an example of manipulating the default files, suppose that a program wishes to perform some text output on a file called F and then revert back to the original initial default output file. This would be done as follows

    -- change default output to F
    SET_OUTPUT (F);

    -- all TEXT_IO output now goes by default to F

    -- revert to initial output file
    SET_OUTPUT (STANDARD_OUTPUT);

Not here that the file F must be opened before calling SET_OUTPUT, otherwise the STATUS_ERROR exception will be raised, and its mode must be IN_FILE, otherwise the MODE_ERROR exception will be raised.

    Finally, it must be emphasised that the ability to manipulate the default files is only provided for convenience. Output can always be sent to a specific file by giving that file explicitly as a parameter in each TEXT_IO subprogram call.

15.8 TEXT OUTPUT

All output operations are performed using the overloaded procedure PUT. The general effect of the PUT operation is to write one or more characters onto the output file starting from the current column, line and page number. As noted above, the length of a line may be bounded or unbounded. If the length is unbounded then the value is always put on the current line. If the length is bounded and the value will not fit on the current line, then it is output instead at the beginning of the next line. If this in turn would cause a bounded page length to be exceeded, then a new page is started before writing the value. Following any PUT operation, the current position in the file is updated to denote the character position immediately following the sequence of characters just written.

PUT procedures for values of type CHARACTER and STRING are provided directly by TEXT_IO. The effect of

PUT ('A');

is just to write the character 'A' at the current character position in the default output file (all examples will use the default files for convenience). The effect of

PUT ("This is a string constant");

is to output each character in the string one by one as for the case of single character output.

In order to output an integer value, an instance of the generic INTEGER_IO package within TEXT-IO must be declared. This package then provides PUT (and GET) for the specified integer type. For example, a package to output values of type INTEGER would be instantiated by

package TEXT_INT_IO is new TEXT_IO.INTEGER_IO(INTEGER);

The PUT (and GET) operations defined by this package can then be made directly visible by

use TEXT_INT_IO;   - - not "use TEXT_IO;" !

The specification of the PUT operation for integers is

procedure PUT (FILE: in FILE_TYPE;
                ITEM: in NUM;
                WIDTH: in FIELD := DEFAULT_FIELD;
                BASE: in NUMBER_BASE := DEFAULT_BASE);

where NUM is the generic integer type and FIELD and NUMBER_BASE are integer subtypes. As always, the FILE parameter may be omitted. The effect of this PUT is to write the value of the integer ITEM onto the output file with no leading zeros, no underscores and with a leading minus sign if it is negative. If ITEM is zero then a single '0' is output. The WIDTH parameter determines the minimum field width (that is, the number of character positions) to be used in the output. If the specified width is less than that required to output the value then it is widened to just that required. Otherwise, the integer value is preceded by sufficient spaces to fill the field. The BASE parameter can be used to output values in bases other than 10. In this case, the format described in Chapter 2 for based literals is used. As a simple example of the use of PUT for integers, the following calls

PUT (128,6); PUT (−3,10); PUT(255,10,16);

would give the following output

$$\wedge\wedge\wedge 128 \wedge\wedge\wedge\wedge\wedge\wedge\wedge\wedge -3 \wedge\wedge\wedge\wedge 16\#FF\#$$

where the $\wedge$'s denote blanks.

At this point it is convenient to introduce some of the facilities available in TEXT_IO for layout control. Suppose that an integer array called NUMBERS is given indexed from 1 to 20 and it is required to print a table of the values in the array with five numbers in each line. In order to do this, it will be necessary to known how to terminate the current output line and start a new one.

A procedure called NEW_LINE is provided in TEXT_IO for just this purpose. Its specification is

procedure NEW_LINE(FILE: **in** FILE_TYPE;
                       SPACING: **in** POSITIVE_COUNT .= 1);

The call NEW_LINE terminates the current output line and starts a new line. The call NEW_LINE(N) terminates the current line and then adds N−1 empty lines.

Using this procedure, the required table of numbers can be generated by the following statements

```
FIELD_WIDTH := 6; NUMS_PER_LINE := 5;
for I in 1 . . 20 loop
    PUT(NUMBERS(I), FIELD_WIDTH);
    if I mod NUMS_PER_LINE = 0 then
        NEW_LINE;
    end if;
end loop;
```

After execution, the following would be output

```
|    397   -468  23567     23      5|
|  49000      0    -87    986   3471|
|   -343  -4567   9884     -3      0|
|   3369    -45     -1   3456    456|
```

where the vertical bars would not appear in the output but are included here just to mark the beginning and ends of the lines.

In the above, a new line is started after every fifth value in the array has been printed and the column structure is implemented using the WIDTH parameter of the PUT operation. Suppose now, however, that the numbers are to be aligned so that the leading digits start in the same column, i.e. left-justified rather than right-justified. This can be done using the SET_COL procedure

procedure SET_COL(FILE: **in** FILE_TYPE; TO: **in** POSITIVE_COUNT);

The effect of a call to this procedure is simply to set the current column position in the specified file to the specified value. This is achieved by outputting a sufficient number of spaces. If the value specified by the TO parameter is less than the current column position then a new line is started followed by TO-1 spaces. Note that as with all TEXT_IO subprograms the FILE parameter may be omitted. In this case, however, such a call would be ambiguous since SET_COL can, in fact, be applied to both input and output files. Hence, it may refer to either the default input or the default output. To resolve this, the general rule is applied in such cases the default file is always the output file.

Using the SET_COL procedure, the required left-justified table can be generated by the following statements

```
FIELD_WIDTH := 6; NUMS_PER_LINE := 5;
for I in 1 .. 20 loop
    SET_COL( ((I-1) mod NUMS_PER_LINE) * FIELD_WIDTH + 1);
    PUT(NUMBERS(I), WIDTH => 0);
end loop;
```

Note here that an explicit call to NEW_LINE is no longer needed since new lines are created automatically by the SET_COL procedure. After execution, the output would now be

```
|397    -468  23567 23     5|
|49000 0       -87   986  3471|
|-343  -4567  9884   -3    0|
|3369  -45    -1     3456  456|
```

In general, the need to calculate and then write the end of each line explicitly can be avoided by setting the line length so that just the required number of

values per line can be accommodated. This is done using the procedure SET_
LINE_LENGTH. For example, the following would give the same output as the
first example but with a bounded line length

```
FIELD_WIDTH := 6;  NUMS_PER_LINE := 5;
SET_LINE_LENGTH(NUMS_PER_LINE*FIELD_WIDTH);
for I in 1 . . 20 loop
    PUT(NUMBERS(I), FIELD_WIDTH);
end loop;
```

Notice that in this case, no call to NEW_LINE is now needed. When the attempt
is made to print the sixth number, the system determines that it will not fit on
the current line and so automatically starts a new line. After setting the line
length to print out a table such as this, it can if desired be reset to zero to
indicate a return to unbounded length lines by the call SET_LINE_LENGTH(0).

Floating-point and fixed-point numbers (see next chapter) are treated in a
similar way to integer numbers, the relevant generic packages being FLOAT_IO
and FIXED_IO, respectively. PUT for both floating-point and fixed-point values
is specified as follows

```
procedure PUT(FILE:  in OUT_FILE
              ITEM:  in NUM;
              FORE:  in FIELD := DEFAULT_FORE;
              AFT:   in FIELD := DEFAULT_AFT;
              EXP:   in EXP   := DEFAULT_EXP);
```

where NUM is the generic type parameter which is replaced by the actual numeric
type name in each package instantiation. The FORE, AFT and EXP parameters
specify the field width to be used for the integer, fractional and exponent parts
of the number, respectively. If EXP is zero then the number is printed with the
format

⟨FORE⟩ . ⟨AFT⟩

otherwise the number is printed in exponential format with the format

⟨FORE⟩ . ⟨AFT⟩E⟨EXP⟩

with the integer FORE part consisting of a single digit. As an example, the
following block

```
declare
    type REAL is digits 8;
    package REAL_IO is new TEXT_IO.FLOAT_IO(REAL);
    use REAL_IO;
    X:REAL := 0.003974;
```

```
begin
    PUT(X);
    NEW_LINE;
    PUT(X, FORE => 7, AFT => 3, EXP =>4);
    NEW_LINE;
    PUT (X, 3, 3, 0);
    NEW_LINE;
end;
```

would give the following output

3.9740000E-03

$^\wedge\wedge\wedge\wedge\wedge\wedge$3.974E-003

$^\wedge\wedge$0.004

The last class of types provided for by TEXT_IO are enumeration types. PUT (and GET) for these types is provided by the generic package ENUMERATION_IO. The PUT operation obtained from this package is specified as

```
procedure PUT(FILE:   in FILE_TYPE;
              ITEM:   in ENUM;
              WIDTH: in FIELD := DEFAULT_WIDTH;
              SET:    in TYPE_SET := DEFAULT_SETTING);
```

The type TYPE_SET is defined as

```
type TYPE_SET is (LOWER_CASE, UPPER_CASE);
```

and the parameter SET is therefore used to select whether the enumeration value should be printed in lower-case or upper-case letters. The WIDTH parameter defines the total field width to be used for the value in a similar way to that described above for integer types. The only difference is that for enumeration types, any spaces needed for padding are added after the value rather than before it.

As an example of printing enumeration types, suppose that the ENUMERATION_IO package was instantiated for the COLOUR type defined in section 3.2, that is

```
package COL_IO is new ENUMERATION_IO(COLOUR);
```

Given this package then

```
for C in COLOUR range WHITE . . BLUE loop
    PUT (C);
end loop;
```

would give the following output

```
WHITEREDYELLOWGREENBLUE
```

since the default width for enumeration types is 0 and the default type set is upper-case. Spaces can be introduced between each value by increasing the field width. For example, changing the call to PUT in the above to

PUT(C, WIDTH => 7);

would give

WHITE∧∧RED∧∧∧∧YELLOW∧GREEN∧∧BLUE∧∧∧

Notice that these enumeration values are left-justified within each field, unlike numeric values which are always right-justified.

Character values can also be output as enumeration values but in the latter case the enclosing single quotes are retained. For example, suppose that the following package is instantiated

package CH_IO **is new** ENUMERATION_IO(CHARACTER);

then

TEXT_IO.PUT('A');

would output the single character A whereas

CH_IO.PUT('A');

would output three characters, i.e. 'A'.

The above paragraphs have described the main features provided by TEXT_IO for output and for most purposes these will be sufficient. It is, however, worth noting that similar facilities for setting bounded page lengths are supplied to those described for setting bounded line lengths. The procedure SET_PAGE_LENGTH can be used to set a bound on the number of lines in a page such that if an output would exceed this bound, a new page is automatically inserted. The procedure SET_LINE can be used to set the current line number and, in a similar fashion to SET_COL, if this line number is less than the current line number then a new page is started followed by the required number of new lines. A new page can also be started by calling the procedure NEW_PAGE. These page control facilities are useful mainly in the preparation of documents.

Finally, TEXT_IO contains a number of functions for determining the current position in a file (COL, LINE and PAGE) and the current line and page lengths (LINE_LENGTH and PAGE_LENGTH). Specifications for all of these subprograms can be found in Appendix D.

15.9 TEXT INPUT

A file used for text input will, in general, consist of a sequence of characters grouped into lines and pages. As with text output, the current position in an input file in terms of its column, line and page number is always maintained. All input operations are performed using the overloaded procedure GET. Versions of GET for reading characters and strings are provided in TEXT_IO directly and versions of GET have two forms, one in which the input file is named explicitly packages mentioned in the previous section. As with the PUT procedures, all version of GET have two forms, one in which the input file is named explicitly and the other in which no file is named. In the latter case, the default input file is assumed.

Individual characters in a file may be read by calling the following procedure

procedure GET(FILE: **in** FILE_TYPE; ITEM: **out** CHARACTER);

The effect of this procedure is to read the next character from the input file and assign its value to ITEM. Any intervening end-of-line or end-of-page markers are automatically skipped during this process but their presence can, if required, be detected using the Boolean functions END_OF_FILE and END_OF_PAGE. As an example, the following procedure will copy the default input file to the default output file preserving the line and page structure.

```
with TEXT_IO; use TEXT_IO,
procedure COPY_TEXT is
    CH: CHARACTER;
begin
    while not END_OF_FILE loop
        if END_OF_PAGE then
            NEW_PAGE;
        elsif END_OF_LINE then
            NEW_LINE;
        end if;
        GET (CH); PUT (CH);
    end loop;
end COPY_TEXT;
```

Each time around the loop, the end-of-page and end-of-line conditions are tested for and when found a new page or line is output as appropriate. Following this, the current input character is copied to the output. Notice that when an end of line or page is detected, the subsequent call to GET automatically skips over it.

When reading an input file, subsequent input can be skipped by using the following procedures

procedure SKIP_LINE(FILE: **in** FILE_TYPE;
                          SPACING: **in** POSITIVE_COUNT := 1);
procedure SKIP_PAGE(FILE: **in** FILE_TYPE);

The effect of calling SKIP_LINE is to skip through the file to the point immediately following the next line mark. In other words, the current position is set to the beginning of the next line. A call to SKIP_LINE with a value of SPACING greater than one simply causes the operation to be repeated SPACING times. SKIP_PAGE has a similar effect except that the input text is skipped till just after the next page mark. It should also be noted that SET_COL and SET_ LINE can be used with input files as well as with output files. Their effect when used with input files is to skip through the text until the specified column or line is reached.

As noted previously, versions of GET are also provided for reading numeric and enumeration types as well as for characters. The general operation of GET for these cases is as follows. Starting at the current character position of the input file, characters are read according to the syntax of the corresponding literals of the type. Any leading spaces, tabs, line marks or page marks are skipped. If the value read does not conform to the required syntax then the exception DATA_ERROR is raised. For numeric types an optional plus sign or minus sign may precede the number. Once the value has been read it is converted to the internal representation and assigned to the ITEM parameter supplied in the call to GET. If this value lies outside of the range of values allowed for this parameter then the exception DATA_ERROR is raised. If the value read is an enumeration literal, then DATA_ERROR will be raised if the literal read is not one of the literals specified by the type of the ITEM parameter. GET for numeric types may also specify a WIDTH parameter. If this parameter is zero, which is the default case, then GET works as just described. If the WIDTH parameter is non-zero then the value of WIDTH sets an upper limit on the number of characters that may be read. Furthermore, line and page marks are not skipped in this latter case but instead cause termination of the input operation.

As an example of reading numeric values, the following statement would read back the table generated from the NUMBERS array in the previous section:

```
for I in 1 .. 20 loop
    GET(NUMBERS(I));
end loop;
```

Here it is assumed that the integer input/output package TEXT_INT_IO is available and that the file containing the table has been opened as the default input file. Notice that because the operation of GET without a WIDTH parameter automatically skips line marks, the line structure of the table can be ignored.

As a more general example, suppose that the default input file contains data arranged as follows:

INTENSITY:	RED	=	207
INTENSITY:	YELLOW	=	493
INTENSITY:	BLUE	=	100
etc.			

It is required to initialise an integer array whose components are indexed by an enumeration type COLOUR and whose values denote the intensities of the corresponding colours. Assume that the following declarations are given

```
type COLOUR      is (RED,GREEN,YELLOW,BLUE, .... );
type INTENSITY   is range 0 .. INTEGER'LAST;
type COL_LEVELS  is array(COLOUR)of INTENSITY;

SPECTRUM:        COL_LEVELS;
```

then a procedure to read the input file and initialise SPECTRUM may be written as follows

```
with TEXT_IO; use TEXT_IO;

procedure INIT_SPECTRUM is

    COL:    COLOUR;
    LEVEL:  INTENSITY;
    CH·     CHARACTER;

    package COL_IO is new ENUMERATION_IO(COLOUR);
    package LEV_IO is new INTEGER_IO(INTENSITY);
    package CNT_IO is new INTEGER_IO (COUNT);

    use COL_IO, LEV_IO, CNT_IO;

begin
    while not END_OF_FILE loop

        - - skip to colon
        loop
            GET(CH);
            exit when CH=':';
        end loop;

        - - read colour
        GET(COL);                -- COL_IO

        - - skip to =
        loop
            GET(CH);
            exit when CH='=';
        end loop;

        - - read level
        GET(LEVEL);              -- LEV_IO

        - - update array and skip to next line
        SPECTRUM(COL) := LEVEL;
        SKIP_LINE;

    end loop;
```

```
exception
    when others =>
        NEW_LINE;
        PUT("Input Error Detected on Line ");
        PUT(LINE(CURRENT_INPUT));          - - CNT_IO
        PUT(" Column ");
        PUT(COL(CURRENT_INPUT));           - - CNT_IO
end INIT_SPECTRUM;
```

As with previous examples, each line of the input file is processed within a while loop terminated by the end of file condition. For each line, characters are skipped until the colon is found, and then the colour is read using COL_IO.GET. Character are then skipped again until the equals sign is found and finally, the level is read using LEV_IO.GET. If an error of any kind occurs, the exception handler outputs an error message to the default output file. For example, if line 3 of the input contained

INTENSITY: RAD   =   198

then the error message output would be

Input Error Detected on Line 3 Column 16

The current line and column number are determined using the functions LINE and COL provided within TEXT_IO. Notice that an explicit file name has to be given for these functions in this case because the default file is the output file.

15.10 STRING INPUT/OUTPUT

The package TEXT_IO also provides GET and PUT operations for the type STRING. When PUT is called with a string as parameter, each character in the string is output in sequence. When GET is called with a string as parameter, the length of the string is first determined and the required number of characters is then read from the input sufficient to fill the string.

As well as these basic GET and PUT operations, there are two extended forms defined by

```
procedure GET_LINE(FILE: in FILE_TYPE; ITEM: out STRING;
                   LAST: out NATURAL);
procedure PUT_LINE(FILE: in FILE_TYPE; ITEM: in STRING);
```

A call to GET_LINE reads characters from the input file into the specified string until either the string is filled or the end of the current line is reached. In the latter case, the input is skipped to the beginning of the next line. In both cases, the parameter LAST denotes the index value of the last character in ITEM which was filled. GET_LINE is thus particularly useful for reading successive lines of a text file into a string. A call to PUT_LINE is equivalent to a call to PUT immediately followed by a call to NEW_LINE.

The final set of facilities provided in TEXT_IO do not actually involve input/output at all. As should now be clear, text input/output involves two main processes: a conversion between internal binary formats and external character formats, and actual input/output operations. However, format conversions are sometimes needed within a program as a completely separate operation. For example, a report generator program may need to build a complete page of text in memory before actually sending it to an output device.

To facilitate this, GET and PUT for numeric and enumeration types have alternative forms in which the file parameter is replaced by a string parameter. For example, the following versions of GET and PUT are defined for integer types

```
procedure GET(FROM: in STRING; ITEM: out NUM;
              LAST: out POSITIVE);
procedure PUT(TO: out STRING; ITEM: in NUM;
              BASE: in NUMBER_BASE := DEFAULT_BASE);
```

The effect of this GET is to read characters from the input string as though it were a file and convert them into an integer returning the result in ITEM. The parameter LAST denotes the index position of the last character read from the string. Similarly, the effect of this PUT is to convert the given ITEM into its external character format storing the result in the string.

15.11 AN EXAMPLE – THE CROSS REFERENCE GENERATOR PROGRAM

In Chapter 11, a cross reference program for Ada source texts was designed as an example of using data structures involving access types. In that program, all the input/output was encapsulated into a package called IO_INTERFACE. However, the body of the package was not given at that time as the necessary knowledge of Ada input/output was not available. Now that the facilities for high level input/output in Ada have been described, the body of the package can be implemented.

For convenience, the specification of the IO_INTERFACE package is reproduced here:

```
package IO_INTERFACE is

    type LINE_NUM is private;
    type IDENT is private;
    NULL_IDENT: constant IDENT;
```

```
procedure GET_ID(ID: out IDENT; LN: out LINE_NUM;
              DONE: out BOOLEAN);
procedure PRINT(ID: in IDENT);
procedure PRINT(LN: in LINE_NUM);

function ">"(ID1,ID2: IDENT) return BOOLEAN;

private

    MAX_ID_SIZE:    constant := 16;
    MAX_LINE_NUM: constant := 10000;

    type LINE_NUM is range 0 .. MAX_LINE_NUM;
    type IDENT      is new STRING(1 .. MAX_ID_SIZE);

    NULL_IDENT: constant IDENT := (1 .. MAX_ID_SIZE=>' ');

end IO_INTERFACE;
```

Recall the functions of the subprograms defined by this package. Firstly, GET_ID scans the input Ada source text and returns each successive identifier along with its line number. When the input text is exhausted, DONE returns TRUE. During this process, GET_ID also prints a listing of the source file with appended line numbers. The two **PRINT** procedures write an identifier and a line number, respectively, into the output file. Remember also that before printing each identifier a new line must be started. Finally, the ">" operator tests for lexical ordering of its two operands.

The private part of the package given here was suggested in Chapter 11. It implements the IDENT type as a simple string type. This implies that an upper limit must be set of the size of identifiers that can be distinguished. This limitation may not be acceptable for some applications, but for the purposes of this example it is quite satisfactory.

As the first stage in the design, the body of IO_INTERFACE may be sketched out as follows:

```
with TEXT_IO; use TEXT_IO;

package body IO_INTERFACE is

    ID_WIDTH: constant := 20;    - - for printing IDENTs
    LN_WIDTH: constant := 10;    - - for printing LINE_NUMs

    SOURCE:   FILE_TYPE;         - - source text file
    LIST:     FILE_TYPE;         - - output list file

    - - instantiate generic input/output packages

    package LN_IO is new INTEGER_IO(LINE_NUM);
    package INT_IO is new INTEGER_IO(INTEGER);
    use LN_IO, INT_IO;
```

```
- - Single Character Input Package

package SOURCE_INPUT is
      CUR_CH: CHARACTER := ' ';   - - current input character
      OLD_CH: CHARACTER := ' ';   - - previous input character
      procedure GET_CH;
      procedure SKIP_TO_NEXT_LINE;
end SOURCE_INPUT;

use SOURCE_INPUT;

package body SOURCE_INPUT is separate;

- - initialisation procedures

procedure INIT_SOURCE_FILE is separate;

procedure INIT_LIST_FILE is separate;

- - scanner

procedure GET_ID(ID: out IDENT; LN: out LINE_NUM;
                 DONE: out BOOLEAN) is separate;

- - print procedures

procedure PRINT(ID: in IDENT) is separate;
procedure PRINT(LN: in LINE_NUM) is separate;

- - compare operator

function ">"(ID1,ID2:IDENT) return BOOLEAN is separate;
begin
      INIT_SOURCE_FILE;
      INIT_LIST_FILE;
exception
      when others =>
           PUT("Error in Initialisation");
end IO_INTERFACE;
```

In addition to the visible subprograms declared in the specification, the body of
IO_INTERFACE contains a package called SOURCE_INPUT and two procedures
INIT_SOURCE_FILE and INIT_LIST_FILE.

The package SOURCE_INPUT is used to read successive input characters
from the source file. The current input character is always stored in CUR_CH
and the previous input character is 'remembered' in OLD_CH. Each new character from the source file is obtained by a call to GET_CH. As a side effect, this
package also takes care of producing the line numbered listing of the source file.
The procedure SKIP_TO_NEXT_LINE causes the rest of the current input line

to be ignored and CUR_CH is set to the first character of the next line. This procedure is used for skipping over comments. The inclusion of this package is yet another example of the use of abstraction. As well as reading in characters one-by-one, the routines that it provides must also take care of converting lower-case to upper-case and printing the line numbered listing. The introduction of a package allows these details to be deferred until later, and thereby avoids unnecessary complication at this stage of the design.

The two procedures INIT_SOURCE_FILE and INIT_LIST_FILE are called to initialise the IO_INTERFACE package. The purpose of these procedures is to open the source and list files. In order to proceed further with the design, some assumptions will have to be made concerning the working environment of the program. It will be assumed here that the program will operate in an interactive environment and that the standard input and output files are linked to the user's console. Hence the user will be asked to name the source and list files when the program runs. The procedures to do this must allow for the possibility of the user mis-typing a name or specifying a non-existent external file. The general style of doing this was indicated earlier in the chapter. The INIT_SOURCE_FILE procedure is the simplest and this can be given directly,

```
separate(IO_INTERFACE)
procedure INIT_SOURCE_FILE is
    OK:BOOLEAN;
begin
    loop
        NEW_LINE;
        PUT("Enter Source File Name:   ");
        declare
            FILE_NAME: STRING(1 .. 20) := (1 .. 20 => ' ');
            LAST: NATURAL;
        begin
            GET_LINE(FILE_NAME, LAST);
            OK := TRUE;
            OPEN(SOURCE, IN_FILE, FILE_NAME);
        exception
            when NAME_ERROR =>
                PUT("File Not Found");
                OK := FALSE;
            when others =>
                PUT("Illegal File Name");
                OK := FALSE;
        end;
        exit when OK;
    end loop;
end INIT_SOURCE_FILE;
```

The general structure of this procedure is quite straightforward although the use of the inner declare block needs explaining. Each time around the loop, the user is asked to type in a file name at his console. The procedure then attempts to open this external file. If it fails, the exception is handled within the inner block thereby allowing the procedure to repeat the process after outputting a suitable error message.

The INIT_LIST_FILE procedure is a little more difficult simply because two possibilities must be considered: either the name of the file supplied by the user is an existing file that he wishes to overwrite, or it is a new file that he wishes to create. The only way to find out is to attempt to open the file first then if the operation fails attempt to create it, i.e.

```
separate(IO_INTERFACE)
procedure INIT_LIST_FILE is
    OK:BOOLEAN;

    procedure OPEN_LIST(NAME: in STRING; OK: out BOOLEAN) is
    begin
        OK := TRUE;
        OPEN(LIST, OUT_FILE,NAME);
    exception
        when others=> OK := FALSE;
    end OPEN_LIST;

    procedure CREATE_LIST(NAME: in STRING; OK: out BOOLEAN) is
    begin
        OK := TRUE;
        CREATE(LIST,OUT_FILE,NAME);
    exception
        when others=> OK := FALSE;
    end CREATE_LIST;

begin
    loop
        NEW_LINE;
        PUT("Enter List File Name:   ");
        declare
            FILE_NAME: STRING(1 .. 20) := (1 .. 20 =>' ');
            LAST: NATURAL;
        begin
            GET_LINE (FILE_NAME,LAST);
            OPEN_LIST(FILE_NAME,OK);
            if not OK then
                CREATE_LIST(FILE_NAME,OK);
            end if;
```

```
              end;
              if OK then
                exit;
              else
                PUT("File Name Error");
              end if;
          end loop;
          NEW_LINE(LIST);
          PUT(LIST, 1, LN_WIDTH);
      end INIT_LIST_FILE;
```

The actual attempts to open and create the list file have been expressed as procedures to allow the calls to CHARACTER_IO.OPEN and CHARACTER_IO.CREATE to be guarded by exception handlers (further nested blocks within the above would obscure the procedure's operation too badly).

Turning now to the implementation of GET_ID, this will need to make use of the SOURCE_INPUT package for reading characters from the source file. At each call to GET_ID, the input source file must be scanned through until the next identifier is found, and then this identifier must be copied into the ID parameter. Therefore, assume that a procedure FIND_NEXT_IDENT is available which scans the input until the next identifier is found, leaving the first character of this identifier in CUR_CH. Given this procedure, GET_ID may be designed as follows:

```
      separate(IO_INTERFACE)
      procedure GET_ID(ID: out IDENT;  LN: out LINE_NUM;
                              DONE: out BOOLEAN) is
          NEXT_ID:IDENT := NULL_IDENT;
          IDX: NATURAL := 1;
      begin
          DONE := FALSE;
          FIND_NEXT_IDENT;          - - find next identifier
          LN := LINE_NUM(LINE(SOURCE));     - - set line number
          - - transfer identifier to ID
          while (CUR_CH in 'A' .. 'Z') or (CUR_CH in '0' .. '9')
                              or (CUR_CH='-') loop
              if IDX <= MAX_ID_SIZE then
                NEXT_ID(IDX) := CUR_CH;
              end if;
              IDX := IDX + 1;
              GET_CH;
          end loop;
          ID := NEXT_ID;
```

```
exception
    when END_ERROR =>
        DONE := TRUE;
        NEW_LINE(LIST,3);
end GET_ID;
```

Notice here the use of the END_ERROR exception to detect the end of the file. This is an alternative to using the END_OF_FILE function. Normally it is not good practice to use exceptions to denote normal termination conditions. Here it simplifies matters considerably, since it avoids having to pass Boolean flags up from GET_CH to all the procedures which use it.

The FIND_NEXT_IDENT procedure must search the input text for letters but ignore any letters within character literals, string literals, based integer literals and comments. Also, it must ignore the 'E' in exponents. This last case and the case of character literals are the most difficult, since they require knowledge of the current context to distinguish them. A character literal is denoted by a single quote mark, but this character may also appear in attribute names. When an 'E' is detected, it may be the start of an identifier or it may be an exponent. This is the reason why SOURCE_INPUT keeps a copy of the previous input character as well as the current character. The previous character can be examined to resolve the ambiguities in the above two cases. The body of FIND_NEXT_IDENT therefore consists of a case statement embedded within a loop in which each case deals with each of the various possible contexts that a letter can be found in.

```
procedure FIND_NEXT_IDENT is
begin
    SKIPPING:
    loop
        case CUR_CH is
            when ' ' ' =>        - - might be a character literal
                if OLD_CH in 'A' . . 'Z' then
                    GET_CH;     - - no, must be an attribute
                else
                    - - yes, skip character literal
                    GET_CH; GET_CH; GET_CH;
                end if;
            when ' " ' =>        - - skip strings
                loop
                    GET_CH;
                    exit when CUR_CH=' " ';
                end loop;
                GET_CH;
```

```
      when '-' =>           - - might be a comment
         GET_CH;
         if CUR_CH='-' then   - - yes, skip it
            SKIP_TO_NEXT_LINE;
         end if;
      when '#' =>           - - skip based literals
         loop
             GET_CH;
             exit when CUR_CH='#';
         end loop;
         GET_CH;
      when 'E' =>           - - might be an exponent
         if (OLD_CH in '0' .. '9') or (OLD_CH='#') then
            GET_CH;    - - yes, skip it
         else
            exit SKIPPING;   - - no, must be an identifier
         end if;
      when 'A' .. 'D' | 'F' .. 'Z' =>
         exit SKIPPING;      - - identifier found
      when others =>
         GET_CH;                  - - skip everything else
   end case;
  end loop SKIPPING;
 end FIND_NEXT_IDENT;
```

Note that, in practice, FIND_NEXT_IDENT would need to be declared within the declarative part of GET_ID.

The remaining subprograms in the IO_INTERFACE package are the two PRINT procedures and the "$>$" function. These are all straightforward and are given immediately.

```
   separate(IO_INTERFACE)
   procedure PRINT(ID:IDENT) is
   begin
      NEW_LINE(LIST);
      PUT(LIST,STRING(ID));
      - - fill out to required field width with spaces
      for I in MAX_ID_SIZE+1  .. ID_WIDTH loop
         PUT(LIST,' ');
      end loop;
   end PRINT;
```

```
separate(IO_INTERFACE)
procedure PRINT(LN: in LINE_NUM) is
begin
    PUT(LIST, LN, LN_WIDTH);
end PRINT;

separate(IO_INTERFACE)
function ">"(ID1,ID2: IDENT) return BOOLEAN is
begin
    return STRING(ID1) > STRING(ID2);
end ">";
```

Note the type conversions necessary to make use of the PUT procedure for STRING types in printing IDENTs and in defining the ">" operator.

Finally, the body of SOURCE_INPUT is given as follows

```
separate(IO_INTERFACE)
package body SOURCE_INPUT is

    procedure GET_CH is
    begin
        while END_OF_LINE(SOURCE) loop
            SKIP_LINE(SOURCE);        - - skip input line marks
            NEW_LINE(LIST);           - - start new line on listing
            PUT(LIST,LINE(SOURCE),LN_WIDTH; - - add line numbe
        end loop;

        OLD_CH := CUR_CH;            - - get next input character
        GET(SOURCE,CUR_CH);
        PUT(LIST,CUR_CH);            - - print it

        if CUR_CH in 'a' .. 'z' then  - - convert to upper case
            CUR_CH := CHARACTER'VAL(CHARACTER'POS(CUR_CH
                        -CHARACTER'POS('a')+CHARACTER'POS('A')
        end if;
    end GET_CH;

    procedure SKIP_TO_NEXT_LINE is
    begin
        while not END_OF_LINE(SOURCE) loop
            GET(SOURCE,CUR_CH);       - - read and print input chars
            PUT(LIST,CUR_CH);         - - upto the end of the line
        end loop;
        GET_CH;                       - - read first char of next line
    end SKIP_TO_NEXT_LINE;
end SOURCE_INPUT;
```

Notice that a line number is printed on the list file each time that the end of an input line is reached (the line number of the very first line was output by the INIT_LIST_FILE procedure).

15.12 EXERCISES

(15.1) An external file called "SAMPLES.DATA" contains a sequence of integer numbers in the range −2048 to 2047. Write a program to read this data and find the minimum and maximum values in the file. The program should write these values to the default output device with suitable formatting.

(15.2) Re-design the body of the INTEGER_STACK package described in section 8.12, Exercise (8.1), so that the size of the stack is only limited by the amount of secondary storage available. In other words, implement the stack so that the first few items of the stack are held in memory and the rest of the stack is stored on a file.

(15.3) An external file called "/usr/exams/comp" is given which contains a sequence of records defined by the following

```
NO_OF_EXAMS: constant := 5;

subtype PERCENT is INTEGER range 0 .. 100;
type MARK_ARRAY is array (1 .. NO_OF_EXAMS) of PERCENT;
type STUDENT_RECORD is
   record
      NAME: STRING(1 .. 20);
      MARKS: MARK_ARRAY;
   end record;
```

Write a program which reads each record from the file and prints the student's name, his marks in each exam and his average mark on a single line of the default output file. Also arrange that an asterisk be placed against any mark that is below 40%.

16

Real data types

Real numbers are used for the measurement of real continuous quantities. Within an Ada program, real numbers may be represented approximately by the real data types. The inherent inaccuracy of real number representation in a computer is an inevitable consequence of a finite-size machine wordlength. In any program using real types the effects of this inaccuracy must be considered. Even in simple uses of reals, small approximations in the real types can lead to significant errors overall. In more complex algorithms, they can lead to instability and total failure of the algorithm to compute useful results.

In the past, ensuring that numerical algorithms can be moved from one machine to another has been very difficult, since the accuracy of real number representation has always been machine dependent. Ada is rather unusual, however, in that it provides facilities for declaring user-defined real data types with a specified accuracy. Thus, it should be possible to write portable numerical algorithms in Ada.

Quite a few aspects of real data types have been covered in earlier chapters. The notation for writing real numbers was presented in Chapter 2, the declaration of real constants was described in Chapter 5, and the input/output of real data types was covered in Chapter 15. In this chapter, the way in which real data types are declared and used will be described. It must be emphasised, however, that the treatment is of necessity brief. A detailed discussion would not only be extremely lengthy but would also require an in-depth knowledge of numerical analysis. Here the intention is simply to give an overview of the facilities provided and to indicate the basic ways in which they can be used.

16.1 FIXED-POINT AND FLOATING-POINT REPRESENTATION

The real data types of Ada are divided into two classes called fixed-point and floating-point. The purpose of this section is to explain what is meant by these terms. To aid understanding, all the examples in this section are presented as if real numbers are stored in decimal, and that all operations applied to them are decimal. (In fact, Ada assumes a binary representation, but this difference will not matter as far as this presentation is concerned. What matters here are the principles, not the number base of the arithmetic.)

A fixed-point number is represented by a fixed number of digits and an 'imaginary' decimal point. The decimal-point is imaginary because it does not exist at the level of the hardware, which treats all fixed-point numbers as simple integers. For example, suppose that a total of four digits are available, then a number such as 2.4 could be represented in fixed-point as 02.40 and the number 0.24 as 0.240. However, both numbers would actually be represented by the underlying hardware as the same four digit integer number 0246. It is up to the programmer to 'remember' where the decimal-point is in each fixed-point number. This is important because the position of the decimal-point must be known in order to perform a fixed-point operation using integer arithmetic. For example, the numbers 02.40 and 0.240 cannot be added directly because their decimal-points are in different positions. Instead, one must be adjusted so that its decimal-point is in the same position as the other. This can be done by either multiplying 02.40 by 10 and then moving the decimal-point left by one position or by dividing 0.240 by 10 and then moving the decimal-point right by one position. The first case would give 2.400+0.240 = 2.640, and is implemented by the underlying hardware as 2400+0240 = 2640. The second case would give 02.40+00.24 = 02.64, and is implemented by the underlying hardware as 0240+0024 = 0264. Notice that the decision as to which way to move the decimal-point must be taken only after careful analysis of the problem. Shifting the point left retains accuracy but can easily lead to overflow. Shifting the point right avoids the possibility of overflow but can result in a loss of accuracy. To emphasise this point, try adding the two fixed-point numbers 100.0 and 00.01!

From now on, the position of the decimal-point in a fixed-point number will be denoted by counting the number of fractional digits. This quantity will be called the *scale* of the number; for example, the scale of 02.40 is 2 and that of 0.240 is 3. The operation of adjusting the position of the decimal-point will be called *rescaling*.

Table 16.1 tabulates the arithmetic operations between two fixed-point numbers X and Y. The scale of each is denoted by Sx and Sy, respectively. For

Table 16.1 Fixed-Point Arithmetic Operations

Operation	Scale of X	Scale of Y	Scale of Result
X + Y	Sx	Sy=Sx	Sx
X − Y	Sx	Sy=Sx	Sx
X * Y	Sx	Sy	Sx + Sy
X / Y	Sx	Sy	Sx − Sy

addition and subtraction, the scales of the operands must be the same and the scale of the result is the same as the scale of the operands. Multiplication and division, however, can be performed on operands with differing scales. Again it is helpful to look at the way in which these operations are actually implemented in integer arithmetic. Consider the multiplication of 02.46 by 2.000. The operands are multiplied as integers, that is, 0246 * 2000 = 0492000. The scale of the result is the sum of the scales of the operands, that is, 5; hence, the result is 04.92000. Notice here that the product is (nearly) double-length, and although multiplication is exact, in practice the result must be truncated, possibly after rescaling, to single-length. For division, the first operand is extended to double-length and then normal integer division performed. For example, to divide 02.46 by 2.000, the first operand is extended to 0246000 (scale 5) and then divided by 2000 to give 0132. The resulting scale is 5 – 3 = 2; hence the result is 01.32.

It should be clear from the above that great care needs to be taken to use fixed-point numbers properly. Within a fixed-point algorithm, frequent rescaling must be performed to ensure that overflow does not occur and that precision is maintained. When the operands are variables, this is rarely a simple task.

Finally, it should be appreciated that from the point of view of error analysis, a fixed-point representation with a given scale allows real numbers to be stored with an accuracy which is absolute. For example, a scale of 2 gives an absolute accuracy of 0.01. Ada calls this accuracy measure the *delta* of the fixed-point number and as will be shown later, this forms the basis of fixed-point number representation in Ada.

The floating-point representation of numbers avoids the problems of scaling associated with fixed-point by storing numbers as a fixed-length mantissa plus an associated exponent. For example, the number 2.46 could be represented in floating point by

> 0.246E1

where the three digit mantissa is 0.246 and the exponent is 1. The value of a floating-point number is given by

> mantissa * (radix ** exponent)

In this case the radix is 10; hence, 0.246E1 is equal to 0.246 * 10 = 2.46. The key feature of floating-point is that the mantissa is arranged to be the largest possible fraction of 1.0. After every floating-point operation, the result is always rescaled so that this condition is true. This process is called *normalisation*. For example, in computing 2.46/10.0, the immediate result would be 0.0246E1, but normalisation rescales this to 0.246E0. This means that there is no loss in precision on truncation back to a 3 digit mantissa.

To summarise, fixed-point provides a simple representation for real numbers which gives a bound on the *absolute* accuracy. In contrast, floating-point involves a more complex representation but it provides a bound on the *relative* accuracy.

The practical consequences of this are that for general numerical work floating-point is much easier to use, since it is relative accuracy rather than absolute accuracy which is important in numeric computations. To put it another way, when working in fixed-point, explicit scaling of the data must be performed to maintain accuracy and to prevent overflow, but in floating-point this is done automatically. However, although floating-point is easier to use it requires either special purpose hardware to implement or each floating-point operation must be simulated in software. The former is expensive and the latter is very slow. Hence fixed-point meets a definite need in the implementation of low-cost real time systems with a requirement for fast arithmetic computations, such as are often found in the areas of digital signal processing and simple control systems.

16.2 FLOATING-POINT TYPES

Every Ada implementation provides a predefined floating-point type called FLOAT. The precision and range of real numbers which can be represented by this type is machine dependent. However, as will be described below, floating-point types can be defined by the user with specified precisions, and so this machine dependence can be avoided.

The same basic operations are provided for floating-point types as for integer types, that is,

monadic:	+	identity
	–	negation
	abs	absolute value
diadic:	+	addition
	–	subtraction
	*	multiplication
	/	division
	**	exponentiation

Hence, if X and Y are of type FLOAT, typical arithmetic operations might be

```
Y := 9.7*X + 4.01;
Y := 1.0/X;          - - Y = reciprocal of X
Y := X**2;           - - Y = square of X
Y := abs X;          - - Y = absolute value of X
```

Notice that constants in a real expression must always be written as real literals; integer literals are not allowed, for example,

```
Y := 1/X;
```

is illegal. Also, the second operand of the exponentiation operation must be an integer, for example, X∗∗0.5 is not allowed. In fact, exponentiation is defined as a repeated multiplication operation, and its effect is shown by the following code:

```
- - compute X_TO_POWER_N  =  X**N
X_TO_POWER_N:=1.0;                        - - initialise
for I in 1 .. abs N loop                  - - multiply by X N times
    X_TO_POWER_N:=X_TO_POWER_N*X;
end loop;
if N<0 then                               - - correct for -ve N
    X_TO_POWER_N:=1.0/X_TO_POWER_N;
end if;
```

As well as the above set of arithmetic operations, the full set of relational operators can be used with any floating-point type. For example,

$$X <= 1.0 \text{ and } Y > 0.0$$

is a condition involving two floating-point comparisons. Beware, however, of using the equality and inequality operators. Due to the approximate nature of real number representations, tests such as X=Y may give unexpected results. For example, the expression

$$(X/Y)*Y = X$$

will very often evaluate to FALSE. It is usually a much better approach to use expressions of the form $X-Y <= E$ where E is a suitably small number.

As a simple example of the use of floating-point, the following program will read a sequence of numbers from the default input file, tabulate them on the default output file, and then print their mean value. The sequence is preceded by an integer number giving the total number of values in the file.

```
with TEXT_IO; use TEXT_IO;
procedure AVERAGE is
    VALS_PER_LINE: constant := 3;
    COUNT: INTEGER range 0 .. INTEGER'LAST := 0;
    VALUE: FLOAT;
    SUM   : FLOAT := 0.0;

    package INT_IO is new INTEGER_IO(INTEGER);
    package FLT_IO is new FLOAT_IO(FLOAT);
    use INT_IO, FLT_IO;
begin
    GET(COUNT);   - - read number of values to be averaged
```

```
      for I in 1 .. COUNT loop                    - - compute sum
          GET(VALUE);                             - - and tabulate values
          SUM := SUM+VALUE;
          PUT(I,WIDTH=>3); PUT(' . ');
          PUT(VALUE, FORE => 2, AFT => 3, EXP => 3
          if I mod VALS_PER_LINE = 0 then
              NEW_LINE;
          else
              PUT(' ');
          end if;
      end loop;

      NEW_LINE(2);                                - - print mean value
      PUT("Mean Value is ");
      PUT(SUM/FLOAT(COUNT),WIDTH=>10,MANTISSA=>4);
  end AVERAGE;
```

Hence, if the input contained

```
12
12.73 14.28 0.63 9.71
2.9 4.7 8.693 27.1
2.39 1.98 20.0 18.2
```

then the output would be

1. 1.273E01	2. 1.428E01	3. 6.300E-01
4. 9.710E00	5. 2.900E00	6. 4.700E00
7. 8.693E00	8. 2.710E01	9. 2.390E00
10. 1.980E00	11. 2.000E01	12. 1.820E01

Mean Value is   1.028E01

The formulation of the AVERAGE procedure is quite straightforward, although three points should be noted. Firstly, in order to input and output values of type INTEGER and FLOAT, appropriate packages must be instantiated. Secondly, the operation of GET for numeric values automatically skips line marks; hence the line structure of the input can be ignored. Thirdly, in order to compute the mean, the division of a real number by an integer number is required. This necessitates the use of an explicit type conversion, that is, SUM/FLOAT(COUNT) must be written, since the direct division SUM/COUNT is illegal (the operands must be of the same type).

   In addition to the predefined type FLOAT, most Ada implementations will provide a further type called LONG_FLOAT with an extended precision. (Some implementations may even supply a range of predefined floating-point types with different precisions, for example, SHORT_FLOAT, FLOAT, LONG_FLOAT, LONG_LONG_FLOAT, etc.) The type LONG_FLOAT can be used to improve the accuracy of arithmetic computations. For example, in the following function for computing a scalar product, a LONG_FLOAT type is used to store the accumulated sum of the products, before conversion back to the standard precision of FLOAT for the result:

```
function SCALAR_PRODUCT(X,Y:FLOAT_VEC) return FLOAT is
    SUM: LONG_FLOAT := 0.0;
begin
    for I in X'RANGE loop
        SUM := SUM + LONG_FLOAT(X(I))*LONG_FLOAT(Y(I));
    end loop;
    return FLOAT(SUM);
end SCALAR_PRODUCT;
```

where the type FLOAT_VEC denotes a one-dimensional array with components of type FLOAT.

As noted at the start of this section, the direct use of the FLOAT and LONG_FLOAT types may cause difficulties with portability, because of the differing precisions provided by different implementations. This is a similar problem to that noted for integer types in Chapter 3, and a similar solution is provided for floating-point types. A user may define his own floating-point types with a specified accuracy. This accuracy is then guaranteed, independently of the implementation. Also, of course, the introduction of distinct types for logically different classes of real numbers improves program readability and security, and so is generally to be encouraged.

The syntax of a floating-point type declaration is given by the following diagrams:

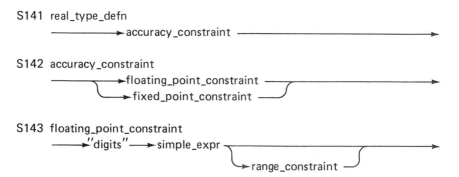

S141 real_type_defn

S142 accuracy_constraint

S143 floating_point_constraint

A floating-point type is declared by writing an accuracy constraint which specifies the number of decimal digits of precision required, optionally followed by a range constraint. For example, the declaration

type MY_FLOAT is digits 8 range −1.0E20 .. 1 . 0E20;

declares a type MY_FLOAT with at least 8 digits of precision, and a range of
−1.0E20 to 1.0E20. Notice that the number of digits specified for the precision
(that is, the number to be used for the mantissa) is only a *minimum* requirement.
An implementation may provide more digits than that requested. Also, since the
mantissa is actually represented in binary, this minimum requirement in terms of
decimal digits is actually translated by the compiler into a minimum number of
bits. In fact, if D decimal digits are specified, then the compiler will provide at
least D∗log(10)/log(2) bits.

As with integer type declarations, the compiler treats the floating-point
declaration

> **type** F **is digits** D **range** L . . R;

as being equivalent to a derived type declaration

> **type** F **is new** *fp-type* **digits** D **range** L . . R;

where *fp-type* is chosen to be that predefined floating-point type (that is,
FLOAT, LONG_FLOAT, etc.) which gives just the requested accuracy.

As with all scalar types in Ada, additional constraints may be placed on a
floating-point object either directly in its declaration or via a subtype. For
example,

> X: MY_FLOAT;
> Y: MY_FLOAT **digits** 6;
> Z: MY_FLOAT **range** −1000 . 0 . . 1000;

declares three objects of type MY_FLOAT called X, Y and Z, but objects Y and
Z have further constraints placed upon them. Object Y is stated to require at
least 6 digits of precision, and object Z has its range constrained to −1000.0 to
+1000.0. In principle, the object Y could be stored with fewer bits than that of
X, although in practice, most compilers would not do this as it would be very
inefficient. An explicit **digits** constraint can be useful, however, both as an aid to
documentation and to improve security. If in a later revision of a program the
type MY_FLOAT were modified, say to give only 5 digits of precision, then the
compiler would report an error when the declaration of X was elaborated. A
subtype or object constraint can never expand the accuracy or the range specified for the type. Also note that range constraints may, in practice, need to be
used with some caution, since the consequent range checking which then needs
to be performed on every assignment operation may be quite significant.

Finally, note that none of the mathematical functions such as SIN, COS,
SQRT, etc. are predefined in Ada. Instead it is expected that implementations
will provide one or more library packages which supply these operations.

16.3 FIXED-POINT TYPES

There are no predefined fixed-point types in Ada. A user must define each and every fixed-point type required in a program. The syntax for declaring a fixed-point type is shown by the following diagram, which should be read in conjunction with diagrams S140 to S142:

S144 fixed_point_constraint

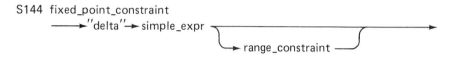

The declaration

type MY_FIXED **is delta** 0.01 **range** −100.0 . . 100.0;

introduces a fixed-point type called **MY_FIXED** with delta 0.01 and range −100.0 to +100.0. Note that the range constraint must be included in a fixed-point type declaration: it can only be omitted in a subtype declaration or object constraint. The delta specifies a bound on the absolute accuracy required for the type.

The exact effect of the above type declaration is best appreciated by examining how it would be represented in a computer. Since fixed-point numbers are actually stored in binary, the specified delta of 1/100 must be reduced to the nearest power of 2, that is, 1/128 which is 2**−7. To achieve this accuracy, therefore, 7 fractional bits are required. Similarly, the implemented range must be the nearest power of two greater than the specified range, that is, −128 . . 127. Hence, 7 bits are also needed to the left of the binary point. Thus, including a sign bit, a total of 15 bits are required to represent an object of type MY_FIXED, that is,

    sbbbbbbb . fffffff

where each b denotes an integer bit, each f denotes a fractional bit and the s denotes the sign bit. On a 16 bit computer, therefore, objects of type **MY_FIXED** would fit very conveniently into a single word, leaving the least significant bit spare as a 'guard' bit.

The operators provided for fixed-point types are shown in Table 16.2 along with the allowable operand types. In this table, F and G each represent any fixed-point type and I represents any integer type. As is shown by this table, the unusual feature of fixed-point is that the multiplication and division operators may have operands of different types or one operand of an integer type. Also, the result type is, in two cases, *universal-fixed*. This type denotes a fixed-point type of arbitrarily fine precision, and is used to denote double-length products and single-length dividends. A universal-fixed result must always be explicitly converted to some actual numeric type by applying a type conversion to it.

The universal-fixed type is necessary to allow scaling operations to be performed. When two fixed-point types are multiplied together, an accurate

Table 16.2 Arithmetic Operators for Fixed-Point Types

Operator	Left Operand	Right Operand	Result
+ − (monadic)		F	F
+ −	F	F	F
*	F	I	F
*	I	F	F
*	F	G	Univ-Fixed
/	F	I	F
/	F	G	Univ-Fixed
Relational Operators	F	F	BOOLEAN

product is generated which will be double the length of the operands (see section 16.1). For example, suppose that A*B is to be computed, where A and B are of type AFIX and BFIX respectively, and are actually represented as follows

AFIX:	sbbb . ff	− − scaling 2
BFIX:	sb . ffff	− − scaling 4

then A*B will have the form

	sbbbb . ffffff	− − scaling 6

which is double the length and has 6 fractional bits. The type of A*B is universal-fixed and must be converted to some numeric type (not necessarily, but usually a fixed-point type). For example, if it were required to assign A*B to C where C was of type CFIX represented as

CFIX:	sbb . fff	− − scaling 3

then the assignment must be written

        C := CFIX(A*B);

The effect of the type conversion CFIX(. .) is effectively a scaling operation in which 2 integer bits and 3 fractional bits of A*B are discarded. Alternatively, if the assignment of A*B to an integer I were required, then

        I := INTEGER(A*B);

would have the desired effect. This time the type conversion INTEGER(. .) has the effect of discarding all of the fractional bits.

In effect, the scaling of fixed-point numbers in an Ada program is achieved entirely through the typing system. Each type effectively denotes one particular size and scaling for a fixed-point number. To change scales in a program, all that is needed is to apply an appropriate type conversion. For example, at the machine level the operation

CFIX(B)

is equivalent to shifting B by one bit left. To add A and B, one or other must be converted, that is, either A + AFIX(B) or BFIX(A) + B. In the former, B is shifted left by 2 bits and in the latter A is shifted right by 2 bits. The difference between these is that the former loses precision in B, and the latter increases the risk of overflow. A compromise might be to convert both to an intermediate representation, for example, CFIX(A) + CFIX(B).

The above discussion has concentrated on explanations in terms of the underlying representation. In fact, of course, fixed-point in Ada is designed so that the programmer need not be too concerned with how each type is implemented. The need to consider the underlying representation usually arises only to check that the total number of bits required for each type can be efficiently represented on the target machine. Fixed-point is most commonly used in real-time applications and so considerations such as these are unavoidable.

Turning now to the use of fixed-point types, the following procedure illustrates several points of note:

```
procedure USE_FIXED is
        type BIG      is delta 10.0 range −1.0E4 . . 1.0E4;
        type SMALL   is delta 0.01 range −100.0 . . 100.0;
        type FRAC    is delta 0.0001 range −0.9999 . . 0.9999;

        B1,B2:  BIG;
        S1,S2:  SMALL;
        F1,F2:  FRAC;

begin
        B1  :=  274.0;          - - Last significant digit of 274.0 will
                                - - be lost on conversion to BIG.
        F1  :=  0.1;            - - Note that 0.1 cannot be stored
                                - - exactly.
        F2  :=  F1+0.2;         - - 0.2 is stored with same precision
                                - - as is used for F1.
        S1  :=  SMALL(B1*F1);   - - Result is approximately 27.0. Note
                                - - that the explicit type conversion
                                - - is essential.
        B2  :=  B1 + BIG(S1);   - - B2 is 300 approx., scale of S1 is
                                - - changed to BIG.
        if B2=300.0 then        - - Legal but dangerous use of "=".
            . . . .             - - B2 will only be approx. 300.0.
```

if B2>S1 **then**	- - Illegal as types of operands in
. . . .	- - ">" operation must be the same.
if B2>BIG(S1) **then**	- - Legal version of previous
. . . .	- - statement.
S2:=SMALL(F1∗S1/F2);	- - Illegal, type conversion must be
	- - applied to F1∗S1.
S2:=SMALL(SMALL(F1∗S1)/F2);	- - Legal version of previous
	- - statement.

    end USE_FIXED;

An example of programming in fixed-point is given in section 16.5.

16.4 THE SEMANTICS OF REAL COMPUTATIONS

Although the ability to specify the precision of real data types gives the potential for writing portable numerical algorithms, it does not by itself entirely solve the problem. In order that accurate error analysis may be performed, the semantics of real operations must be defined. The problem is, however, to define these semantics so that they can be implemented efficiently on different hardware and yet be precise enough to meet the demands of the numerical analyst. In this section, the main properties of real data types in Ada will be outlined. These properties provide the basis for error analysis in Ada, although the detailed methods of such analysis are beyond the scope of this book.

Consider first floating-point types. The type declaration of a floating-point type defines a minimum length for the mantissa. For example, assume that a type F is declared as

    type F **is digits** 5;

then the minimum number of bits for the mantissa is $5∗\log(10)/\log(2)$ which is 17. The mantissa of type F can be written in hexadecimal to show the actual binary representation. For example, 0.5 would be

    16#0.10000#   - - exactly 0.5

This denotes a minimal representation for F and as a consequence it determines a set of values of F which can be represented exactly on any machine, for example,

    16#0.10000#   - - exactly 0.5
    16#0.10001#   - - exactly 0.5000076294
    16#0.10002#   - - exactly 0.5000152588

These numbers are called the *model numbers* of F and are the basis on which analysis is performed.

Although an implementation of F must provide at least the model numbers, it may (because it allocates more than 17 bits) also provide further numbers 'in between' these. It is the possibility of these numbers which leads to most of the difficulties in real arithmetic. For example, the number 0.1 cannot be represented exactly in binary. In hexadecimal notation 0.1 is

$$16\#0.19999999999 \ldots \#$$

Hence, a number which is not a model number cannot be guaranteed an exact representation. Instead, such a number is said to be bounded by a *model interval*. In this case, the nearest model number below 0.1 is $16\#0.19999\#$ and the nearest above 0.1 is $16\#0.1999A\#$. Hence the model interval for 0.1 is

$$16\#0.19999\# \ .. \ 16\#0.1999A\#$$

An Ada compiler will guarantee that the actual value used to represent 0.1 will be within this range. Hence, model intervals can be used to determine the errors introduced by the approximation of constants in a program.

In a similar way, the errors introduced by floating-point operations can be defined in terms of model intervals. Given two operands X and Y and an operation **fop**, then for each of X and Y there will be a model interval. The operation is then applied to these two intervals using exact arithmetic, to give a range of possible values for X **fop** Y. This range is then extended, if necessary, to a model interval which gives the bounds of the actual value computed for X **fop** Y.

As a further aid to numerical analysis, a variety of attributes are defined for a floating-point type, based on its model numbers. These are listed in full in Appendix A but for classical error analysis the most useful are

F'EPSILON: the absolute value of the difference between 1.0 and the next model number above 1.0.

F'SMALL: the smallest possible model number of F.

In addition to the attributes of a floating-point type based on its model, there are also attributes which allow the way the type is actually implemented to be determined. For example, F'MACHINE_MANTISSA gives the number of bits actually used to represent the mantissa of type F. Again, the full list of these is given in Appendix A.

The properties of fixed-point types are also treated in terms of model numbers. If a fixed-point type G has a delta specified as D, then this determines a maximum actual delta which can be used in the representation. This actual delta will usually be the power of two which is less than or equal to D, and can always be determined via the attribute G'ACTUAL_DELTA. From this actual delta, the model numbers for the type G are given by

$$\text{sign} * M * G'\text{ACTUAL\_DELTA}$$

where M is in the range 0 to $2*N-1$ for some N. The same sort of analysis can then be performed on fixed-point types as for floating-point types. The main difference between the two is that the model numbers of a fixed-point type cannot normally be determined without reference to a particular implementation, since the actual deltas may differ. Hence it is more difficult to guarantee the properties of a fixed-point algorithm across a range of implementations. Finally, as with floating-point types there are a variety of attributes defined for fixed-point types, and these are listed in Appendix A.

16.5 AN EXAMPLE – FIXED-POINT IMPLEMENTATION OF A DIGITAL FILTER

As an example of the use of fixed-point arithmetic, a typical problem in digital signal processing will be examined. Suppose that a digital signal is to be low pass filtered using the 3rd Order Chebyshev filter described by the following difference equation

$$y(nT) = 0.011956 * (x(nT) + 3x(nT-T) + 3x(nT-2T) + x(nT-3T))$$
$$+ 1.9749y(nT-T) - 1.5243y(nT-2T) + 0.4538y(nT-3T)$$

where $x(nT)$ denotes the value of the input signal at the time nT (T is the sample period) and $y(nT)$ is the computed output of the filter.

The following task implements the above filter using fixed-point arithmetic. Input is performed via a call to the READ entry of an ADC (Analogue to Digital Conversion) task which returns an integer input sample in the range -2048 to 2047 every T seconds. Similarly, output is performed by a call to the WRITE entry of a DAC (Digital to Analogue Conversion) task.

```
task FILTER;

task body FILTER is

      type XFIX    is delta 1.0           range -16384.0 .. 16383.0;
      type YFIX    is delta 2#1.0#E-4     range -2048.0 .. 2047.0;
      type ZFIX    is delta 2#1.0#E-17    range -8192.0 .. 8191.0;
      type C1FIX   is delta 0.000001      range 0.0 .. 0.02;
      type C2FIX   is delta 0.0001        range 0.0 .. 2.0;

      C1:  constant C1FIX := 0.011956;
      C21: constant C2FIX := 1.9749;
      C22: constant C2FIX := 1.5243;
      C23: constant C2FIX := 0.4538;

      XN,XN1,XN2,XN3: XFIX := 0.0;
      YN,YN1,YN2,YN3: YFIX := 0.0;
      Z: ZFIX;

      INPUT_DATA: INTEGER range -2048 .. 2047;
```

```
      begin
        loop
            - - read input
            ADC.READ(INPUT_DATA);
            XN := XFIX(INPUT_DATA);

            - - compute output
            Z := ZFIX(C1*(XN + 3*(XN1+XN2) + XN3));
            YN := YFIX(Z + ZFIX(C21*YN1)
                         - ZFIX(C22*YN2)
                         + ZFIX(C23*YN3) );

            - - output to DAC
            DAC.WRITE(INTEGER(YN));

            - - update variables
            XN3:=XN2; XN2:=XN1; XN1:=XN;
            YN3:=YN2; YN2:=YN1; YN1:=YN;

        end loop;
      end FILTER;
```

The key points in this design are the choice of fixed-point types. It has been assumed here that the program will run on a 16-bit machine. All X and Y values are therefore given types which can be represented within 16 bits. The Xs always denote integer values; hence XFIX has a delta of 1.0. The range of XFIX is set to accommodate the maximum value of the expression XN+3*(XN1+XN2)+XN3 which is 8*XN. The filter has a maximum gain of 1.0; therefore the Ys are bounded by the same range as the Xs. Hence the type YFIX is chosen to give the maximum precision possible within a 16-bit computer word. All intermediate results are represented by ZFIX, which has been made 'double-length' to preserve accuracy. To determine the exact type specification for ZFIX, first of all the range must be determined and then the delta chosen to use the remainder of a 32-bit double word. The maximum value of the type ZFIX is given by the maximum of

(a) C1*(XN + 3*(XN1+XN2) + XN3)
(b) C21*YN1
(c) C22*YN2
(d) C23*YN3
(e) any partial sum of (a), (b), (c) or (d)

Taking the worst all round case gives

$$C1*8*Xmax + (C21+C22+C23)*Ymax$$

Setting the Xmax=Ymax=2048 gives 8296; however, the Y values are not independent variables, and it can be shown that a range of –8192 to 8191 is quite safe. This leaves 17 bits for the fractional part and this sets the delta accordingly.

Finally, note that it has been assumed in the above that the compiler will use the minimum number of bits for the actual delta of each type. This in general is a reasonable assumption, although it is worth noting that the actual delta can be set explicitly by using a representation specification as described in the next chapter.

16.6 EXERCISES

(16.1) Given the following declarations

> **type** FLTX **is digits** 6;
> **type** FLTY **is new** FLTX;
> **type** FIXA **is delta** 0.005 **range** −100.0 .. 100.0;
> **type** FIXB **is delta** 0.01 **range** −100.0 .. 100.0;
>
> X:FLTX; Y:FLTY; A:FIXA; B:FIXB;

then locate the errors in the following statements

(a) X := X / 100;

(b) Y := X * Y;

(c) A := A * B;

(d) B := B * 8#778.0#;

(e) B := FIXB(B/A + A/B);

(16.2) Extend the **AVERAGE** procedure given in section 16.2 to compute the standard deviation as well as the mean. It may be assumed that a package MATH_LIB is available which provides the function SQRT with argument and result of type **FLOAT**.

(16.3) A simple first order digital filter can be defined by the equation

> OUTPUT := INPUT − 0.9*PREVIOUS_OUTPUT

write a package which provides a procedure FILTER_1 defined as

> **procedure** FILTER_1(INPUT: **in** DATA_VAL; OUTPUT: **out** DATA_VAL);

where

> **type** DATA_VAL **is new** INTEGER **range** −128 .. 127;

Implement the procedure using fixed-point arithmetic and assume that it must be optimised to run on a 16-bit computer.

17

Low level programming

In general an Ada program can be considered to be an abstract description of a set of computations to be performed by a computer. The description is abstract in the sense that it is independent of the actual computer to be used and it is the job of the compiler to map this abstract description into the appropriate set of instructions for the actual machine. Sometimes, especially in real time programming, it is necessary to have closer control over the way that the compiler performs this mapping and in Ada this control is achieved through the use of representation specifications.

A representation specification can be used to specify precisely how certain kinds of language construct are to be implemented. For example, when a type is defined, it is normally the compiler which decides how much storage will be needed to represent objects of that type in memory. Similarly, when a variable is declared, the compiler decides where to store that variable in memory. A representation specification can be used to override these compiler decisions.

Representation specifications are useful in two main areas. Firstly, they allow input/output operations to be programmed at the machine level. This is particularly important in real time systems, which often include non-standard peripheral devices such as analogue to digital convertors. Secondly, they allow a program to be optimised for running on a particular target machine, which may be important if memory space or execution speed is critical.

17.1 REPRESENTATION SPECIFICATIONS

Representation specifications may be used to define precisely how a record or enumeration type is to be represented in memory and where particular variables are to be stored. They allow the programmer to specify the maximum number of bits which are to be allocated to objects of a given type; to specify the amounts of storage which are to be allocated to tasks and collections; and to specify the actual delta of a fixed-point type. Also, they allow interrupts to be associated with entry calls.

Representation specifications are written immediately after the list of declarative items in a declarative part (see syntax diagram S56 in section 5.2) and may only refer to entities declared in that same declarative part.

There are four kinds of representation specification, as is shown by the following syntax diagram:

S145 representation_specification

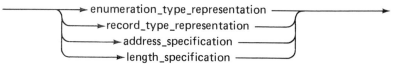

The first three of these are of direct use in low level input/output programming, as will be explained in the next section. The fourth is used principally for optimisation, and is described in section 17.3.

17.2 LOW LEVEL I/O PROGRAMMING

In order to program an i/o device directly at the hardware level, two things are generally needed. Firstly, there must be some mechanism for accessing the status, control and data registers of the device. Secondly, there must be some mechanism for handling interrupts.

In order to access a device register in Ada, the following steps must be taken:

(1) Describe the abstract properties of the register by means of a data type;
(2) Specify how that data type must be mapped into memory;
(3) Declare an object of that type;
(4) Locate the object at the address in memory occupied by the device register (note that memory mapped input/output is being assumed).

As an example, suppose that an analogue to digital convertor has a 16-bit control/ status register defined as shown in Fig. 17.1 (this is actually an AD11K convertor on a PDP11 minicomputer).

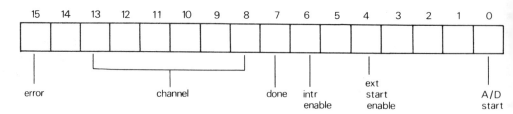

Fig. 17.1 – Control/Status Register of a Typical ADC

It is possible to write to this register to control the ADC's operation, and to read it to determine its status. The meaning of the various bits and fields of the register are:

A/D Start	– set to 1 to start a conversion
Ext Start Enable	– if set, a conversion may be started by external hardware (– not used in the examples here)
Intr Enable	– if set, enables the ADC to generate an interrupt when Done goes true
Done	– goes to 1 when the current conversion is complete
Channel	– the ADC has up to 64 analogue input channels. The value written into this field of the register (range 0 .. 63) selects the input channel to be converted
Error	– set when an error occurs

This register can be described in Ada by the following type declarations

```
subtype CHANNEL is INTEGER range 0 .. 63;

type BIT is (OFF,ON);

type ADC_CSR is
    record
        AD_START:       BIT;
        EXT_START_EN:   BIT;
        INTR_ENABLE:    BIT;
        DONE:           BIT;
        CHAN:           CHANNEL;
        ERROR:          BIT;
    end record;
```

These types describe the abstract properties of the device register as a record with component names chosen to reflect the function of the various bits and fields. The type BIT is introduced to denote a control or status bit, rather than using BOOLEAN directly. This is because the representation of the type BIT must be explicitly specified, and this can only be done for user-defined types.

To map the ADC_CSR record onto the correct bit positions of the register, a record type representation must be used, whose syntax is given by the following diagrams:

S146 record_type_representation

S147 location

$\longrightarrow$ "at" $\longrightarrow$ simple_expr $\longrightarrow$ "range" $\longrightarrow$ range $\longrightarrow$

S148 alignment_clause

$\longrightarrow$ "at" $\longrightarrow$ "mod" $\longrightarrow$ simple_expr $\longrightarrow$

The record type representation enables the location of each component within the record to be specified in terms of the storage location it occupies relative to the start of the record and its bit position within that storage location. For example, if COMP is a record component, then

COMP **at** I **range** M . . N;

locates COMP in the Ith storage location between bits M to N inclusive. The size of a storage location is implementation dependent but can be determined via the constant STORAGE_UNIT in package SYSTEM. An alignment clause, if included, is used to indicate that any object declared of the given record type must be located at a starting address which is a multiple of the value given by the expression. For example,

at mod 8

would mean that the record may be located at any address which is a multiple of 8, that is, address 0, 8, 16, 24, 32, etc.

Returning to the example, the representation for ADC_CSR depends on the size of a storage unit. Here it will be assumed that the underlying machine is byte-oriented and that word-sized data must be aligned on an even address boundary (cf. the PDP11). The record type representation for ADC_CSR is therefore as follows:

for ADC_CSR **use**

record at mod 2;	
AD_START	**at** 0 **range** 0 . . 0;
EXT_START_EN	**at** 0 **range** 4 . . 4;
INTR_ENABLE	**at** 0 **range** 6 . . 6;
DONE	**at** 0 **range** 7 . . 7;
CHAN	**at** 1 **range** 0 . . 5;
ERROR	**at** 1 **range** 7 . . 7;
end record;	

In a similar way to the above, the mapping of the enumerated type BIT must be specified. This is done using an enumeration type representation with syntax as follows:

S149 enumeration_type_representation

$\longrightarrow$ "for" $\longrightarrow$ name $\longrightarrow$ "use" $\longrightarrow$ aggregate $\longrightarrow$ ";" $\longrightarrow$

where the aggregate is used to specify the underlying integer value to be used to represent each of the enumeration literals. In this case, the value of OFF must be 0 and the value of ON must be 1 (actually this would have been the default choice of the compiler anyway). Hence, the required representation specification is

for BIT **use** (OFF=>0, ON=>1);

The types required to represent the control/status register have now been fully defined. All that remains is to declare a variable of type ADC_CSR and to locate it at the memory location used by the actual register. The variable declaration is normal, that is,

CSR: ADC_CSR;

Its location in memory is fixed by an address specification whose syntax is described by the following diagram:

S150 address_specification

⟶►"for" ►name ⟶►"use"⟶►"at" ►simple_expr ⟶►";"⟶

where simple_expr denotes the address of the named object. In this case, if the control/status register is located at address 170400 (octal), then the appropriate specification is

for CSR **use at** 8#170400#;

Once the various registers associated with an input/output device have been defined in the manner described above, access to them is achieved simply by reading and writing to the corresponding variable. For example, to test the DONE bit of the ADC, all that is needed is

if CSR . DONE=ON **then** .....

The following procedure illustrates how the ADC could be programmed to read a sample value from a given channel. It assumes that the types CHANNEL, BIT and ADC_CSR have been previously declared as above and that the converted value is read from a 16-bit buffer register located at 170402 (octal). Notice that the procedure uses polling to determine when the conversion has completed. During this time, the calling program or task is *busy waiting*.

```
     procedure READ_ADC(CH: in CHANNEL;  VALUE: out INTEGER;
                                         OK: out BOOLEAN) is
          CSR:ADC_CSR;                    - - declare cont/status reg
          BFR:INTEGER range 0 . . 4095;  - - declare data buffer reg

          for CSR use at 8#170400#;      - - locate them in memory
          for BFR use at 8#170402#;
```

```
begin
    - - start conversion on specified channel
    CSR := (AD_START        => ON,
            EXT_START_EN  => OFF,
            INTR_ENABLE   => OFF,
            DONE          => OFF,
            CHAN          => CH,
            ERROR         => OFF);

    - - wait for end of conversion by polling DONE bit
    while CSR . DONE<>ON loop
        null;
    end loop;

    - - check for errors
    OK := CSR . ERROR=OFF;

    - - if none then read converted value from data buffer
    if OK then
        VALUE := BFR;
    end if;
end READ_ADC;
```

In practice, busy waiting must normally be avoided in order to prevent wasting processor time. At the level of the hardware, busy waiting is avoided by the use of interrupts. At the language level, an interrupt can be handled by associating it with the entry of a task. When used in this way, the task is effectively the equivalent of the *device handler* or *device driver* of assembly language programmed systems.

To link an interrupt to a task entry, an address specification is used, the stated address being the vector address associated with the interrupt. Such an address specification must appear in the specification part of the task after all the entries of that task have been declared. In fact, this is the only kind of representation specification which can appear in a task specification.

As an example, the following task specification declares two entries

```
task ADC_DRIVER is
    entry READ(CH: in CHANNEL; VALUE: out INTEGER;
                            OK: out BOOLEAN);
    entry INTERRUPT;

    for INTERRUPT use at 8#340#;
end ADC_DRIVER;
```

The entry READ is a normal entry. The INTERRUPT entry, however, is associated with an interrupt by the address specification. Here it is assumed that the interrupt vector address of the ADC is 340 (octal). Thus, in use, the READ entry will be called by other tasks and the INTERRUPT entry will be called automatically by the ADC hardware. The ADC_DRIVER task is therefore the interface between the software system and the device hardware. Note that, although it does not happen in this example, it is quite legal to call an entry associated with an interrupt from the software in the normal way.

The body of the ADC_DRIVER task consists of an endless loop in which an **accept** READ statement is continuously executed. The body of this statement has to start a conversion and then wait for an interrupt to be returned before reading the converted value, that is, it has the following general structure

```
accept READ( .... ) do
    - - start conversion and enable interrupts
    accept INTERRUPT;
    - - disable interrupts and read converted value
end READ;
```

This structure is typical of most interrupt-driven input devices. A further example of an input device handler and also of an output device handler can be found at the end of this chapter. The body of the ADC_DRIVER task is

```
task body ADC_DRIVER is
    CSR:ADC_CSR;                      - - declare cont/status reg
    BFR:INTEGER range 0 .. 4095;      - - declare data buffer reg
    for CSR use at 8#170400#;         - - locate them in memory
    for BFR use at 8#170402#;
begin
    loop
        accept READ(CH: in CHANNEL; VALUE: out INTEGER;
                                OK: out BOOLEAN) do
            - - start conversion on specified channel
            CSR := (AD_START      => ON,
                    EXT_START_EN=> OFF,
                    INTR_ENABLE  => ON,
                    DONE         => OFF,
                    CHAN         => CH,
                    ERROR        => OFF);
            - - wait for interrupt to signal the end
            - - of the conversion
            accept INTERRUPT:
            - - check for errors
            OK := CSR.ERROR=OFF;
            - - if none then read converted value from data buffer
```

```
                    if OK then
                        VALUE := BFR;
                    end if;
                end READ;
            end loop;
        end ADC_DRIVER;
```

From the caller's point of view, the procedure call

> READ_ADC(CHAN,VALUE,OK);

is functionally similar to the entry call

> ADC_DRIVER . READ(CHAN,VALUE,OK);

The vital difference, however, is that in the latter case the calling task will be suspended for the duration of the ADC conversion, thereby allowing the cpu to execute other tasks. In the former case, the calling task is not suspended and therefore prevents execution of other tasks, thereby slowing down the system.

Finally, note that access to device registers, as described above, assumes that they are memory mapped. Where this is not the case, or where the techniques described above are not thought to be appropriate, Ada supplies a package called LOW_LEVEL_IO specified as follows:

```
package LOW_LEVEL_IO is
    - - declare possible types for DEVICE and DATA
    - - declare overloaded procedures for these types:

    procedure SEND_CONTROL      (DEVICE:device_type;
                                 DATA:in out data_type);
    procedure RECEIVE_CONTROL   (DEVICE:device_type;
                                 DATA:in out data_type);
end;
```

This package contains a procedure SEND_CONTROL and a procedure RECEIVE_CONTROL for every device supported by the package. The former may be used to send control information to a device, and the latter may be used to request information from a device. The DEVICE parameter identifies the device and the DATA parameter denotes control information to be transferred. The kinds and format of both these parameters are implementation dependent.

17.3 LENGTH SPECIFICATIONS

A length specification can be used to control the amount of storage associated with various program entities. The syntax of a length specification is given by the following diagram

S151 length_specification

```
───▶"for"─▶ attribute ───▶"use"───▶ expr ───▶";" ──────────────▶
```

The effect of a length specification depends on the given attribute which must be T'SIZE, T'STORAGE_SIZE or T'SMALL.

A length specification for T'SIZE, where T is any type other than a task type, sets a maximum limit on the number of bits which can be allocated for objects of type T. The number of bits specified must be denoted by a static expression and must be sufficient to represent all values of the type. As an example, a CHARACTER object may be represented by as few as 7 bits, but a compiler may well allocate a full word for each character for convenience. A more compact representation of the character type could be introduced as follows:

```
type PACKED_CHARACTER is new CHARACTER;
for   PACKED_CHARACTER'SIZE use 8;
```

When an object of type PACKED_CHARACTER is declared, the compiler may allocate at most 8 bits for it. Note, however, that in general a better way to optimise the use of memory in the case of structured data types is to use the PACK pragma, whose form is

```
pragma PACK(T);
```

where T is the name of a record or array type. The effect of this pragma is to request the compiler to minimise the gaps between adjacent components of the data structure in memory.

Representation specifications force the compiler to map types in a precisely specified way, and this lack of flexibility may cause problems, especially with portability. The use of a pragma, however, is less rigid, since it is merely a recommendation to the compiler to emphasise one particular criterion when choosing a mapping.

Perhaps the most important use of length specifications concern the T'-STORAGE_SIZE attribute, where T is either the name of an access type or the name of a task type. In the case of an access type, a length specification is used to reserve a given amount of storage for the associated collection. The requirement for this facility was discussed in section 11.7. As an example, suppose that it was required to reserve a fixed amount of storage for the collection of ITEM objects defined in section 11.2. This could be done as follows:

```
NO_OF_ITEMS: constant := 150;

type ITEM;

type ITEM_POINTER is access ITEM;

type ITEM is
    record
        NAME: PERSON_NAME;
        NEXT: ITEM_POINTER;
    end record;
```

-- specify size of the collection of ITEM objects

for ITEM_POINTER'STORAGE_SIZE **use**
    NO_OF_ITEMS * ((ITEM'SIZE/SYSTEM.STORAGE_UNIT)+1);

The expression in the length specification (which need not be static) gives the total number of storage units to be allocated to the collection. This is calculated by making use of the SIZE attribute to find the number of bits required to store an ITEM object, and then dividing it by the number of bits in a storage unit as defined by SYSTEM.STORAGE_UNIT. Notice, however, that the number of ITEMS which can actually be allocated to the collection may be slightly less than NO_OF_ITEMS, since the memory management system may use some of the available space for house-keeping information.

The storage required for the workspace of a task can be specified in a similar way. For example, if USER is the name of task type, then

for USER'STORAGE_SIZE **use** 1000;

specifies that each task activated of type USER will be allocated a workspace of 1000 storage units. As with the previous case, the expression denoting the number of storage units need not be static but can be computed at run-time.

Finally, the actual delta of a fixed-point type can be explicitly specified via a length specification. For example, if a type FIX is defined as

type FIX **is delta** 0.01 **range** -100.0 .. 100.0;

then if 7 fractional bits are to be used for the actual delta,

for FIX'SMALL **use** 1.0/128.0;

will achieve this.

17.4 MACHINE DEPENDENT CONSTANTS

As noted earlier, every Ada implementation must supply a package called SYSTEM which defines a number of constants describing various aspects of the system. An actual implementation can include any number of these constants, but the following will always be provided

SYSTEM_NAME	— an enumeration value identifying the name of the system
STORAGE_UNIT	— the number of bits per storage unit
MEMORY_SIZE	— number of storage units in memory
MIN_INT	— smallest integer value supported by a pre-defined type
MAX_INT	— largest integer value supported by a pre-defined type

17.5 AN EXAMPLE – THE LINE_INTERFACE PACKAGE

In section 12.13 an example was given of a communications interface package in which the interface to the actual serial input and output lines was represented by a package called LINE_INTERFACE specified as follows:

```
package LINE_INTERFACE is
    procedure TX_OUT(CH: in CHARACTER);
    procedure RX_IN(CH: out CHARACTER);
end LINE_INTERFACE;
```

In this section an implementation of the body of this package will be given assuming that the underlying hardware has the architecture of a PDP11 mini-computer. With this architecture, all devices are memory-mapped and serial lines have two device registers associated with them. The first is a control/status register of which the only relevant bit is bit 6 which, when set, enables an interrupt from the device. The second is the buffer register which is also 16 bits but only the lower 8 bits are actually used.

The following package body describes the main features of the implementation. For clarity, the device register addresses and associated interrupt vector addresses are declared as constants.

```
with BUFFER_TYPE;

package body LINE_INTERFACE is

    - - Device Addresses
    TX_VEC: constant := 8#64#;
    RX_VEC: constant := 8#60#;
    TX_CSR: constant := 8#177564#;
    TX_BFR: constant := 8#177566#;
    RX_CSR: constant := 8#177560#;
    RX_BFR: constant := 8#177562#;

    - - Register Types
    type BIT is (OFF,ON);
    type CSR_REG is
        record
            INTEN: BIT;
        end record;

    - - Instantiate Character Buffer Package
    package CHAR_BUF is new BUFFER_TYPE(CHARACTER);
    use CHAR_BUF;
    RX_BUFFER,TX_BUFFER: BUFFER(SIZE=>64);

    - - Specify Representations
    for BIT use (OFF=>0, ON=>1);
```

```
for CSR_REG use
    record at mod 2;
        INTEN at 0 range 6 . . 6;
    end record;
- - Driver Tasks
task TX_DRIVER is
    entry INTERRUPT;
    for INTERRUPT use at TX_VEC;
end TX_DRIVER;

task RX_DRIVER is
    entry INTERRUPT;
    for INTERRUPT use at RX_VEC;
end RX_DRIVER;

task body TX_DRIVER is separate;
task body RX_DRIVER is separate;

- - Interface Procedures
procedure TX_OUT(CH: in CHARACTER) is
begin
    PUT(TX_BUFFER,CH);
end TX_OUT;

procedure RX_IN(CH: out CHARACTER) is
begin
    GET(RX_BUFFER,CH);
end RX_OUT;

begin    - - initialise character buffers
    INIT(TX_BUFFER);  INIT(RX_BUFFER);
end LINE_INTERFACE;
```

As can be seen, this package makes use of the generic BUFFER_TYPE package designed in section 14.5. Two buffers are declared of type BUFFER called RX_BUFFER and TX_BUFFER. These are used to link the interface procedures to the actual device driver tasks. Buffering is essential here to prevent incoming characters being lost and to prevent tasks calling TX_OUT being held up while each character is transmitted.

The actual driver tasks are fairly straightforward. The body of the TX_DRIVER task is

```
separate (LINE_INTERFACE)
task body TX_DRIVER is
    CSR: CSR_REG;
    BFR: CHARACTER;
    for CSR use at TX_CSR;
    for BFR use at TX_BFR;
```

```
begin
   loop
      GET(TX_BUFFER,CH);
      CSR.INTEN := ON;
      BFR := CH;
      accept INTERRUPT;
      CSR.INTEN := OFF;
   end loop;
end TX_DRIVER;
```

The task executes an endless loop. Each cycle, a character is first extracted from the TX_BUFFER. Interrupts are then enabled and the character is written into the device's buffer register. At this point the task must wait until the device signals that it is ready to receive another character by raising an interrupt. It therefore executes an accept statement to wait for this interrupt. When it is received, interrupts are disabled and the cycle is repeated.

The RX_DRIVER task is similar except that interrupts are left enabled permanently to ensure that no incoming characters are lost.

```
separate (LINE_INTERFACE)
task body RX_DRIVER is
   CSR: CSR_REG;
   BFR: CHARACTER;
   for CSR use at RX_CSR;
   for BFR use at RX_BFR;
begin
   CSR.INTEN := ON;
   loop
      accept INTERRUPT;
      CH := BFR;
      PUT(RX_BUFFER,CH);
   end loop;
end RX_DRIVER;
```

This completes the design of the LINE_INTERFACE package.

Appendix A

Predefined Language Attributes

The following attributes are predefined in Ada, for various kinds of entity. To obtain an attribute A of an entity E, write E'A. In the following descriptions, where possible each attribute is declared as it would be in Ada. Note that the descriptions are abbreviated in some cases. The language reference manual should be consulted for a complete definition of each attribute.

Attribute of any object or subprogram X

1. ADDRESS : *universal_integer*;
   The address of X in memory.

2. SIZE : *universal_integer*;
   The number of bits allocated to hold the object.

Attributes of any type or subtype T (except a task type)

3. BASE
   Applied to a subtype, yields the base type; applied to a type, yields the type itself. This attribute may be used only to obtain further attributes of a type, for example, T'BASE'FIRST.

4. SIZE : *universal_integer*;
   The minimum number of bits required to hold an object of type T.

Attributes of any scalar type or subtype T

5. FIRST : T;
   The minimum value of T.

6. LAST : T;
   The maximum value of T.

7. **function** IMAGE (X:T) **return** STRING;
   Converts the value X to its external display form, for example, INTEGER'IMAGE(20) returns the string "20", DAY'IMAGE(MON) returns the string "MON".

8. **function** VALUE (S:STRING) **return** T;
Converts the string S representing a value of type T from its external display form to its actual value, for example, INTEGER'VALUE("20") returns the integer value 20, DAY'VALUE("MON") returns the enumeration value MON.

Attributes of any discrete type or subtype T

9. **function** POS (X:T) **return** *universal_integer*;
Returns the position number of X in the ordered sequence X'FIRST . . X'LAST, the position of T'FIRST is itself for integer types and zero for enumeration types.

10. **function** VAL (I:*universal_integer*) **return** T;
Returns the value of type T with position number I.

11. **function** PRED (X:T) **return** T;
Returns the value preceding X in the range T'FIRST . . T'LAST.

12. **function** SUCC (X:T) **return** T;
Returns the value succeeding X in the range T'FIRST . . T'LAST.

13. WIDTH : *universal_integer*;
The minimum image length of all values of T.

Attributes of any fixed-point type or subtype T

14. DELTA : *universal_real*;
The delta specified in the declaration T.

15. AFT : *universal_integer;*
The number of digits needed after the point to accommodate the precision required for T.

16. FORE : *universal_integer*;
The number of characters needed for the integer part of the decimal representation of any value of type T.

17. LARGE : *universal_real*;
The largest model number of T.

18. MACHINE_ROUNDS : BOOLEAN;
True if the machine rounds to the nearest even value when computing values of type T.

Attributes of any floating-point type or subtype T

19. DIGITS : *universal_integer*;
The number of digits specified in the declaration of T.

20. MANTISSA : *universal_integer*;
The number of bits used for the mantissa of the representation of model numbers of type T.

21. EMAX : *universal_integer*;
The largest exponent value of the representation of model numbers of T. The smallest exponent value is −EMAX.

22. SMALL : *universal_real*;
The smallest positive model number of type T.

23. LARGE : *universal_real*;
The largest model number of T.

24. EPSILON : *universal_real*;
The difference between unity and the smallest model number of T greater than unity. Both unity and T'EPSILON are model numbers of T.

25. MACHINE_RADIX : *universal_integer*;
The radix of the exponent of the underlying machine representation of T.

26. SAFE_EMAX : *universal_integer*;
Largest exponent value of the safe numbers of T. (The safe numbers of T are an implementation dependent set which include the model numbers of T but which span a greater range.)

27. SAFE_LARGE : *universal_real*;
The largest positive safe number of T.

28. SAFE_SMALL : *universal_real*;
The smallest positive safe number of T.

29. MACHINE_MANTISSA : *universal_integer*;
The number of digits in the mantissa of the underlying machine representation of T.

30. MACHINE_EMAX : *universal_integer*;
The largest exponent value of the underlying machine representation of T.

31. MACHINE_EMIN : *universal_integer*;
The smallest exponent value of the underlying machine representation of T.

32. MACHINE_ROUNDS : BOOLEAN;
True if the machine rounds to the nearest even value when computing values of type T.

33. MACHINE_OVERFLOWS : BOOLEAN;
True if the exception NUMERIC_ERROR is raised when a value is computed which is too large to be represented correctly by the underlying machine representation of T.

Attributes of any constrained array type, subtype or object A

34. FIRST(I) : A'RANGE(I);
The lower bound of the Ith index.

35. LAST(I) : A′RANGE(I);
    The upper bound of the Ith index.

36. LENGTH(I) : *universal_integer*;
    The number of elements in the Ith dimension.

37. RANGE(I) - - a subtype
    The subtype A′FIRST(I) . . A′LAST(I), whose base type is the Ith index type of A.

In each of the above attributes, I must be a static integer expression. If I=1 it may be omitted.

Attributes of any object or subtype R of any record type with discriminants
38. CONSTRAINED : BOOLEAN;
    True if and only if the discriminant values of R cannot be modified.

Attributes of any record component C
39. POSITION : INTEGER;
    The offset within the record, in storage units, of the first unit of storage occupied by C.

40. FIRST_BIT : INTEGER;
    The offset, from the start of C′POSITION, of the first bit used to hold the value of C.

41. LAST_BIT : INTEGER;
    The offset, from the start of C′POSITION, of the last bit used to hold the value of C.

Attribute of any access type T
42. STORAGE_SIZE : *predefined_integer*;
    The total number of storage units reserved for the collection associated with T.

Attributes of any task or object of a task type T
43. TERMINATED : BOOLEAN;
    True when T has been terminated.

44. CALLABLE : BOOLEAN;
    True when T has been activated but not yet terminated.

45. PRIORITY : *universal_integer*;
    The static priority of T.

46. STORAGE_SIZE : *predefined_integer*;
    The number of storage units allocated for the execution of T.

Attribute of any entry E
47. COUNT : INTEGER;
    The number of calling tasks currently waiting on E.

Appendix B

Predefined Language Pragmas

CONTROLLED   Takes an access type name as argument and specifies that automatic storage reclamation must not be performed on objects of the type except upon leaving the scope of the access type definition.

ELABORATE   Takes one or more simple names denoting library units and indicates that these should be elaborated before the succeeding compilation unit.

INLINE   Takes a list of subprograms as arguments and specifies that the bodies of each subprogram should be expanded in-line at each call.

INTERFACE   Takes a language name and a subprogram name as arguments. It specifies that the body of the subprogram is written in the named language.

LIST   Takes ON or OFF as argument. It is used to turn listing on and off during compilation.

MEMORY_SIZE   Takes an integer number as argument, denoting the number of memory storage units required.

OPTIMIZE   Takes TIME or SPACE as argument and specifies a criterion for the compiler to use in translating the associated block or program unit body.

PACK   Takes a record or array type as argument and specifies that storage should be minimised in choosing a representation for the type.

PAGE   Starts a new page on the output listing, if any.

PRIORITY   Takes a static expression as argument denoting the priority of the associated task.

SHARED   Takes the name of a scalar or access variable and denotes that the variable is shared by two or more tasks.

STORAGE_UNIT   Takes an integer value as argument denoting the number of bits in a storage unit.

SUPPRESS   Used to suppress checks such as range and index constraints.

SYSTEM_NAME   Takes a name as an argument which specifies the name of the object machine.

In each of the above cases, there are rules concerning the places in a program where the pragma can be written. Refer to the language reference manual for these, and for the names of the checks which can be specified in the SUPPRESS pragma.

Appendix C

Predefined Language Environment

This appendix outlines the specification of the package STANDARD which defines the Ada Language Environment and the package SYSTEM which defines the Implementation Dependent Environment.

```
package STANDARD is

    type BOOLEAN is (FALSE,TRUE);


    -- The predefined relational operators for this type are
    -- as follows

    -- function "="  (LEFT,RIGHT:BOOLEAN) return BOOLEAN;
    -- function "/=" (LEFT,RIGHT:BOOLEAN) return BOOLEAN;
    -- function "<"  (LEFT,RIGHT:BOOLEAN) return BOOLEAN;
    -- function "<=" (LEFT,RIGHT:BOOLEAN) return BOOLEAN;
    -- function ">"  (LEFT,RIGHT:BOOLEAN) return BOOLEAN;
    -- function ">=" (LEFT,RIGHT:BOOLEAN) return BOOLEAN;

    -- The predefined logical operators and the predefined
    -- logical negation operator are as follows

    -- function "and"(LEFT,RIGHT: BOOLEAN) return BOOLEAN;
    -- function "or" (LEFT,RIGHT: BOOLEAN) return BOOLEAN;
    -- function "xor"(LEFT,RIGHT: BOOLEAN) return BOOLEAN;

    -- function "not"(RIGHT: BOOLEAN) return BOOLEAN;


    -- The universal type 'universal_integer' is predefined

    type INTEGER is 'implementation_defined';

    -- The predefined operators for this type are as follows

    -- function "="  (LEFT,RIGHT:INTEGER) return BOOLEAN;
    -- function "/=" (LEFT,RIGHT:INTEGER) return BOOLEAN;
    -- function "<"  (LEFT,RIGHT:INTEGER) return BOOLEAN;
    -- function "<=" (LEFT,RIGHT:INTEGER) return BOOLEAN;
    -- function ">"  (LEFT,RIGHT:INTEGER) return BOOLEAN;
    -- function ">=" (LEFT,RIGHT:INTEGER) return BOOLEAN;
```

```
-- function "+"  (RIGHT: INTEGER) return INTEGER;
-- function "-"  (RIGHT: INTEGER) return INTEGER;
-- function "abs"(RIGHT: INTEGER) return INTEGER;

-- function "+"  (LEFT,RIGHT: INTEGER) return INTEGER;
-- function "-"  (LEFT,RIGHT: INTEGER) return INTEGER;
-- function "*"  (LEFT,RIGHT: INTEGER) return INTEGER;
-- function "/"  (LEFT,RIGHT: INTEGER) return INTEGER;
-- function "rem"(LEFT,RIGHT: INTEGER) return INTEGER;
-- function "mod"(LEFT,RIGHT: INTEGER) return INTEGER;

-- function "**"(LEFT: INTEGER; RIGHT: INTEGER) return INTEGER;
```

```
-- An implementation may provide additional predefined integer
-- types.  It is recommended that the names of such additional
-- types end with INTEGER as in SHORT_INTEGER or LONG_INTEGER.
-- The specification of each operator for the type universal_
-- integer, or for any additional predefined integer type, is
-- obtained by replacing INTEGER by the name of the type in the
-- specification of the corresponding operator of the type
-- INTEGER, except for the right operand of the exponentiating
-- operator.
```

```
-- The universal type 'universal_real' is predefined.

type FLOAT is 'implementation_defined';

-- The predefined operators for this type are as follows

-- function "="  (LEFT,RIGHT:FLOAT) return BOOLEAN;
-- function "/=" (LEFT,RIGHT:FLOAT) return BOOLEAN;
-- function "<"  (LEFT,RIGHT:FLOAT) return BOOLEAN;
-- function "<=" (LEFT,RIGHT:FLOAT) return BOOLEAN;
-- function ">"  (LEFT,RIGHT:FLOAT) return BOOLEAN;
-- function ">=" (LEFT,RIGHT:FLOAT) return BOOLEAN;

-- function "+"  (RIGHT: FLOAT) return FLOAT;
-- function "-"  (RIGHT: FLOAT) return FLOAT;
-- function "abs"(RIGHT: FLOAT) return FLOAT;

-- function "+"(LEFT,RIGHT: FLOAT) return FLOAT;
-- function "-"(LEFT,RIGHT: FLOAT) return FLOAT;
-- function "*"(LEFT,RIGHT: FLOAT) return FLOAT;
-- function "/"(LEFT,RIGHT: FLOAT) return FLOAT;

-- function "**"(LEFT: FLOAT; RIGHT: INTEGER) return FLOAT;
```

```
-- An implementation may provide additional predefined floating
-- types.  It is recommended that the names of such additional
-- types end with FLOAT as in SHORT_FLOAT or LONG_FLOAT.
-- The specification of each operator for the type universal_
-- real, or for any additional predefined floating type, is
-- obtained by replacing FLOAT by the name of the type in the
-- specification of the corresponding operator of the type
-- FLOAT.
```

```
-- In addition, the following operators are predefined for
-- universal types.

-- function "*" (LEFT:u_int;  RIGHT:u_real) return u_real;
-- function "*" (LEFT:u_real; RIGHT:u_int ) return u_real;
-- function "/" (LEFT:u_real; RIGHT:u_int ) return u_real;
```

```
-- where u_int denotes universal_integer and u_real denotes
-- universal_real

-- The type universal_fixed is predefined.  The only operators
-- for this type are as follows

-- function "*" (LEFT:fxt; RIGHT:fxt) return universal_fixed;

-- function "/" (LEFT:fxt; RIGHT:fxt) return universal_fixed;

-- where 'fxt' denotes any fixed point type

-- The following characters form the standard ASCII
-- character set.  Character literals corresponding to
-- control characters are not identifiers.  They are
-- indicated in lower case type in this definition

type CHARACTER is

(nul, soh, stx, etx, eot, enq, ack, bel,
 bs,  ht,  lf,  vt,  ff,  cr,  so,  si,
 dle, dc1, dc2, dc3, dc4, nak, syn, etb,
 can, em,  sub, esc, fs,  gs,  rs,  us,

 ' ', '!', '"', '#', '$', '%', '&', ''',
 '(', ')', '*', '+', ',', '-', '.', '/',
 '0', '1', '2', '3', '4', '5', '6', '7',
 '8', '9', ':', ';', '<', '=', '>', '?',

 '@', 'A', 'B', 'C', 'D', 'E', 'F', 'G',
 'H', 'I', 'J', 'K', 'L', 'M', 'N', 'O',
 'P', 'Q', 'R', 'S', 'T', 'U', 'V', 'W',
 'X', 'Y', 'Z', '[', '\', ']', '^', '_',

 ''', 'a', 'b', 'c', 'd', 'e', 'f', 'g',
 'h', 'i', 'j', 'k', 'l', 'm', 'n', 'o',
 'p', 'q', 'r', 's', 't', 'u', 'v', 'w',
 'x', 'y', 'z', '{', '!', '}', '~', del );

for CHARACTER use -- 128 ASCII character set without holes
    (0, 1, 2, 3, 4, 5, ...., 125, 126, 127);


-- The predefined operators for the type CHARACTER are the
-- same as for any enumeration type.

package ASCII is      -- control characters

    NUL : constant CHARACTER := nul;
    SOH : constant CHARACTER := soh;
    STX : constant CHARACTER := stx;
    ETX : constant CHARACTER := etx;
    EOT : constant CHARACTER := eot;
    ENQ : constant CHARACTER := enq;
    ACK : constant CHARACTER := ack;
    BEL : constant CHARACTER := bel;
    BS  : constant CHARACTER := bs;
    HT  : constant CHARACTER := ht;
    LF  : constant CHARACTER := lf;
    VT  : constant CHARACTER := vt;
    FF  : constant CHARACTER := ff;
    CR  : constant CHARACTER := cr;
    SO  : constant CHARACTER := so;
    SI  : constant CHARACTER := si;
    DLE : constant CHARACTER := dle;
```

```
DC1 : constant CHARACTER := dc1;
DC2 : constant CHARACTER := dc2;
DC3 : constant CHARACTER := dc3;
DC4 : constant CHARACTER := dc4;
NAK : constant CHARACTER := nak;
SYN : constant CHARACTER := syn;
ETB : constant CHARACTER := etb;
CAN : constant CHARACTER := can;
EM  : constant CHARACTER := em;
SUB : constant CHARACTER := sub;
ESC : constant CHARACTER := esc;
FS  : constant CHARACTER := fs;
GS  : constant CHARACTER := gs;
RS  : constant CHARACTER := rs;
US  : constant CHARACTER := us;
DEL : constant CHARACTER := del;

-- other characters

EXCLAM        : constant CHARACTER := '!';
SHARP         : constant CHARACTER := '#';
DOLLAR        : constant CHARACTER := '$';
QUERY         : constant CHARACTER := '?';
AT_SIGN       : constant CHARACTER := '@';
L_BRACKET     : constant CHARACTER := '[';
BACK_SLASH    : constant CHARACTER := '\';
R_BRACKET     : constant CHARACTER := ']';
CIRCUMFLEX    : constant CHARACTER := '^';
GRAVE         : constant CHARACTER := '`';
L_BRACE       : constant CHARACTER := '{';
BAR           : constant CHARACTER := '|';
R_BRACE       : constant CHARACTER := '}';
TILDE         : constant CHARACTER := '~';

-- lower case letters

LC_A  : constant CHARACTER := 'a';
LC_B  : constant CHARACTER := 'b';

  -- etc

LC_Z  : constant CHARACTER := 'z';

end ASCII;

-- predefined subtypes

subtype NATURAL   is INTEGER range 0..INTEGER'LAST;
subtype POSITIVE  is INTEGER range 1..INTEGER'LAST;

-- predefined string type

type STRING is array (POSITIVE range <>)of CHARACTER;

pragma PACK(STRING);

-- The predefined operators for this type are as follows

-- function "="  (LEFT,RIGHT:STRING) return BOOLEAN;
-- function "/=" (LEFT,RIGHT:STRING) return BOOLEAN;
-- function "<"  (LEFT,RIGHT:STRING) return BOOLEAN;
-- function "<=" (LEFT,RIGHT:STRING) return BOOLEAN;
-- function ">"  (LEFT,RIGHT:STRING) return BOOLEAN;
-- function ">=" (LEFT,RIGHT:STRING) return BOOLEAN;
```

```
-- function "&" (LEFT:STRING;    RIGHT:STRING)    return STRING;
-- function "&" (LEFT:CHARACTER;RIGHT:STRING)     return STRING;
-- function "&" (LEFT:STRING;    RIGHT:CHARACTER)  return STRING;
-- function "&" (LEFT:CHARACTER;RIGHT:CHARACTER) return STRING;

type DURATION is delta ... range ... ;    -- impl defined

-- The predefined operators of the type DURATION are the
-- same as for any fixed point type

-- predefined exceptions

CONSTRAINT_ERROR : exception;
NUMERIC_ERROR    : exception;
PROGRAM_ERROR    : exception;
STORAGE_ERROR    : exception;
TASKING_ERROR    : exception;

end STANDARD;




package SYSTEM is          -- machine dependent

type ADDRESS is implementation_defined;
type NAME    is impl_defined_enumeration_type;

SYSTEM_NAME: constant NAME := impl_defined;

STORAGE_UNIT : constant :=    impl_defined;
MEMORY_SIZE  : constant :=    impl_defined;

-- System dependent Named Numbers

MIN_INT       : constant :=    impl_defined;
MAX_INT       : constant :=    impl_defined;
MAX_DIGITS    : constant :=    impl_defined;
MAX_MANTISSA  : constant :=    impl_defined;
FINE_DELTA    : constant :=    impl_defined;
TICK          : constant :=    impl_defined;

-- other system dependent declarations

subtype PRIORITY is INTEGER range impl_defined;

.....

end SYSTEM;
```

Appendix D

Standard I/O Packages

This appendix gives the specifications of the SEQUENTIAL_IO, DIRECT_IO and TEXT_IO packages described in Chapter 15.

```
with IO_EXCEPTIONS;
generic
   type ELEMENT_TYPE is private;
package SEQUENTIAL_IO is

   type FILE_TYPE is limited private;

   type FILE_MODE is (IN_FILE, OUT_FILE);


   -- File Management

   procedure CREATE (FILE: in out FILE_TYPE;
                     MODE: in FILE_MODE := OUT_FILE;
                     NAME: in STRING := "";
                     FORM: in STRING := "");

   procedure OPEN   (FILE: in out FILE_TYPE;
                     MODE: in FILE_MODE;
                     NAME: in STRING;
                     FORM: in STRING := "");

   procedure CLOSE  (FILE: in out FILE_TYPE);
   procedure DELETE (FILE: in out FILE_TYPE);
   procedure RESET  (FILE: in out FILE_TYPE; MODE: in FILE_MODE);
   procedure RESET  (FILE: in out FILE_TYPE);

   function MODE (FILE: in FILE_TYPE) return FILE_MODE;
   function NAME (FILE: in FILE_TYPE) return STRING;
   function FORM (FILE: in FILE_TYPE) return STRING;

   function IS_OPEN(FILE: in FILE_TYPE) return BOOLEAN;


   -- Input Output Operations

   procedure READ  (FILE: in FILE_TYPE; ITEM: out ELEMENT_TYPE);
   procedure WRITE (FILE: in FILE_TYPE; ITEM: in  ELEMENT_TYPE);

   function END_OF_FILE (FILE: in FILE_TYPE) return BOOLEAN;
```

```
    -- Exceptions

    STATUS_ERROR : exception renames IO_EXCEPTIONS.STATUS_ERROR;
    MODE_ERROR   : exception renames IO_EXCEPTIONS.MODE_ERROR;
    NAME_ERROR   : exception renames IO_EXCEPTIONS.NAME_ERROR;
    USE_ERROR    : exception renames IO_EXCEPTIONS.USE_ERROR;
    DEVICE_ERROR : exception renames IO_EXCEPTIONS.DEVICE_ERROR;
    END_ERROR    : exception renames IO_EXCEPTIONS.END_ERROR;
    DATA_ERROR   : exception renames IO_EXCEPTIONS.DATA_ERROR;

private
    -- implementation defined
end SEQUENTIAL_IO;



with IO_EXCEPTIONS;
generic
    type ELEMENT_TYPE is private;
package DIRECT_IO is

    type FILE_TYPE is limited private;

    type FILE_MODE is (IN_FILE, INOUT_FILE, OUT_FILE);
    type COUNT      is range 0 .. implementation_defined;
    subtype POSITIVE_COUNT is COUNT range 1 .. COUNT'LAST;

    -- File Management

    procedure CREATE (FILE: in out FILE_TYPE;
                      MODE: in FILE_MODE := INOUT_FILE;
                      NAME: in STRING := "";
                      FORM: in STRING := "");

    procedure OPEN   (FILE: in out FILE_TYPE;
                      MODE: in FILE_MODE;
                      NAME: in STRING;
                      FORM: in STRING := "");

    procedure CLOSE  (FILE: in out FILE_TYPE);
    procedure DELETE (FILE: in out FILE_TYPE);
    procedure RESET  (FILE: in out FILE_TYPE; MODE: in FILE_MODE);
    procedure RESET  (FILE: in out FILE_TYPE);

    function MODE (FILE: in FILE_TYPE) return FILE_MODE;
    function NAME (FILE: in FILE_TYPE) return STRING;
    function FORM (FILE: in FILE_TYPE) return STRING;

    function IS_OPEN(FILE: in FILE_TYPE) return BOOLEAN;

    -- Input Output Operations

    procedure READ  (FILE: in FILE_TYPE; ITEM: out ELEMENT_TYPE;
                     FROM: POSITIVE_COUNT);
    procedure READ  (FILE: in FILE_TYPE; ITEM: out ELEMENT_TYPE);

    procedure WRITE (FILE: in FILE_TYPE; ITEM: in  ELEMENT_TYPE;
                     TO:   POSITIVE_COUNT);
    procedure WRITE (FILE: in FILE_TYPE; ITEM: in  ELEMENT_TYPE);

    procedure SET_INDEX(FILE: in FILE_TYPE; TO: in POSITIVE_COUNT);

    function INDEX (FILE: in FILE_TYPE) return POSITIVE_COUNT;
    function SIZE  (FILE: in FILE_TYPE) return COUNT;
```

```
    function END_OF_FILE (FILE: in FILE_TYPE) return BOOLEAN;

    -- Exceptions

    STATUS_ERROR : exception renames IO_EXCEPTIONS.STATUS_ERROR;
    MODE_ERROR   : exception renames IO_EXCEPTIONS.MODE_ERROR;
    NAME_ERROR   : exception renames IO_EXCEPTIONS.NAME_ERROR;
    USE_ERROR    : exception renames IO_EXCEPTIONS.USE_ERROR;
    DEVICE_ERROR : exception renames IO_EXCEPTIONS.DEVICE_ERROR;
    END_ERROR    : exception renames IO_EXCEPTIONS.END_ERROR;
    DATA_ERROR   : exception renames IO_EXCEPTIONS.DATA_ERROR;

private
    -- implementation defined
end DIRECT_IO;



with IO_EXCEPTIONS;
package TEXT_IO is

    type FILE_TYPE is limited private;

    type FILE_MODE is (IN_FILE, OUT_FILE);

    type COUNT     is range 0 .. implementation_defined;
    subtype POSITIVE_COUNT is COUNT range 1 .. COUNT'LAST;
    UNBOUNDED: constant COUNT := 0; -- line and page length

    subtype FIELD is INTEGER range 0 .. implementation_defined;
    subtype NUMBER_BASE is INTEGER range 2 .. 16;

    type    TYPE_SET  is  (LOWER_CASE,  UPPER_CASE);


    -- File Management

    procedure CREATE (FILE: in out FILE_TYPE;
                      MODE: in FILE_MODE := OUT_FILE;
                      NAME: in STRING := "";
                      FORM: in STRING := "");

    procedure OPEN   (FILE: in out FILE_TYPE;
                      MODE: in FILE_MODE;
                      NAME: in STRING;
                      FORM: in STRING := "");

    procedure CLOSE  (FILE: in out FILE_TYPE);
    procedure DELETE (FILE: in out FILE_TYPE);
    procedure RESET  (FILE: in out FILE_TYPE; MODE: in FILE_MODE);
    procedure RESET  (FILE: in out FILE_TYPE);

    function MODE (FILE: in FILE_TYPE) return FILE_MODE;
    function NAME (FILE: in FILE_TYPE) return STRING;
    function FORM (FILE: in FILE_TYPE) return STRING;

    function IS_OPEN(FILE: in FILE_TYPE) return BOOLEAN;

    -- Control of Default Input and Output files


    procedure SET_INPUT  (FILE:in FILE_TYPE);
    procedure SET_OUTPUT (FILE:in FILE_TYPE);

    function STANDARD_INPUT  return FILE_TYPE;
    function STANDARD_OUTPUT return FILE_TYPE;
```

```
function CURRENT_INPUT  return FILE_TYPE;
function CURRENT_OUTPUT return FILE_TYPE;


-- Specification of line and page lengths

procedure SET_LINE_LENGTH(FILE: FILE_TYPE; TO: in COUNT);
procedure SET_LINE_LENGTH(TO: in COUNT);

procedure SET_PAGE_LENGTH(FILE: FILE_TYPE; TO: in COUNT);
procedure SET_PAGE_LENGTH(TO: in COUNT);

function LINE_LENGTH(FILE: FILE_TYPE) return COUNT;
function LINE_LENGTH return COUNT;

function PAGE_LENGTH(FILE: FILE_TYPE) return COUNT;
function PAGE_LENGTH return COUNT;

-- Column, Line and Page Control

procedure NEW_LINE(FILE: in FILE_TYPE; SPACING:in POSITIVE_COUNT:=1);
procedure NEW_LINE(SPACING:in POSITIVE_COUNT:=1);

procedure SKIP_LINE(FILE: in FILE_TYPE; SPACING:in POSITIVE_COUNT:=1);
procedure SKIP_LINE(SPACING:in POSITIVE_COUNT:=1);

function END_OF_LINE(FILE: in FILE_TYPE) return BOOLEAN;
function END_OF_LINE return BOOLEAN;

procedure NEW_PAGE(FILE: in FILE_TYPE);
procedure NEW_PAGE;

procedure SKIP_PAGE(FILE: in FILE_TYPE);
procedure SKIP_PAGE;

function END_OF_PAGE(FILE: in FILE_TYPE) return BOOLEAN;
function END_OF_PAGE return BOOLEAN;

function END_OF_FILE(FILE: in FILE_TYPE) return BOOLEAN;
function END_OF_FILE return BOOLEAN;

procedure SET_COL(FILE: in FILE_TYPE; TO:in POSITIVE_COUNT);
procedure SET_COL(TO:in POSITIVE_COUNT);

procedure SET_LINE(FILE: in FILE_TYPE; TO:in POSITIVE_COUNT);
procedure SET_LINE(TO:in POSITIVE_COUNT);

function COL(FILE: in FILE_TYPE) return POSITIVE_COUNT;
function COL return POSITIVE_COUNT;

function LINE(FILE: in FILE_TYPE) return POSITIVE_COUNT;
function LINE return POSITIVE_COUNT;

function PAGE(FILE: in FILE_TYPE) return POSITIVE_COUNT;
function PAGE return POSITIVE_COUNT;

-- Character Input-Output

procedure GET(FILE: in FILE_TYPE; ITEM: out CHARACTER);
procedure GET(ITEM: out CHARACTER);
procedure PUT(FILE: in FILE_TYPE; ITEM: in CHARACTER);
procedure PUT(ITEM: in CHARACTER);
```

```
-- String Input-Output

procedure GET(FILE: in FILE_TYPE; ITEM: out STRING);
procedure GET(ITEM: out STRING);
procedure PUT(FILE: in FILE_TYPE; ITEM: in STRING);
procedure PUT(ITEM: in STRING);

procedure GET_LINE(FILE: in FILE_TYPE; ITEM: out STRING;
                   LAST:out NATURAL);
procedure GET_LINE(ITEM: out STRING; LAST:out NATURAL);
procedure PUT_LINE(FILE: in FILE_TYPE; ITEM: in STRING);
procedure PUT_LINE(ITEM: in STRING);

-- Generic package for Input-Output of Integer Types

generic
   type NUM is range <>;
private INTEGER_IO is

   DEFAULT_WIDTH : FIELD := NUM'WIDTH;
   DEFAULT_BASE  : NUMBER BASE := 10;

   procedure GET(FILE: in FILE_TYPE; ITEM: out NUM;
                 WIDTH: in FIELD :=0);
   procedure GET(ITEM: out NUM; WIDTH: in FIELD :=0);

   procedure PUT(FILE: in FILE_TYPE;
                 ITEM  : in NUM;
                 WIDTH : in FIELD := DEFAULT_WIDTH;
                 BASE  : in NUMBER_BASE := DEFAULT_BASE);
   procedure PUT(ITEM  : in NUM;
                 WIDTH : in FIELD := DEFAULT_WIDTH;
                 BASE  : in NUMBER_BASE := DEFAULT_BASE);

   procedure GET(FROM:in STRING; ITEM: out NUM;
                 LAST: out POSITIVE);
   procedure PUT(TO    : out STRING;
                 ITEM  : in NUM;
                 BASE  : in NUMBER_BASE := DEFAULT_BASE);

end INTEGER_IO;

-- Generic packages for Input-Output of Real Types

generic
   type NUM is digits <>;
package FLOAT_IO is

DEFAULT_FORE : FIELD := 2;
DEFAULT_AFT  : FIELD := NUM'DIGITS-1;
DEFAULT_EXP  : FIELD := 3;

procedure GET(FILE: in FILE_TYPE; ITEM: out NUM;
              WIDTH: in FIELD := 0);
procedure GET(ITEM: out NUM; WIDTH: in FIELD := 0);

procedure PUT(FILE: in FILE_TYPE;
              ITEM: in NUM;
              FORE: in FIELD := DEFAULT_FORE;
              AFT:  in FIELD := DEFAULT_AFT;
              EXP:  in FIELD := DEFAULT_EXP);
procedure PUT(ITEM: in NUM;
              FORE: in FIELD := DEFAULT_FORE;
              AFT:  in FIELD := DEFAULT_AFT;
              EXP:  in FIELD := DEFAULT_EXP);
```

```
   procedure GET(FROM: in STRING; ITEM: out NUM; LAST: out POSITIVE);
   procedure PUT(TO:   out STRING;
                 ITEM: in NUM;
                 AFT:  in FIELD := DEFAULT_AFT;
                 EXP:  in FIELD := DEFAULT_EXP);
end FLOAT_IO;

generic
   type NUM is delta <>;
package FIXED_IO is

   DEFAULT_FORE : FIELD := NUM'FORE;
   DEFAULT_AFT  : FIELD := NUM'AFT;
   DEFAULT_EXP  : FIELD := 0;

   procedure GET(FILE: in FILE_TYPE; ITEM: out NUM;
                 WIDTH: in FIELD := 0);
   procedure GET(ITEM: out NUM; WIDTH: in FIELD := 0);

   procedure PUT(FILE: in FILE_TYPE;
                 ITEM: in NUM;
                 FORE: in FIELD := DEFAULT_FORE;
                 AFT:  in FIELD := DEFAULT_AFT;
                 EXP:  in FIELD := DEFAULT_EXP);
   procedure PUT(ITEM: in NUM;
                 FORE: in FIELD := DEFAULT_FORE;
                 AFT:  in FIELD := DEFAULT_AFT;
                 EXP:  in FIELD := DEFAULT_EXP);

   procedure GET(FROM: in STRING; ITEM: out NUM; LAST: out POSITIVE);
   procedure PUT(TO:   out STRING;
                 ITEM: in NUM;
                 AFT:  in FIELD := DEFAULT_AFT;
                 EXP:  in FIELD := DEFAULT_EXP);
end FIXED_IO;

-- Generic package for Input-Output of Enumeration Types

generic
   type ENUM is (<>);
package ENUMERATION_IO is

     DEFAULT_WIDTH : FIELD :=0;
     DEFAULT_SETTING : TYPE_SET := UPPER_CASE;

     procedure GET(FILE: in FILE_TYPE; ITEM: out ENUM);
     procedure GET(ITEM: out ENUM);

     procedure PUT(FILE:  in FILE_TYPE;
                   ITEM:  in ENUM;
                   WIDTH: in FIELD := DEFAULT_WIDTH;
                   SET:   in TYPE_SET := DEFAULT_SETTING);
     procedure PUT(ITEM:  in ENUM;
                   WIDTH: in FIELD := DEFAULT_WIDTH;
                   SET:   in TYPE_SET := DEFAULT_SETTING);

     procedure GET(FROM: in STRING; ITEM: out ENUM;
                   LAST: out POSITIVE);
     procedure PUT(TO:  out STRING;
                   ITEM: in ENUM;
                   SET:  in TYPE_SET := DEFAULT_SETTING);

   end ENUMERATION_IO;
```

```
-- Exceptions

STATUS_ERROR : exception renames IO_EXCEPTIONS.STATUS_ERROR;
MODE_ERROR   : exception renames IO_EXCEPTIONS.MODE_ERROR;
NAME_ERROR   : exception renames IO_EXCEPTIONS.NAME_ERROR;
USE_ERROR    : exception renames IO_EXCEPTIONS.USE_ERROR;
DEVICE_ERROR : exception renames IO_EXCEPTIONS.DEVICE_ERROR;
END_ERROR    : exception renames IO_EXCEPTIONS.END_ERROR;
DATA_ERROR   : exception renames IO_EXCEPTIONS.DATA_ERROR;

private
  -- implementation defined
end TEXT_IO;
```

Appendix E

Syntax Diagrams

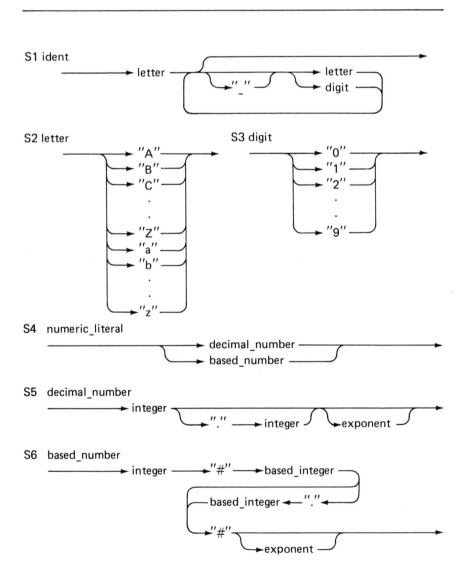

S1 ident

S2 letter   S3 digit

S4 numeric_literal

S5 decimal_number

S6 based_number

S7 integer

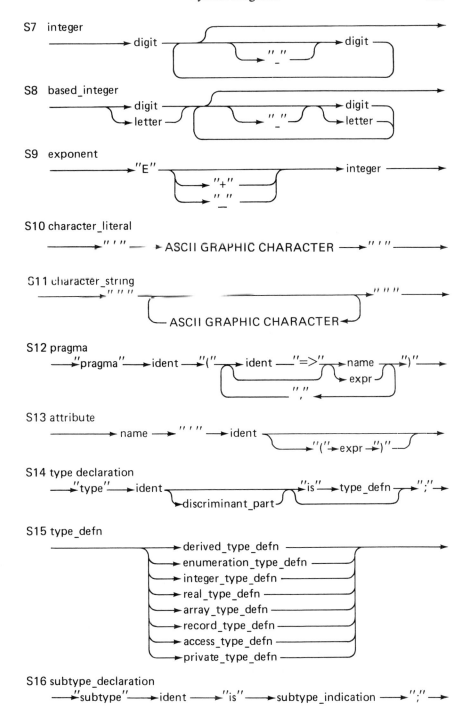

S8 based_integer

S9 exponent

S10 character_literal

S11 character_string

S12 pragma

S13 attribute

S14 type declaration

S15 type_defn

S16 subtype_declaration

S17 subtype_indication

S18 constraint

S19 range_constraint

S20 range

S21 derived_type_defn

S22 enumeration_type_defn

S23 integer_type_defn

S24 expr

S25 relation

S26 simple_expr

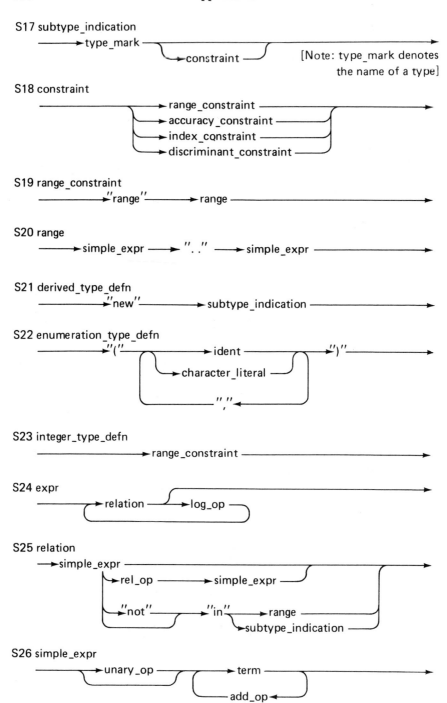

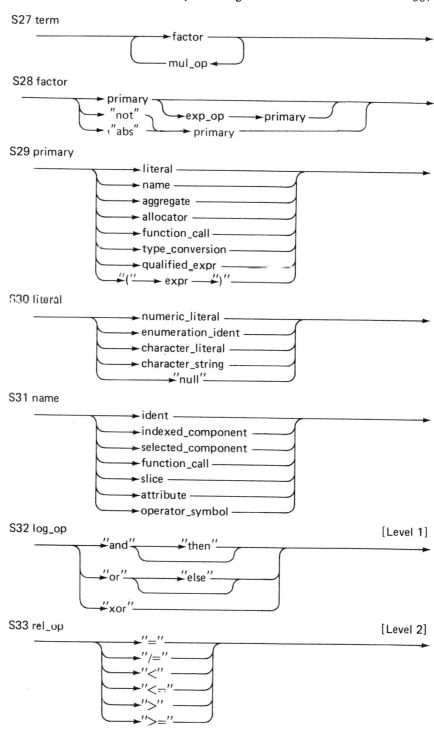

S27 term

S28 factor

S29 primary

S30 literal

S31 name

S32 log_op   [Level 1]

S33 rel_op   [Level 2]

S34 add_op   [Level 3]

S35 unary_op   [Level 4]

S36 mul_op   [Level 5]

S37 exp_op   [Level 6]

S38 type_conversion

S39 sequence_of_statements

S40 statement

S41 label

S42 simple_statement

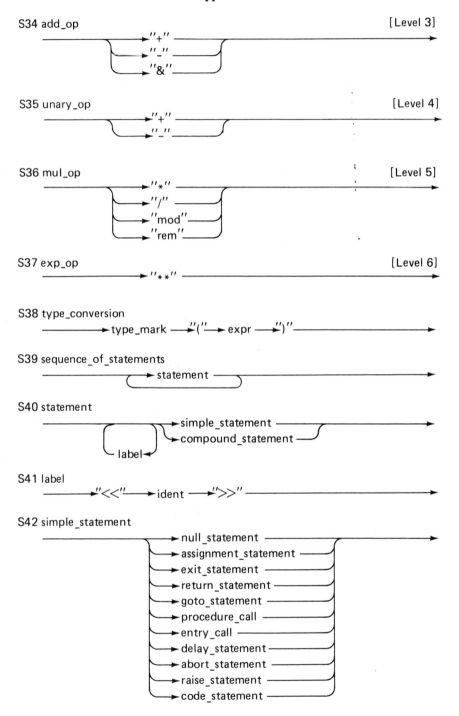

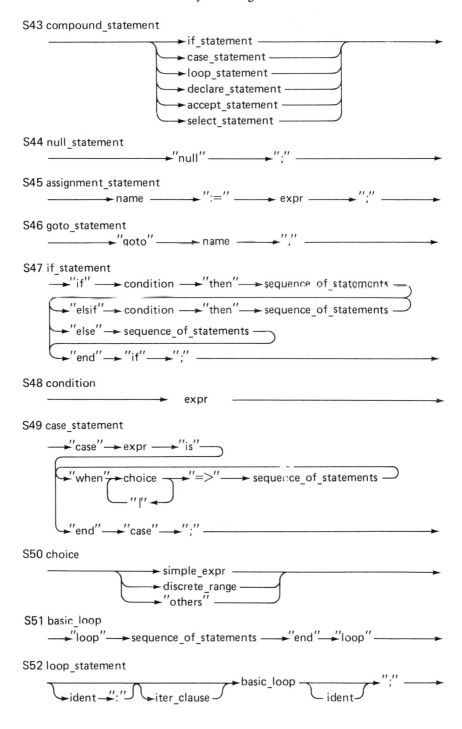

S43 compound_statement
- if_statement
- case_statement
- loop_statement
- declare_statement
- accept_statement
- select_statement

S44 null_statement
"null" ";"

S45 assignment_statement
name ":=" expr ";"

S46 goto_statement
"goto" name ";"

S47 if_statement
"if" condition "then" sequence_of_statements
"elsif" condition "then" sequence_of_statements
"else" sequence_of_statements
"end" "if" ";"

S48 condition
expr

S49 case_statement
"case" expr "is"
"when" choice "=>" sequence_of_statements
"|"
"end" "case" ";"

S50 choice
- simple_expr
- discrete_range
- "others"

S51 basic_loop
"loop" sequence_of_statements "end" "loop"

S52 loop_statement
ident ":" iter_clause basic_loop ident ";"

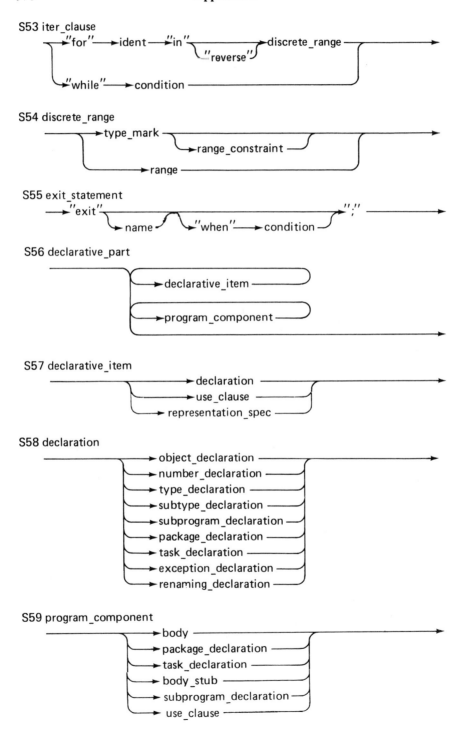

S53 iter_clause

S54 discrete_range

S55 exit_statement

S56 declarative_part

S57 declarative_item

S58 declaration

S59 program_component

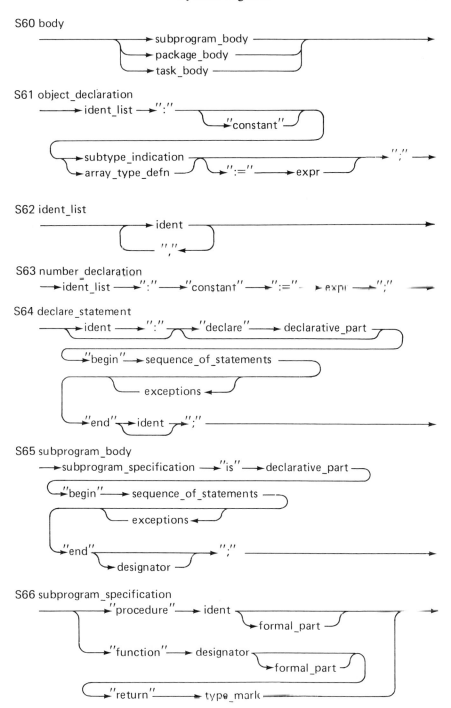

S60 body
  → subprogram_body →
  → package_body →
  → task_body →

S61 object_declaration
  → ident_list → ":"
      → "constant"
  → subtype_indication
  → array_type_defn
      → ":=" → expr
  → ";" →

S62 ident_list
  → ident →
  ← ","

S63 number_declaration
  → ident_list → ":" → "constant" → ":=" → expr → ";" →

S64 declare_statement
  → ident → ":" → "declare" → declarative_part
  → "begin" → sequence_of_statements
  → exceptions
  → "end" → ident → ";" →

S65 subprogram_body
  → subprogram_specification → "is" → declarative_part
  → "begin" → sequence_of_statements
  → exceptions
  → "end" → ";" →
      → designator

S66 subprogram_specification
  → "procedure" → ident
      → formal_part
  → "function" → designator
      → formal_part
  → "return" → type_mark

S67 designator

S68 operator_symbol

S69 return_statement

S70 formal_part

S71 parameter_declaration

S72 mode

S73 procedure_call

S74 function_call

S75 actual_parameter_part

S76 parameter_association

S77 formal_parameter

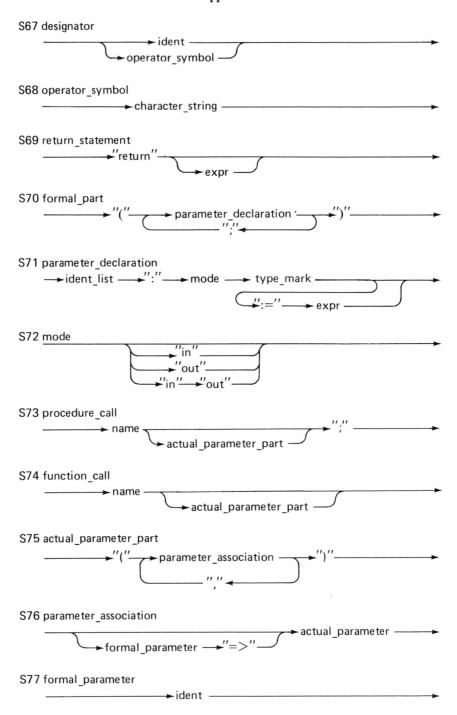

S78 actual_parameter

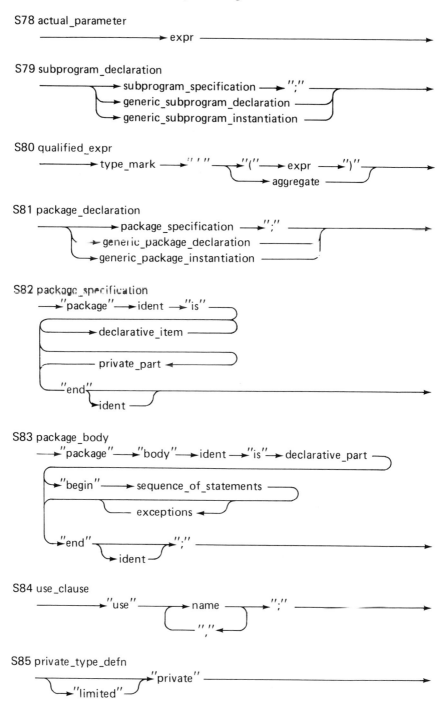

S79 subprogram_declaration

S80 qualified_expr

S81 package_declaration

S82 package_specification

S83 package_body

S84 use_clause

S85 private_type_defn

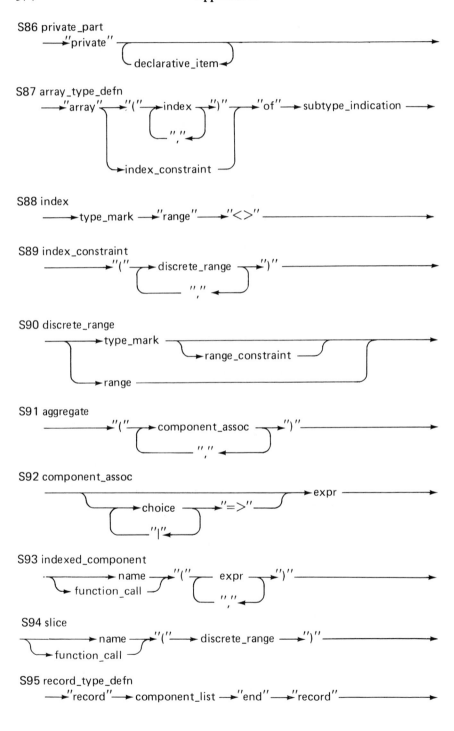

S86 private_part
→"private"
└─ declarative_item ◄

S87 array_type_defn
→"array"→"("→index→")"→"of"→subtype_indication→
","
→index_constraint

S88 index
→type_mark→"range"→"<>"

S89 index_constraint
→"("→discrete_range→")"
","

S90 discrete_range
→type_mark→range_constraint
→range

S91 aggregate
→"("→component_assoc→")"
","

S92 component_assoc
→choice→"=>"→expr
"|"

S93 indexed_component
→name→"("→expr→")"
→function_call
","

S94 slice
→name→"("→discrete_range→")"
→function_call

S95 record_type_defn
→"record"→component_list→"end"→"record"

S96 component_list

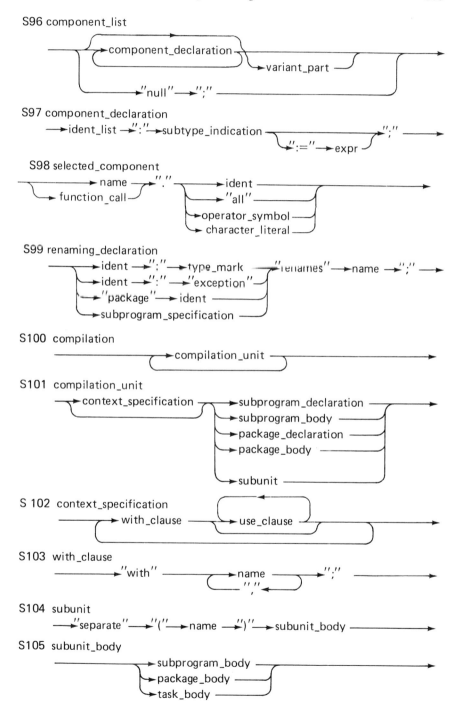

S97 component_declaration

S98 selected_component

S99 renaming_declaration

S100 compilation

S101 compilation_unit

S 102 context_specification

S103 with_clause

S104 subunit

S105 subunit_body

S106 body_stub

```
  ┌──►subprogram_specification ────►"is" ──►"separate"──►";" ──────────────►
  ├──►"package"──►"body"──►ident ─┤
  └──►"task" ──────►"body"──►ident ┘
```

S107 discriminant_part

```
  ──────────────►"(" ──┬──►discriminant_declaration ──┬──►")" ──────────────►
                        └──────────◄──";"──────────────┘
```

S108 discriminant_declaration

```
  ──►ident_list ──►":" ──► type_mark ───────────────────────────────────────►
                                          └──►":=" ──► expr ──┘
```

S109 variant_part

```
  ───────►"case"──►name ──►"is" ──┐
  ┌──────────────────────────────◄┘
  │
  │  ┌──►"when" ──┬──►choice ──┬──►"=>"──►component_list ──┐
  │  │            └──◄──"|"────┘                            │
  └──┤                                                      │
     └──►"end" ──►"case"──►";" ─────────────────────────────────────────────►
```

S110 discriminant_constraint

```
  ──────►"(" ──┬──►discriminant_specification ──┬──►")" ──────────────────────►
               └────────────◄──","──────────────┘
```

S111 discriminant_specification

```
  ┌──────────────────────────────────────────┬──► expr ──────────────────────►
  └──┬──►name ──┬──►"=>" ──┘
     └──◄──"|"──┘
```

S112 access_type_defn

```
  ──────────►"access" ──────────────► subtype_indication ──────────────────►
```

S113 allocator

```
  ──►"new" ──┬──►· subtype_indication ──┬──────────────────────────────────►
             └──► qualified_expression ─┘
```

S114 task_declaration

```
  ──────────────────────────►task_specification ───────────────────────────►
```

S115 task_specification

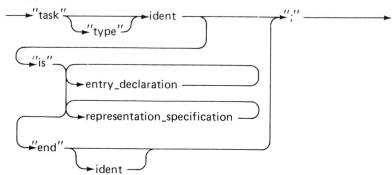

S116 task_body

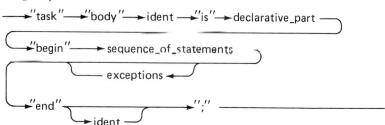

S117 entry_declaration

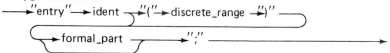

S118 entry_call

S119 accept_statement

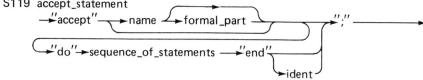

S120 select_statement

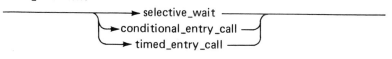

S121 selective_wait

S122 select_alternative

S123 delay_statement

S124 conditional_entry_call

S125 timed_entry_call

S126 abort_statement

S127 exception_declaration

S128 raise_statement

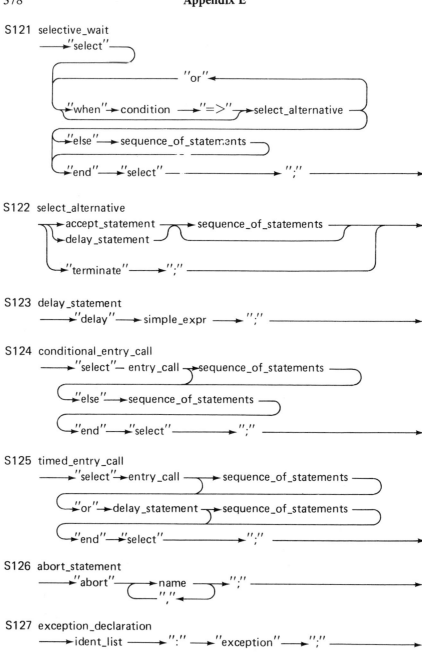

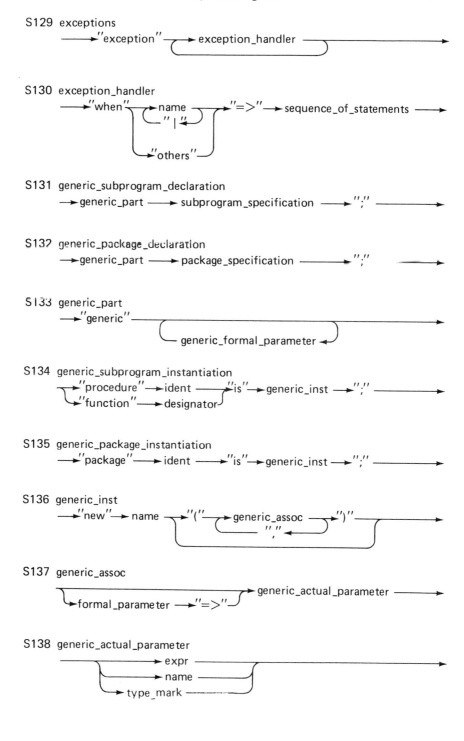

S129 exceptions
→"exception" → exception_handler →

S130 exception_handler
→"when" → name → "=>" → sequence_of_statements →
"|"
"others"

S131 generic_subprogram_declaration
→ generic_part → subprogram_specification → ";" →

S132 generic_package_declaration
→ generic_part → package_specification → ";" →

S133 generic_part
→"generic"
generic_formal_parameter

S134 generic_subprogram_instantiation
→"procedure" → ident → "is" → generic_inst → ";" →
→"function" → designator

S135 generic_package_instantiation
→"package" → ident → "is" → generic_inst → ";" →

S136 generic_inst
→"new" → name → "(" → generic_assoc → ")" →
","

S137 generic_assoc
→ generic_actual_parameter →
→ formal_parameter → "=>"

S138 generic_actual_parameter
→ expr →
→ name →
→ type_mark →

S139 generic_formal_parameter

S140 generic_type_defn

S141 real_type_defn

S142 accuracy_constraint

S143 floating_point_constraint

S144 fixed_point_constraint

S145 representation_specification

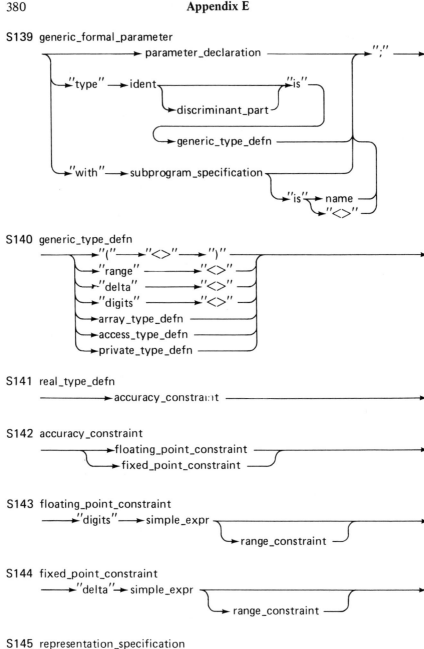

S146 record_type_representation

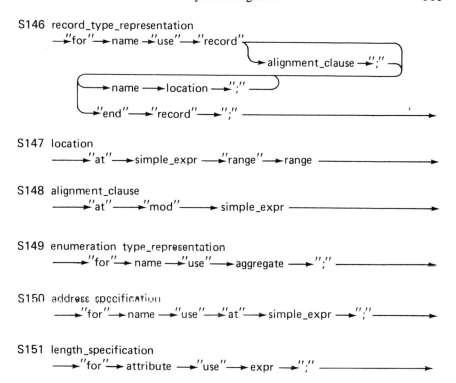

S147 location
→"at"→simple_expr →"range"→range

S148 alignment_clause
→"at"→"mod"→ simple_expr

S149 enumeration type_representation
→"for"→ name →"use"→ aggregate →";"

S150 address specification
→"for"→name →"use"→"at"→ simple_expr →";"

S151 length_specification
→"for"→ attribute →"use"→ expr →";"

Appendix F

Solutions to Selected Exercises

SECTION 3.8

1.   **type** DEVICE **is** (PRINTER,   TERMINAL, DISC,
                           MAG_TAPE, CARD_RDR, CARD_PUNCH);

        subtype USER_DEVICE **is** DEVICE **range** PRINTER . . DISC;

4.   (A) CHARACTER'VAL(I + CHARACTER'POS('0'))

        (B) I **mod** 2 = 1 **and** J **mod** 2 = 0

        (C) CH **in** 'A' . . 'Z' **or** CH **in** 'a' . . 'z'

        (D) 2 ** (N−1) − 1

5.   (A) 28   (F) TRUE

        (B) TRUE   (G) 4

        (C) Illegal − type mismatch   (H) 83

        (D) −5   (I) Illegal − brackets needed

        (E) 1   around S=6

SECTION 4.10

2.   **for** LAST_CH **in** 'A' . . 'Z' **loop**
          NEW_LINE;
          SPACES(CHARACTER'POS('Z')−CHARACTER'POS(LAST_CH)+1);
          for CH **in** 'A' . . LAST_CH **loop**
             PUT(CH);
          end loop;
          for CH **in reverse** 'A' . . CHARACTER'PRED(LAST_CH) **loop**
             PUT(CH);
          end loop;
        end loop;

3.   - - basic solution: no error checking
          N := 1;
          loop
              FACT_N := FACT_N/N;
              exit when FACT_N=1;
              N := N+1;
          end loop;

SECTION 5.7

2.   In DS1:   I:=DS1.J;   - - ok
                 I:=DS2.K;   - - DS2.K not in scope
                 I:=DS3.L;   - - DS3.L not in scope

       In DS2:   I:=J;   - - type mismatch
                 COUNT:=INTEGER(I)   - - type mismatch
                 J:=K;   - - ok, J is DS1.J
                 DS1.I:=J;   - - ok, J is DS1.J
                 A:=ON;   - - type mismatch A is DS2.A
                 J:=DS3.L;   - - DS3.L not in scope

       In DS3:   L:=I;   - - ok, I is DS1.I
                 L:=K;   - - K not in scope
                 L:=DS2.K;   - - DS2.K not in scope

SECTION 6.9

1.   - - basic outline − no error checking
          procedure READ_INT(VAL: **out** INTEGER) **is**
              CH: CHARACTER;
              SUM: INTEGER := 0;
              NEGATIVE: BOOLEAN := FALSE;
          begin
              GET(CH);
              if CH = '+' **then**
                GET(CH);
              elsif CH = '−' **then**
                NEGATIVE := TRUE;
                GET(CH);
              end if;
              while CH **in** '0' .. '9' **loop**
                SUM := SUM∗10 + CHARACTER'POS(CH)−CHARACTER'POS('0');
              end loop;

```
      if NEGATIVE then
        VAL := -SUM;
      else
        VAL := SUM;
      end if;
   end READ_INT;
```

5.   **procedure** HANOI(NO_OF_DISKS: **in** NATURAL) **is**

```
   type POLE_NAME is (LEFT, RIGHT, MIDDLE);
   type EXTERNAL_NAME is array(POLE_NAME) of CHARACTER;

   EXT_NAME: constant EXTERNAL_NAME := ('L','R','M');

   procedure PRINT_MOVE(SOURCE,DEST: in POLE_NAME) is
   begin
      NEW_LINE;
      PUT(EXT_NAME(SOURCE) );
      PUT(' '); PUT('K'); PUT(' ');
      PUT(EXT_NAME(DEST) );
   end PRINT_MOVE;

   procedure MAKE_MOVE(N: in NATURAL;
                       SOURCE,DEST,SPARE: in POLE_NAME) is
   begin
      if  N=1  then
         PRINT_MOVE(SOURCE, DEST);
      else
         MAKE_MOVE (N-1, SOURCE, SPARE, DEST);
         PRINT_MOVE(SOURCE, DEST);
         MAKE_MOVE (N-1, SPARE, DEST, SOURCE);
      end if;
   end MAKE_MOVE;
begin
   MAKE_MOVE(NO_OF_DISKS, LEFT, RIGHT, MIDDLE);
end HANOI;
```

SECTION 7.7

1.   The following package provides simple graphics. All output takes place
      at the current cursor position which is set by the MOVE procedure.
      Initially the cursor is at (0,0). After any output operation, the cursor
      is left at the last character printed. The procedures for drawing lines
      increment the appropriate co-ordinate modulo the size of the screen
      causing wrap-around of long lines on the screen.

```
package SIMPLE_GRAPHICS is

  procedure DRAW_H_LINE(CH: in CHARACTER; LENGTH: in NATURAL);
  procedure DRAW_V_LINE(CH: in CHARACTER; LENGTH: in NATURAL);
  procedure DRAW_CH(CH: in CHARACTER);
  procedure MOVE(X: in ABSCISSA; Y: in ORDINATE);

  function X_POS return ABSCISSA;
  function Y_POS return ORDINATE;

end SIMPLE_GRAPHICS;

package SIMPLE_GRAPHICS is

  use SCREEN;

  XMAX: constant := ABSCISSA'LAST+1;
  YMAX: constant := ORDINATE'LAST+1;

  X0:ABSCISSA := 0,
  Y0:ORDINATE := 0;

  procedure DRAW_H_LINE(CH: in CHARACTER;LENGTH: in NATURAL) is
  begin
    for I in 1 .. LENGTH loop
      OUT_CH(CH,X0,Y0);
      X0 := (X0+1) mod XMAX;
    end loop;
  end DRAW_H_LINE;

  procedure DRAW_V_LINE(CH: in CHARACTER;LENGTH: in NATURAL) is
  begin
    for I in 1 .. LENGTH loop
      OUT_CH(CH,X0,Y0);
      Y0 := (Y0+1) mod YMAX;
    end loop;
  end DRAW_V_LINE;

  procedure DRAW_CH(CH: in CHARACTER) is
  begin
    OUT_CH(CH,X0,Y0);
  end DRAW_CH;

  procedure MOVE(X: in ABSCISSA; Y: in ORDINATE) is
  begin
    X0 := X; Y0 := Y;
  end MOVE;

  function X_POS return ABSCISSA is
  begin
    return X0;
  end X_POS;
```

```
function Y_POS return ORDINATE is
begin
   return Y0;
end Y_POS;
```
```
begin
   CLEARSCREEN;
end SIMPLE_GRAPHICS;
```

SECTION 8.12

1.
```
package body INTEGER_STACK is

      STACK_SIZE: constant := 100;

      STACK:    array (1 .. STACK_SIZE) of INTEGER;
      STK_PTR: INTEGER range 0 .. STACK_SIZE := 0;

      procedure PUSH(X: in INTEGER) is
      begin
         STK_PTR := STK_PTR + 1;
         STACK(STK_PTR) := X;
      end PUSH;

      procedure POP(X: out INTEGER) is
      begin
         X := STACK(STK_PTR);
         STK_PTR := STK_PTR - 1;
      end POP;

   end INTEGER_STACK;
```

2.
```
package INTEGER_STACK_TYPE is

      type STACK is limited private;

      procedure PUSH(S: in out STACK; X: in INTEGER);
      procedure POP   (S: in out STACK; X: out INTEGER);

   private
      STACK_SIZE: constant := 100;
      type BUFFER is array (1 .. STACK_SIZE) of INTEGER;
      type STACK is
         record
            DATA: BUFFER;
            PTR:    INTEGER range 0 .. STACK_SIZE := 0;
         end record;

   end INTEGER_STACK_TYPE;
```

```
package body INTEGER_STACK_TYPE is

    procedure PUSH(S: in out STACK; X: in INTEGER) is
    begin
        S.PTR := S.PTR + 1;
        S.DATA(S.PTR) := X;
    end PUSH;

    procedure POP(S: in out STACK; X: out INTEGER) is
    begin
        X := S.DATA(S.PTR);
        S.PTR := S.PTR - 1;
    end POP;

end INTEGER_STACK_TYPE;
```

SECTION 9.8

3.   No, P.X and P.Y are unambiguous references to the record P.
       Yes, a local use of the name P would make P.X hidden. The assign-
       ments would then have to be changed to ONE.P.X := 0; etc.

4.   Overloading of ON in enumeration types and function is legal, but over-
       loading of ON and CONNECTED as variables is illegal. Overloading of
       SWAP is legal, since procedure specifications are distinguishable.

SECTION 10.7

1.   type MODE is (CARTESIAN, POLAR);

```
type POINT(M: MODE) is
    record
        case M is
            when CARTESIAN =>
                X: ABSCISSA;
                Y: ORDINATE;
            when POLAR =>
                R: RADIUS;
                THETA: ANGLE;
        end case;
    end record;
```

2.   First Case

```
type STATUS is (NATIONAL, ALIEN);
```

```
type PERSON_RECORD(ST:STATUS := NATIONAL) is
  record
    NAME: PERSON_NAME;
    GENDER: SEX;
    BIRTHDAY: DATE;
    case ST is
      when NATIONAL =>
        BIRTHPLACE: PLACE_NAME;
      when ALIEN =>
        ORIGIN: COUNTRY;
        ENTRY_DATE: DATE;
    end case;
  end record;
```

Second Case

Data for Aliens can be represented by a nested variant record as follows;
notice that default discriminant values are given to allow the nested
component to be unconstrained

```
type ALIEN_CLASS is (VISITING, TEMP_RESIDENT);
```

```
type ALIEN_RECORD(CLASS: ALIEN_CLASS := VISITING) is
  record
    ORIGIN: COUNTRY;
    ENTRY_DATE: DATE;
    case CLASS is
      when VISITING =>
        null;
      when TEMP_RESIDENT =>
        PERMIT_ISSUED: BOOLEAN;
        PERMIT_NO: PERMIT_NUMBER;
        EXPIRY_DATE: DATE;
    end case;
  end record;
```

the PERSON_RECORD then becomes

```
type PERSON_RECORD(ST:STATUS := NATIONAL) is
  record
    NAME: PERSON_NAME;
    GENDER: SEX;
    BIRTHDAY: DATE;
    case ST is
      when NATIONAL =>
        BIRTHPLACE: PLACE_NAME;
```

```
   when ALIEN =>
        ALIEN_DATA: ALIEN_RECORD;
   end case;
 end record;
```

SECTION 11.9

1.   The following implementation of the BUFFER package assumes that
        the system will perform automatic garbage collection. In practice, it
        would normally be preferable to maintain a free-list of message cells,
        as described in section 11.7

package body BUFFER is

     - - define buffer as a two-way linked list of message cells

     type CELL;

     type LINK **is access** CELL;

     type CELL **is**

        record

           M: MESSAGE;

           P: PRIORITY;

           PREVIOUS, NEXT: LINK;

        end record;

     - - CELLS are linked primarily in order of priority and

     - - then in order of arrival. HEAD designates the

     - - highest priority entry in the list (that is, the next

     - - message to be received). TAIL designates the lowest

     - - priority entry in the list.

     HEAD, TAIL: LINK;

     procedure SEND(M: **in** MESSAGE; P: **in** PRIORITY) **is**

        THIS: LINK := TAIL;

        TEMP: LINK;

     begin

        if THIS=null **then**   - - buffer is empty

           HEAD := **new** CELL'(M,P,null,null);

           TAIL := HEAD;

        else   - - find where to insert message

          while THIS/=null **and then** THIS.P<P **loop**

            THIS := THIS.NEXT;

          end loop;

          if THIS/=null **then**   - - insert new cell before THIS

            TEMP := **new** CELL'(M,P,THIS.PREVIOUS,THIS);

```
              THIS.PREVIOUS := TEMP;
              if  TAIL=THIS then                    - - no previous cell
                 TAIL := TEMP;
              else                                  - - link previous cell
                 TEMP.PREVIOUS.NEXT := TEMP;
              end if;
           else                                     - - insert at head of list
              TEMP := new CELL'(M,P,HEAD,null);
              HEAD.NEXT := TEMP;
              HEAD := TEMP;
           end if;
        end if;
     end SEND;

  procedure RECEIVE(M: out MESSAGE) is
  begin
     if  HEAD=null then
        - - Error, buffer is empty!
     else
        M := HEAD.M;                    - - extract message and
        HEAD := HEAD.PREVIOUS;          - - delink empty cell
        if  HEAD=null then
           TAIL:=null;
        else
           HEAD.NEXT := null;
        end if;
     end if;
  end RECEIVE;

end BUFFER;
```

Notice that, in the above, the case of an attempt to receive a message from an empty buffer has not been dealt with. One possibility would be to raise an exception, as described in Chapter 13.

SECTION 12.14

2.   task body LP_CONTROL is
           FREE:BOOLEAN := TRUE;
        begin
           loop
              select
                 when FREE =>
                    accept SECURE(HIGH);
                    FREE := FALSE;

```
          or
             when FREE and SECURE(HIGH)'COUNT=0 =>
                accept SECURE(MEDIUM);
                FREE := FALSE;
          or
             when FREE and SECURE(HIGH)'COUNT=0
                       and SECURE(MEDIUM)'COUNT=0 =>
                accept SECURE(LOW);
                FREE := FALSE;
          or
                accept RELEASE;
                FREE := TRUE;
          or
             when FREE =>
                terminate;
          end select;
       end loop;
  end LP_CONTROL;
```

4.   To allow multiple concurrent readers, the READ and WRITE entries
      are replaced by package procedures. Within the package is a control
      task which schedules access to the shared variable TIME_NOW.

```
package PROTECTED_TIME is
   procedure READ(T: out TIME);
   procedure WRITE(T: in TIME);
end PROTECTED_TIME;

package body PROTECTED_TIME is
   TIME_NOW: TIME;

   task CONTROL is
      entry START;
      entry STOP;
      entry UPDATE(T: in TIME);
   end CONTROL;

   task body CONTROL is
      READER_COUNT: INTEGER range 0 .. INTEGER'LAST := 0;
   begin
      loop
         select
            when UPDATE'COUNT=0 =>
               accept START;
               READER_COUNT := READER_COUNT + 1;
```

```
            or
               accept STOP;
               READER_COUNT := READER_COUNT - 1;
            or
               when READER_COUNT=0 =>
                  accept UPDATE(T:in TIME) do
                     TIME_NOW := T;
                  end;
                  loop
                     select
                         accept START;
                         READER_COUNT := READER_COUNT + 1;
                     else
                         exit;
                     end select;
                  end loop;
               end select;
            end loop;
         end CONTROL;

         procedure READ(T:out TIME) is
         begin
            CONTROL.START;
            T := TIME_NOW;
            CONTROL.STOP;
         end READ;

         procedure WRITE(T:in TIME) is
         begin
            CONTROL.UPDATE(T);
         end WRITE;

      end PROTECTED_TIME;
```

Note that the inner loop after the **accept** WRITE statement in the CONTROL task is to prevent repeated calls to WRITE from locking out tasks wishing to read the time. In practice, this example is a little unrealistic, in the sense that the variable TIME_NOW will be a small data structure (or even a simple scalar). This kind of approach really only pays off when the protected variable is a large data structure and concurrent reading can then reduce execution times.

SECTION 13.8

```
1.      package INTEGER_STACK is
           procedure PUSH(X:in INTEGER);
```

```
procedure POP(X:out INTEGER);
UNDERFLOW, OVERFLOW: exception;
end INTEGER_STACK;

package body INTEGER_STACK is

    STACK_SIZE:constant := 100;

    STACK:     array (1 .. STACK_SIZE) of INTEGER;
    STK_PTR: INTEGER range 0 .. STACK_SIZE := 0;

    procedure PUSH(X:in INTEGER) is
    begin
       if  STK_PTR=STACK_SIZE then
          raise OVERFLOW;
       else
          STK_PTR := STK_PTR + 1;
          STACK(STK_PTR) := X;
       end if;
    end PUSH;

    procedure POP(X:out INTEGER) is
    begin
       if  STK_PTR=0 then
          raise UNDERFLOW;
       else
          X := STACK(STK_PTR);
          STK_PTR := STK_PTR - 1;
       end if;
    end POP;

end INTEGER_STACK;
```

SECTION 14.6

3.
```
       generic
          STACK_SIZE:NATURAL;
          type ELEMENT is private;
       package GENERIC_STACK is
          procedure PUSH(X:in ELEMENT);
          procedure POP(X:out ELEMENT);
       end GENERIC_STACK;

       package body GENERIC_STACK is

          STACK:     array (1 .. STACK_SIZE) of ELEMENT;
          STK_PTR: INTEGER range 0 .. STACK_SIZE := 0;

          procedure PUSH(X:in ELEMENT) is
```

```
begin
   STK_PTR := STK_PTR + 1;
   STACK(STK_PTR) := X;
end PUSH;

procedure POP(X:out ELEMENT) is
begin
   X := STACK(STK_PTR);
   STK_PTR := STK_PTR – 1;
end POP;
end GENERIC_STACK;
```

Alternatively using discriminated types

```
generic
   type ELEMENT is private;
package GENERIC_STACK_TYPE is
   type STACK(SIZE:NATURAL) is limited private;
   procedure PUSH(S:in out STACK; X:in ELEMENT);
   procedure POP(S:in out STACK; X:out ELEMENT);
private
   type BUFFER is array (NATURAL range <>) of ELEMENT;
   type STACK(SIZE:NATURAL) is
      record
         DATA: BUFFER(1 .. SIZE);
         PTR:    INTEGER range 0 .. SIZE := 0;
      end record;
end GENERIC_STACK_TYPE;

package body GENERIC_STACK_TYPE is
   -- similar to that shown in Section 8.12 Q2.
```

The merits of the above two approaches are discussed in section 14.5.

SECTION 15.12

```
2.     package body INTEGER_STACK is
          BLOCK_SIZE:constant := 256;
          type BLOCK is array (1 .. BLOCK_SIZE) of INTEGER;
          type STACK_POINTER is
          record
             BLK:       INTEGER := 1;
             OFFSET:   INTEGER range 0 .. BLOCK_SIZE+1 := 0;
          end record;
```

```
TOP_BLK: BLOCK;              - - top of stack in memory
SP: STACK_POINTER;

package BLK_IO is new DIRECT_IO(BLOCK);
use BLK_IO;

BLK_FILE: FILE_TYPE;

procedure LOAD_BLOCK(N: in INTEGER) is
begin
   if  N<1 then
      raise UNDERFLOW;
   else
      READ(BLK_FILE, TOP_BLK,N);
   end if;
exception
   when others =>
      raise STACK_ERR;
end LOAD_STACK;

procedure STORE_BLOCK(N: in INTEGER) is
begin
   WRITE(BLK_FILE,TOP_BLK,N);
exception
   when others =>
      raise OVERFLOW;
end STORE_BLOCK;

procedure BLOCK_CHECK is
begin
   if  SP.OFFSET=0 then
      SP.OFFSET := BLOCK_SIZE;
      SP.BLK := SP.BLK - 1;
      LOAD_BLOCK(SP.BLK);
   elsif SP.OFFSET>BLOCK_SIZE then
      SP.OFFSET := 1;
      STORE_BLOCK(SP.BLK);
      SP.BLK := SP.BLK + 1;
   end if;
end BLOCK_CHECK;

procedure PUSH(X: in INTEGER) is
begin
   SP.OFFSET := SP.OFFSET + 1;
   BLOCK_CHECK;
```

```
    TOP.BLK(SP.OFFSET) := X;
end PUSH;

procedure POP(X: out INTEGER) is
begin
    X := TOP_BLK(SP.OFFSET);
    SP.OFFSET := SP.OFFSET - 1;
    BLOCK_CHECK;
end POP;

begin
    CREATE(BLK_FILE,INOUT_FILE);
exception
    when others =>
        raise STACK_ERR;
end INTEGER_STACK;
```

Note that exception OVERFLOW is raised following any WRITE error on the assumption that the most likely reason will be lack of file space. STACK_ERR is raised for all other unanticipated exceptions.

SECTION 16.6

1.   (A)   X is a real type hence X/100 must be written as X/100.0

        (B)   X and Y are different types, both operands of * must be of the same type. Hence should be Y := FLTY(X)*Y;

        (C)   Type of A*B must be fixed. Hence should be A := FIXA(A*B);

        (D)   778.0 is not a valid octal number.

        (E)   Types of A/B and B/A must have their types fixed individually. Should be B := FIXB(B/A) + FIXB(A/B);

Index